Stephen W Titterington was born in Penrith, Cumbria in 1961. He was educated at Ullswater School and then Cumbria College of Agriculture – Newton Rigg.

His early working life was spent on the family farm in the shadow of Blencathra and he went on to become a self-employed dry stone waller and expert molecatcher. He now lives in Penrith.

Dedication

My mother Ann Titterington for her input, encouragement and initial proof reading; my brother Angus; my sister-in-law Anne; my sister Heather, and Katie Parker for their help in computer work and emailing literary agents and publishers. The local writing group for their help in the layout of the book. All my friends for their support and encouragement.

Stephen Wilson Titterington

THE WHITE MOLE'S STORY –
MAKING MOUNTAINS
OUT OF MOLEHILLS

A Life in the Balance

AUSTIN MACAULEY PUBLISHERS™
LONDON • CAMBRIDGE • NEW YORK • SHARJAH

Copyright © Stephen Wilson Titterington (2017)

The right of Stephen Wilson Titterington to be identified as author of this work has been asserted by him in accordance with section 77 and 78 of the Copyright, Designs and Patents Act 1988.

All rights reserved. No part of this publication may be reproduced, stored in a retrieval system, or transmitted in any form or by any means, electronic, mechanical, photocopying, recording, or otherwise, without the prior permission of the publishers.

Any person who commits any unauthorised act in relation to this publication may be liable to criminal prosecution and civil claims for damages.

A CIP catalogue record for this title is available from the British Library.

ISBN 9781787100527 (Paperback)
ISBN 9781787100534 (Hardback)
ISBN 9781787100541 (E-Book)
www.austinmacauley.com

First Published (2017)
Austin Macauley Publishers™ Ltd.
25 Canada Square
Canary Wharf
London
E14 5LQ

Acknowledgements

Thanks go to Roger Townsend for his stunning front cover photograph. Thanks also to the Scottish and English mental health services, without them I don't know where I'd be now.

My final thanks go to my ever-enduring family who I have put through the wringer but were always there to support me.

Introduction

My name is Stephen W Titterington, I am 52 years old and I was born in Penrith, Cumbria and raised on a farm called Highgate Close in the Lake District. My early life was what was expected of a farmer's son on a hill farm, apart from attending agricultural college for nine months at the age of eighteen. It was changed though in 1986 when a friend introduced me to the game of golf and I joined the local Keswick Golf Club, situated at the nearby village of Threlkeld. The game soon got a tremendous hold of me and I found myself playing more and more often, at the expense of my farm work. So after two years of juggling both endeavours I decided to leave the farm and take a month's holiday in Switzerland, with a view to maybe finding work there. I had a superb time walking, drinking and playing golf in the Jungfrau Region and I even fell in love with a walking guide, but it was only a holiday romance and with only vague offers of work, I returned home at the end of the month away. I took up working with friends, going self-employed doing garden work, dry stone walling, fencing and mole trapping, at which I am an expert and it has led to the title of this book, because in my circle of friends I have gained the nickname, 'White Mole'. The main reason for this is explained in Part 5.

For two years I worked at this type of work and also did so much self-employed work back on the home farm. However, in 1990 I got the chance to work in the building trade, sub-contracting to a builder based in Keswick. The work was new to me on the whole and the money was good, leading me to push the boat out and buy a powerful Ford Capri, 2.8 injection. The car was bright red and the purchase of it blew away all the bad jokes at the golf club about my previous car – a Lada Riva! The work was very stressful, however and after eighteen months of infighting with the other members of my work gang I had had enough. It did not end well; enough to say I should have laid some of those bastards flat out on their backs! But that is another story.

So I went back, cap in hand, to my dad and asked him if I could come back and work on the farm. He said yes, but because he had sold half the stock from the farm when I left in 1988, he said I would have to take a huge reduction in pay from what I had been used to! This meant of course that I had difficulty keeping up the repayments on the Capri and after a while of struggling, I was hauled up before my accountant and told that I had to either give up smoking or the Capri would have to go! Now, I loved smoking (I was on twenty a day!) but I loved the car more, so I gave up smoking and I did it by going cold turkey on the twentieth of January 1992. I even burned the last five cigarettes on the fire! Giving up was the hardest thing I have ever done and I did it without the nicotine replacement stuff you can use now!

I settled back into the rhythm of the farm, at least as much as my craving for cigarettes would let me! Then in 1994 my whole world was turned on its head by a sequence of events which I shall call 'episodes' and these occurred over the period of the next five years until I was finally diagnosed with a form of bipolar, which is the modern interpretation of manic depression.

For years I struggled on without medication but I finally had to succumb and am now at this moment in 2014 stable on the drug Depixol and doing well.

Anyway I hope this has led the reader into the beginning of *The White Mole's Story* in June 1994.

Part 1

Grindelwald, Switzerland
June 1994.

I had saved hard for my summer holiday to Grindelwald in the Swiss Alps and the months preceding it had seemed to drag. This period had included lambing time on the family farm and as any sheep farmer will know, this is a tiring period. Consequently I was mentally feeling a bit jaded, but physically I was in good shape.

Grindelwald is a large village near the town of Interlaken in the Bernese Oberland region and it is a popular hiking and skiing destination. It is my favourite place and preceding this trip I had been there four times, both in winter and summer. I am a good skier and had several unusual experiences while skiing in the Grindelwald area. Before Grindelwald I had not done much hiking or high level walking and the mountains of my home county of Cumbria were largely unexplored by me.

The holiday started normally enough on the nineteenth, with my dad driving me down to Manchester airport. The flight was good and also the coach transfer to the village of Grindelwald at one thousand one hundred and fifty metres (three thousand seven hundred and seventy-three feet) in altitude. The view of the Eiger Mountain up to the right on entering the village was impressive. It stands at the height of three thousand nine hundred and seventy metres (thirteen thousand and twenty-five feet).

During the transfer journey I had met and got to know another single passenger – a bloke called Fred who was also a keen walker and having seen the article about the hiking award you could achieve in the holiday brochure, we agreed to team up and try for it together. He was staying in the same hotel as me, the three-star Jungfrau where I had stayed several times in the past. The coach dropped us off outside the hotel and we checked in. After unpacking and freshening up in my single room I joined Fred in the bar for a couple of beers. I put some music on the jukebox which had an excellent selection. I got out a map of the area and we discussed a variety of hikes that had been listed in the holiday brochure as good ones to do towards achieving the hiking award.

The barmaid informed us that dinner was ready and we went through into the dining room, where we enjoyed an excellent meal. After this we walked up through the village, calling at and enjoying a beer in some of the popular bars as we went. The mighty Wetterhorn at three thousand seven hundred and one metres (twelve thousand one hundred and forty-two feet) rose up, bathed in the setting sun, ahead of us at the end of the valley. We returned to the hotel Jungfrau and retired.

The next morning I rose about seven, went down to breakfast where Fred joined me and we enjoyed some traditional alpine fare. I then went back upstairs, packed my rucksack, donned my hiking boots and then joined Fred in the foyer. The weather was fine and clear as we set off up the street on Monday the twentieth to find the tourist information. On locating it, we picked up a couple of yellow hiking pass award booklets which listed about twenty hikes to choose from. You had to get the booklet stamped at a train or cable car ticket office at the start and finish of each hike to verify them. The stamp had a start and finish time on it so that you could not shorten the hike and cheat by taking public transport. The award schedule shown consisted of four hikes to be awarded a bronze boot, six hikes for a silver boot, and ten hikes for a gold boot.

We left the office and walked to the train station, where we got the booklets stamped at the ticket office. From here we crossed the main street and struck off down a walking path to head for the valley bottom, having decided to do the Grindelwald to Alpiglen hike from the booklet. As we went, we had a good view of the Finsteraarhorn at four thousand two hundred and seventy-four metres (fourteen thousand and twenty-two feet) – the highest mountain in the area, rising up above the lower glacier ahead of us.

Upon reaching the floor of the valley we made our way to the glacier gorge attraction that we had seen signposted. After paying our two Swiss francs entry fee at the kiosk we set off on a narrow path beside and above the churning river from which there rose a chilly breeze. After about twenty-five metres the path entered a narrow tunnel just where the river exited a tall slit in the rock. Emerging from the short tunnel, we stepped onto a wooden walkway bolted to the side of the gorge, which here had widened to about six metres. We walked for about a quarter of a mile, occasionally passing through more tunnels taking photos as we went. The sides of the gorge rose high above us, at one point almost narrowing to meet. Here there was a giant boulder jammed. We reached the end of the path and ahead of us we were faced with a view of the snout of the lower glacier, blocking the gorge some two hundred metres distant. It was covered by old snow, which had avalanched from the high peaks above. We retraced our steps to the start, agreeing that it had been well worth a visit.

Looking at the map, we saw that the Alpiglen path struck off up the side of the gorge nearby, and we found this marked by a signpost showing a walking time of approximately three hours. Also on the sign was a red and white flag denoting that this was a more difficult mountain path.

We set off up through the conifers and although the air was cool we were soon sweating out the beer from the night before. The narrow path zigzagged up through the trees steeply and after about a quarter of an hour they thinned out and we emerged above the gorge on a rocky plateau, a path branched off to the left down to a little footbridge across the chasm, looking at the map we saw it eventually lead to the cable car station at Pfingstegg.

We struck off in the opposite direction back into the trees and continued up the side of the valley which was part of the lower slopes of the Eiger Mountain; presently we came to the base of a ten metre cliff where there was a well-placed set of steel steps which enabled us to surmount this obstacle. Reaching the top of these we continued on a more level path for two hours, passing over several small streams, some of which were avalanche chutes still containing old snow from the winter. As we went, we talked about our jobs, me telling Fred about how I was an agricultural contractor specializing in mole catching and dry stone walling while he told me he was a fork lift truck driver.

The trees thinned out and we reached the little hamlet of Alpiglen at one thousand six hundred and fifteen metres (five thousand two hundred and ninety-eight feet), which is situated next to the cog railway from Grindelwald/Grund to Kleine Scheidegg. Here we got our hiking pass booklets stamped at the railway station and then got a table at the mountain restaurant nearby as we were past ready for our lunch. The waitress came out and we ordered beers and gulashsuppes, which is a thick broth containing meat and vegetables and is served with thick slices of black bread. As we sat back to wait for our meal, we appreciated the fine view back over the valley to the village below and noticed the sheep, pigs, goats and cattle grazing on the high alpine pastures nearby. A parasol sheltered our table from the strong sun and although a few thunderclouds had built up it was still a fine day. Our beers (Feldschlosschen brew) arrived and we took long, well-earned draughts from the foaming half-litre glasses. Our meal was served and we ate heartily, talking together between mouthfuls.

Upon finishing the excellent food and drink we got out the map and hiking pass booklets and saw that the return walk to the village was not listed as an awarded one, but we decided to do it anyway rather than catch a train ride, being still quite fresh. We paid our bills, thanked the waitress, shouldered our rucksacks, left the restaurant and set off down the wide gravel path in the direction of the village. The going was easy and fast, being downhill and in what seemed no time at all we were back at Grund in the valley bottom, having passed through the lower pastures where the farmers were making sweet-smelling hay. From Grund we walked up a tarmac footpath half a mile past the open-air swimming pool to our hotel in Grindelwald. It was only mid-afternoon and I decided to retire to my room for a lie down before dinner.

After I had enjoyed a couple of hours' sleep I went down to reception and asked for a key for the bathroom, my room only having just a wash basin, collected my toiletries from my room and went along the corridor to the bathroom, which was in the centre of the building but contained a small window which opened into a linen room. I ran the bath, got undressed and because the room was steaming up I opened the window. Just at that moment a maid came into the linen room and noticing me looking through the window, smiled, nodded back and feeling slightly embarrassed, I closed the window, thinking this was not a very private set-up but slightly amusing.

I enjoyed soaking my aching legs for an hour then returned to my room, where I wrote up my diary, having donned a change of clothes after my bath. I then went down to the bar where I found Fred talking to the holiday company rep, Karen, who was visiting on her hotel rounds. I bought three beers (Rugen Braus) for the three of us and then joined the other two. Karen was interested in our plans to try and achieve the hiking awards but said to be careful, especially on the red and white marked walks. She then told us about the death of a rep from another company who had fallen from the path to the Gleckstein hut, high above the upper glacier. It had taken the rescuers days to find his body, him having fallen several hundred feet down into the gap between the rock and the ice. This unnerved us slightly but we then felt better afterwards when we saw that that hike was not listed in the booklets.

After a couple of beers and a good crack we parted from Karen and went and enjoyed our evening meal. Upon finishing this we went up the village for a repeat of last night's pub crawl, returning to the hotel about eleven p.m. and retiring to bed.

Tuesday the twenty-first. Rising about seven, I got myself together and joined Fred at breakfast and having brought the map and hiking booklet, we made plans to try for two interlinking hikes, seeing as how the weather looked good; these would comprise walking up from the village to the top gondola station of First, and then walking around the mountain to the col of Grosse Scheidegg.

We finished our meal, picked up our gear from our rooms and set off up through the village, looking for a signposted route that would take us to our objective. We soon found one and the sign showed First, three hours. It was yellow and without the red and white flag denoting that this was a standard grade hike. The gondola station was nearby and we got our booklets stamped at the ticket counter to start the hike, and set off up the path in bright sunshine. The way took us up the eastern side of the valley, between pretty alpine houses and out onto green pastures, some of which were mown for hay. As yesterday, we were soon sweating as we climbed steeply towards the mid station of the gondola at Bort. The path zigzagged up the slope, occasionally passing beneath the trundling gondola cabins, each able to seat six people.

After about an hour and a half's stiff walking we reached Bort and stopped for a rest and a bite to eat from the chocolate bars we had bought at the little supermarket on the way up the village. We set off again after ten minutes or so and toiled on up towards the top gondola station at First. It soon came into view, high up in the distance, perched on a rocky promontory. Another hour and a half saw us reach First at two thousand one hundred and sixty-eight metres (seven thousand one hundred and thirteen feet) and there we had an excellent lunch of bratwurst with rosti (sausage and fried potatoes) accompanied by beer at the restaurant. We ate outside on the veranda above a steep drop; the fine view stretched out over the valley to the magnificent peaks of the Wetterhorn, Schreckhorn (four thousand and seventy-eight metres – thirteen thousand three hundred and seventy-nine feet) and Eiger.

Just then Fred exclaimed, "Hell's teeth, we will have to remember to get our booklets stamped at the gondola station."

I laughed, 'Hell's teeth' being one of my sayings and agreed with him. Finishing our meal, we paid the attractive waitress who was dressed in a traditional Swiss outfit. Shouldering our rucksacks we walked to the gondola lift station and got our booklets duly stamped by the attendant to complete our first hike of the day. We also got a stamp to start the next hike and noticing on the map that there was no cable car or train station at the end of it at Grosse Scheidegg, we consulted the attendant and he told us there was a hotel there, which would stamp the booklets for us.

We walked a short distance and found a signpost, which said 'Grosse Scheidegg two and a half hours'. This was again without the red and white flag so we knew it was an easier walk. We struck out on a wide gravel road, which stretched ahead on the level around the lower slopes of the Schwarzhorn Mountain (two thousand nine hundred and twenty-eight metres – nine thousand six hundred and six feet). I would climb this on a later holiday. The road passed across high mountain pastures which in the winter were ski pistes. (I had skied on these on a previous winter holiday with my sister.)

The going was flat and easy and we were able to let our attention stray to the magnificent view of the high peaks and glaciers to our right. Many other people were walking this route and in typical hiking camaraderie we exchanged the traditional Swiss greeting of *Gruss Gott* as we passed.

In what seemed like no time at all, we reached Grosse Scheidegg at one thousand nine hundred and sixty-two metres (six thousand four hundred and thirty-seven feet). This is a col, which stands right at the head of the valley and is the boundary between the valley of Grindelwald and the valley above the Reichenbach Falls near Meiringen. A good tarmac road joins the two valleys and a regular bus service connects the two villages. The Hotel Grosse Scheidegg is the only building at the col, nestling beneath the mighty cliffs of the Wetterhorn. We got our booklets stamped by the receptionist here to verify the hike and asked her what time would the next bus be calling and she told us they ran on the hour. It was three thirty p.m. so we decided to quench our thirsts with a beer and then take the easy way by bus back to Grindelwald.

We passed a pleasant half hour talking and drinking our beer and then caught the bus back to the village. It was crammed and we had to stand, holding onto the dangling straps as the vehicle traversed the switchback down the high mountain pass. The journey took about twenty minutes and we were dropped off in the middle of the village.

Fred said, "I want to buy some postcards," so we agreed to meet up later and I left him and walked back to the Hotel Jungfrau. On entering reception, I was given a message from the rep Karen. On reading it I learned that it was her day off and she expressed her wish to join Fred and me on a hike, if this was okay. She would meet us at the Hotel Derby reception at nine a.m. on the morrow. Presently Fred arrived back with his cards and we discussed Karen's proposal, deciding we liked the idea.

We parted again and I got the key for the bathroom again and went up for a shave and shower, then had another lie down before going down to the bar for a drink and to put some tunes on the jukebox. Fred soon joined me with a map and his hiking booklet and poring over these, we made plans to again link two hikes together on the morrow. We decided to walk from the village in the same direction as Monday, being towards the gorge, but climbing up to the left of it this time and taking the path to the Steiregg restaurant, high above the lower glacier, where we would have lunch then retrace our steps to do a second, easier looking hike around the lower slopes of the Schreckhorn to the Milchbach restaurant at the upper glacier. By the time we had sorted this out, it was dinner time. Finishing our drinks we joined the other guests (many of whom were British) in the dining room and enjoyed another good meal. Later we went back in the bar and enjoyed more drinks and exchanged hiking stories with other guests then turned in early to prepare for what we thought would be a tough day on the morrow.

Wednesday the twenty-second. I rose early and prepared my hiking gear before joining Fred at breakfast. We left the hotel and made our way up to the Hotel Derby, which was at the railway station. We were right on time and Karen was waiting there for us, suitably equipped with good quality hiking gear. We told her what we had planned for the day and she was pleased because she had not done either of those hikes. The weather was not as good as the previous day's, with low cloud and a little drizzle but Karen said that the forecast was for it to clear up later on.

Fred and I got our booklets stamped at the station and we asked Karen if she was going to try for a hiking award in between her duties as a rep, she said that it was still fairly early in the season but that she may do it later on!

From the station we struck off down into the valley bottom, at one point just avoiding a huge snail slithering across the path in the damp conditions. We crossed a bridge over the turbulent river rushing down from the upper glacier and found a signposted path for Steiregg, marked three hours and also, by the red and white flag. The drizzle had become a little heavier by this time and we were forced to don our coats. The conversation flowed as we set off up the path through grassy pastures; soon we left these and entered the trees. Zigzagging up the slope we became very warm and being sheltered by the trees, were able to remove our coats again.

Karen was quite an attractive woman and Fred and I were soon vying for her attention! After about half an hour's climbing we stopped for a drink and a rest. Sitting down between the tree trunks, we listened to an excited chittering coming from the tree tops.

I said, "What's that racket?"

Karen told me it was black squirrels and suddenly one of them appeared. It scampered down the tree trunk in front of me, coming to a standstill a metre in front of my face. It eyeballed me for a few seconds and then tore off back up the tree. I decided that this was a rare experience and was quite a treat; Karen said that it was unusual for them to come so close.

We set off again and after a while, came to a place where our path joined a wider one coming in from the left and then stretching away to the right beneath a cliff face. Here there was a sign pointing to the left, which said 'Pfingstegg thirty minutes, Milchbach two and a half hours' and pointing to the right, said 'Steiregg two hours'. The cable car was at Pfingstegg, accounting for the fact that there were suddenly a lot more people about. We struck off to the right and as the weather began to lift, we cleared the trees.

The way now took us round into the narrow lower glacier valley, passing across tiered cliffs high above the ice. In places, there were gut-swooping drops down to the right, where we were protected by fencing.

The path rose at a steady rate with a few zigzagging sections and ahead of us the cloud began to break up, offering us tantalizing glimpses of tributary glaciers and high peaks. Presently we rounded a left hand corner and the valley opened out to present a fine view of the main glacier ahead and below us. To our right, about two hundred metres away, tucked back on the side of the valley was a fairly large, prettily flower decked building, this being obviously the Steiregg restaurant, which lay at one thousand seven hundred and two metres (five thousand five hundred and eighty-four feet).

We made our way across to the hostelry and were surprised to see sheep grazing nearby! We joined many other walkers there and sat down at a table. A waitress came and seeing as gulashsuppe was on the menu, we ordered that, accompanied by the mandatory beers.

As we waited for our meal, the sound of an approaching helicopter reached our ears. It soon came into view from the direction of Grindelwald and came into land in a flurry of flying dead grass, near to the restaurant. The pilot got out and proceeded to unload packages from the cargo bay of the machine. A member of the restaurant staff went to help him carry the evident supplies to the restaurant, this obviously being the only way to supply the hostelry! And it was reflected in the menu prices. Our meal duly arrived and we asked the waitress if she could stamp our hiking booklets. She said yes and that she would go and find the stamp. We tucked into our meals, enjoying the sun, which had begun to peep out from between the breaking clouds.

On finishing, Fred got out the map and pointed out to Karen and me that the path continued a long way on up the twisting glacier valley, to terminate at the high Schreckhorn hut. Karen said that this route was reserved for mountaineers and bearing in mind what had happened to the other rep above the upper glacier, I realised that I would only be able to attempt one of these routes when I had more experience.

We summoned the waitress and paid for our meals, leaving a tip. She then stamped our booklets to verify the hike, then stamped them again to start the next hike and told us we were the first hikers to receive the stamp that season.

We sat for a bit longer and Karen informed us that tonight was 'Bring your own drink' night at the nightclub and that all the other reps would be there.

Fred said, "That sounds like a good party."

Karen said that it was usually a good night out. We left Steiregg and retraced our steps to the place where the paths divided. About halfway back we were startled by a loud crack and roar. Turning, we were just in time to catch sight of a large ice avalanche cascading down from the Eiger onto the glacier below, I was quick and was able to get a photo of this, thinking we had been treated to a grand display of nature's might.

We walked on, past the top station of the cable car at Pfingstegg (one thousand three hundred and ninety-one metres – four thousand five hundred and sixty-three feet) towards Milchbach. This path was more level and we made fast progress. We were right at the limit of the tree line and at intervals were able to catch good views out across the valley, over the village, down towards the town of Interlaken hidden in the distance.

At one point we came across a fairly large stream, which flowed over bare rock scoured clean by avalanches from the cliffs of the Schreckhorn above during the winter. We picked our way across this area and continued on, eventually arriving at the Milchbach restaurant at one thousand three hundred and forty-eight metres (four thousand four hundred and twenty-two feet). Here we got a beer each and sat on the veranda, after getting our booklets stamped by one of the staff. I was intrigued by the view of a narrow path with a toll-gate, which began at the side of the restaurant and snaked up the cliffs beside the upper glacier. There appeared to be ladders in places to get over the steeper sections. As I watched, I picked out two figures climbing up a cliff section off to the side of the path, high up near the point where the path disappeared over a lip into the upper glacier valley. Suddenly one of the figures appeared to drop from the cliff and disappear.

I shouted out, "Jesus, one of those people has fallen."

One of the waitresses was nearby and she came over to ask what I was making a fuss about. I told her what I had witnessed.

She said, "Are you sure?"

"Of course I'm sure," I retorted in a strident voice.

She rushed off inside to get her boss. He came out and told us he would get in touch with the rescue services, but just then we looked up and saw that the fallen climber had reappeared on a ledge and his/her partner had climbed back down to him/her! They started back down the path towards us, stumbling in places and after a while came through the toll-gate. They were a young English couple and it was obviously the girl who had fallen because her face, legs and arms were all covered in bloody grazes. The restaurant staff helped them to a table and got them a couple of brandies. They were both visibly shaken but were now in good hands, so we left thinking this could be a very dangerous environment and made our way down to the signposted 'ice grotto', which proved to be a tunnel bored into the snout of the upper glacier. There was a small entry fee! We paid and entered the intensely blue tunnel; it had boards on the floor to stop you slipping and went in for thirty metres or so, to end in a chamber decorated with ice carvings of various animals. We took photos and then retraced our steps, back out into the afternoon sunshine.

We struck out, heading back towards Grindelwald, passing the Hotel Wetterhorn where there was an old restored cable car on display. Karen pointed out that there had once been a cableway up to a point, high to the left of the upper glacier and she pointed up to show Fred and me the old concrete bunker which formed the top station, high on the cliffs.

We walked on, the going was easy and the afternoon was hot as we left the trees and trekked through the mountain pastures where hay was being made. At one point we stopped to watch a group of haymakers near the path. There was one middle-aged woman working a hay rake and she had a skirt on. I thought that was brave considering there were lots of horseflies about, these nasty sods can give you a painful bite. Just then one of the pesky insects landed on her leg. She waited for a few seconds and then calmly reached down and crushed it in her fingers! There were many people working in the fields, some with hand tools and some on machines, as we continued on back into the village.

Karen parted from us near the gondola station, saying that she would meet us at nine p.m. that evening at the Espresso bar. She said how much she had enjoyed walking with us. Fred and I said the pleasure was mutual and then headed off down the street to our hotel.

We got ready in the usual fashion, had our evening meal and then went out on the town. I took my bottle of duty free Bacardi with me, (up until that night I had only been taking nips out of it) and Fred took something similar for the 'Bring your own drink' bash at the nightclub.

We had a beer in each of the popular bars, enjoying the crack and were feeling a bit squiffy by the time we entered the packed Espresso bar. We were a bit late and Karen was already there, dressed in her party gear. She was accompanied by five other reps from different holiday companies and she introduced Fred and me to them as, 'The two intrepid hikers from the Jungfrau.' There were a couple of pretty women in the group and I took a shine to one of them.

We got a good crack going, had a couple of rounds of drinks and then left the bar and headed up the street to the nightclub, which was under the five star Hotel Sunstar and was called the Plaza Club. We descended a flight of steps and I was surprised to find that there was no entrance fee. On entering the club, I surveyed the scene, noticing that there was only one bar, albeit a large one, and only one dance floor. The fittings were plush and very upmarket. We made our way to the bar and bought bottles of soft drinks to mix with the spirits we had all brought with us. The prices were steep even for these and I was glad we didn't have to buy alcohol!

There were seated alcoves all around the dance floor and we bagged one of these. Glasses had been supplied from the bar and we all charged them. Karen stood and raised a toast to good hiking and to good health. My Bacardi and Coke was delicious and slid down my throat very easily, me being a bit bloated from the beer I had drunk so far! The music was loud and there was an excellent light display from both above and below the transparent dance floor. I was feeling confident and my dancing feet came upon me when I heard the opening bars of a Billy Ocean number. I got up and asked the rep I had taken a shine to, whose name was Susan, if she would like to dance with me. She nodded 'Yes' and we made our way out onto the dance floor. A cloud of dry ice greeted us as we stepped onto the flashing coloured squares of the floor. I soon began to relax and show some good moves, which matched Susan's, who was a very good dancer. Some of the other members of our group soon joined us, including Karen but Fred stayed firmly in his seat!

After a couple of tunes Susan and I returned to our seats. I took a pull at my drink and could have sworn that my glass was fuller than before we started dancing. Fred seemed very quiet as I turned my attention fully to Susan. I found her very easy to talk to and conversation flowed easily. We were soon out on the dance floor again but Fred refused to join us. We kept having breaks from dancing to get a drink and every time I returned to the table my glass seemed fuller and the bottle of Bacardi emptier!

As the night went on, I became more and more inebriated, even though I was burning the alcohol off by dancing. On one occasion when returning to the table, I discovered the reason for my drink seeming fuller – I caught Fred topping up my glass with Bacardi.

I said, "That's enough of that mate, I can get my own drink, thank you!"

He just laughed and then looked sheepish. I was quite annoyed but bit back any reaction. The bottle of Bacardi was by now nearly empty as I took a long swig from my glass. This time there was a peculiar bitter taste to the liquor but at the time I never gave it another thought. It was now nearly two a.m. and the nightclub was preparing to close. The slow dances came on and I tugged Susan back onto the floor for a final smooch. We were both pretty sozzled and she was putty in my hands. We enjoyed a couple of dances and then it was time to go home. I kissed Susan as we came off the dance floor, but she made it plain that she did not want to take things any further! All of us were pretty well oiled as we left the club and as we did so the night air hit me and I fell into some nearby bushes, Fred must have pulled me out but that's the last thing I remember until the next day!

The reader will have to bear with me because I cannot remember parts of the days which followed!

Thursday the twenty-third. I was still drunk, but must have got ready in the usual way. I may have eaten breakfast! But I found myself on the train to Kleine Scheidegg, which is the train station and hamlet on the ridge between the valleys of Grindelwald and Wengen. Fred was with me and told me that we had made plans last night to go across to the village of Murren, taking in a listed hike on the way. I can't remember making any such plans but here I was, so I would have to get on with it! It was mid-morning, so I must have slept late. The little train rattled its way up the cog railway, stopping briefly at Alpiglen to allow passengers to alight and board, then trundled on to our destination.

We alighted at Kleine Scheidegg amid a torrent of Japanese tourists. This is the start of the train ride to the Jungfraujoch, the highest railway station in Europe, where the Japanese Emperor paid a visit.

I said to Fred, "I'm not feeling too well today, mate, you will have to look after me!"

He replied, "I'm not surprised, you were really knocking it back last night!"

I shot back, "I had a little help from you!"

We went to the ticket office and got our booklets stamped to begin a hike to Wengen. The duration would be about two and a half hours and we set off, my rucksack seemed particularly heavy, so thank God the route was all downhill. The weather was good but a few ominous thunder clouds had started to build to the southwest. Fred wasn't very talkative and I assumed he was jealous of me because of my apparent success with the women on the previous night! Therefore there wasn't much crack. This was, I suppose, the start of a rift between us, but if I'm honest, things began to go wrong between us when I caught him tampering with my drink! The path was wide and busy with other walkers, taking us down through summer pastures, which in winter form part of the Lauberhorn run ski piste, famous as the longest downhill run of the season for the champion skiers.

The going was fast in spite of my ever-present hangover, and we were soon down in Wengen, which is similar in size to Grindelwald, but is traffic free. We must have got lunch somewhere but I can't remember. After getting our booklets stamped at the station we continued on foot down into Lauterbrunnen in the valley bottom. (This was not a listed hike in the booklets.) We then got tickets for and took the funicular railway up the other side of the valley to Grutchalp. As we travelled up the steep gradient, we observed the mighty cliff on our left, down which fell the waterfall described by Lord Byron as 'the tail of the pale horse ridden by death'.

I think we walked from Grutchalp to the village of Murren, I do not recall but I do remember taking the cable car to the peak of the Schilthorn at two thousand nine hundred and seventy metres (nine thousand seven hundred and forty-five feet), where there is a revolving restaurant called Piz Gloria, made famous in the Bond film *On Her Majesty's Secret Service*. I had skied down from here with my sister in the afore-mentioned winter holiday. There are magnificent vistas all around from this fine viewpoint. Fred was still with me and we must have spent some time here, then gone back down on the cable car to Murren. I remember getting our booklets stamped at the bottom cable car station and doing a listed hike back to a village between Murren and Grutchalp.

The afternoon had become very hot and thundery, my water supply had run out; I was dehydrated from all the drink the night before and I recall accepting drinks off Fred, who had a blue and a red flask. He always offered me the red flask and after a while walking and a few pulls at the red flask I became very silly and giggly, I would burst out laughing at the slightest thing Fred said. (He had begun to talk more again by now.) He told me that he had experimented with various street drugs in his time and I giggled.

I asked him if he was 'using' at that moment.

He said, "I might be."

I told him I was feeling strange and asked him if there was anything other than water in the red flask. He became very evasive and would not give me a straight answer. Because of this my euphoric mood began to evaporate and be replaced by one of suspicion and paranoia. Just then there was the most colossal bang, which echoed around the valleys! It frightened me and I asked Fred what he thought it was.

He was pleased to have the subject changed and said, "They must be blasting some rock somewhere."

The sound was like thunder but much louder. I looked to the sky to find that it had become filled with towering thunderheads. They were almost like nuclear explosions and I became very afraid!

We finished the hike and got stamped somewhere and returned to Grindelwald, probably by train through the valleys. The rest of the day and evening is a blank; whether I had anything to eat or drink I can't say!

Friday the twenty-fourth. I awoke and getting up opened the bedroom window. There was no view, only a few bushes, in which sat a small brown bird. It was singing loudly and it seemed to say to me, 'Get up, get out and get moving!'

I hurriedly packed my gear, donned my boots and left the hotel. As I did so, I noticed a red Ford Mondeo parked in the layby opposite the hotel. A man was leaning against the driver's door, reading a newspaper.

When he saw me, he folded the paper and got into the car. I set off to walk down the pavement at the side of the main road in the general direction of Interlaken. On occasion, I looked back to see if the car had set off after me; it had not! The paranoid feeling from the day before was still with me and I also began to feel I was entering some kind of different dimension, where everyone and everything else was behaving strangely, when in fact I was the one who was behaving oddly!

I left the main road onto a walking path through the outskirts of the village and through the pastures, heading down the valley. Suddenly a large flock of carrion crows took flight from a tree nearby with a raucous cawing. I had shot hundreds of these nasty sods in my time on the family farm back home, and it seemed to me in my fevered mind that they were calling out to me, mocking me for taking so many of their number's lives back home. I hurried on, yesterday's thunderclouds had dispersed and the day was fine and hot.

I passed through several hamlets and presently came into the village of Burglauenen, where there is a station on the main railway line from Grindelwald to Interlaken. The main valley road also passes through here. I was now on a single-track road with houses on one side. It ran parallel to the main road. On hearing the sound of a car engine behind me, I turned to see the same red Ford that had been outside the hotel; the driver was watching me intently! I waved him by but he continued to crawl along behind me. Suddenly I panicked and ran off down a side road and straight across the main road, narrowly avoiding being run over! I shot straight over into another side road, which took me over a bridge spanning the main valley river. I then left the road and scrambled up a steep grassy bank and into the trees. I tore up the steep slope until I was out of breath; collapsing on the ground I tried to regain my breath. I was now out of sight of the road and getting up, I continued on up the slope much more slowly. Presently I came upon a clearing in the trees where there sat a huge boulder. I crept into the overhang of this and sat down on a smaller rock, put my head between my knees and began to shake uncontrollably!

I don't know how long I remained in this position but I must have got up and returned to Grindelwald at some point, for I awoke in my hotel room early the following morning.

Saturday the twenty-fifth. It must have been about three a.m. when I rose and although I probably hadn't eaten anything the day before, I wasn't hungry! Whether I had slept much I can't say, but the hunted, paranoid feeling was upon me once more and after hurriedly packing my gear I left my room and crept downstairs. There was no-one about at this hour as I unlocked the front door of the hotel with my room key, then re-locked it behind me. It was still dark as I made my way down the main road from the hotel; there was some ambient light from the street lamps and I was able to see quite a bit at this point. Suddenly the lights of a vehicle appeared down the road and I jumped over the roadside barrier into the adjoining pasture. The grass was long and wringing wet with dew. As I ran through the pasture, my legs became drenched by the cold dew. It became darker as I got further from the road and I fell over a couple of fences before encountering the train track from the village down into Grund in the valley bottom. I picked my way across this and soon found a proper path, which took me down towards the river. There is a big car park at Grund, which services the train to Kleine Scheidegg and the gondola cableway up to Mannlichen. Here I encountered several cars with their lights on and engines running. I skirted the car park and set off to run in the direction of the glacier gorge. The cars left the park and spread out round the nearby roads; I thought they were looking for me and I dropped to the ground as one of them roared towards me, passing close. After it had passed I saw it turn right and in the beam of its headlights I could see that it was going over one of the few bridges over the main river. I got up, ran after it and crossed the bridge.

 The sky was now beginning to lighten in the east behind me and visibility was therefore improving. Having crossed the river and avoiding the cars, I struck off the road up through more pastures, eventually coming to the tree line, where I got briefly tangled up in a single electric fence wire, so positioned to keep the cattle out of the trees. I felt strangely energised as I climbed up the steep slope, which forms the lower slopes of the Eiger. I must have been running on pure adrenalin. The trees were quite well spaced and I was able to make quite rapid progress up the mountain side in the dim early dawn light.

 How long I climbed for I can't say, but somewhere along the way I acquired two sticks about an inch thick and two feet long, which I packed in my rucksack. Eventually I struck a path crossing my line of travel and realizing that this must be the Alpiglen path that we had walked on the first day, I followed it.

 It was by now fully daylight and the sky was beginning to cloud over from the south, behind the Eiger. Just then, small white particles began to fall from the sky and as they settled on the ground I expected them to melt, thinking they were snow, but they did not. This alarmed me and I thought back to two days ago, when I had seen what looked like nuclear explosions in the sky and drew the conclusion that the white flakes were some kind of fallout. The Bosnian war was being fought at the time and I thought there must have been some kind of escalation. This made an already troubled mind even worse! I put my coat and hat on to protect myself from this stuff and continued along the path, but instead of heading for Alpiglen I struck off to the left, up steep slopes where the trees soon thinned out and the ground became rock-strewn. I climbed steadily towards the infamous mighty north face of the Eiger; occasionally traversing patches of old snow. I reached the base of the great cliff and looked up at the towering edifice. I reached out to touch the icy cold rock and although my mind was tortured, it wasn't that far gone that it suggested me trying to climb this obstacle! I made my way along the base of the great face for a mile or so, eventually coming out on the grassy slopes above Kleine Scheidegg.

To my left was the little railway station called Eigergletcher, on the Jungfraujoch line. I made my way to this and sat down in the ticket office. One of the station workers approached me and said something in German; I replied that I was English. He then spoke to me in English, asking me where I had come from, (it being still early morning.) I said Grindelwald and made up some cock and bull story about me setting off early to get clear of the Eiger north face before the sun loosened rocks to avalanche from the top of the face! He then gave me a funny look suggesting that I was quite mad and he was probably right! I asked him if I could buy a ticket for the train ride to the top here and he said yes, so I did this at the desk and went out onto the platform to wait for what must surely have been the first train of the day.

I was pretty exhausted by now and I thought a nice train ride would give me a rest! Presently the little cream and brown train came trundling up the cog railway and pulled up to let me board; there were no other passengers getting on here. Even at that early hour the train was quite crowded, but I found a seat. I attracted quite a few curious glances from other passengers, aimed in the direction of the two sticks that were poking out of my rucksack!

The train set off again and soon entered the tunnel bored into the side of the Eiger. From here the track extends up through the mountain, passing the north face, where there are narrow side tunnels at right angles to the track which allow passengers to walk through and look out of windows set in the face towards Kleine Scheidegg and Grindelwald. The railway then turns to the right and there are more side tunnels at Eismeer, which allow you to walk through and look out of the south side of the

Eiger over impressive glaciers. The track then continues inside the rock under the peak of the Monch to the top station of the Jungfraujoch at three thousand four hundred and fifty-four metres (eleven thousand three hundred and thirty-three feet). Because I had been up here on the previous winter holiday I did not visit any of these attractions on the way up and apart from falling asleep on the train, I can't remember what else I did up there, although there are many things to do!

Some time must have passed and I must have returned down to Kleine Scheidegg, for the next thing I remember is walking down the wide path back towards Grindelwald. Strange dark clouds were streaming out of the two glacier valleys ahead of me to my right! I realized that this was smoke coming from what I thought at the time was some great conflict to the south. Thinking that there was fallout in the air I tied my handkerchief around my nose and mouth. This of course attracted strange looks from other walkers.

Suddenly one of them spoke to me, saying, "Hell's teeth, Steve, why have you got that hanky tied round your face!" I was surprised to find Fred standing in front of me! I replied with something like, "Christ, Fred can't you see World War Three has broken out, get yourself to safety!"

He laughed and said, "Shit, you are losing it, mate, get yourself to a doctor!"

I gave him a hard stare and pushed past him to continue down the path thinking what a coincidence, meeting him at this time and place! Nothing more can be remembered until the following day!

Sunday the twenty-sixth. I found myself sitting in the hotel Jungfrau reception, mid-morning, with my hiking gear at hand, watching a group of Japanese guests carrying their suitcases down a nearby passage. I went across to the desk and asked the girl there if they had closed the country's borders yet.

She said, "You need to relax, Mr Titterington. A doctor is coming to see you in a little while."

This spooked me and I gathered my gear and fled from the hotel!

I must have made my way across the valley to the Mannlichen area, because I found myself climbing out of the valley again in this area. It was very hot and I made my way off the path through the pastures into a grove of trees, where I lay down and promptly fell asleep,

It was late afternoon when I was awoken by the sound of distant thunder. I wearily hoisted my rucksack and continued on up the slope. It was a long way up to the top gondola station of Mannlichen and it was nearly dark as I approached this. My state of mind was still one of suspicion and paranoia. It was almost like I was in some kind of alternative dimension! Yesterday's smoke had dispersed, but the air had become very heavy and oppressive. Just then a bright beam of light shone out from the lift station, down towards me and thinking it was some kind of searchlight, I ducked down and scuttled across the slope to avoid it. From my memory I knew there was a good, level, wide path, which connected Mannlichen with Kleine Scheidegg, so, wishing to avoid other people, I made for this.

Night had now closed in and the air crackled with energy, the thunder had moved much closer and lightning flashed out close by. I donned my Gore-Tex coat but I had no waterproof trousers at that time, so had to make do. Although I knew a powerful thunderstorm was beginning, I was aware that the lightning would show me the path I had embarked upon. Great fat drops of rain began to fall and it soon became a torrential downpour, the lightning flashed and the thunder roared and I was very frightened, but I ploughed stubbornly on along the path. There is a place where the path passes around the flanks of the Tschuggen Mountain and there are steep drop-offs here so I had to be very careful.

I eventually reached the hamlet of Kleine Scheidegg. My trousers were soaked and the rain had begun to run off into my boots; however, the good quality coat was keeping my top half dry. I stopped and crept into the doorway of a snow tractor shed. Just then the sky in front of me, near the Jungfrau Mountain, lit up! A string of lightning was seen to descend from the broiling clouds and on the end of it was a ball of light. This suddenly exploded in a sheet of bright light, I had never before or have since seen the like – this was ball lightning. As it turned out this was the peak of the storm and the rain began to ease, the thunder moved away and the cloud began to lift.

After a short while I left my temporary shelter and set off down the path towards Wengen. I was familiar with this route as it was the same one Fred and I had taken a few days ago. The cloud began to break, revealing a half moon and the visibility began to improve. Strangely, I was still not hungry, but even if I had been I only had a few squares of chocolate left in my soaked rucksack. I made good progress but stumbled occasionally where there were rough patches in the path, concealed by the gloomy moonlight shadows of trees. I eventually came into Wengen, but didn't stop, carrying on down into Lauterbrunnen in the valley bottom. Here I sought out the railway station, found a bench seat and curled up to sleep, but although the station was deserted I could only manage to doze.

I remained here for about a couple of hours until the dawn began to show. I got up with the knowledge that there would soon be people about and set off again. It was amazing that by this time I was not footsore but I had on the best pair of boots I have ever owned – Scarpa Attacks!

Monday the twenty-seventh. I made my way across the valley to the conifer woods, down range from the Grutschalp funicular railway station and struck up the steep slope through the trees. Daylight strengthened as I fought my way through the undergrowth. I toiled on for several hours until suddenly I came out onto a wide roughly paved path. On the ground in front of me was a piece of paper wedged under a stone. I picked it up and on it were scribbled some of what looked like words in a very shaky hand. In my fevered mind, I thought the 'little people' had left me some kind of message and although the words were not decipherable, they seemed to be telling me to follow the path upwards.

In all this charging around the countryside, I guess I was looking for some place of safety, a kind of Shangri-la, or a doorway back into the normal world! I struck off up the wide path and presently came to a place where there was a small limestone crag next to the path. On impulse I took off my rucksack and set about trying to climb it. I got halfway up and suddenly there was a furious beating of wings behind my head. I nearly fell off and was forced to retreat to a narrow ledge where I turned to find I was under attack by an extremely pissed off raven. I stopped moving and it moved away to alight on the crag some ten feet away, then amazingly it appeared to begin talking! I remember thinking I must really have lost it now, but it may be not that far-fetched, there are such things as talking birds. It must have been speaking German for I could not understand it, but I got the general drift of its meaning being, "Get the hell off my territory!" It obviously meant business so I climbed back down, picked up my rucksack and continued on my way. The path levelled out and presently cleared the trees, entering high mountain pastures. It led me to the top station of the Grutschalp funicular railway. I must have still had enough cash with me because I was able to buy a ticket for the little train to Murren. It must have been around midday as I boarded the train, it was almost empty and as it travelled along the level track, I took the opportunity to go forward and speak to the driver. I cannot remember much of what I said to him but I do recall asking him how the war was going! His only response being, "Please return to your seat, sir."

I obeyed and we soon arrived at the village of Murren. Last night's thunderstorm had cleared the air and it was now fine and clear again, but becoming hot. Having had little response from the train driver about the state of the world, I decided to phone home. I found a public telephone and dialled my home number, but was unable to make a connection. (Looking back, I was using the wrong code) This made me feel more that there was indeed some global conflagration! I must have mooched around the village for a while and then walked all the way back to Grutschalp. My water bottles were empty and had been for some time, but I was suspicious of the cattle water troughs that were placed at intervals along the way, because of what might be falling from the sky! I would only drink from natural springs, which were few and far between so therefore I wasn't getting enough hydration.

When I got back to Grutschalp, I set off to retrace my steps on the path I had walked earlier that day. The afternoon was very hot and being exhausted by this time, I soon left the path and found a quiet place in the undergrowth where I could rest. I tried to sleep but was again unsuccessful, so I just lay flat out until the day had begun to cool.

Later I got up and resumed walking the path, heading south around the wooded side of the mountain. Eventually I came out onto a gravelled forestry road and I followed it as it zigzagged uphill. After a bit there was a turning to the left and following it I came to a cliff into which a vehicle-sized tunnel was bored. Sounds of machinery and drilling came from it, so I didn't go in. Instead I noticed a large ladder made from sections of trees to the left of the tunnel mouth and I climbed up it, coming out about forty feet up onto the top of the cliff. There was a level area here where a large tree had been felled, it had been cut off about four feet from its base and there was a metal spike hammered into the middle of the stump. Looking out across the valley from here, I determined fancifully that this was the mount for a machine gun! Upon hearing voices from below I turned and headed into the trees, along a faint path.

It was now late in the day and the temperature was falling away quickly. I realized that I was quite high up and that the coming night would probably be very cold. To avoid hypothermia, (my survival instincts were kicking in) I would have to find somewhere to spend the night. Just then the trees thinned out and I came upon a high mountain farm. I went to the farmhouse and knocked on the door. It was opened by a burly man and I asked him in English if he had anywhere I could sleep. He replied in German, but with a few English words, which formed the distinct impression to me that he was telling me to bugger off. I looked past him to see the rest of his family tucking into their evening meal and I was suddenly very hungry. However, the farmer shook his fist at me, therefore sending me away with a flea in my ear, (now I know how Joseph felt when he was told there was no room at the inn!) I left hurriedly and headed off up a valley, now clear of the trees, night had closed in but the moon was out and I was able to pick my way across the rough pastures. However I soon realized that I was heading farther and farther from habitation, so I turned around and headed back in the direction of the farm. I was thoroughly worn out and felt the farmer had behaved very badly towards me. I therefore decided I would rest in one of his barns anyway.

On getting back to the farm, I crept under the side of a shed, but the cows grazing nearby smelled me out, came across and licked at me. This was no good because I wasn't going to get a minute's peace so I got out of there and entered a cowshed. By the moonlight, I could see that there were a number of young calves tied by the neck, so I let them loose and chased them out into the open air! I then curled up in the empty stall and tried to sleep but of course the disorientated calves were making a racket, so fearing this would attract attention I went outside once more. There were some pigs grunting in another shed and I thought to myself, I'll teach those sods in the farmhouse to treat me like shit. So I let the pigs out! This caused pandemonium and I legged it into the trees to head back down the mountain.

I stopped after a couple of miles and curled up at the base of a tree and tried to sleep again. I nodded off for a while but was soon woken by the cold seeping through my clothing. I got up and wearily continued downhill, eventually coming out on the forestry track again. I followed it until I came to a house, there were lights on and I could hear voices. There was a Diahatsu truck parked nearby and as I was worn out, I thought, what the hell, I wonder if the keys are in it; they were. I got in. It was left hand drive of course and I started it up; however, I could not find the switch for the lights and could only engage reverse gear! I reversed the vehicle into a side turning then put it in neutral and allowed it to freewheel down the road. I was able to see fairly well by the moonlight filtering through the trees and steered the truck down the road for a couple of miles. I then abandoned it on the roadside, realizing that it would be no further use to me when I got onto the flat, having still not been able to find a forward gear. I hoisted my rucksack once more and for some reason set off back up the road. After a short distance I encountered a huge bulldozer parked in a layby, I got on it but there were no keys so I couldn't start it. I then continued on my way. It was the early hours of the morning before I passed the house where I had acquired the truck.

Tuesday the twenty-eighth. It was all quiet at the house as I sneaked past; I continued along the road for a while and came to a little hamlet. The first building on the right hand side looked like a small barn and being desperate to get out of the cold, (there was frost on the grass by now!) I investigated it. Going round the front, I found a door and a window. It looked deserted and as I thought the whole world had gone to hell in a hand cart and it didn't matter what I did any more, I broke a pane of glass in the window, reached in, unfastened the window catch and climbed into a little room. There was a table and a few chairs; also in the gloom I spotted a folded deck chair leaning against the wall. I unfolded the deck chair, dropped my rucksack and gratefully sank into the chair. I tried to sleep again but there was obviously no heating and I only managed to doze. After a few hours the dawn light came creeping in through the window and I got up for a better look around. At the back of the room I found a small flight of wooden steps. On climbing these, I found myself in a kind of loft, on the left was an area where hay might be stored and on the right was a relatively new door, which appeared to access another room. I knocked on it, just in case there was somebody in this part of the building, but judging by the amount of dust on the furniture downstairs I thought this unlikely. I then noticed that the door handle was securely tied shut with baler twine. I untied this and opened the door, going through I was amazed to find myself standing in a tiny, self-contained flat. Looking around, I saw a little table and chair, a two berth bunk bed and various cupboards fastened to the pine panelled walls. There was also a window, of course. I wondered if there was any food and upon exploration of the cupboards found a selection of tinned goods. There was Spam, beans and fruit in syrup! I was amazed; here there was food, sheets and duvets on the beds and just as important – a place to lie up. It really was heaven sent! In the table drawers, I found a tin opener and cutlery. There were plates in the cupboards and I was soon tucking into a fine meal of cold pork and beans followed by delicious, thirst quenching tinned fruit. After eating my excellent meal I stripped off my clothes and slipped under the duvet of the bottom bunk bed. I was asleep finally and instantly!

 I awoke around mid-afternoon, having had the best sleep for ages, but for a minute I didn't know where I was, then it all came back to me. Suddenly it was as if I had awoken back in the normal world and I began to think rationally again.

 I said out loud to myself, "Jesus, I've been away from my hotel for nearly three days, they will be looking for me!"

I got out of bed and dressed. I rubbed my face and found several days' growth there. I thought I must look like a down and out, but thankfully there was no mirror to confirm this. There was no sink or running water in the flat so I took the dirty meal utensils downstairs. I found a key for the back door in the table drawer and went outside into the afternoon sunshine. Just outside was a little wooden trough into which water was pouring from a metal pipe. I scooped water out of the trough to wash the dirty dishes then took them back upstairs. I put the utensils back where I found them and put the empty tins into a bin bag. My bowels were moving and so, there being no toilet; I crapped into the bin bag and left it in the dustbin outside the flat door. I tidied up the bed and the rest of the flat as best I could, packed my rucksack, tied up the flat door again, re-locked the back door and left the building by a large trapdoor that I had found on the front of the structure.

In the daylight, I could see that there were eight or ten other buildings in the hamlet. There didn't appear to be anybody about, thank God! Looking back now I think the hamlet must only have been used possibly by hay making farmers later in the season. I set off down the hillside and soon found a path, signposted to the train station of Zweilutschinen in the valley bottom. I followed this route, knowing that the train was the quickest way of getting back to Grindelwald. I was feeling well rested and mentally I was fine again. I had refilled my water bottles at the little trough where I had rested up, being now unafraid of the water. I was in a hurry to get back and resume normal life. There were no threatening clouds in the sky and no loud bangs to make me nervous! I made good progress down through trees and meadows and was soon down at the next village, Isenfluh. There was a footpath sign here which in pointing back the way I'd come, named the hamlet where I had rested up as Sulwald.

I continued on through Isenfluh and down to Zweilutschinen, where I bought a ticket at the station for Grindelwald. The trains ran on the hour, every hour and I just had time to get a drink at a little restaurant nearby. I had mineral water, having made up my mind to keep off alcohol for a bit! After I had enjoyed my refreshment I went to the station with only a few minutes to spare before the train from Interlaken got in. I boarded the brown and yellow train and found a seat; it was quite crowded at this time of day, it being by now about five o'clock. As the train set off up the valley, I began to think about what I might find when I got back to my hotel and became apprehensive! The train ride to Grindelwald took about twenty minutes. I got off as it pulled into the station and walked down the road to the Hotel Jungfrau.

On entering reception the girl there exclaimed, "Mr Titterington, thank God! Where have you been?"

I replied, "I got lost in the mountains for a bit but I finally found my way back."

She then said, "I will telephone Karen and tell her you are back. Please wait here till she is able to come, we have all been very worried about you!"

I sat down in the lounge nearby and waited for Karen. She arrived after about twenty minutes in a fluster and promptly threw her arms round me, giving me a bear hug!

She said, "Thank God you're all right, where on earth have you been? The authorities were just about to launch a search and rescue operation; it would have cost your family thousands!" (If you go missing and have to be rescued in Switzerland, you have to pay for it, unlike the U.K.)

I said, "I'm sorry I've been such a worry, but I haven't been feeling well since the night out at the club and I felt an overwhelming urge to get away for a bit."

She said, "That's okay but you should have told someone where you were going." I couldn't tell her not even I knew where I was going!

She said, "Fred told me he saw you on Saturday and he said you were acting all weird"

I replied, "I'm not surprised I was, because of the amount of Bacardi he was putting in my glass that night!"

I told her I had become worried by the loud bang I had heard and by the smoke coming from the south! She told me that there had been some large forest fires to the south of the Jungfrau range, so that explained the smoke I had seen. She also told me that there was always a certain amount of blasting going on in the area! We sat down and I told her what I had been up to the last few days and she was amazed, but also a little worried, especially about the theft of the vehicle and breaking into the flat! Just at that moment I had a thought and I began rummaging in my rucksack.

I said, "Damn, I can't find my camera. I'm sure I had it at the flat where I laid up!"

Karen said, "Are there any pictures of you on it?"

I replied, "Shit, yes. I will have to go back and get it!"

She said, "Yes, I suppose you will, but not before you've had a good rest and got some proper meals inside you."

I was forced to agree. I thought to myself, *how could I have been so stupid as to leave my precious camera at the flat!*

The receptionist called over to me, "I assume you will be eating here tonight?"

I said, "Yes, of course."

Just at that moment the large glass door into the dining room was slid back and dinner was served.

Karen said, "Before you eat, can I ask, do you want to see a doctor after your meal? I mean, just to check you over!"

I replied, "No, I'm feeling fine now, thanks!" It was true, I really was okay again. I had no time to get shaved and washed before dinner, so I just went into the dining room and dumped my rucksack by my table. Karen had left and gone about the rest of her duties. I received some odd looks from the other guests, but the serving girls said some nice things to me! Fred was at another table and just gave me the odd cursory glance.

After enjoying a nice filling meal I left the dining room, got the key for the bathroom from reception, went upstairs and had a much needed shave and a good soak in the bath. I returned the bathroom key and went straight to bed, where I went out like a light!

Wednesday the twenty-ninth. I awoke around eight thirty a.m., got myself together and went down for breakfast, where I ate like a horse! There was no sign of Fred, he must have gone walking. I sat in the dining room and planned what I would do next. I determined that first I would make use of the laundrette across the road from the hotel and wash my very sweaty clothes. Then I would make use of my German phrase book and compose a letter of apology and thanks for the owners of the flat where I had rested up. I would then take this, with some money to pay for any damages and leave it at the flat when I went back to recover my camera on the morrow.

It took me all day to do these things and the composition of the letter was especially difficult! I had enjoyed lunch in the public restaurant of the hotel, eating a most excellent omelette, eggs being my favourite food.

The evening followed the same course as the one before; Karen visited again and we had a drink in the bar, (non-alcoholic for me). She was keen to know my plans for the coming days and I told her about the letter I had written and my plan to take it and retrieve my camera. She was impressed and told me that I was a decent person.

I had also been thinking about the hiking award. I had done seven of the listed hikes and needed three more to achieve the golden boot award, but I only had three days of my holiday left. One day would be taken up with recovering my camera.

Since the beginning of the holiday I had been hankering after doing the longest hike in the booklet – the one from First to Schynige Platte – the classic high mountain hike! There and then I decided to go for it on the Friday. I told Karen of my thoughts and she responded by advising caution, considering what I had just been through. At this time of my life, at thirty-three years old, I was at my peak of fitness, especially after just having finished working the lambing season on the farm at home! I told her that in spite of the events of the past week, I would never have a better chance to do the said hike!

She said, "I can see you've made up your mind, but please be careful, I have been so worried about you these last few days, I would have joined you on that hike as I have not yet seen the alpine gardens at Schynige Platte, but I can't get the time off work."

I said, "I would have enjoyed your company!"

She replied, "I'm sure Fred would go with you if you asked him."

I told her that I had lost all confidence in Fred and that I didn't want to walk with him anymore. We parted company and I got an early night.

Thursday the thirtieth. I rose early, packed my gear, got my breakfast and caught the train down to Zweilutschinen. After I got off the train I donned my Gore-Tex coat and put the hood up, in spite of it being a fine hot day! This was mainly a disguise as I didn't want to be recognised on my camera recovery operation.

I hadn't realized how far it was back up the mountain to Sulwald and the flat. It took me most of the morning to get there and I was very warm with the coat on. I approached the hamlet warily; however, there was still nobody about and I was able to re-enter the flat unobserved. My camera was there and I quickly stowed it in my rucksack, left the letter of apology and as much money as I could spare on the table, re-tied the flat door and on impulse got down on my knees to offer up a prayer. This place had probably saved my life and I needed to acknowledge this! I then left the building and legged it down the hill.

It was about four p.m. when I got back to Grindelwald and I had a drink at the Hotel Derby at the station. This was Karen's main base and she just happened to be in reception, talking to some of her other clients. I sought her out and told her about my expedition; she thought I had been lucky not to be discovered. We then both had a bit of a laugh about it. I returned to my hotel and went about getting ready for the evening meal.

After this I turned in early to prepare for what would be a big day on the morrow.

Friday the first of July. I was up in good time and had my gear packed, having re-loaded my camera and enjoyed a good breakfast. On this day, I told the receptionist where I was going and set off up the village to the First gondola station. The weather was fine with only a few patchy clouds.

At the gondola I bought a one way ticket to First and boarded one of the little cabins. This lift had only recently been converted from a two-seater chairlift and had been known as the longest chairlift in Europe. The gondola lifts you from Grindelwald at three thousand four hundred and sixty-four feet to First at seven thousand one hundred and thirteen feet. I was alone in the cabin as it trundled out of the station. I had re-stocked with chocolate on the way up the village and my water bottles were full. I sat back to enjoy the ride and take in the magnificent views of the great peaks unfolding to my right. After a while, my cabin entered the first station of Bort and the automatic doors opened; you can get out here if you wish. It then continued on up to the second station of Egg, (most appropriately named for me, I think) where the direction of the lift turns ninety degrees to the left. It is then just a short hop up to First.

When I arrived at First, I got the lift operator to stamp my hiking booklet to get me started. I had noticed that there was a second hike listed in the booklet, from Schynige Platte down to Breitlauenen, the mid station on the cog railway, servicing Schynige Platte from Wilderswill near Interlaken. I thought that if I had enough energy left I would try and link the two hikes together. The signpost near the lift station showed Schynige Platte, five and a half hours and was marked with the red and white flag.

I set off from First at ten a.m. for my first stop-off point of the Faulhorn, where I had been told there was a restaurant, which would provide a good opportunity for lunch, being as it was about two hours away. After about half an hour I came to the extremely picturesque reservoir of Bachalpsee, where I got some superb photos looking back over the water to the great peaks beyond.

The weather was great and the reflection of the great mountains in the water was stunning. There were a few other hikers travelling the path as I continued on towards the Faulhorn. The going had been easy up to this point but it soon grew trickier as I began to climb through patches of old snow. I had donned my shorts for this trip and the sun was burning the backs of my legs so I stopped to apply some sun cream.

I reached the Faulhorn, which stands at two thousand six hundred and eighty metres (eight thousand seven hundred and ninety-six feet) high, just before midday and found that the restaurant was nestled against the west-facing slope of a rocky peak, just below the summit.

I parked my rucksack next to a vacant table on the outside terrace where the Swiss flag flew proudly. I then went into the building and ordered some soup. The staff indicated that they would bring the food out to me and I went back outside to wait for it.

I sat at my table admiring the tremendous vista to the south, from left to right there towered the Wetterhorn, the Schreckhorn, the Finsteraarhorn, the Eiger, the Monch (four thousand and eighty-nine metres – thirteen thousand four hundred and sixteen feet) and finally the Jungfrau (four thousand one hundred and fifty-eight metres – thirteen thousand six hundred and forty-two feet).

Just then I heard a bleating and around the corner of the building came a large dark brown Brienz goat; it eyed me with a confident look! I thought, *there is no grass up here, how does it survive?* Then I watched as it approached one of the recently abandoned tables and guzzle some leftover bread!

I said to myself, "Ah, that's how it gets by."

I thought I would have to be on the ball or that cheeky sod would steal my lunch!

The proprietor brought my soup out and said, "Enjoy."

I then tucked into the huge bowl of soup and the thick slices of black bread and did a bit of people watching. Unlike the summit of Helvellyn back home, where you could find walkers dressed in their Sunday best or stilettos, these hikers were all kitted out in impressive gear!

I finished my meal without interference from the goat, paid the bill, (the prices were quite reasonable considering the isolation of the place) hoisted my rucksack and continued on my way. The well-worn path was marked every now and again by red and white flags painted on rocks. The route took me downhill now, through screes and patches of old snow; it twisted and turned through shallow valleys but the going was quick.

After a while I came to another, smaller restaurant right next to the path, where there were quite a lot of hikers who were stretched out, enjoying the sunshine. I took a brief break here to take a pull at my water bottle then carried on. There were smashing views to the north, down towards the vivid blue lakes of Thun and Brienz, with the town of Interlaken between.

As I drew closer to Schynige Platte, the landscape became less rocky and grassy areas began to appear, with sheep grazing on them. Up at the Faulhorn there had been quite a chilly breeze but now it had become very warm!

I arrived at Schynige Platte at about three p.m., having done the hike in a fast four hours thirty-five minutes with thirty minutes added on for lunch. I was fairly tired but thought I could manage the other hike, so I got my booklet stamped at the train station to finish the first hike, and again to start the second. There were many people about here; some were hikers but most were there to visit the famed alpine gardens. I was not interested in flowers and I didn't think I had time to visit the gardens anyway, so I gave them a miss.

I set off down the path in the direction of Breitlauenen at a good pace and soon found I had left all the people behind! The path was steep and rough in places so I had to watch my footing. It only took me an hour to do the hike and I was soon getting my booklet stamped at the little railway ticket office at Breitlauenen. Having done this and bought a ticket for the train down to Wilderswill I mooched about the station, waiting for the train. There was only one other person waiting, this being an old woman sitting on one of the platform seats. I approached her and said, "Hello." She looked up at me and returned my greeting in English.

She then said, "Have you been walking?"

I replied, "Yes, I have come all the way from First!"

Then she said, "How long did it take you?"

"Five and a half hours" I said.

She told me that that was a fast time and that I must be a very strong man; I thought that after what I had just been through, it must be true! She asked me where I was from and I told her. She then told me she was a Swiss national and that she lived in Interlaken. She described how in her youth she had hiked all the way from Grindelwald to Schynige Platte many times; she also told me that nowadays there were many more hikers doing the route! The conversation flowed easily as her English was so good and she went on to tell me that a lot of rich foreigners were buying their way into Switzerland these days.

After a while the little green train came trundling down the track from the top station and we boarded it. Both of the carriages were pretty full but I managed to find a seat for the old lady. I stood next to her and we continued to talk as the train rattled its way down to Wilderswill.

About half an hour later we reached Wilderswill and got off the train. The old lady was going back to Interlaken and I of course back up to

Grindelwald, so we parted with a handshake to make our way to our respective platforms on the linking main line.

As I boarded the Grindelwald train, I thought back upon the events of the day. The hikes had been very rewarding, the encounter with the goat amusing, the chat with the old lady interesting and the train ride restful! The journey up to Grindelwald took about half an hour and as the train approached the village I was once again able to appreciate the grand view of the Eiger up to the right. It was now about five thirty p.m. as I got off the train and I just had time for a drink on the terrace of the Hotel Derby.

As I sat at my table beneath the cooling trees, a voice hailed me from behind. "There you are, have you had a good day?"

It was Karen, she sat down with me, bringing her own drink and we discussed the details of my trip. She was particularly taken with my tales of the goat and the old lady!

She asked, "What do you intend doing tomorrow?"

I replied, "Well, I only need one more listed hike for the gold boot, so looking at the booklet I think I will do the one back along the shore of Lake Brienz, after taking a steamer ride."

She said, "That sounds like a nice restful way to end your eventful holiday!"

I agreed. We parted company and I returned to the Hotel Jungfrau. I had no time to get cleaned up so I just went straight in for dinner. Fred came over to me in the dining room and asked me how I was, I told him I was fine and that I had had a good day. I thought that was a nice gesture.

After an enjoyable meal I went up and got a shave and bath then came back down to the foyer, where I found Fred sitting.

I said, "Can I buy you a drink?"

He said, "Yes, thanks."

So we went into the bar. He had a beer but I made do with a Coke. We talked about each other's days and it transpired that he had taken the gondola to Mannlichen and then walked to Kleine Scheidegg, the same walk I had done in the thunderstorm. He had then come back to the village by train. I told him what I intended to do on the morrow and he said he might walk down the valley to Lutschental to get his tenth hike in for his gold boot award. I was glad we had sort of made up, even if I still didn't entirely trust him. We talked till ten thirty p.m. then I went to bed.

Saturday, the second of July. I had a bit of a lie-in and a late breakfast, got my things and caught a mid-morning train down to Interlaken and then a bus to the steamer pier at the western end of Lake Brienz. The great thing about Swiss transport is that it all links up and having bought a ticket, I was soon boarding a steamer bound for the other end of the lake. The weather was glorious as I took my seat. The boat was quite crowded and people wore tee shirts and shorts, as I did, in the hot sun. The steamer got under way and the blue water was soon surging past. There were fine views in all directions but particularly towards the foothills of the Bernese Oberland including Schynige Platte. The breeze was in my hair and I felt great. The traumatic events of the last week seemed a million miles away.

All too soon the steamer was docking at the other end of Lake Brienz and I was departing. I got my hiking booklet stamped on the relevant page at the steamer ticket office and was soon on my way back along the northern shore of the lake. The going was very flat and therefore quick; soon I was back at the steamer pier on the western end of the lake, getting my booklet stamped again to close and complete my attempt on the gold boot hiking award. I decided that it had been a very rewarding experience.

I was soon aboard the bus back to the railway station and thenceforth the train back up to Grindelwald. When I got back to the village, the shops were still open and I took the opportunity to buy a few presents for family back home. I also bought a tee shirt and peaked cap with 'Grindelwald' printed on them for myself.

I walked back down to my hotel, visiting the tourist information on the way and leaving my completed hiking booklet with them. The helpful lady at the desk said I had done well and that the hiking award certificate and gold boot would be posted to me in England.

I went through the usual routine of the evening and just after dinner, the receptionist told me that Karen wished to meet Fred and me for a drink at the Hotel Derby at nine p.m. Fred was nearby and I told him of the message. We walked up to the Derby for the appointed time and Karen was waiting there for us.

She sat us down in the bar and ordered three beers. When they came, she raised her glass to us and said, "Here's to the gold boot!"

We raised ours and chorused, "The gold boot!"

This was my first alcoholic drink since the big night out before my bad patch and I drank it carefully!

We struck up a good conversation about the hikes that had gone into achieving the gold boot award. Our beers were soon finished and we moved off up the village to tour our other favourite bars. I was soon back to enjoying my beer and a normal night out on the drink to celebrate the holiday.

We finished the night off in the Espresso bar at midnight and then made our way home to bed.

Sunday the third of July. It was home time but I didn't have an early journey so I had a lie-in and a leisurely breakfast. The coach for the airport didn't leave until two p.m. so having packed our suitcases I suggested to Fred, who was on the same transfer, that we take a last walk up the village and grab a spot of lunch at one of the restaurants. We did this and finally settled on the Derby for lunch, I had an omelette while Fred had bratwurst with rosti. This was washed down with a beer each.

Halfway through my beer I went to the toilet and when I came back Fred said, "Come on, sup up, Steve. We had better get going if we want to catch that coach!"

I put the glass to my lips and tasted the beer; it had that funny bitter taste to it that I remembered from the nightclub! I didn't comment on this but just said that I was suddenly feeling full and left the glass on the table. Fred just laughed but as we paid for the meal I was left with an uneasy feeling.

We walked back to the Jungfrau and were soon loading the cases we had left in reception into the waiting coach. We said our goodbyes to the hotel staff, boarded the coach and were soon on our way to Zurich airport.

The journey took about two hours. On entering the terminal building, Fred and I parted company with a handshake. He was flying to Gatwick and I to Manchester so we would be checking in at different parts of the terminal. That was the last I ever saw of Fred! The check-in, customs and boarding the flight went smoothly and I was soon winging my way back to Manchester. The flight was smooth and in two and a half hours I was touching down at my home airport. I quickly retrieved my suitcase from the carousel and cleared customs. My dad was waiting for me at arrivals and we were soon loading my suitcase into his van. He told me that the police had been to the farm twice, once to tell him that I was missing and again to tell him that I had been found; they had all been really worried! I told him I was sorry for causing such a fuss. On the way back home to the Lake District, I told him of the events of my holiday.

I spent the next day relaxing to get over my demanding trip. When I weighed myself, I was amazed to find I had lost a stone and a half! The following day I threw myself into hay making which was in full swing. It was a week before I was able to visit the doctor and tell him of my strange experience abroad; all he said was not to drink so much in the future! The hiking award certificate and the gold boot, in the form of a lapel badge, arrived from Switzerland after that week and I display them proudly to this day.

Part 2

Kaprun, Austria
August 1995.

Wednesday the ninth. I had been on a good skiing holiday to the French Alps in January and things had gone well, so when I got back I booked a walking holiday for two weeks in Kaprun, Austria which, like Grindelwald, doubles up as a ski resort in winter and a hiking resort in summer. The nearby resort of Zell Am Zee is probably better known. There is a world-class golf course between the two villages and being a keen golfer, I took my golf clubs with me.

The reader will have to bear with me again because I forgot to take my diary on this trip so therefore details are a bit sketchy.

I drove up to Glasgow in my beloved Ford Capri 2.8i and left it at the airparks facility, which took a bit of finding, in the city and then boarded a shuttle bus to the airport with my suitcase, small hand luggage rucksack and my golf clubs. This was quite a handful. I was soon at the airport and checking in; there was no extra charge for the golf clubs! I received my boarding card and proceeded through passport control to the duty free shop where I bought a litre bottle of Bacardi. There was a short wait in departures for the flight but I was soon boarding the plane, the flight was to Salzburg and we were soon in the air.

The flight was about two and a half hours and being a good flyer, I enjoyed the nice in-flight meal. It was also a bump-free ride and we were soon touching down at the small airport of Salzburg. I retrieved my luggage and cleared customs. There was a rep from the holiday company (a different company from the previous year) waiting for me with a sign at arrivals and I was soon boarding the coach to Kaprun. The journey took about one and a half hours. There were plenty of other young people on the coach but they were all couples so I didn't crack on with anybody.

I was soon offloading my gear in Kaprun outside the hotel, the name of which I have forgotten, along with four other people. It was pouring with rain and this was particularly disappointing because I had just come from a heatwave back home. I scuttled inside the hotel and checked in, got the room key then took my luggage up to my single room which was on the first floor, right at the front of the hotel. It was about five thirty p.m. as I unpacked and I thought I would just have time for a beer before dinner. I investigated the bar, finding that it was right at the front of the building and I thought, *oh dear, I wonder if it's right underneath my room!* I ordered a beer – some Austrian brand, and settled down to do some people watching.

There were quite a few customers in the bar at this time but it was open to the general public so it was difficult to tell who was a resident. My beer was quite nice but not as good as the Swiss brands. I could hear from the conversation round about that there were quite a few English people present, but I didn't crack on with anyone.

I finished my beer and made my way back into the lounge, where other guests had gathered for dinner. My board arrangements were evening meal and breakfast (half board) the same as the Swiss holiday. I met a nice older couple from Yorkshire in the lounge. They asked me if I would like to sit with them at dinner and I accepted.

When dinner was served, the waitress moved the cutlery from my single table onto the Yorkshire couple's table and there we enjoyed a good meal, accompanied by interesting and stimulating conversation. I told them about the previous year's holiday and about my achievement of the gold boot award but omitted the details of my apparent breakdown! I also told the couple that I intended to find the tourist information in the village on the morrow and see if the authorities did a similar hiking award in Austria. The couple, whose names were John and Margaret, said that they were mainly there for the sight-seeing but would probably take in a bit of low level walking as well.

After dinner we continued our crack over a few drinks in the lounge until about ten p.m. and then we all turned in. I soon found to my dismay that my room was indeed above the bar and it was some time before the noise died down and I was able to get off to sleep.

Thursday the tenth. I was up reasonably early and enjoyed a nice continental breakfast with John and Margaret and then we went our separate ways. I left the hotel with my Gore-Tex coat and small rucksack and went off to explore the village. The weather had cleared up a bit but still wasn't brilliant. I found a little supermarket where I bought chocolate and bananas for my hikes. I then found the bank and got some of my traveller's cheques changed into Austrian Schillings. After this I found the tourist info and made my enquiries. The people there told me that the only hiking award they did was for a big walk in the mountains to the north of Zell Am Zee! I thought that this would perhaps be worth trying for. I bought a local map with all the available hikes shown on it and was disappointed that the area did not seem to be as gifted with good walking as Grindelwald!

I left the tourist info and made my way back through the village. The local architecture was typically alpine with the usual flower-decked wooden houses intermingled with concrete and wood hotels.

Kaprun lies at the junction of two valleys at the foot of the Kitzsteinhorn Mountain and the lower slopes of the surrounding mountains rise up quite close to the village.

When I got back to the hotel reception, I was addressed by a young man there, who asked me if I was the guest who had brought his golf clubs with him. I acknowledged this and he then went on to introduce himself as the proprietor's son.

He extended his hand and said, "I am Dennis."

I took his hand and gave it a good old fashioned Cumbrian squeeze and said, "I am Steve."

He went on to tell me that he was a keen golfer and that he was a member of the renowned Schmittenhohe club just down the road. He said he was going to play a round on Saturday the twelfth with his doctor friend and he wondered if I would like to join them and make up a 'three ball.'

I said, "Wow, yes. That would be great, thank you."

The rest of the day was spent around my hotel, preparing for a good hike the next day. I had a bite of lunch in the hotel restaurant and in the evening I once again joined John and Margaret for dinner, where the crack was excellent again. I had a few beers with them after and then turned in early but once again, found it difficult to sleep until the bar beneath me closed.

Friday the eleventh. I was up in good time and breakfasted before most of the other guests were up and about. During my meal I pored over the map I had bought and made my mind up to walk to the high Gleiwitzer hut; a mountain hut in the hills to the south east of the village.

I went back to my room and got my stuff together and then left the hotel and made my way out of the village to the east, where I found a good path signposted to the Gleiwitzer hut with a walking time of three and a half hours. The signpost system seemed very similar to the Swiss one. I set off up the path in relatively good weather and the first section of the hike took me up through conifer woods. There were few other walkers about as I made my way up the winding route. After about half an hour the trees thinned out and I entered high mountain pastures where cattle were grazing. There were many wooden water troughs supplied by springs and I made use of these to quench my thirst in the warm conditions, saving my bottled water for the higher slopes.

The path wound upwards through rolling hills, becoming rockier the higher I got. There were no buildings anywhere in sight and I determined that the cattle must be milked at a farm somewhere down near the tree line.

I walked on for hours, twisting and turning through valleys and high cols, thinking that I had been walking for a long time and that the guide time on the signpost at the start could not be very accurate! Eventually a building hove into view and I made my way to it. As I drew close, I could see the name 'Gleiwitzer' painted on it. I looked at my watch and saw I had been walking for over four hours! There were one or two other hikers about as I sat down at a table on the outside eating area.

It was about one p.m. and I had worked up quite an appetite. Presently a young lad came out of the hut and approaching me, he said, "Hello."

I said, "Hello," back,

And he said, "Are you English?"

I replied, "Yes."

He then gave me a menu and asked me if I wanted anything to drink. His English was excellent and I complimented him on it. I ordered a beer and the lad went back into the building.

I sat back and enjoyed the sun. The views were of round-topped mountains similar to the Cairngorms of Scotland, the higher snow-capped peaks being hidden behind a ridge to the west.

The lad soon re-emerged from the hut with a foaming beer for me and on delivery; I ordered the soup of the day, the menu of the hut being very similar to the Swiss ones.

The lad said, "Enjoy!" as I took a long pull at the beer.

My soup soon followed the beer and I tucked in. It was very similar to the soups I had enjoyed in Switzerland and was accompanied by the same black bread. The soup and beer were delicious and I was soon paying for them, hoisting my rucksack and making my way back to Kaprun. The map showed that there was a different route that could be taken for the return journey so I took it.

The path from the hut took me uphill to the west and before long I was cresting the ridge and gazing out towards the Kitzsteinhorn Mountain with its glacier and further in the distance was the highest mountain in Austria, the Grossglockner. After the ridge, the route took me downhill, passing first across screes and then down into mountain pastures. A couple of hours had passed as I entered the tree line. The way was easy to follow as there were no turnoffs in the path and the occasional signpost kept me right.

I arrived back in the village in the late afternoon and on entering my hotel I sought out the bar and ordered a beer. As I was tucking into this, Dennis entered and sat down next to me. He asked me where I had been walking and how long it had taken me to do the hike. He did not join me in a beer as he was still too young to drink! We talked for a while, mainly discussing the planned golf day on the morrow then I finished my beer and went upstairs to get ready for dinner. On this holiday, I had a room with en-suite facilities so I was able to do my ablutions without having to get a bathroom key from reception.

When I came back down to the lounge, the holiday company rep was there talking to John and Margaret and they beckoned me over and told me there was going to be a quiz in a nearby bar the following night. I, being keen on the occasional quiz, said I would be interested in making a team up with John and Margaret. We talked for a while, me telling them about my hike and then the rep left. I enjoyed a good evening meal with John and Margaret and a few beers after before turning in.

Saturday the twelfth. On this morning, I had a short lie-in then breakfasted and sought out Dennis, who was doing some paperwork in reception. He said that he would be ready to go to the golf course in half an hour and that his mother would drive us there. I then went and got my golf clubs from the ski room and left them in reception while I went back to my room to get my golf shoes and a few other bits and bobs.

After returning to reception I read the holiday company folder until Dennis was ready, then we loaded our clubs into his mother's car and she drove us to the Schmittenhohe club. On arrival, Dennis took me to the professional's shop where I was introduced to his doctor friend, whose name was Karl. Karl had a good firm handshake and his English was excellent as he told me we had a tee time slot for eleven thirty a.m. All I had to do now was pay for my round and this proved to be a heavy toll – I can't remember how much, but I know the green fee was more than the average British one. I also purchased some chocolate to eat on the way round and I thought about buying some new golf balls but these were expensive, so I had to make do with the used ones from my bag! I had also had to present a handicap certificate to the professional to prove I was a member of a club and therefore a competent golfer.

From the shop we moved to the driving range area after changing into our golf shoes in the locker room. The weather was dry but cloudy and quite warm, so I had dressed in tailored shorts and a tee shirt with a collar. We got a basket full of balls each from the machine, having put a few coins in to pay for them and then proceeded to hit them down the range, going through our repertoire of clubs to warm up for the main event. It was then nearly time to tee off and we moved to the first tee. We had to wait for another group to start their round but our turn soon came. Dennis and Karl agreed that as their guest I should be the first one to tee off so I got my metal headed driving club out, teed the ball up and took my stance. I was quite nervous as I addressed the ball in front of my playing partners. My swing when it came was very quick and I narrowly avoided lifting my head and missing the ball. However, I made contact, hitting a low daisy cutter, which travelled about a hundred metres! I let out a sigh of relief and stepped off the tee. Dennis and Karl then teed off, both of them hitting good drives down the par five first hole.

I had the highest handicap of our group; at the time I was off a fifteen handicap and my standard of play reflected this! The course was generally flat, being in the valley bottom and the fairways were quite narrow and tree-lined. I think I scored a double bogey seven on the first hole but I can't remember much about the rest of our game apart from I think the par three, eighth hole where I had a real purple patch. The hole was close to a hundred and sixty-six metres so I hit a metal three wood, connecting with the ball really well and it flew beautifully to land right in the middle of the green. Dennis and Karl both hit good tee shots but failed to make the green. When we got down to the green, the other two chipped up close to the flag and then it was my turn. I was faced with a flat six-metre putt but it was a tricky right to left one! I lined myself up and made a practice swing before hitting a beautiful putt which curled round and dropped in the centre of the cup. I let out a shout of glee; I had scored a birdie two.

This was, however, the only bright point in an otherwise uninspiring performance on my part. The other two both had pars on that hole and we continued to play round to the fifteenth hole, where Dennis and Karl announced that they were calling it a day because they had a competition round the next day. Dennis told me that Karl was taking him back to Kaprun and that if I wanted a lift I would have to go with them. I was not too happy about this state of affairs because I had paid for eighteen holes, but I went along with them anyway. We walked back to the clubhouse and changed our shoes before loading our gear into Karl's car.

As we drove back to Kaprun, I reflected on what had not been a very rewarding day and curse it, we had not even had time to get a drink in the clubhouse! I asked Dennis and Karl if they would mind if I walked round with them during their competition round on the morrow and they agreed that it should be okay, providing the third member of their group didn't object.

It was about four p.m. when Karl dropped Dennis and me off outside the hotel in Kaprun and as he said goodbye, he mentioned how much he had enjoyed my company. I told him I had enjoyed the crack too – the Cumbrian phrase mystifying him slightly!

I put my golf clubs away in the ski room and made my way to the bar where, being thirsty after my efforts on the course, I ordered a large stein glass of beer. Dennis joined me with his Coke and we discussed the events of our round and the coming game on the morrow. The stein holds nearly two litres of beer and I was a bit squiffy by the time I had finished it! I thought about having another, normal sized beer, but realizing that I would have to be reasonably sober for the quiz that evening I decided to go up and get a shave and bath.

It was about six p.m. by the time I had got shaved and bathed so I made my way down to the lounge, where I found John and Margaret. They told me they had taken a bus that morning to neighbouring Zell Am Zee and gone up the cable car to the top of the mountain there. They said the views from the top were stunning. I told them about my golf day and particularly my fine birdie, but they were a bit disappointed for me with the cost and only having got fourteen holes out of it.

We had dinner together and then walked up the street to the bar where the quiz was being held. It started at eight thirty p.m. and we only just got there in time. We managed to get a table in the crowded bar and ordered drinks from the waitress. I had a large beer, the first of many that night, and overhearing the conversations nearby realized that the participants for the quiz were largely British.

There were the usual quiz subjects and the rounds and the beers came and went and it all became a bit of a blur! This was apart from one defining moment for me when the question – which was the last Bond film to feature Roger Moore – was asked and I immediately whispered to John that it was *A view to a kill*. He and Margaret disagreed with me, saying it was something else, which I allowed them to go with. When the answers for that round were read out, my instant suggestion proved right but having gone with something else we got it wrong. This pissed me off somewhat.

The quiz must have lasted a couple of hours and I can't remember what position our team finished in but I can recall being pretty well oiled. We left the bar without a prize and returned to our hotel, it was time to call it a night.

Sunday the thirteenth. I was awake fairly early, having learned the previous day that Dennis and his companions had a tee off slot at the club for eleven a.m. I breakfasted with John and Margaret, our slight tiff over the wrong answer at the quiz forgotten, and then sought out Dennis, who was in reception. He told me that Karl was going to pick us up and take us to the golf club at nine forty-five a.m., where we would meet the other player in the group, whose name was Christian. I went back upstairs and packed my small rucksack with a few bits and bobs for the day. I wore my shorts and tee shirt again and also my trainers. The weather was dry but cloudy and it looked like rain later so I took my Gore-Tex coat with me as I returned to the lounge. John was there and he told me that he and Margaret intended to take the funicular railway up to the Kitzsteinhorn glacier for a look around and hopefully get above the cloud.

I waited around in the lounge after John had gone and presently Dennis appeared and told me Karl had arrived and was asking if I was ready. We went through to reception where I shook hands with Karl. We then loaded our gear and ourselves into Karl's car, which was a top of the range Mercedes, and set off for the Schmittenhohe club.

On arrival, we got our gear together and proceeded to the pro shop where I was introduced to Christian, who told me in perfect English that he was a ski instructor in the winter and a walking guide in summer. The three of them then paid their competition fees, got their score cards (I also picked one up to record their scores and I still have it to this day) and then we made our way to the driving range, it being about ten thirty a.m.

They got their baskets of balls and proceeded to hit them down the range. I stood back and studied the form, noting that Christian had a particularly good swing. When the balls were finished, we made our way to the first tee. The competition was an individual stableford, which means you score points for each hole. The three of them teed off, with Christian, who had the lowest handicap of nine, going first, followed by Karl and then Dennis. Karl's handicap was eleven and Dennis's thirteen.

They all hit good tee shots down the par five first but I am not going to bore the reader with the details of all the scores on all the eighteen holes of their rounds. Suffice to say that Dennis had a bogey six on the first hole and completed the front nine holes in a respectable forty-five shots, scoring sixteen points. He then did the back nine in an even better thirty-nine shots, scoring twenty points, making a total of thirty-six points for his round, which is par for the eighteen hole course.

My walk round with the trio consisted of looking for lost balls, attending the occasional flag and talking! I couldn't help noticing on my way round that there were moles working on the course. I commented on this to the players, asking them what the German word for a mole was. Dennis told me that it was *mousen volen* and I went on to tell the group that I was a mousen volen trapping specialist!

The mood of the group was quite upbeat as we made our way from the eighteenth green to the club house, both Karl and Christian having had good rounds also. The trio put their clubs away in the cars and then said to me to go to the outside sitting area of the clubhouse to wait for them while they changed their shoes in the locker room. I was not allowed in the main clubhouse area because I had trainers on. I made my way to the veranda area, found a vacant table and waited for my friends. The weather had held fair and a weak sun had now appeared, it being about three thirty p.m. I indulged in a spot of people watching while I waited and soon formed the opinion that the golfers sitting at the nearby tables were at the top of the earnings range! And I vowed to ask my friends what was the annual subscription fee for their club.

The trio soon joined me and a waiter approached. Karl asked me what I wanted to drink and I said, "A large beer, please."

He ordered three large beers and a Coke for Dennis.

When the drinks arrived, I raised my glass and said, "To golf and the mousen volen."

They all laughed, joined me in the toast and we tucked into our drinks. We talked for about half an hour while enjoying our drinks, during which I asked the question about the subscriptions, the answer to which I can't remember exactly but I know the cost was several times that of my own club.

We finished our drinks and made our way to the car park, where Christian shook my hand and said how much he had enjoyed my company. We parted and Karl drove Dennis and me back to Kaprun.

On arrival back at the hotel, Dennis went off to do a few chores, while I made my way to the bar where I found John and Margaret. I got a beer and then told them of my day. They then related their tale of the visit to the glacier and I was surprised to learn that they had got above the cloud and that there were people skiing up there! We enjoyed a good crack as only northerners together can! Then went and got ready for dinner.

After the meal I had a few more drinks with John, while Margaret went for a walk through the village. During this time we got talking to a young couple, who told us they had hiked a path up into the hills to the south, in the direction of the glacier, where they had come across the remains of what they had been told was an old World War Two prisoner of war camp. I was fascinated by the tale and there and then made up my mind to give it a visit on the morrow. I therefore turned in early but slept poorly due to the noise from the bar and the boy racers charging about outside on the road until the early hours.

Monday the fourteenth. I awoke about six feeling a bit groggy, got my gear together and took an early breakfast. As I set off southward, out of the village, the weather was overcast but dry. The young couple from the night before had told me that I had to walk up the road up the valley for a couple of miles until I found a signpost pointing up a path to the right, saying 'Kitzsteinhorn', so this is what I did.

After about three quarters of an hour's walking up the road, dodging the occasional car, I found the sign and the path; the way seemed to go straight up the side of the valley steeply. I set off up through pastures and then patchy scrub which soon changed to mature conifer trees. After about two hours the path levelled out and I came to a clearing. It began to rain so I put on my coat and put the hood up. In the clearing, there were a number of large concrete pads and at one end of one of them were the remains of a hut. I approached this, passing several mounds of what looked like ashes and melted tar. I surmised that this then were the remains of the prisoner of war camp. There was a quite sinister and nerve jangling atmosphere about the place as I explored further. I was becoming rather frightened as I made my way back through the camp and suddenly there was a kind of tapping and scraping on the back of my hood. I whirled round to find that there was nothing behind me but the remains of the camp, the trees and the rain. I fled terrified, back into the trees at a run, found the path and headed at a fast pace further up into the mountains. When I had put a good distance between myself and the camp, I stopped for a rest and a drink. I had never visited such a site before and had never considered the fact that the camp might be haunted but it had none the less given me quite a turn.

I had now reached the edge of the tree line and ahead of me the land sloped up towards the snout of the Kitzsteinhorn glacier. Some distance away I could see the chairs and cable of a ski lift so I set off again, heading towards this. I was becoming hungry, as it was now past the middle of the day. Just then I noticed a hut near the bottom of the ski lift with a tendril of smoke rising from its chimney. I approached the hut and saw a figure who appeared to be chopping wood nearby. As I got up to the person, I said, "Hello," and the figure turned to reveal an old man, whose most prominent feature was a pair of piercing glacier blue eyes.

He stared at me and then responded by saying, "What do you want?" in English.

I said, "Have you got anything to eat, please? I have money to pay you."

He told me he had some soup on the stove that I could have and he beckoned me to follow him into the hut. On entering the hut, I noticed that it was decorated in typical alpine fashion. I then had a sudden thought and got out my wallet to find it was nearly empty – I had forgotten to change any more money. I knew then a moment of panic as I asked the old man how much would the soup cost. He told me and I searched the wallet and my small change, finding that I had only three-quarters of the amount he was asking. I told the man that I only had so much cash on me and he appeared to stiffen slightly as he worked over the stove.

He brought the steaming bowl of soup, accompanied by a few slices of black bread, over to the table and said, "Sit down and enjoy."

I did as he said, feeling quite uncomfortable and picked up the spoon. I dipped the spoon into the soup and raised it to my mouth. On instinct, I smelled the spoonful of soup and found it to have a very spicy tang. I then took a taste while the old man stood there staring at me with those intense eyes. The soup tasted very fiery but there was also another taste that almost seemed like ashes. Although I was baulking at the taste I bolted the meal down, paid the man with all I had, apologising for not having the full amount, telling him where I was staying so he could collect the rest of the money from me there and fled from his unsmiling face, out of the hut and back down the path towards the trees.

When I had gone a reasonable distance from the hut and feeling a pain coming on in my stomach, I stuck my fingers down my throat and retched up the meal. Suddenly some of the old feelings from the previous year began to resurrect themselves and my mood began to darken. Had that old bastard tried to poison me because I didn't have enough money to pay for his soup? Or because I was wearing a black tee shirt and him being from the second world war generation had taken exception to this, being as the Nazis who had presumably operated in that area had regiments called 'the blackshirts'. Perhaps this was a bit of a leap of my imagination but I never will know.

Instead of returning to the main valley on the path that I had come up, I struck off to the left, through heavy undergrowth. I began to experience the unfortunate hunted feeling that I had got the previous year and I tore through the brush as if the very devil was after me. I crossed a ravine with a dry stream bed and pushed on uphill. Just then some stones rolled down by me; there was obviously someone or something above me in the trees. I proceeded more cautiously and nervously but I never encountered another soul. Eventually I emerged out of the undergrowth onto a ridge along which ran a path. To my right I could see that the ridge stretched away back in the general direction of Kaprun, so I headed that way.

After some time and distance the ridge ended in a hill top, where there were some buildings and a road. I continued onto the road, giving the buildings a wide berth and headed downhill in the direction of the village, which I could now see in the distance. I stopped for a rest and a drink from my almost empty water bottle, at a bend in the road. As I stepped off the road onto the grass, something shiny on the ground caught my eye. I bent down and picked up a silver coloured ring about two and a half centimetres across and about half a centimetre thick. The circle of the ring was completed by a crude weld, suggesting that it had not been made for a person's finger; however at the time I had just read *The Lord of the Rings* and in my increasingly fevered imagination decided that this object was something to do with that tale. Looking back, I found out later that day that there had been a downhill mountain bike race on that hill a few days previously and the ring had probably dropped off a crashed bike. I still have it as a keepsake.

I pocketed the ring and walked on back down to the village. Again the reader will have to bear with me because my recall of the events of the following few days is a bit patchy but I will detail what I can remember.

I must have returned to my hotel. Whether I ate or drank anything else that day I can't say. I also must have changed some of the rest of my traveller's cheques at reception because I had enough cash to buy most of the things that I would need in the days ahead.

I remember leaving the hotel in the dark hours before dawn the next day and making my way with my rucksack along the road towards the neighbouring village of Zell Am Zee. As I went there, was very little traffic save the occasional boy racer, which I avoided contact with by jumping over the barriers into the fields beyond.

My mind seemed to have dissolved into turmoil, those feelings of being pursued were uppermost in it and the desire to keep moving was ever present.

On entering the village of Zell Am Zee, I followed the signs for the cable car station. As I was walking up the street in the dawn of the new day, I came across a young man curled up on a doorstep. He was of eastern European cast and being as the Bosnian war was going on at the time I determined that he must be a refugee. I got out my wallet, took out a twenty Schilling note and pushed it beneath his sleeping body. I continued on up the street, eventually coming to the cable car station. Of course, at that hour it wasn't running so I struck off up the path beside it to climb the mountain that it serviced. The name of the mountain which is the main ski area of that village escapes me.

The weather was fair but cloudy as I toiled up the steep slopes, passing across mountain pastures, which would be ski pistes in the winter. I was tired but strangely not hungry and was able to top up my water bottle at the occasional cattle watering trough on the way. On this occasion, I was not afraid to drink from these troughs when I got the chance. I passed an area where plastic pipes were being dug in, presumably for building snow-making infrastructure for skiing.

After what seemed like a long time I reached the top of the mountain, where there was the cable car terminus and a large mountain restaurant. Of course, it only being early morning I was the first walker to arrive. I approached the restaurant and tried the doors, finding them to be unlocked. I suppose it must have been around eight a.m. because there were staff just coming on duty, whom I guessed must live above the facility. Seated at one of the tables as I went in was a group of local workers, who eyed me suspiciously as I passed them on my way to the service hatch. In a normal state of mind, I would have been nervous about entering such an establishment under those circumstances but I was too exhausted to care! Upon reaching the hatch I ordered a mineral water off the serving girl and she gave it to me, giving me a curious look. I moved onto the till area and paid the money for the drink to the same girl, who had moved with me. As I made my way to a table, I was aware that all eyes were upon me and as I sat down the table full of workers began conversing in German. Upon hearing the English words 'pseudo masochist', I turned towards them to find that they were all staring at me.

Suddenly they all burst out laughing. I quickly finished my water and hurriedly departed the restaurant.

The return journey to Zell Am Zee and on back to Kaprun is a blur, as is the period through until the early hours of the following morning, during which I can only remember one thing and that is a brief conversation with John, who said he and Margaret were worried about me. Whether I ate anything over this period I can't say.

I found myself leaving the hotel again in the early hours of the morning. Whether I went to bed and slept I don't know; my state of mind was very fragile. I felt paranoid and hunted. I soon left the streets and entered the fields surrounding Kaprun. It was raining and there was only just enough light to be able to proceed.

I found myself heading in the general direction of the path to the Gleiwitzer hut once more. I climbed over fences and through the occasional back garden and eventually found the sign, which marked the start of the path to the hut. As I started off up the route, I entered the trees and the going became even more difficult. It was almost pitch black and I found myself feeling round in the pockets of my coat. My right hand closed around the ring I had found two days ago. I gripped it tightly and grimly continued on into the darkness. I was terrified for a while but just then something happened which made the going a little easier. As I looked down at the ground, small flecks of what appeared to be a phosphorous-like material started to show up. These glowed and seemed to be only in the area where booted feet had disturbed them; therefore they showed up the line of the path. I struck on up through the forest guided by the glowing flecks.

Eventually the darkness began to lighten and I reached the upper limit of the trees. I had no food with me, not even a few squares of chocolate, but I had water in my flask, which I kept refilling at the cattle troughs along the way.

After what seemed like an eternity of twists and turns in the path I found myself approaching the Gleiwitzer hut. It was just breaking dawn as I tried the front door. It was open, of course, (the mountain hut doors are rarely locked) and I went inside the almost darkened building. A small nightlight burned and by the light of this I was able to drag my exhausted body over to a vacant bunk. I threw down my gear, took off my boots, stripped off down to my shirt and small clothes and crept under the blankets on the bunk.

The events of the next few days are a bit patchy in my memory but I will again attempt to detail them.

I was awoken several hours later by the bustle of the hut and I got out of my bunk, dressed and got the rest of my gear together. I was feeling a little better, having had some rest but I still had no appetite. The people who were in charge of the hut went about their chores and did not seem to recognise me as a recent addition to their clientele so I didn't make them any the wiser. There were hikers of all nationalities moving around, getting ready to depart the hut. A small group of what emerged to be Dutch hikers approached me and asked me if I was going down the mountain. They must have sussed out I was English because they spoke to me in my native tongue. I replied that I was and they invited me to accompany them.

So I departed from the hut, forgetting to leave any money for my stay and joined the Dutch party to descend the path that I had come up earlier. I was feeling a little more normal but was still somewhat paranoid and this state of mind began to worsen as we went down the mountain. This was mainly due to disturbing topics of conversation being held by my fellow walkers and also by the fact that some of them appeared to be smoking joints.

When we reached a point some two miles from Kaprun, we passed a point where a small side path branched off to the left. Being at the back of the single file of walkers I seized my opportunity to be rid of the rest of the group and darted off down this new route.

I must have made it back to the village. Whether I called in at my hotel I can't say but I found myself trekking across the valley floor and arriving at a railway station, which serviced a track running down an adjacent valley. An old steam engine was just arriving, pulling a long line of carriages and as it came to a standstill I boarded it, there being no reason not to!

Having taken on passengers, the train chuffed out of the station, down the valley. It was quite crowded and I had to stand out in the open air at the end of my carriage. This was not a problem however because it had got out into a lovely day.

Presently I was approached by a conductor and asked for my ticket. I replied that I did not have one and asked the man in English what the price of the fare was.

He replied, "Are you a guest?"

And with a bit of improvisation I boldly said, "Yes."

He declared with a smile that the price was five Schillings. I paid the conductor and then looking back into the carriage, realised that the majority of passengers were all decked out in their best clothes and that this must be a special train, perhaps going to a wedding! Fancy that, me declaring that I was a guest, being of the unshaven appearance of a man who had just come down out of the mountains after summiting some great peak.

The train travelled for some time down the valley and I enjoyed a brief respite from my troubled state of mind, relaxing to the rocking motion of the carriage in the warm midday sun. Eventually the train pulled into a station at what appeared to be the end of the line. All the passengers got off, with the wedding guests making their way to their function and leaving me to decide what to do next. Just outside the station was a large map displayed on a board; it showed the local area and on it I picked out the Grossglockner, (the highest mountain in Austria) and near to it, but also not far from where I was, was a well-known waterfall cataract. At least to the locals it was well known, but I forget its name.

I decided to pay the waterfall a visit, having got my camera with me. I followed signs for the falls up through the little village that the railway serviced, joining a flow of other tourists intent on the same destination. The well-marked path snaked through the trees after I left the village and soon crossed the roaring torrent of a river by a well-constructed footbridge. The route then began to climb up the side of the churning, milky-coloured flow and soon I arrived at a viewing platform area. Ahead of me the river crashed down, over a series of falls. A fine spray rose up all around, wetting everything and everyone in sight. I took several photos of the spectacular scene and then continued on up the path to visit each stage of the waterfall. There were viewing platforms at each level and I got some good shots with my camera. By the time I got to the top of the falls, I was feeling decidedly weary once more. There was a sign at the top which pointed in the direction of the Grossglockner but thankfully I had the good sense not to go that way and descended back to the village, seeking the bus stop.

The route map at the stop showed that the service would take me back to Kaprun. After a while a bus arrived. On boarding it, I asked the driver if he was going to Kaprun and he said that he was, so I bought my ticket and sat down. I was very tired and by this time it was late afternoon. I fought to stay awake on the journey and made a mistake by getting off the bus too early, meaning I had to walk a couple of miles to get back to Kaprun.

During the journey I had made up my mind to go home. I still had a week of my holiday left but I was just charging around from pillar to post, wearing myself out. My state of mind was not good and I wasn't communicating very well with the people around me! I had virtually lost touch with John, Margaret and Dennis.

Upon entering my hotel, I got my room key and went upstairs without speaking to anyone. I gathered up all the relevant equipment for the journey home into my rucksack and then packed my suitcase, putting it and my golf clubs next to the bed. I left these items to the holiday company, to hopefully return them to my home.

I then left the hotel again, carrying only my rucksack and coat, also the room key, which I forgot to leave. It was now late in the evening and starting to get dark. I set off once more in the direction of Zell Am Zee. Although I had a rough plan worked out of how I was going to get home I was very tired and had difficulty concentrating. There was quite a bit of traffic on the road at this time of day as I made my way along the grass verge and several boy racers sounded their horns at me as they tore past, making me angry.

It must have been around ten or eleven p.m. when I walked into Zell Am Zee. My plan was to try to catch a train to Innsbruck and then hopefully get a flight back to the U.K. from there. I made my way to the railway station and asked at the ticket office for a ticket to Innsbruck. The man on duty supplied me with the appropriate ticket, taking my money and told me that a train would be arriving in approximately half an hour. He also told me that it was the night train coming from the east and that it would probably be nearly full.

When the train rolled into the station, the guard got off and escorted me to his carriage at the back, where I was shown into the mailbag area. There were no seats so I settled down in amongst the mailbags, thinking the train must indeed be packed for them to have put me in here. However it was reasonably warm and I was just glad to get off my feet. The train began to move and I soon fell asleep.

I was awoken some time later by the guard shaking my shoulder. The train was at a standstill as the man escorted me off it; I had to jump down onto the side of the track as we were not in a station. The guard walked me up the train to a second class carriage and I got on, found a seat and then quickly fell asleep again.

When I opened my eyes again, I found myself gazing into the eyes of one of the most beautiful women I had ever seen, she was sitting in the seat opposite and must have got on while I was asleep. It was still dark outside the train windows but the lights burned brightly inside the carriage. I shyly averted my gaze from the attractive sight, turning to look to my left where I encountered two other pretty women, sitting on the opposite side of the carriage. They were engaged in conversation with each other and they must have felt my gaze upon them for they turned to look at me, I looked away and they giggled and then resumed their talk. It didn't matter where I directed my eyes; I seemed to be looking at one of these women. I thought I had died and gone to heaven! Having had some rest by this time my thought pattern had begun to return to normal. The woman opposite was now reading a book but she kept glancing up at me. She had the look of an eastern European about her. I began to indulge in a small fantasy. I was wearing my mountain climber's hat that I had bought the previous year, with the words, 'Mountain climbers' school Grindelwald' inscribed on it and imagined that the woman thought I was a famous mountain guide, therefore finding me attractive. Thinking these pleasant thoughts, my eyelids grew heavy once more and I drifted off to sleep again.

The next time I woke, the train was at a standstill and looking out of the window I saw a station sign reading 'St Anton'. Now I knew that we were at a ski resort near Innsbruck and I didn't have far to go. Looking around, I realised that the three women were gone; therefore, like the story of my life, I had missed the opportunity to chat them up! The train began to move again and I nodded off once more.

Whether the train stopped at Innsbruck I will never know because I slept through until I was awoken by the tannoy, which was broadcasting in a variety of languages. Listening to the English announcement I heard to my astonishment that the train was approaching the Swiss border and would all passengers have their passports ready for inspection by the border guards. I frantically searched my rucksack for my passport and was relieved to find it there, just as the guards entered the far end of the carriage. I knew a moment of panic as they approached me; although I hadn't done anything wrong the reality of my situation dawned on me. I was about to enter another country and perhaps I had been reported missing in Kaprun and there was now a search going on for me! However, my fear that I would be hauled over the coals for something was soon dispelled as the guards addressed me. They inspected my passport and asked me for my ticket. On seeing the ticket, they remarked that it only covered my journey to Innsbruck and gave me a searching look. I panicked a bit and stuttered that I had slept right through the Innsbruck stop. The men smiled and asked me where I wanted to go from there. I asked them where was the train going and they said Zurich, so I said I would go there.

They told me how much the fare was and I said, "I only have Austrian Schillings."

"They will be fine," the men said and took a couple of large denomination notes off me in exchange for a ticket.

They then said, "Danke," (thank you) and went on into the next carriage.

I stayed awake for the rest of the journey to Zurich, which was uneventful. On arrival at the station at Zurich, I made my way to the airport, which was directly above. I sought out the British Airways information desk and enquired about flights to the U.K. They told me that there was a flight leaving shortly for Gatwick with availability and that the price of a ticket would be four hundred pounds. My jaw dropped and I was forced to tell them that I couldn't afford the fare!

I had been feeling a bit better up until that point but as I made my way, with feet dragging, away from the desk and out of the airport I began to feel tired and somewhat paranoid once more. Before I left the terminal, I got a traveller's cheque changed into Swiss Francs at the bureau de change and bought a map of the Zurich area at the tourist information. I walked away from the airport and soon found myself travelling down the verge of a major highway. It was very hot and sunny, being now around late morning. Above me the air seemed hazy with the fumes of aircraft taking off and landing at the busy airport. How far I walked, or for how long, I can't say but eventually I came to a slip road off the highway and following this; I came to a small village.

I walked around this village for a bit and upon finding a bus stop, decided that the course of action I had been taking was not doing me any good and that I would therefore better try to get a bus back to the airport and try and find a cheaper flight.

A bus pulled up eventually and I boarded it, experiencing a few initial difficulties in explaining to the driver where I wanted to go but he finally gave me a ticket, which I paid for with my newly acquired francs. The bus seemed to travel away from the airport at first but it circled back round and I was soon alighting at the terminal building.

Once more in the airport, I sought out the Dan Air desk, having remembered that I had heard somewhere that this company did cheaper flights. The lady there was very helpful, probably having taken pity on this poor dishevelled traveller and she told me that there was a flight leaving for Gatwick later that day and that the price of a ticket would be two hundred pounds. I jumped at this chance and was soon paying her the fare with the traveller's cheques from my dwindling supply.

I had several hours to kill before check-in time so I mooched around the airport, even managing to grab a snack and coffee at a café, my appetite having mysteriously reappeared on buying the plane ticket.

The time went by and at last I was able to put my faithful rucksack through the Dan Air check-in desk and receive my boarding pass. I cleared passport control after a bit of scrutinizing by the official due to my unshaven appearance and made my way to the departure gate. At the gate I looked out of the window and saw that the plane was already in position and it was of a type that I had never flown on before. It was fairly small but had four engines.

After a while the call came to board and I made my way onto the plane and found my seat. After a short delay we taxied out and took off. I found that my mood was lightening all the time as the flight proceeded and by the time the in-flight meal was served I was feeling quite normal again, with a burgeoning appetite. I wolfed the meal down and then settled down for a short sleep.

I awoke as we were descending towards Gatwick. The plane landed smoothly and taxied to the terminal building. After we were cleared to leave the plane I made my way through passport control to the baggage reclaim.

I retrieved my rucksack from the baggage carousel and then made my way through the airport to the British Airways information desk, where I enquired about flights to Glasgow. The lady there said that there was a flight leaving shortly and that if I was quick I could catch it. I asked how much was the cost of the ticket and the lady said eighty pounds. I rummaged in my wallet and fished out my remaining traveller's cheques, finding that I had just enough left for the ticket. I paid the fare, received my ticket and hurried to the B.A. check-in desk. I handed over the ticket and watched my trusty rucksack disappear once more up the conveyor belt. I repeated the Zurich airport routine and soon found myself winging my way over the familiar English countryside and up into Scotland.

After landing I picked up my rucksack from baggage reclaim and on doing so, noticed that one of the side pockets was unfastened. On investigating, I found that my expensive pair of sunglasses that had been in that compartment had vanished. I was not amused but realising that there was little I could do about it, I went on my way.

I made my way out to the bus stop for the company who had been looking after my car. After a while the bus came and I was whisked back into the city of Glasgow and to the depot where my car was parked. It was now very late in the evening and on arrival at the said depot, the disgruntled man in charge there reluctantly gave me the keys for my car, complaining that I was not due back for nearly another week!

My car started easily and the journey back to Cumbria was uneventful, apart from the fact that a peculiar light rain fell on my windscreen on the way, which slicked on and was difficult to remove even with the screen wash. Apparently, the weather had stayed hot and dry while I was away so maybe the slicking on the windscreen was caused by the rain washing the pollutants hanging over the motorway out of the air!

I arrived home at the farm in the early hours, letting myself into the house and then awakening my surprised parents to tell them the holiday had gone wrong but I was home safely!

Later in the day a call from the holiday company was received, asking if I was home and okay. My folks dealt with this. My suitcase and golf clubs arrived back by delivery van a week later.

On this occasion, I didn't seek medical help to explain the events of my holiday and life continued on as normal, for a while anyway.

Part 3

Banff, Canada
February/March 1997.

I had worked hard and saved well towards a ski holiday since the fateful Austria trip. I had planned on going to Breckenridge in the U.S.A., but the single room supplements were as much as the total price of the holiday so I opted for Banff in the Canadian Rockies, which was much cheaper, with a better exchange rate for my pound. It was still a lot of money, however and I was forced to go self-catering.

I was flying out of Manchester and had arranged to stay with friends the night before, who had a holiday house near our farm and whose main house was on the outskirts of the city.

I drove down to Manchester in my Capri on Tuesday the twenty-fifth of February, arriving in the evening after getting lost several times. A black cat crossed the road in front of me as I was entering the estate where my friends lived! They showed me where to park my car so that it was out of the way for the duration of my holiday and then welcomed me into the house, where I was served a nice meal. I went to bed early to prepare for what undoubtedly would be a long and arduous journey, as it consisted of three flights and then a further transfer to my destination.

Wednesday the twenty-sixth of February. My friends took me to the airport at seven forty-five a.m., where I said goodbye then checked my skis and suitcase in for the coming three flights. I would not see them again until the Canadian airport of Calgary. I went through the usual airport routine, buying a bottle of duty-free whisky on the way and flew out at approximately ten thirty a.m. for Schiphol airport in Amsterdam, where I changed for the flight to Minneapolis in the U.S.A. The plane was waiting at the gate and I could see that it was a Boeing 747 jumbo jet. It was massive, appearing to be twice as big as the planes around it. I had never flown on one of these before and was excited by the prospect! Upon boarding the giant I found my seat halfway along the standard class cabin, with the first class cabin being above me. As I got comfortable, I was delighted to see that there were T.V. screens suspended from the cabin ceiling at regular intervals. I had heard about in-flight movies on these big planes and I was relishing the thought of these.

After a while the huge plane taxied out to the end of the runway, where it waited for a few moments, then the pilot applied the throttles and I was pushed back in my seat by the massive power of the four engines. The plane roared along the runway and took off in what seemed like a short distance with incredible ease! We quickly reached cruising altitude and as the journey progressed I was astonished how little turbulence there was, it was just as though we were still on the ground! The in-flight meal was served and then drinks, of which I had a few. The in-flight movie came on and it was, *The Ghost and the Darkness*, starring Michael Douglas and Val Kilmer. The film was about two big game hunters in Africa hunting two man-eating lions terrorising a gang of railroad workers building a railway across the wilderness. I had never seen it before and it was excellent!

I can't remember the exact duration of that flight but it must have been around nine hours. I didn't sleep during the journey and spent the time talking to my fellow passengers, drinking (both alcoholic and soft drinks) and admiring the view from my window seat, down to the Atlantic Ocean below. This was particularly good when passing over the southern end of Greenland and then later over Hudson Bay.

As the great plane descended towards Minneapolis, I reflected on what had been a memorable flight. They used to call the American P51 Mustang fighter 'the Cadillac of the skies' during the second world war and I decided that the Boeing 747 was worthy of the same title during the modern age.

We landed at Minneapolis and on making my way to transfer I experienced my first taste of the U.S. immigration system. They are very careful about who or what they let into their country and I seemed to queue for over an hour to go through this rigmarole. Eventually I got through and was able to make my way to and board the flight to Calgary in Canada. I can remember little of this stage in my journey apart from flying on a standard jet and the leg being about two and a half hours in length.

The plane touched down in Calgary about ten thirty p.m. local time. I went through security and retrieved my suitcase and skis from the baggage reclaim, being slightly surprised to see them after three flights. A rep from my holiday company was waiting to greet me at the welcome point and she escorted me to the waiting transfer coach. During the journey to Banff along the Trans-Canada Highway, which took about two hours, I found myself thinking back to an incident at home, at a party at the hotel where my sister worked. I had been pretty well oiled (well gone on drink) that night but I remember standing on the edge of the dance floor and a male voice behind me saying, "Be careful what you do in Canada." when I turned round, there was nobody behind me! I have always remembered this as it gave me a chill that night and also on the night of the coach transfer. It was obviously dark outside the coach and the snow drifting across the road in the headlights in front made me drowsy. I drifted in and out of sleep as we travelled.

The coach finally arrived in Banff at one thirty a.m. and dropped me off outside the Rundle apartments. There was a night porter on duty and he showed me to my apartment, which was in the basement; it seemed nice enough though. I quickly unpacked and poured myself a stiff whisky from my duty free, drank it down and then went to bed feeling pretty exhausted.

Thursday the twenty-seventh of February. I got up fairly early and had a closer inspection of the apartment, noting that it had quite good cooking facilities, a fridge, a good bathroom with shower and obviously, the double bed that I had slept in. There was of course no food in the apartment, so having got dressed in my skiing gear I ventured out to the reception area, where I consulted the staff on the subject of breakfast. They told me there was a good restaurant called the Ptarmigan just down the street, so I went outside and walked to the said establishment.

On the way, I took in the views of the great peaks of the Rockies, rising up all around the town. I also became aware of the intense cold, which seemed more noticeable than on my alpine skiing adventures. Upon entering the Ptarmigan my spectacles steamed up, a hazard of all specs wearers when coming in out of the cold into a warm building. I sat down at a vacant table, wiping my specs on my handkerchief and an attractive waitress approached me. I told her it was my first day in Canada and asked her what she recommended for breakfast. She said the pancakes with maple syrup were very good so I ordered these and coffee. The meal arrived shortly and I was astonished at how many pancakes there were in the helping. I was very hungry, however and was soon tucking into the pile, pouring maple syrup onto it as I went. As I ate, I observed that there were many other skiers eating here and decided that I would do this again if I didn't feel like making breakfast in the apartment! The food was delicious and a very reasonable price, too.

After finishing my meal I returned to my apartment to prepare for a day's skiing. I had my own boots, (an old pair of Salomen SX90s, top of the range in their time!) which I had brought in my suitcase and, of course, my own skis. I had also purchased the appropriate lift pass from the rep on the transfer bus so fixing this on a cord round my neck; I was now almost ready to go skiing. I squeezed into the old Salomens, which was always a bit of a performance, and gathered up my skis, then locked up the apartment and asked at reception where the ski bus stop was. Having received this information I made my way down the street to the bus stop. Now, I knew via information from the rep that Banff did not have its own ski area and that it serviced three ski areas; these were Mount Norquay, Sunshine Village and Lake Louise, each of which was reached by bus.

As I waited for a bus, I inspected my wallet, finding that I was running low on the Canadian dollars that I had brought from England and would have to get some traveller's cheques changed at the bank later in the day or early the next. I had enough cash for lunch, though and right now I just wanted to go skiing. I had made up my mind to try Sunshine Village for my first outing so when three buses arrived at the same time, I picked the one displaying the appropriate sign and following the other skiers, put my skis in the carrying rack on the back of the bus. I then boarded and sat in the seat immediately behind the driver.

The bus departed at approximately ten twenty a.m., moving through the town, which seemed to be about the same size as Keswick in the Lake District back home. We headed out of town onto the Trans-Canada Highway. The day was quite fine but with isolated snow flurries. At first I didn't know whether it was appropriate to talk to the driver, but anyway he began to speak to me. He was obviously a very sociable type and we soon had a good conversation going. He gave me a lot of good information about the skiing in the various areas and also the best bars to visit in Banff.

The journey took about half an hour but passed quickly due to the good crack with the driver. He dropped us off at a large car park at the base of a wooded mountain. I retrieved my skis from the bus rack. This proved to be a bit of a scrum, with everybody jostling to get theirs off at the same time! I then got out the piste map that I had got from the rep with my welcome pack. I could see from it that a gondola lift ran from the car park up a long valley up to the main ski area. I walked to the lift and was pleased that the tarmac had been cleared of snow, (as any skier knows, walking over hard-packed snow or ice in ski boots can be a tricky business). I boarded the gondola after showing my lift pass to the official. My skis were placed in a bucket attached to the outside of the cabin and my poles went inside with me. The cabin seated six people and this one was nearly full! The cabin trundled out of the station and we were off. It was quite stuffy in the enclosed space and halfway through the journey up the valley somebody farted, causing accusing looks to be exchanged all around! I got up and opened the little sliding window and the atmosphere soon cleared up.

We all got out at the top station and I again consulted my piste plan. There was much more snow here at my destination of Sunshine Village. I could see from the plan that a chairlift ran from nearby to the highest point of the area servicing a blue run (easy) and a red run (medium difficulty). I clipped on my skis, (Dynastar Laser 195s with Look racing bindings). The snow was crisp and firm under foot and the air was very cold. I am an experienced skier of advanced standard and can get down most slopes but the first few turns of a holiday are always a bit rusty and wooden. The area around me was dotted with lift stations and mountain restaurants comprising the village. Being in a bowl, lifts fanned out up the mountain sides in all directions. The chairlift I had chosen was only about a hundred yards away but the intervening space was crowded by skiers, some beginning their run down the blue run back to the car park, underneath the gondola I had arrived on. I pushed off down the gentle slope towards the lift, putting in a few shallow turns, avoiding the other skiers as I went. Arriving at the lift, I showed my pass and slid my way through to the departure ramp, joining three other skiers there. The chair came round the huge winding wheel behind us and scooped up the four of us who were lined up perfectly. As we rose up, we reached above our heads and pulled down the safety bar, which on this lift was attached to a large Perspex window cover that would keep the wind off us during our journey.

I was soon able to strike up a good conversation with the other occupants of the chair during our ride to the top.

It has been said by people in the years in between this holiday and the present day that I am not a very sociably adept person, but I know this to be a falsehood and that I can get a conversation going under most circumstances!

I was glad of the protection from the Perspex window cover as the temperature must have been minus six to minus seven degrees centigrade and the wind chill even more!

At the top of the lift we all slid off the arrival ramp without colliding with each other. I looped my pole straps over my wrists and set off to ski down the well-marked blue run. The condition of the snow was excellent and I was soon into my rhythm, making wide long parallel turns (skis close together). I was quickly back down to the bottom of the chairlift and soon on my way back up it again. On the next run down, I tried the red run and found it to be quite difficult due to a 'mogul field' (bumps of snow about a metre high) halfway down, but I managed to stay on my feet.

I had a few more runs down the same pistes and then stopped for a bite of lunch at one of the restaurants in the village. Upon using the toilets and looking in the mirror there, I was surprised to see icicles hanging from my bushy moustache, which I had grown in the last couple of years. My face was also very cold and starting to show a few white patches. I had noticed other skiers wearing a kind of mask to protect their faces from frostbite so upon leaving the restaurant, I made my way to the ski service and accessories shop to buy one of these masks. I did not have enough cash left so I had to use my credit card. The mask was made of a type of foam rubber and wrapped round the face to fasten at the back of the head with Velcro. It had perforations at the nose and mouth areas to allow breathing and reached up the face to just below the eyes. I put the mask on and then spent the rest of the afternoon skiing the other pistes around the village. These were mainly blue and red standard with the occasional black (difficult), which I steered clear of.

The lifts closed at four p.m. and so I made the return run under the gondola to the car park at this time. There were buses ready waiting to take skiers back to Banff; the cost of these journeys was included in the lift pass purchase. I put my skis in the back of one and boarded it. I was pleasantly surprised to find that the driver was the same one who had brought me here, so I again sat in the seat behind him, whereupon he remembered me and we resumed our conversation during the journey back to Banff.

On arrival back in the town, I retrieved my skis from the back rack of the bus and then made my way to a bank where I got some traveller's cheques changed; then I visited a supermarket to pick up milk, eggs, bread and cereal for breakfasts. I had decided that I would eat out in the evenings, in view of the good exchange rate. It was snowing as I left the store and made my way back to my apartment, struggling slightly under my load of food and equipment.

After I had had a nice bath which revived my stiff muscles, I put on my going out gear and ski jacket and set off out into the night to find a place to eat and then maybe visit some of the bars I had heard about. The

Ptarmigan had provided a good breakfast so I headed there to try it for an evening meal. I can't remember what I ate there but it must have been good because it set me up for a good night on the town! I got in late and had a nightcap out of my whisky bottle then went to bed.

Friday the twenty-eighth of February. I got up in good time after quite a good sleep, although the apartment had proved a bit stuffy during the night, being virtually below ground level and having only a couple of letter box type windows at the top of one wall. My head felt a bit woolly from the drink of the previous night but otherwise I was raring to go! I am not much of a cook but I can do eggs in most forms and that morning I made scrambled eggs on toast, with cereal to start, followed by coffee that I had also bought the night before. During the meal I weighed up my options for the day ahead; I could see by looking out of my narrow windows that it was a fine day and I made up my mind to try Lake Louise.

I put on my skiing clothes and boots, gathered up my skis and left the apartment for the ski bus stop. I was out and about earlier than the previous day and there were many more skiers waiting at the stop for the buses. When the buses arrived, I singled out the Lake Louise one and fought in the usual scrum to get my skis into the back rack, then boarded and found one of the few remaining seats, this time away from the driver.

The journey took fifty minutes and I passed the time talking to the guy sitting next to me. The village of Lake Louise lies just to the north of the Trans-Canada Highway and the ski area just to the south. The valley is wide, with the lower slopes clad in trees. The lake lies up a side valley with a huge Victorian hotel, the name of which I forget, at the end of it.

The bus dropped us off in a large car park with a restaurant and chairlift nearby. The sign on the side of the chairlift station showed minus fourteen degrees centigrade and you could certainly feel it. I put my face-mask on, clipped on my skis and made my way to the chairlift.

The lift took me high above the trees to a ridge, from where the pistes stretched down into another valley. I spent the day skiing this area because it was in sunlight. It was bitterly cold, with the occasional light snow flurry and you had to keep moving to stay warm. At lunch time I stopped at a mountain restaurant for a bite to eat and a Coke. The antics of a grey jay-like bird amused me on the veranda; it would wait until the skiers weren't looking and then steal food from their plates, then make its getaway into a tree nearby.

Late in the day I returned to the ridge and stopped for a minute to take a photo and appreciate the fine view out across the valley to the lake, with the higher peaks of the Rockies rising up either side of it. One of the pistes back to the car park was graded a black diamond run and feeling confident, I took it on. The snow conditions were superb as I carefully picked my way down the steep but smooth run. (This piste is the FIS Lake Louise Ladies' downhill run!). I was breathless with exertion and excitement by the time I emerged at the car park and feeling a need to celebrate, I made my way to the restaurant bar where I got talking to the driver of one of the piste grooming machines. He was grabbing a quick drink before he went on night duty to prepare the pistes for the next day. I had four large beers in that bar and they went down very nicely indeed.

I was feeling half cut as I boarded the bus back to Banff and had a little kip during the journey back.

On arrival back in the town, I returned to my apartment, shaved and showered and went out to the Ptarmigan again for supper. From here I toured the bars, including the Hard Rock Café, where I got talking to a couple of local blokes, one of whom worked on the ski lifts at Lake Louise. They took me to a nightclub and things got a bit hazy after that!

Saturday the first of March. I got up with a hangover, being not too sure of the events of the previous evening or indeed, how or what time I had got in. I managed breakfast, however and was soon out and about and making the bus journey to the third ski area of Mount Norquay. This was the nearest of the areas to Banff and the trip only took twenty minutes. This area was also the smallest, having only four chairlifts. It did, however, have a double black diamond run which I tackled and found to be extremely difficult, having loads of moguls. I therefore skied this piste only once!

I worked the pistes all day, chatting on the lifts with the other skiers and helping the occasional child on and off the chairs. The weather had been a little kinder than the day before, with higher temperatures but also with constant light snow, making the visibility a little poor. When the lifts closed, I retired to the ski lodge, where I again got stuck into the beer, which was good taking. There was a rather good country and western singer performing and I sang along to the tunes I recognised. The buses back to Banff ran up to six p.m. and I caught the last one back.

Back in the town I visited the supermarket and bought a few simple things for my supper then returned to my flat and cooked a light meal before relaxing with a few whiskies and the book I had brought with me. I turned in early, beginning to become aware that I was burning the candle at both ends!

Sunday the second of March. Having had an early night and a reasonable sleep, I was out and about early and soon on my way to Lake Louise, where I planned to meet and ski with the 'ski friends' group that I had heard about from the rep at the start of the holiday. The meeting place for this group was at the bottom of the main chairlift, just off the car park. I found the group quite easily and saw that it consisted of two guides wearing blue ski jackets and a bunch of other skiers like me, who had come in from Banff. The guides turned out to be retired people who lived locally and who were of an expert standard of skier.

We were soon up at the top of the main ridge, which was at about two thousand five hundred and ninety metres (eight thousand five hundred feet) and the highest point of all three ski areas.

Here at the top of the chairlift I heard a shout of, "Hi, Steve."

I turned and saw the lift operator waving at me. He was one of the guys I had been at the nightclub with a couple of nights ago!

I waved back and shouted, "Hello."

He had told me he worked one of the highest and coldest lifts and that he got to and from his job in an old snow tractor. This machine was parked nearby with the engine (a gloriously burbling six cylinder) running to stop it from freezing up.

The guy shouted, "Have a good day."

And I replied, "I will," and then I set off to join the back of the group, which was heading off into the next valley. Skiing with the 'ski friends' proved to be quite a frustrating business because the group was made up of different standards of skier and we kept having to stop to allow the slower members to catch up!

I stuck with the group all day though, even when I lost my body heat on occasion due to the constant stopping. Luckily the day was warmer than the last time I had skied these slopes.

At the end of the day we gathered in the bar at the car park and enjoyed a few celebratory beers. I enjoyed sharing skiing stories with the other group members but didn't manage to make any significant connections with any of them, especially the women!

Back in Banff, I noticed a group of large elk hanging around the outskirts of the town and recalled an amusing tale I had heard from the piste grooming machine driver about these persistent deer having a habit of standing in house/shop doorways, with their ample backsides shoved up against the doors, preventing people from getting in or out of their buildings!

I ate out that night and toured a few bars before turning in about midnight. Earlier I had met one of my holiday reps enjoying a drink with other reps in one of the bars and he had told me that there was going to be a carvery at one of the mid-mountain restaurants in Lake Louise, followed by a torchlit ski descent afterwards and this was on the next day! So on agreeing to join this activity I paid him the cost of it and then went home.

Monday the third of March. The carvery started at four p.m. so having got to Lake Louise in good time on this day, I determined to get as much skiing done as possible before the event. The weather was mainly fair, with the temperature hovering at about ten degrees below zero. I explored all of the pistes in the area and about three thirty p.m. I returned to the main ridge, now knowing where the restaurant was that was holding the event. You would have thought that I would not have difficulty stopping in the right place; however, I made a balls up of it by skiing very fast down the approach piste and overshooting the restaurant by about five hundred metres! With the lifts about to close, I did not have time to ski to the bottom, come back up on the lift and make a second attempt so I unclipped my skis and set off, carrying them, to hike back up the quite steep slope to the restaurant. It seemed to take an eternity.

I arrived hot, tired and sweaty at the venue about a quarter of an hour late. I stuck my skis into the snow alongside what seemed like hundreds of others and went up the steps into the building. It was packed and there were very few available spaces left at the tables. I grabbed one of these, throwing off my ski jacket onto the back of my chair as it was roasting, in out of the cold. Waitresses were plying the tables with drink and there was loud music playing.

Just then the music died down and a master of ceremonies picked up a microphone and asked, "How many people here are from England?" and as if as one the whole of the restaurant's occupants raised their hands. After this I grabbed a beer but made up my mind not to have too many, in view of taking on my first ever torchlit ski descent! Most of the people around me seemed to be plastered already and I wondered if they had been drinking in there since lunch time!

The carvery was served and it was a massive haunch of beef. Everybody queued up for their portion and there was more than enough to go round. The beef was served with potatoes and vegetables and was succulent.

After we had eaten and had a few more drinks, it was announced that everybody should take up their belongings, make their way outside and prepare for the torches to be lit and the descent to begin. I put my outer gear back on and went out into the frigid night air. As I was clipping into my skis, a middle-aged woman approached me and asked if I was a good skier. I told her I was and she then asked if I would go down the slope in front of her because she had had a little too much to drink! She told me her name was Susan. I said I would do my best to lead her down. Just then the local ski guides, of which there must have been around twenty, lit their flares and the piste outside the restaurant was suddenly bathed in light! There must have been over a hundred skiers gathered for the run down and some of them were obviously the worse for wear! The lead guide shouted to the crowd that he would lead off and would everybody form a single file as we went down the mountain. The rest of the guides would then space themselves out along the chain of skiers to light the way. We all formed a rough queue and Susan stuck to me like glue!

All at once the order to begin was shouted and the line of skiers began to move. I was about six places from the front and when my turn came I set off slowly diagonally down the slope, keeping a safe distance from the skier in front. I could hear the swishing of my new found friend's skis behind me and gained confidence from this. The slope was not steep and the guides skiing alongside lit it well with their bright torches. I made the first turn easily and then began the long zigzag to the bottom. I found it quite easy and the moderate amount of alcohol that I had consumed seemed to help! I was even able to glance back occasionally to check on my charge, but was only able to see as far back as the last bend in the piste and was not aware at that point that things were starting to go wrong further back.

I was enjoying myself and I shouted back to Susan, "Are you okay?" She replied, "Yes, fine, thank you. Thank God you are a good skier." I smiled to myself and felt even better.

The run down was maybe a couple of miles long but it was over all too soon. We finished the run at the main car park and the holiday reps, whom I had not noticed until that point, marshalled those who had completed the course into the nearby bar. We took off our skis and my new found friend said she would stand me a beer. I accepted the offer gratefully and we went into the bar. Roughly only half of the original crowd had made it to the bottom at that time and there seemed to be a long gap with nobody coming off the slope. The reps were running around in a worried fashion, telling us that the two buses that would take us all back to Banff would be arriving shortly. I downed the beer that Susan had bought me and told her my name was Steve. She finished her drink and then we both agreed that we should be getting ready to leave.

We joined those skiers who had got down and made our way to the waiting buses. There were enough of us to fill one of the vehicles so when we had loaded our skis and boarded our bus; we left for the return journey to Banff. I would not find out the fate of the other half of the original group until later the next day!

Susan sat next to me on the way back and I enjoyed a good conversation with her. I had enjoyed the whole day immensely and I suppose it was around this time that my mood began to approach a more heightened state! Susan told me that her husband had left her that lunch time, him being not too keen on skiing by torchlight and that he had gone back to Banff on an early bus to do a bit of shopping.

On arrival back in the town, we got off the bus, grabbed our skis and then Susan gave me a peck on the cheek and thanked me again for my help and company. She then said she would maybe see me again on the slopes and then left me; I never saw her again! I walked back to my flat, threw off my gear and poured myself a large whisky. It was by now getting fairly late so I finished my drink and then turned in.

Tuesday the fourth of March. On this day, I decided to head for Sunshine Village again so I got ready in the usual fashion and caught an early bus. During the journey I decided to find a ski service shop at Sunshine, having become aware that my skis were not running as smoothly as they might, and so upon leaving the bus I headed for the gondola station and when reaching it I discovered a ski rental/service establishment, right next to the ski lift. I took my skis inside and asked the staff if they could service them for me. They said it would be no problem but that it would take a while and so would I like to hire a pair of skis at a reduced rate while they saw to mine? I agreed to this attractive deal and they then asked me what standard of skier I was. I told them, advanced to expert and they brought a pair of obviously brand new skis from a rack, stating that although they were not as long as my own, they were of a stiffer flexibility and were the latest racing skis. This made me glow with pride and feel like the downhill racer I had always wanted to become! I asked them how long I could have the skis for and they said to take them for the day and pick up my own when returning them.

I marched out of the shop and headed into the lift station in a jaunty fashion then boarded one of the cabins, which then whisked me up to

Sunshine. It was overcast and snowing when I got off the lift but this meant that it was not quite as cold as it had been recently and I was able to dispense with the face-mask, which could be quite stifling at times. I clipped on the new skis and headed for the same chairlift that I had taken at the beginning of my holiday. Once at the top I set off down the blue run. At first I made the turns gingerly as I got used to the new feeling of the stiffer skis. I gained in confidence quickly, though and was soon tearing down the slope, carving out fast, tight turns. It began to snow more heavily and a layer of freshly fallen snow soon built up on the piste, slowing it down somewhat.

I skied all morning, trying out most of the other runs around the village. The new skis were working well but I had developed a niggling pain in the side of my left ankle. I stopped for lunch at one of the restaurants in the village and had a couple of large beers with my meal. On coming back out onto the slopes, I headed to a chairlift just in front of the restaurant. There was no queue so I swiftly slid through the boarding area and took my place in line with the approaching chair. The lift operator was a young woman and she was standing right next to where the chairs passed. Just as my chair was passing her, she grabbed it and swung it back on its pivot. She then threw it at me just as I was crouching to sit. Fortunately, I had my head turned towards the chair and was able to catch it and slow it down before the edge of the seat slammed into the back of my legs! The chair scooped me up and I looked back at the lift operator to find her staring after me in a most unpleasant way. I thought to myself, *why the bloody hell did she do that?* Then I began to wonder; did she see me coming out of the restaurant and did she then smell alcohol on me as I passed and thought she would test me with that manoeuvre to find out if I was pissed! I would find out later that day that drinking alcohol on the slopes in Canada and the U.S.A. is frowned upon; unlike in the ski resorts of Europe and so maybe I had come to the right conclusion as to the woman's actions. As it was, I avoided using that particular lift again that day.

After a couple more runs, the pain in my ankle became unbearable and I made my way to the repair shop in the village where I took off my sweaty, pongy left boot and got the probably nauseated technician to examine it. Upon inspection, the head of a rivet had worn through the fabric of the inner boot, causing it to rub against my ankle! The technician told me that he could maybe fix the boot up temporarily but that I really needed a new pair of boots. The guy strapped some tape over the head of the offending rivet and then put the boot back together. I paid him and then went back out to continue skiing. I could still feel the rivet in my boot but the chafing of it was much reduced. During the final run of the day down the easy blue piste under the gondola to the car park, I had time to contemplate the unfortunate development of the problem with my boots; would I be able to afford the considerable expense of a new pair? At the car park I took my hired skis back to the shop next to the gondola station and retrieved my own freshly serviced pair, whereupon I paid the staff and told them how much I had enjoyed the racing skis! I loaded my skis onto the waiting ski bus and boarded it for the return journey to Banff.

When I got back to town, I went back to my flat with my skis and upon examination of my finances, found that I still had a substantial amount of my spending money left so, knowing that the shops and banks were still open I went back out into town, still wearing my ski boots and taking my passport and book of traveller's cheques, I went to the nearest shop selling ski equipment. It was a large store, well stocked with all the latest equipment and I was soon engrossed in the search through the somewhat bewildering display of new ski boots. Presently one of the staff approached me and asked me if I needed any help.

I said, "Yes, please."

He then started to tell me about the selection process for a new pair of boots, with questions like what standard of skier I was and what type of skis did I have? I gave him all the relevant information and then he sat me down, went back to the rack of boots and pulled out a pair of green ones in my size. He brought them over and explained that these were the latest 'comfort fit' type. They were Lange Banshees and the outer plastic skin of the boot was semi-transparent, making it possible to see through to the inner shell. Each boot had two adjustable fastening clips on the foot and two on the ankle, unlike my old rear entry pair, which just had the one clip on the heel and a small lever on the foot which tightened a strap across the top of the foot.

The assistant said, "Try them on and walk up and down in them," so I did. They were much easier to put on than my old ones and once on, were incredibly comfortable!

I walked up and down, and the guy said, "What do you think?"

I said, "They feel amazing."

I then asked him how much they cost and he gave me a figure in Canadian dollars, which computed to about two hundred and forty pounds; this was a fair price considering they were a top of the range boot! I am always a bit impulsive when buying things and it didn't take me long to weigh up the pros and cons and also consider that the boots would look good on me in a ski lift queue with the word 'Banshee' emblazoned across the sides! I told the guy I would take them but that I would have to get some cheques changed.

He said, "It's no problem, we take traveller's cheques here."

And so I paid the guy. Obviously the cheques I had given him did not match the exact cost but were rather over it so he gave me the change in dollars.

The guy said, "Keep the new boots on to break them in and give me your old ones and we will dispose of them."

I did this then thanked him for his very excellent service and then left the shop.

There is something about spending money that puts you on a high and I was already high on the day's events before I went in the shop, so afterwards I was positively stratospheric. I headed to the nearest bar and ordered a beer and also, because it was well past supper time, something to eat. The food and drink went down well and I was soon making my way on to other bars, sporting my new boots as I went. In one of these bars I came across one of the reps who had been involved in the torchlit ski descent and on asking about it, discovered the fate of the other half of the group. She told me that about halfway down the run, there had been a crash and that the participants had become disorientated in their drunken state and some of them had wandered off the piste into the trees! The hairs began to stir on the back of my neck as she related the rest of the tale. Apparently it had taken half the night to reassemble the group, get them to the bottom of the run and back to Banff! Also that there were known to be grizzly bears hibernating in their winter dens in the area but that during March, they had been known to wake up temporarily and prowl the pistes for a bit before returning to their sleep! This meant that men carrying high powered rifles were said to patrol the pistes during this pre-spring period. (I did not see any evidence to support this scary rumour, however). I left the rep and then continued on to more bars, becoming more and more inebriated! I don't think I went as far as going to a nightclub and dancing in my new boots but who knows? I did, however, get in very late and fell into bed without showering!

Wednesday the fifth of March. I awoke to another hangover but managed to clear it away somewhat with a good long shower. After a light breakfast I got my gear together and headed for Lake Louise. On the way out of town on the bus, I noticed a man walking by the side of the road, he was carrying a large rucksack and seemed to be heading out onto the Trans-Canada Highway. I wondered where he might be heading for at that time of year. For the moment I put him out of my mind.

The weather was fine and dry but very cold as on arrival at Lake Louise I noted the thermometer read minus fifteen Celsius. I was feeling quite a bit better by now and was keen to get started, to try out my new boots and newly serviced skis. I took the usual lift to the ridge where I kept an eye out for my acquaintance, the lift operator, but he was nowhere in sight, it must have been his day off. The condition of the snow was excellent with only about an inch of new snow, unlike at Sunshine Village the day before where it had laid a new layer of six inches. (There had been very little new snow in Banff.)

Due to an ongoing irritable problem with my sinuses, (I was taking decongestant medication for this) the rise in altitude of the lift left me with a build-up of pressure in my ear canals, which I had to clear by holding my nose, closing my mouth and blowing out. Looking back, this condition was probably caused by constantly inhaling creosote fumes while treating fence posts and wooden sheep troughs back home on the farm!

After clearing my tubes I set off to ski down into the next valley. At first the new boots and sharpened skis felt a little strange but I soon became used to these new sensations and by the time I had reached the valley bottom, I was brimming with confidence. For some reason that day I had donned a different hat; my new headgear was a bright red woolly hat with a large pom-pom on the top. It was very warm but must have looked slightly ridiculous because while waiting in the lift queue I became the object of much sniggering and guffawing, resulting in one guy saying to me, "Nice headgear, friend, where did you get it at? A joke shop?"

I gave him a dirty look and then went through to board the next lift feeling somewhat self-conscious. This incident pissed me off a bit and the feeling stayed with me for the rest of the day, re-emerging at each lift queue I came to, with sporadic comments and giggling from my fellow skiers. Nowadays way-out headgear is the norm on the slopes!

I ate lunch in the same restaurant I had previously visited, namely the one with the cheeky jay-like birds. The boots and skis were performing admirably and during the afternoon I skied the whole range of pistes in the area, not knowing at the time that it would be the last day's skiing I had in Canada!

I finished off the day with a gut-swooping fast run down the black diamond piste to the car park and then wet my whistle in the bar there!

The rest of the day followed the usual routines but I became aware of a growing feeling of discontent, probably fuelled by the jibes about my hat!

Thursday the sixth to Sunday the tenth of March. (This period is a blank in my diary so I have attempted to relate the ongoing events from memory alone). I awoke in a very strange mood and began to pack my dad's old rucksack I had brought with me with provisions for a long hike. I felt claustrophobic in the little flat, partly below ground and some of the symptoms of the previous two episodes began to re-emerge. The urge to get out and get going was upon me and also a feeling of wanting to hide away from others! I got out a piece of paper and wrote a kind of goodbye letter. In it, I asked for my remaining belongings to be returned home and that was it – the MIND TRAP had been sprung! I left the letter on the kitchen worktop, put on my hiking boots and my ski jacket, shouldered the rucksack and left the flat, probably without eating.

As I walked out of town in a southerly direction, I disturbed a large flock of ravens and magpies feasting on scraps on the outskirts. The magpies were the biggest I had ever seen, being almost as large as their cousins, the ravens and there were a hell of a lot of them! Perhaps you know the magpie rhyme:
One for sorrow
Two for joy
Three for a girl
Four for a boy
Five for silver
Six for gold
Seven for a secret
Never to be told

Anyway, there were many more than seven and as they took to the wing they set up a tremendous clambering cackle and croaking which seemed to sound like they were laughing at me! Magpies are notorious robbers of small birds' nests and I consider myself to be a champion of the small birds' cause. A few years previously I had shot five of these sods with one barrel of my twelve gauge shotgun; they were lined up one behind the other on the top wire of a fence. Just after they dropped, another one flew out of the trees nearby and I got it with the other barrel!

I quickly moved on and out onto the side of the Trans-Canada Highway. The weather was quite fine but it was very cold. I had dispensed with my salopettes and now wore only a pair of ordinary jeans and I could feel the cold coming through them!

They drive on the right in Canada and so I walked south on the northbound side of the dual carriageway. There was no hard shoulder and only about six inches of tarmac between the white side-line and the grass. There was, however, a fairly broad grass verge for me to walk along. Banff lies in a broad flat bottomed valley which runs north to south. Both the carriageways of the Trans-Canada Highway running through the valley are raised up above the surrounding land; this I suppose is to make the wind blow the snow off the road and also probably to enable the snow ploughs to have somewhere to push the snow if the road does get blocked!

As I went south, I had no idea of where I was going or indeed of how far I would walk, or for how long! I just felt driven to get out and away. It had come on me so quickly, with so few of the warning signs I could have recognised from the previous episodes! This time it was even stranger than before, I supposed that outwardly I would appear normal but on the inside, I was in turmoil.

Back in the early nineties I had subcontracted my labour to a builder, who I had come to dislike and distrust intensely before we finally went our separate ways. He had driven a big Volvo and so as I walked, every time I saw a Volvo coming towards me I would stick two fingers up at it! I was angry with the world! There was, however, a part of me that was operating normally because I could not fail to notice the beauty that was around me. To the west side of the valley rose the towering peaks of the Rockies and among my belongings I had brought a disposable camera with the ability to take wide angle photos (I had bought this a few days previously at the supermarket) and so I took pictures as I went. Canada is such a massive country and you get some idea of its size when you walk through it, e.g. by the time the middle of the day had come I was still passing the same mountain as when I started!

During the early afternoon I became thirsty. Having not brought any water with me, this was a problem. At intervals, streams ran down under the road from the low hills to the east; however, the mouths of the culverts were at the other side of an eight foot high deer fence at the side of the highway! I knew I had to get to the water somehow but I was becoming tired. My need overwhelmed my fatigue and I was forced to take off my rucksack and scale the fence. This I did with difficulty and almost injured myself in the process! I had my little Thermos flask in my pocket and I filled this from the stream. I then got down on all fours and took a long drink from the sparkling clear flow. (I was not experiencing an apocalyptic scenario like the Swiss episode, so I was not afraid of the water!) Having scrambled back over the fence, I continued on my way.

As the miles went by, I gradually became more and more fatigued, but there were no service stations or indeed any habitation of any sort; nor were there any people, although back at the stream I had seen boot marks in the snow, suggesting somebody else had also been there on foot at some time recently. There was only a thin covering of snow on the verge, meaning the walking was not difficult. The gradient was level also, but the days of hard skiing and burning the candle at both ends were catching up on me. I had brought some food with me, including quite a few bars of chocolate, which I nibbled on as I went. Also, I had prepared for most eventualities by having the rest of my spending money and my passport with me.

Around late afternoon I found myself approaching a place where the hills on my side of the road rose much more steeply and presently formed a cliff at the side of the road. The verge disappeared and I was forced to stop and consider my options. If I continued along this side of the road, I would be probably be hit by an oncoming vehicle and be seriously injured! I looked over to my right across the other carriageway and saw that the railway, (the Canadian Pacific) ran parallel to the road. I decided to head for this. I waited for a gap in the traffic and then sprinted across to the centre barrier, jumped it and then picked a gap in the traffic on the other carriageway and ran across it. Having reached the other side of the road I found there was no footway here as well and I now, with dismay, contemplated another barrier that I had not counted on – the river! There was a short drop to the bank and as I lowered myself down to it I felt, for the first time that day, real fear! The river was maybe ten yards wide but was not completely frozen over, there were patches of open water! There was no telling how thick the ice was but if I was going to continue my journey I would have to brave the crossing! With my heart in my mouth, I got down on all fours to help spread my weight and crawled slowly out onto the ice. It creaked slightly but held as I crept across, trying not to think about how deep or how cold the water was beneath. I reached the other side and let out a huge sigh of relief! You could say that there was a part of me that was enjoying this, it was exciting, even thrilling; it was like being in a movie except that it was real and it was happening to me right now!

I was well used to crow shooting expeditions back home, ranging over a variety of different terrains so I was no stranger to being out in the sticks. Helped by the adrenalin rush of the river crossing and the consumption of more chocolate, my energy levels began to pick up again as I fought my way through deeper snow towards the railway. On the way, I passed an area of bushes and from these I extracted a stout staff about a metre and a half long which I kind of used as a third leg. It was also useful to probe the snow in front of me to feel for obstructions.

At the railway there was no fence to climb over and I got up to the track quite easily. I walked on south between the rails but had slight difficulty in doing so as some of the pieces of ballast were lying on the cross timbers, making it feel like I was walking on marbles! There were no trains, however, at this time and I was able to make quite good progress.

After a mile or so the railway crossed a bridge over the river. I made the crossing and then, as the valley had widened out once more and the highway was still nearby, I crossed back onto it and continued my journey down the roadside verge. After a while, as dusk was drawing in, I came to a place where the road ran alongside a frozen lake. At the other side of this were the huge buildings and conveyors of a mine. I would find out in the fullness of time that this was the largest and most productive phosphate mine in Canada. I walked on past the lake and mine and darkness fell as I then changed onto the southbound carriageway, because the lights of the oncoming traffic were dazzling me! It was easier going with the traffic as I was able to use the vehicle headlights to show up any obstructions on the verge.

Several hours must have passed before I came across a road sign saying 'Canmore,' which pointed right. Shortly after this a slip road ran off to the right and I followed it. The road then swung back underneath the main highway and on following it, I came to the lights of a largish town. I made my way into the outskirts and presently came across a small grove of conifers at the roadside. The new-found energy of earlier had long since worn off and I decided that this was a good place for a rest, so I took off my rucksack and lay down on the bare ground beneath the branches of one of the trees. It was a small tree and I was able to kind of curl up around the trunk. Still warm from my walking, I soon fell asleep but it could only have been for a short while because I was awoken by the intense cold creeping through my clothing! I got up, picked up my belongings and continued on into the town. I have since found out that Canmore is the town featured in the movie, *Last Of The Dogmen* starring Tom Berenger and Barbara Hershey, an interesting film about a tribe of native American Indians living on in modern times in a secret valley in the mountains of Montana.

I reached the quiet main street (it was late in the evening by now) and was about to continue down it when a man called out nearby.

"Where are you going at this hour, sir?"

I had not noticed the police car parked nearby. The officer got out of his car and approached me. I had had several encounters with the police in England over the years, not all of them good so as he got closer and began to unbutton the holster of his sidearm, I panicked a bit and as I was still carrying my staff, I raised it in front of me. This was the first person who had spoken to me all day and here he was, threatening to pull a gun on me!

I said, "If you pull that gun, you had better be prepared to use it or I will knock it out of your hand with this stick!"

He backed off a bit and then said, "If you put the stick down, I will leave my gun where it is. We have had a report of a man who has gone missing in Banff and if you are him, I only want to help you!"

I felt slightly embarrassed and ashamed and quickly lowered my staff.

The officer said, "You look done in. If you get in the car, I will take you to the hospital and they can look you over."

I replied, "Okay, thank you."

I left my staff on the pavement and got into the back seat of the police car.

The cop got in and I said, "Please don't lock the doors. I won't try to get out."

He didn't and we moved off down the street.

We pulled up in front of the glass doors of the hospital and we both got out of the car.

The cop said, "If you go in, they will take care of you."

I said, "Are you not coming in with me, then?"

And he said, "No, I must be getting on with my other duties!"

I walked up to the glass doors and then suddenly I was seized by a moment of panic. What were they going to do to me when I got in there?

The cop said, "Goodbye and good luck."

I waved to him and then waited for him to get back in his car and drive off, then I took one last look at the friendly, welcoming faces waiting for me inside the hospital and then bolted down a road to the side of the building, lowered myself over two and a half metre high drop of a retaining wall and sprinted for the trees on the edge of town! Once in the trees and using the ambient light from the streetlights of the town, I found some more bushes and selected a stout branch, twisting it off at the base and again about two and a half metres up to fashion another staff. I then continued along the edge of the trees, skirting the edge of town to make my way back out into open country. Out here it was possible to see quite well, even though there was no moon. The stars were very bright and also there was a certain amount of light coming from the spectacular Hale/Bopp comet, which hung in the sky above me. I had also seen the comet in our own skies before I left England, but it was much brighter in Canada!

I left the trees once I cleared the town and located the railway again, steering clear of the highway for the time being in case there was now a full blown search for me going on! As I climbed up onto the track bed once more, I disturbed a small herd of elk foraging in a meadow nearby, causing them to stampede into the trees. The walking along the track was even more difficult in the poor light and I stumbled several times as I headed on south. I was very tired again by now and incredibly, I began to nod off while still kind of stumbling along! I must have been asleep when I was brought back to awareness by a bright light shining into my face. For a split second I hesitated, not knowing what it was and then I heard a rumbling and the blaring of a klaxon.

I shouted out loud, "Christ Almighty, a train!"

I dived off the track to the right into a snow bank just as the massive diesel engine was about to hit me! The train thundered by as I picked myself up. I was shaking, that had been a very close call and it had unnerved me. I could see the lights of the occasional vehicle on the highway not far away and I decided that it would be the safer option to try that route again. Luckily I only had a flat, snow-covered meadow to cross to get to the road, the river being nowhere in sight at this point. The snow was quite deep in the field, coming up to my knees and I used even more energy getting across it.

I made it back onto the road after a bit of a struggle and continued on south down the verge of the left-hand northbound carriageway. It must have been in the early hours of the morning when I trod on the raised edge of the tarmac and slightly twisted my right ankle! It was painful but I was able to continue with a limp. Of course at this hour there was very little traffic. However, shortly after the ankle incident a car slowed down on the opposite carriageway and amazingly, pulled off the road, drove through the dip between the carriageways and swung out onto my side, pulling up beside me. It was another police patrol car! The cop inside rolled down the passenger side window and shouted at me.

He said, "What the hell do you think you are doing? Don't you know it's illegal to walk on the side of the highway?"

I replied, "Sorry, officer. I didn't know."

I then said, "Can you give me a lift to Calgary, please?" (I had now decided that this was my destination).

He said, "No chance. I'm not a taxi driver. Just get the hell off the highway, will you?"

With that, he roared off back northwards. I thought he was not very helpful unlike the cop back in Canmore.

As I limped on, the countryside around me began to flatten out and the lights of what must have been scattered farmsteads twinkled out, several hundred metres from the road. I thought about going to one of these and seeking help but I was afraid I would get a hostile reception at this hour!

Dawn broke and I found that my water reserves were now depleted, so I left the road and scrambled down the bank at the side to get to the river which had now appeared again, although perhaps it was not the same river I had crossed the day before, it seeming much wider here. The ice extended about two metres out into the flow but the water level was about half of a metre below the edge of it. I thought, *how the hell am I going to get to it?* I took off my rucksack and rummaged around in it, my tired mind trying to come up with a solution. Finally I fished out my electric shaver cord (Yes, I had brought this with me!). I thought if I tied one end of the cord around the handle of my Thermos and then lower it down to the water; I might be able to get a drink like that! So I crept out gingerly onto the edge of the ice and lowered the flask to the water's surface. The plan worked and I was able to half fill the flask. I drank this and then repeated the process before returning to the bank and then back up onto the highway. The whole process had hurt my ankle even more and as I continued walking up the side of the road, my limp became even more pronounced. My staff was a help but I was very sore and weary. The farmland through which I had been passing now became more populated and shortly I entered the outskirts of a small town called Cochrane. Presently I came to a café on the roadside; it was open and I decided to go inside and maybe get a coffee.

I sat down heavily at one of the tables, relieved to be off my sore feet. A waitress approached me with a concerned look on her face and said, "You look done in, have you come far?" I replied, "Yes, from Banff."

Her mouth fell open and she said, "But that's over 40 miles away!"

I said, "Yes, it certainly felt like a long way."

My attempted avoidance of other people had now been broken down by my need for help and I asked the girl if she could get me a coffee and could she tell me how to get a taxi to take me to Calgary. She told me there was a payphone in the back of the café with a list of taxi firm numbers and then she went off to get my coffee.

When she brought the drink to me, she said, "Can I get you some pancakes? They are on the house!"

I was of course hungry and I said, "Yes, please."

She went off to get the food and I sipped my coffee, while rather self-consciously observing the other occupants of the café. It must have been around eight or nine a.m. and it was good to be in out of the freezing temperatures outside.

The waitress brought my pancakes and I thanked her and then drizzled the accompanying maple syrup over them. I tucked into the meal with gusto; it had been a long time since I had eaten anything substantial. After I had finished I paid for my coffee at the counter, thanking the staff for their gift of the free meal and then went into the back to use my change to call for a taxi.

The taxi only seemed to take a few minutes to arrive and seeing it do so from the café window, I went outside to meet it, waving goodbye to the friendly staff as I went. On the way, I passed my trusty walking pole that I had left propped against the door side and I gazed at it wistfully, thinking that it had been a good, helpful friend to me! But I now had no further use for it so I left it where it was.

I got into the back seat of the taxi with my rucksack and the driver, who was black and proved to be very jovial, asked me where I wanted to go. I told him that I would like to go to the airport at Calgary, please.

He said, "No problem," and set the meter running and drove off down the main street.

The journey to the airport seemed to be very short and I thought, *Christ I have nearly walked all the way from Banff to Calgary and it must be about fifty miles.*

On the taxi ride, the driver asked me a few too many questions and I told him a few 'porkies' about the events of the last few days, basically fabricating a story about having my ski trip cut short by an emergency call from home. He seemed to swallow it but my indiscretion would come back to haunt me shortly afterwards.

On arrival at the airport, I paid the driver and thanked him, then went into the terminal building to seek out the information desk. On finding it, I asked the staff if there were any flights leaving shortly for the U.K. They told me I would have to go to the British Airways desk, so I sought this out and made my enquiry again. There was a flight leaving later that day but upon asking the price of it I was shocked to find it was many hundreds of dollars more than I had left! I went away, feeling flattened and in somewhat of a panic as to what to do next. I sat down for a bit to think and after a while came to the only conclusion I could and that was that I would have to go back to Banff!

I got up and made my way to the Bureau De Change, where I got some more traveller's cheques changed into cash to pay for my return trip to Banff. I then went back out of the terminal building to the taxi rank, where I was surprised to see the same taxi waiting that had brought me there! I approached it rather nervously, wondering what I would tell the driver when I asked him if he could take me back to Banff. My earlier meal had given me some thought energy back and I came up with an extension plan to my story.

The driver saw me walking towards his car and he got out and said, "Is everything okay?"

I replied, "Well, yes thanks, but there has been a bit of a mix up and the emergency call turned out to be a false alarm, so would it be possible for you to take me back to Banff, please?"

He said, "Sure, no problem, but it will cost you about sixty dollars". I told him I had enough money and then got into the car.

The journey back to Banff took over an hour and during this I managed to nod off to sleep for a bit. The driver, whose name was Joe, woke me while passing the huge mine I had observed during my walk, with his preamble about the statistics of the facility.

My taxi ride allowed me to recuperate somewhat and by the time Joe dropped me off outside the Rundle apartments in Banff, I was feeling much refreshed. I paid him and thanked him for his help; he told me it had been a pleasure and then drove off. As I turned to head into my apartment building, I noticed a police patrol car parked nearby with an officer standing by it. He was accompanied by a male rep from my holiday company. They approached me and asked me my name. The rep, whom I had not seen before and who I had only identified by his outfit, asked me if I was all right. I told him I was okay and then he said they wanted to take me to the town hospital, having found the note I had left in my flat; and that I had been reported as being seen in Canmore. The rep said he was very worried about me and would I please go with them for treatment? Now the word 'treatment' filled me with a feeling of panic! Although I was somewhat aware that I had been behaving irrationally, I did not see the need to be admitted to hospital, so I told the rep that I would come with him after I had picked up a few things from my flat. I left him and the policeman and went into the apartment building. Upon entering my flat I found that everything had been rummaged through and that some of my decongestant tablets had disappeared. I thought, *Christ, they must think I have been taking drugs!*

I re-stocked my rucksack with food supplies from the fridge and then left my flat and the building by another door, to make my way out of town once more. I had not walked far through the outskirts on my much less painful ankle when a car pulled up alongside me. It was not the patrol car but rather an ordinary saloon with the rep at the wheel. He rolled down the window and asked me where I was going and I told him I was just taking a stroll to ease my bad ankle. With that, I panicked and stumbled off the roadside and into the trees.

I soon left the road behind and headed once more down the valley in the same direction as the previous journey, but this time keeping to the cover of the trees. The hunted feeling was upon me once more as I stumbled between the trees, forging through the snow, which was quite deep in places. Strangely, my ankle began to hurt less as I went. It was now past midday and I began to feel an overwhelming desire to cross to the west side of the valley but this meant crossing the Trans-Canada Highway, the Canadian Pacific Railway and the river.

I made my way down out of the low, tree-covered hills on the eastern side of the valley and crossed the flat meadow-like area to reach the highway. The weather was again kind to me; although it was very cold it was fair, with even a weak sun shining. As I approached the road, I saw the deer fence and my spirits dropped even further; how would I climb it with my dicky ankle and then of course there was the fence at the other side of the road as well! When I got to the fence, I walked along it for a bit and in doing so, was lucky to find a gap underneath the wire, just big enough to get my rucksack through. I pushed it underneath the fence and then with a resigned sigh, set about climbing the wire. My ankle hurt a bit but it was easier than I had thought, especially without the encumbrance of the rucksack and I was soon over the top and descending the other side.

I picked up my sack again and made my way up onto the highway. There was quite a bit of traffic but I was soon able to find gaps and kind of scuttle across both carriageways. I was then faced with the other fence and I again walked along it. This time I was even luckier, as I came across a stream running out from underneath the road and where it flowed under the fence there was a kind of swinging water gate. I was able to push this open and scramble through with my rucksack in my hand.

From here I crossed another flat area, with quite deep snow, to reach the railway. This was not as much of an obstacle as the highway, having no fence and I was soon across it and heading for the river. When I got to the riverbank, I looked down to see that this section was ice free, there must have been hot springs in places in the valley to keep parts of the river free from ice. The water course was maybe ten metres wide at this point but did not look to be very deep; however there was a quite fast flowing current! Up to this point I had not yet fashioned another staff to assist my walking, having been in such a flap to get away from Banff! I now found some nearby bushes and snapped off a stout branch to form my new staff. As I approached the water, I contemplated taking off my boots and socks, but decided against it because I knew I would need both hands free to use my staff and maintain my balance in the swift flow. With much trepidation, I entered the river and began my crossing. The water was soon up to my knees and as I reached the centre of the flow it rose to my groin. The cold water numbed my legs and the powerful current tugged at me, threatening to sweep me away but I held on, using the invaluable staff to keep me upright. The riverbed was gravel and it kind of slithered beneath my feet, feeling strange and for a minute I experienced an awful vision and sensation. Canmore was upstream and I thought in my fevered mind it meant 'can more flesh' and it seemed like I was walking over the rotting flesh and bones of people and animals that had died in that town! That was probably the most unpleasant experience of my life, up to that time anyway. I forced my way on, trying to clear my mind of the awful feeling. The water became shallower and I was soon making my way out to climb the far bank. I could not feel my legs and I rubbed them to try and get some sensation back into them. I then crawled through the knee-deep snow and the dry, powdery consistency of it seemed to draw the water out of my soaked jeans.

I got up after a while and continued walking through the low wooded hills of the western side of the valley. The warmth and feeling gradually returned to my legs as I went south. I had become thirsty again and I found a small stream running down from the higher slopes of the valley and was able to get a good drink from it, refilling my flask at the same time.

I came to a place where I could see quite a good distance through between the trunks of the thinning trees and in the distance, I saw what appeared to be a figure standing and carrying a yellow rucksack. I felt an overwhelming urge to approach this person and make contact. As I scrambled through the snow over the intervening gap, the person seemed to move, sway and change shape. By the time I reached the person figure it resolved itself into nothing more than a rotting tree trunk broken off some six feet above the ground. I thought that what with my experience crossing the river and now this, things were getting stranger and stranger, but more was to follow! A little further on, the ground levelled out and I approached what appeared to be a snow-covered road through the trees. From a distance of maybe thirty-five metres (a long shot with the choked barrel of a shotgun), I could see the head of what could have been a wolf. It was grey and white and seemed to be eyeing me up from the snow bank at the edge of the road! I only saw it for about ten seconds and then it seemed to vanish. Perhaps it was a hallucination, I will never know.

I stopped for a rest after this experience, reflecting on the possibility of being attacked by hungry wolves or maybe a grizzly emerging from its winter den! I ate some chocolate and some cheese, sitting on an old tree stump, and felt very tired.

Not knowing where I was really going any more, I continued down the side of the valley, always keeping to the cover of the trees. The valley began to turn towards the east and I climbed a fairly steep slope to emerge on a ridge. I entered a clearing, which was largely snow-free, having been scoured by the wind. The late afternoon sun shone down warmly on me from between two towering peaks to the west and I sat down on the brown grass. Before I knew it, I had curled up and gone to sleep!

I was awoken in the fading light by the cold, the sun having now dropped behind the high peaks. I got up and made my way back towards the highway, which I could see from the clearing. My water supply was again depleted so I found a fast flowing stream coming down from the higher slopes. Unfortunately, it was down in a gully and the flow was hemmed in by banks of ice; however, I was able to scramble to the edge of it and employ the same tactic I had used to get water from the river near Cochrane on the previous jaunt.

When I had pulled up my flask on the cable and got a drink, I moved out of the trees to approach the highway. For some reason there was no deer fence at this point and I was able to access the roadway without difficulty. There were some buildings across the other side of the highway and I could see a sign, which had the chilling words 'Dead Man's Flattes' written on it. I thought, *that is a place to avoid*, and I started walking up the verge of the southbound carriageway. I had only gone a few metres when I came to a lay-by and in it was parked a familiar car. It was the rep's car that I had last seen on the outskirts of Banff and I could see by the exhaust pipe that the engine was running. Had the rep just arrived or had he been waiting there for some time and kept the engine running to keep himself warm? What a coincidence that he should be at the same point where I had come down out of the trees and at the same time; or was it? I became very suspicious and paranoid, with the thought coming into my head that he or the police had somehow fixed some kind of tracking device to the stuff that I had picked up from the flat!

I approached the idling car and the driver's door opened.

The rep, whose name I forget, got out and said, "Right, Mr Titterington you will come with us right now. We are taking you to the airport at Calgary, where we will put you on a flight home, seeing as you continue to refuse our help here!"

It felt like I was being captured and for a moment I thought about legging it into the trees once more, but I was exhausted so I threw my staff onto the side of the lay-by and said, "Okay, I will come with you." I got into the car and was surprised to see that there were two other occupants besides the rep. I didn't recognize either of them. Perhaps they were some kind of health professionals.

We drove off fast after the rep had taken the wheel, almost squealing the tyres. I had become angry and I tried to take it out on the young lady sitting in the back seat with me, by accusing her of carting me off against my will. I soon settled down though, and after a while I actually began to enjoy the ride. The rep was driving very fast and all of a sudden there came the wailing of a siren from behind. I looked round and saw the flashing red and blue lights of a police car right behind us.

The rep shouted, "Oh, shit!" and slowed down. He pulled in to the side of the road and stopped. The patrol car pulled up behind and the copper got out to approach our car. The rep wound his window down and engaged in a discussion with the officer, which resulted in the rep being given a speeding ticket. I found this quite amusing and enjoyed a little chuckle with myself.

We drove off again and eventually arrived at the airport where we parked and my captors escorted me into the terminal building. The rep took me to the toilets where he told me to get a shave (I had my electric shaver with me in my rucksack). I set about shaving, but the cold had sapped the batteries and there was no connection to the mains so the shaver expired when I had only got halfway through. I washed my face, thinking that I must now look ridiculous and a glance in the mirror told me it was true! The rep had brought all my remaining luggage from Banff and from the toilets he escorted me to the British Airways check-in desk, while explaining that I was booked on a direct flight to Gatwick. The rep handed over a ticket to the official and my skis and suitcase were checked in.

I was asked if I wanted to check my rucksack in as well and I said, "No, thanks, I will keep it as hand luggage."

From here I was escorted through customs to the departure gate.

Here the rep said, "Goodbye, I hope you have a good trip. Make sure you see your doctor when you get home."

When he had gone, I was left with the other passengers who were mainly Londoners and it being late in the evening, they had been drinking! I was still suffering from my nasal problem and the stuffy atmosphere of the departure lounge irritated it. I held my nose and blew to clear the back pressure in my tubes.

Some of the nearby passengers noticed my behaviour and one loud-mouthed sod sang out, "Look at that dickhead, he has been snorting cocaine!"

The cry was taken up by others nearby and then it seemed like the whole waiting crowd was baying at me. I picked up my rucksack, turned and fled through the nearest door! I proceeded at a run through various other exits and before I knew it, I was leaving the terminal building.

I struck out, away from the airport along a street lit highway, towards the glow of light from the city of Calgary.

I had not gone far when a car pulled up beside me and a man shouted, "Can I give you a lift? You will get yourself killed walking on the highway like you are!"

I accepted his offer and got into the car. The driver was the only occupant and he asked me where I wanted dropping off.

I said, "Can you take me to a decent motel in the city, please?" He said, "Sure, no problem."

We pulled away and the guy drove steadily into the huge city. I have not been in many cities but this one certainly seemed huge! We talked a bit on the way but I was still a bit paranoid and was careful about what I told him. He dropped me off outside a large motel in a side street. I thanked him and gave him a few dollars, then went inside the building. It was a bit of a seedy joint but I plucked up courage and went to reception. I booked a single room, which I paid for with my debit card. The young guy on the desk gave me my key card and directions to my room and I went upstairs to find it.

Having located the room, which was accessed by the card's magnetic strip, I set about tidying myself up by finding a shaving point and finishing off the job I had started earlier; then I ran a hot bath. After a good soak I climbed into bed and tried to sleep, but I had eaten little since first thing that day and although I was not very hungry, I couldn't rest and my uneasy, driven feeling returned. I got up, dressed, went downstairs wearing my ski jacket and exited the motel.

It was bone-chillingly cold out on the street as I made my way deeper into the city and I was soon freezing, even in my jacket. There was a large wheelie bin at the side of the pavement, a few hundred yards from the motel, with a piece of carpet lying next to it. I wrapped this around myself and walked on. It must have been after midnight and there were few other people about. For the next few hours I wandered the streets, ranging in and out of people's back gardens, climbing fences and scrambling over walls, not really knowing where I was going or what I was trying to achieve. Eventually I must have found my way back to the motel and gone to bed, for that's where I found myself the following morning.

At some point I must have gone to bed because I can remember getting out of it, packing my gear up and leaving my room. I had booked my accommodation on a room-only basis and I now considered my options. I was feeling fairly hungry so I went down to the dining room and ordered a spot of breakfast. It must have been around nine or ten a.m. so they were still serving. I can't remember what I had to eat but do recall having difficulty eating it! I pondered on what I should do next; it was a funny sort of situation. I was sort of starting again from scratch, being still someway from my normal state of mind but in a new place where nobody knew me. I was also in a populated area so I would have to interact with other people, even if it sometimes went against the grain.

I paid for my meal and left the motel, making my way out towards the outskirts of the city in a more or less aimless fashion. As I began to get clear of Calgary, I found the place where the main railway (I think it was still the Canadian Pacific) entered the city and I got over the fence onto the track bed. I started to walk down the side of the track, heading south west. It was a bright sunny day and still, but very cold. My ankle was hardly bothering me at all by now and I stepped out briskly. The city fell away behind me and I entered flat, open countryside dotted with farms. The fields were covered with old, hard packed snow and I was able to see over them to the Rocky Mountains in the distance, it was really quite stunning. There came a low rumbling from ahead and presently an approaching train came into view from behind a low hillock. When the massive diesel engine pulling the train got up to me, the driver waved but I did not know whether it was a wave of greeting or one of, 'Get the hell off the track!' The engine thundered past, towing about twenty freight trucks and then it went quiet again and I was once more alone.

I walked on for hours and at one point I passed the carcass of a coyote lying between the rails, it had either been hit by a train or shot by a farmer! The sun was getting low in the sky and I found myself drawing into a small town whose name I forget. I left the railway and headed into the built-up area. After a while, walking down the main street I found a hotel that I liked the look of and went inside where I booked a room, again using my debit card to pay. There was a lot of ranching memorabilia hanging from the walls of the reception area, which was not surprising, being close to the famous Calgary Stampede rodeo! I got my room key and went upstairs to find my room and repeat the process of the night before.

When I came back down, I went into the dining room and asked if I could eat. This was fine, it being evening by now. They actually had a form of fish and chips on the menu, so that is what I ordered. The meal came with the beer that I had also asked for. (This would be the first alcohol I had partaken of for some time) Again I had difficulty eating; the food seemed dry and stodgy. I left some of it and did not have a sweet. The beer went down readily enough, though and after paying for the food and drink, I went through to the huge bar area to consume more beer. A country and western band struck up and before I knew it the place had filled up and there was a right old 'hoe down' going on! I did not get up to dance, but rather kept myself to myself.

After a couple of hours I went to bed but once more, sleep eluded me, the alcohol seeming to fuel the re-emerging desire to get up and get going! So I packed up my rucksack once more and left the hotel to head off into the night. Few people saw me leave and I was soon walking out of town into the open countryside. It was bitterly cold and the sky was crystal clear, the stars and the awesome Hale Bopp comet, with its bright twin tails, shone out brightly overhead. I had to keep moving to stay warm but the earlier drinks had left me with a raging thirst, so I headed downhill towards what appeared to be a river about half a mile away. Although there was no moon, there was enough light coming from the sky to see some distance.

Upon reaching what was indeed a river, I was confronted by the same obstacles as before to getting a drink. There was ice stretching out from either bank with only a narrow strip of open water in the middle. In the dim light, I took off my sack, got out my flask and shaver cord and then ventured out gingerly onto the ice. It cracked and squeaked beneath me, but held and I was able to crawl to the edge of the open water, dangle my flask, fill it and get a drink. Unlike the sweet water of the mountains, this stuff tasted foul but it quenched my thirst. I refilled the flask, crept back to shore, donned my sack and continued into the countryside.

It was while I was climbing a low hill over hard frozen snow that I began to feel unwell. A churning, gurgling noise came from my guts and suddenly I was violently sick! I walked on and was sick several more times.

I said to myself, "This is awful, I must have poisoned myself with the river water. I must try to get in, out of the cold!"

Just then a low mound loomed up out of the gloom and as I drew close, it resolved itself into a massive stack of big, round-baled hay. I found a gap between two bales and crawled into it. There was some protection from the cold as I curled up into a ball and tried to sleep, but it was difficult with my guts still in turmoil. After a couple of restless hours the cold again got to me and I raised myself, left the shelter of the stack and headed off in a sort of eastward direction.

Dawn was starting to break when I spotted the lights of a farm not far away, so I approached it. When I drew closer, I could hear an engine running and on entering the farmyard in the growing daylight, I spotted a large yellow school bus ticking over by the side of the farmhouse. I went up to the house door and knocked on it. There was a short delay and then the door was opened by a huge man with a thick black beard. He eyed me suspiciously and for a moment I thought I was dead!

But I stuttered out the words, "Please, can I have a drink of water?"

The giant's face split into a huge grin and he said, "Sure, come in and I will get you one. You must be frozen, being out there in this temperature!"

I was shown into a cosy kitchen where there was a woman and two children. The woman sat me down at the kitchen table and asked me if I wanted a hot drink as well as the water. I nodded and she went to the stove to pour me a drink of coffee. Fortunately my retching up had subsided and I didn't make a mess of her nice clean kitchen floor. The two kids, a boy and a girl studied me with interest and several searching questions followed about how I came to be at their farm at this hour! I made up a tale of being out hiking and getting lost in the dark and left it at that. The farmer's wife brought me a glass of water and a steaming mug of coffee and asked me where I was from. I told them I was English and that I also lived on a farm, but I was careful not to reveal that I had been staying in Banff on a skiing holiday.

The drinks went down well and I was soon feeling much better! The farmer's wife asked me if I was hungry and I told her I was, but declined the offer of food due to my dicky stomach. The farmer said he would give me a lift back to the town I had earlier departed if I wished. He said that his wife would shortly be doing the school run in the bus warming up outside, but that I would not be able to get a lift in that.

Once I had finished my drinks and got warmed up, I said goodbye to the farmer's wife and her children, thanking them for their hospitality and then went outside with the farmer. We got into his impressive pickup truck, which was parked in the yard.

He fired the engine up and noting the sound of it I remarked, "That sounds like a big engine."

And he said, "Yes, it's one of the most powerful trucks you can buy."

He went on to describe how the engine capacity was measured in cubic inches, unlike the European measurement of cubic centimetres. I can't remember how many cubic inches the engine was but it seemed like a lot.

We roared off out of the yard and down the track to join a small side road nearby, talking farming crack as we went! It only seemed like a short journey back to the town and I was soon shaking hands with the burly farmer and expressing my thanks for his help. He dropped me off outside the hotel I had used briefly and said goodbye and good luck, then drove away.

I can't remember what happened during the following couple of hours but I wound up back at the airport at Calgary! It was now Monday the tenth of March.

Once in the terminal building, I was surprised to immediately encounter my holiday rep. He was in no mood for 'niggle naggle'; in fact he was furious. He shouted, "Where the bloody hell have you been? Don't you know you delayed that flight to Gatwick I got you on for six hours while they offloaded your unaccompanied luggage?"

I said I was sorry but privately I thought the other passengers deserved their delay for poking fun at me. The rep said that he could get me on the same flight system I had arrived in Canada on, that afternoon, meaning that I would be travelling home a day earlier than the original finish of my holiday. I declared that that would be fine and that this time I would definitely get on the plane.

I went through the normal check-in routine with my luggage, which had remained in the airport in my absence, but only up until security, where I was hauled off to one side and told to open my suitcase and ski bag. Everything I owned was spread out on a large table and meticulously gone through with a fine-toothed comb (figuratively speaking, of course).

During the process, two officials walked past and one said to the other, "There's that nut. Hell, he has caused us a lot of work!" I tried to ignore the comment, but was niggled by it. Also, the rep, who was still with me, said that he agreed with the opinions of the officials. After the inspection I was allowed to repack my things and proceed to the departure gate. The rep came with me up to this point and here we parted, with him wishing me good luck and me apologising for causing him a lot of extra work. In fact, I probably proved to be the most difficult client he had ever dealt with, maybe causing him to change his job but I will never know!

While I was sitting waiting at the departure gate a man came and sat beside me. He was dressed in a suit and was carrying a laptop. He struck up a conversation with me, which included certain searching questions. I was still feeling somewhat out of phase so I was careful what I told him. I imagined that he was some kind of health professional who had been asked by the airport authority to travel with me and keep an eye on me, but this proved to be yet a bit more fanciful thinking!

I boarded the flight to Minneapolis and it left at one fifty p.m. I must have slept through most of it and the next thing I remember is sitting in the transfer area of Minneapolis St Paul Airport, with my head lolling and fading in and out of sleep.

Just then I was roused from my reverie by a Cockney voice saying, "Are you English? You certainly look like you are!"

I sat up and observed a bunch of young blokes gathered round me.

I said, "Yes, I'm from Cumbria."

One of the group said, "You look knackered, what have you been up to?"

I told them that I had been on a hard skiing trip in Canada. They remarked that it must have been a very strenuous trip indeed to leave me looking like I was! They told me that they were en route back to Gatwick from Miami and judging by their sun tans I saw that it was true. This group of Londoners were much friendlier than the bunch I had fled from in Calgary airport and I enjoyed a good crack with them. There was little else to do; being as the flight out to Amsterdam wasn't until nine forty p.m. (The reader will have to allow some discrepancy in the times shown as although I wrote them in my diary, I don't know if I took into consideration the time differences!)

Eventually I moved through to the shopping area, having said goodbye to the Londoners and here I bought myself a cool tee shirt. Printed on the front and back were scenes from the wilderness. These comprised bears, eagles and elk set against a spectacular mountain backdrop. I had the shirt up until recently, when it dropped to bits following excessive wear!

After what seemed an interminable wait, I moved on to board the waiting Boeing 747 and then flew out to Amsterdam. The flight must have been smooth because I slept through most of it, arriving in Amsterdam much refreshed and feeling more like my old self. I did some more shopping in the Dutch airport, buying a few presents for my family using my debit card, before catching the onward flight to Manchester. Here I was once again surprised to see my luggage appear on the carousel after three flights!

Once through the airport system, I found a payphone and called the friends who I had stayed with before the start of my holiday. They were surprised to hear from me, it being now three p.m. on Tuesday the eleventh of March, a day earlier than expected. They asked me what had happened and I just sort of gave them a vague story about getting ill, leaving it at that. I had a short wait before they came to pick me up in their Volkswagen camper van and then I was transported back to their home on the outskirts of the city.

I spent the night there, avoiding too much questioning about the holiday and then, reunited with my beloved Capri, I drove home on the morning of Wednesday the twelfth of March.

On arrival at home, my folks were also surprised to see me and also somewhat worried by my account of the events of my trip! I weighed myself in the bathroom and was not surprised to find that I had lost a stone and a half, the same as on the previous two episodes.

Again, I did not seek a medical opinion on what had happened to me or indeed, what might be likely to happen to me in the future and life returned to normal, with me throwing myself into the farm work, golf and later, my contract mole trapping.

Part 4

England
October 1997 to Mid-June 1998.

The period stretching from the end of my strange Canadian ski holiday in March to October 1997 had proceeded very much as normal, but early in October I was taken somewhat out of my comfort zone by my brother Angus, who works for the Lake District National Park Authority, asking me to help him with a big contract to repair the massive retaining wall of the Swart Beck above Greenside, Glenridding. I would be working with Angus and also another sub-contractor to the National Park – Thomas Arkle, whom I had only just met. The job was scheduled to take many weeks and we would be working in all weathers at a somewhat unfavourable time of year.

We started preparing for the job on Monday the sixth of October with Angus and me taking the park Land Rover and trailer to a tool hire firm in Penrith, to pick up two large turfer winches and three pulleys. Having loaded the equipment into the trailer we drove up to Greenside and out up the track above the youth hostels, to a place above the large mine spoil heap, which was the closest we could get to the job site. From here we carried the heavy equipment up a vague path and across the Swart Beck, to store it next to the retaining wall.

The wall was, I think, built in the early 1900s at the edge of a blasted channel to divert the waters of the beck across the fell side, away from another large spoil heap, therefore preventing the beck from eroding the spoil heap down into the valley and inundating the village of Glenridding with debris. The wall is over a hundred metres long, two and a half metres high in the channel, four and a half metres high on the outside and two metres wide. It is built like a traditional dry stone wall, of large blocks and boulders to form the sides, with the centre being filled with smaller stones and gravel. Before we started the job, there was quite a bit of damage to the wall, caused by the power of the beck flowing through the channel. There were several large gaps and holes in the structure, enabling the beck water from the channel to escape and flow uncontrolled down into the edge of the spoil heap. The channel was also choked with boulders and gravel that had avalanched in from the scree above.

After stowing the equipment we drove back to the park depot at Threlkeld and exchanged the small trailer for a much bigger one. We then drove out to Bolton, (a village near Penrith) to a farm where Angus had purchased some telegraph poles. With the help of the farmer, we loaded six of these stout poles onto the trailer and then drove back to Greenside with them. The load was too heavy to tow up to the unloading point earlier reached, so we dropped them off on a level area just above the hostels and near the beck. I had asked Angus what the poles would be used for and he just told me that all would become clear in the fullness of time!

The next day, Thomas met Angus and me at the small national park depot at Troutbeck (a hamlet about two miles away from our farm) and the three of us travelled to Greenside in the park Land Rover. We parked at the top unloading spot and then got some equipment out of the back of the vehicle; this comprised a long rock-climbing rope, a petrol driven power winch, a battery driven drill and bits, various rock bolts and a selection of spanners. We carried all the tackle up to the job site and there we drilled holes in an outcrop of bedrock adjacent to the lower side of the wall. The power winch was then bolted into these holes with the rock bolts. Angus then told me to pay out the climbing rope down the rock-strewn slope to the place where we had dumped the telegraph poles. It was a distance of about two hundred and forty metres! We then spent most of the day winching the poles up the slope to the wall. It was a gruelling task, with one of us operating the plucky little power winch while the other two pushed and pulled at the poles to ease them on the slope, as they seemed to get stuck behind every obstruction possible!

The day after that, we erected the poles into two tripods, one each side of the first gap in the wall. One leg of each tripod stood at the base of the wall while the other two legs stood on the bedrock, actually in the beck channel. Each pole was bolted to the rock and then the tripods were each drilled at the top and bolted together to secure them. This was also a trying task as the apex of each tripod was about two metres above the centre of the wall and had to be reached by a small aluminium ladder that we had brought to the site.

Having completed building the tripods, we used slings to hang a pulley beneath each of them. Then we passed the cable of the larger of the two turfer winches over the two pulleys and bolted each end of the cable to the bedrock on the lower side of the wall. The largest of the three pulleys we had brought was then hung from the cable between the tripods. The cable of the smaller turfer winch was then passed over the large pulley and alternating with the power winch with the climbing rope, was then used during the coming days to draw boulders out of the channel. The boulders ranged in size from a half metre across to one and even two metres across, and each had to be secured by a chain or fabric sling. We eased each boulder into position in the gap in the wall with crowbars and it was hard, uncompromising work.

On one occasion, a boulder the size of an armchair slipped out of its sling when suspended above the wall and went bounding down the fellside into the bottom of the gulley below! The boulders, of course, formed the outside skin of the gap in the wall but we also had to find infill for the wall. This we accomplished by dredging the bottom of the channel. We shovelled gravel and small stones into plastic buckets and hoisted them up onto the wall using the power winch and pulley. Every now and then the weather would turn against us and we would be forced to pull out of the job for a day or so to let the raging torrent of the beck subside.

We developed a good camaraderie during the job and we enjoyed much good crack in our bait cabin, which was a construction made from a two and a half metre length of three by two wedged between two rocks, supporting a plastic sheet to keep the rain off. The bait cabin was situated about twenty-five metres below the wall and was just big enough to hold the three of us. On occasion, there would be snow on the roof, which we had to clear to stop the plastic roof sheet from caving in on us. We worked eight hour days with a coffee, lunch and tea stop. These hours were enough because we were pretty pooped out at the end of each day!

There were three large gaps in the wall and many smaller holes in it, each of which had to be filled and rebuilt. Of course, each time we finished one of the gaps the tripods had to be dismantled and moved to the next gap and reassembled. This was a time consuming operation and was also very strenuous.

On one occasion, we were faced with a huge slab of rock that had cracked off from the upper side of the channel and toppled in to partially block it. In the absence of explosives expertise, we had to break up the slab using sledgehammers and steel wedges and then winch the broken pieces out of the channel.

Each time we were rained off from the job I would go dry stone walling for our neighbouring farmer and also, mole trapping for Keswick Golf Club. Combined with going out and ending up at the nightclub at Penrith every Saturday night, it was a pretty full-on period!

On one night out in particular, I had a fantastic experience. I was standing in one of the 'in' pubs of town when I had what can only be described as a vision! I had consumed maybe four pints of lager and was eyeing up the local talent when a white glow seemed to form in the crowd and out of it walked the most beautiful girl I have ever seen! She was wearing a gorgeous white dress. She walked towards me through the crowd and then passed me on her way to the toilets. My eyes followed her all the way and I was dumbstruck! The white glow I had seen was something akin to Scotty beaming somebody down in *Star Trek*! The girl returned from her comfort break and made her way back through the crowd to her friends. I asked my mates who she was but they did not seem to know. I thought about going over to talk to her but I am quite shy and chatting up women is not one of my strong points! Over the next few weeks I saw the girl several times and on one occasion she actually spoke to me. I was standing outside one of the other popular pubs in town when one of the local hooligans cut his hand badly on a broken bottle. The blood flowed and soon formed a pool on the pavement. I had not seen the girl approach me and was somewhat startled by her voice right beside me.

She said, "That looks awful, I bet he is in a lot of pain." I agreed but my shyness then handicapped me and I was unable to continue the conversation and she moved away. I watched her go back into the pub, appreciating her profile as she went. She was about five foot two tall and had a figure to die for; her silky long black hair reached down almost to her waist!

On one of the following occasions that I saw her, I overheard some of a conversation she was having with a young bloke and I'm sure I heard him call her Rachel. I was in love, albeit unrequited and I went to work each day with a song in my heart. However, things were spoiled slightly for me when I found out from one of my golfing buddies that she was only a teenager and me being thirty-six, there did not seem to be a future in it!

Getting back to the Swart Beck job, we had finished the second big gap in the wall and moved our tripods up to the third gap. This one presented a whole new level of difficulty as it was near the top end of the wall, at a place where the beck turned a corner. There was a pool at the base of the gap and the raging water had scoured out the foundation of the wall, meaning that we had to find a way to lower the water level so that we could get our boulders down onto the bedrock. So we set about building a dam just above the pool, with rocks and also incorporating three six-inch bore plastic pipes of some fifteen feet in length. These pipes were used to divert the flow of the beck away from our working area. Having lowered the water level in the pool we were able to clean out the bottom of the gap and get our foundation stones in, down onto bedrock. However, we soon ran out of handy building material and a new plan had to be devised to find some. Angus came up with a novel idea – we could get the material from the massive spoil heap that was now close by. I could not see how this could be done but Angus was confident and after a small break in the work, we met one morning at the Troutbeck depot to find him waiting for us with the Land Rover and trailer. In the trailer was some new equipment; this consisted of a spool of one point five centimetre thick steel cable and a weird looking contraption made from a builder's barrow!

Once back on site, we had to carry the new equipment up to the job. The barrow contraption did not present much of a problem but the cable did; it was very heavy and had to be carried by two people, using a crowbar slotted through the centre of the cable spool. It was a difficult operation and Thomas and I were selected to carry it out. We slipped and slid up the uneven slope and with some trepidation, forded the beck with the cable on our shoulders. We nearly lost hold of it several times during the climb and we were worn out, but much relieved, by the time we got it to the top of the wall.

It was coffee time by the time we had got the new equipment to the top end of the wall and we were just enjoying a hot drink and a sandwich when we heard voices. Angus crawled out of our shelter to see what all the commotion was about, but he quickly returned to tell Thomas and me that the bosses were here for a site inspection! We quickly finished our bait and made our way out of the shelter and up onto the wall. Angus introduced Thomas and me to the group of officials and then we all walked up to the top of the wall, where Angus set about explaining to us all what he intended to use the new equipment for. The bosses were much impressed by the work we had carried out so far and by Angus's plan to finish building up the top gap and then they left us in good tune.

Having gained some idea of the plan, we set about putting it into operation. We took one end of the cable and fastened it around the trunk of a small larch tree growing out of the rock on the top side of the channel, securing it with a U-bolt. The cable was then paid out across over the wall onto the spoil heap, a distance of about fifty metres, where the other end of it was secured in the same fashion to another small larch. It took all three of us to pull the cable tight and then fasten it. The cable end had been passed through the two wheel rims mounted on the barrow contraption as it was extended to the spoil heap. Now it was possible to see the fruition of Angus's plan; seeing the barrow contraption suspended by its wheels on the cable, it was obvious that it was a cargo cable car.

A long piece of the climbing rope was tied to each end of the cable car and then I assumed position on the spoil heap, whence I pulled the cable car across to me. It trundled merrily along on the cable and when it was halfway across, it was maybe ten metres above the ground. Once I had got it to the spoil heap I proceeded to fill the skip of the contraption with rocks. It held about a hundred kilograms and it proved to be too heavy for Angus and Thomas to pull back across to the wall by hand, so they had to use the power winch!

We spent several days winching rocks and rubble across the gap to the wall. The spoil heap had a gradient of forty-five degrees and because the loading point was fixed, I had to climb up the heap and avalanche material down to the loading area. It was exciting work and I enjoyed it immensely.

With our latest efforts, we were able to finish the job and all that was left to do was dismantle the cableway and tripods and carry the equipment back to the Land Rover and trailer, all bar the telegraph poles which we just left stored at the base of the wall on the outside of the channel. But before we did this, Angus and then I rode across to the wall in the cable car, it was real fun. It was by now the nineteenth of November and to celebrate finishing the job, Angus and I had brought our driving clubs and we hit about five balls each from the top of the lower spoil heap, out across to the other side of the valley! We then drove back to the depot at Troutbeck to offload the equipment and then went our separate ways with a handshake. I was feeling good – it had been a difficult, tiring and sometimes dangerous job, but it was also very rewarding!

I have been back to look at the wall on the way back from a hill walk recently and it is still intact!

For the next six days I did some mole trapping for a farmer near Dockray, Matterdale and caught thirty-one moles in that time. Then on the twenty-sixth of November I joined Angus for a new contract for the National Park Authority. The river Caldew had recently burst its banks near the village of Mosedale, on the eastern edge of the Skiddaw range of fells. The river had punched a twenty-five metre hole in the levee and inundated the surrounding fields. The flood had now receded and our job was to rebuild the levee, using a truck load of boulders dumped nearby and also walling stone and rubble from a derelict stone barn almost a mile away down a narrow lane. We had on site a medium sized tracked digger of some seven tonnes, a wheeled JCB digger and an articulated wheeled dumper. My job was to load the dumper, using the JCB, with the material from the old barn and then drive the dumper to the hole in the levee where I would tip it, ready for Angus to sort through with the tracked digger. Also the boulders had to be loaded and brought to the site; these would form the skin of the levee in the river channel, like giant dry stone walling.

The job would last five days and although I had handled big machinery before I was unfamiliar with these beasts. We started off by moving the boulders onto the site and I was able to learn the quite difficult technique of steering the dumper in the adjoining field, where there was plenty of room. Then I was on to bringing the material from the old barn. Angus had driven the JCB down to the barn and I now had to take the dumper down the lane to load up. It was a big machine and the lane was very narrow – there was only about eight centimetres to spare at each side between the wheels and the dry stone walls. The fun started when I had to load the dumper; I soon encountered a problem with the JCB, in that the controls for the back hoe were different from those I had on the tractor-mounted digger back home. I found out much later that the hydraulic pipes on the farm digger had been put on the wrong valves! I was hard wired into operating the farm digger and soon found it difficult and very tiring trying to get used to working the JCB, therefore it was a slow job loading up and I was under a bit of pressure to get the loads to the levee to keep Angus going with the tracked digger. Angus used the tracked digger to sort out large pieces of walling stone from the loads I brought to the site and every now and then, we would cease the machine operations to do a bit of walling by hand to bring the skin of the levee up to full height on top of the boulders. The majority of the content of the loads I brought was of walling stone so we employed a local farmer with his tractor and trailer to bring loads of gravel (loaded by Angus) from further up the river to fill the middle of the levee.

On the whole, the weather was kind to us; the rain kept off, meaning that the river did not flood; in fact it was the opposite. It was hard frost and on one occasion we had to start the JCB with the jump leads!

Having completed the main of the reconstruction of the levee, all that remained was for Angus to landscape the top and side of the levee with a truck-load of delivered topsoil, using the digger. We then re-erected the stock fence that had been swept away in the flood, and the job was finished.

It was a very interesting and rewarding job but I was worn out at the end of each day! I was also doing quite a bit of carrion crow shooting with my mates in the evenings around that time and getting quite a bit of drink afterwards – I was burning the candle at both ends!

The period up to Christmas was spent working on the farm and then I took it easy over the first part of the holiday period. I was drinking a fair bit and at times feeling unwell physically but also, looking back; my mental state was deteriorating also! I remember going into town to buy a respirator mask to protect me from the fumes while I was doing some creosoting work and being very suspicious and paranoid about the fact that I could not buy one anywhere! The last entry in my diary for 1997 was for the twenty-ninth of December and it involved Angus coming over to help me with a big wall gap on the roadside at Mungrisdale. The gap was seven metres long, two metres high on the field side and half a metre high on the road side. There was a blind corner in the road, just up from the gap and according to the local farmer, a car had come into the corner, met one coming the other way and skidded into the wall, knocking it down! I had been told that repairing the wall was an insurance job.

We set about taking the gap down to its foundations and then we began to rebuild. Angus, who is a better waller than me, took the higher field side while I concentrated on the roadside section. I was in ebullient mood and talked non-stop as we worked.

Angus kept looking at me in a funny way and at one point he said, "Will you shut the fuck up, you're talking geese shite!"

I quietened down a bit after that. Because of the size of the gap, we cannot have finished rebuilding it that day and although I have no written record of it, we must have completed the job because it is still standing today!

The period up to Sunday the fourth of January 1998 is unrecorded but I will attempt to lay it out from memory. Soon after the twenty-ninth of December 1997 I remember going for a drive in my Capri, down round the south lakes and then returning to the farm, putting my faithful working sheepdog, Tina, (named after Tina Turner!) into the back of my car and setting off up Scotland. It was of course dark by now as I made my way over the border on the M74. I can remember stopping once just off the motorway to give Tina the opportunity to have a pee!

I must have got up through the industrial belt and taken the A82 to Fort William, because I remember pulling up the hill out of Tyndrum at fifty miles per hour and being overtaken by a fully loaded articulated lorry carrying concrete blocks! I had various C.D.s in the car and I definitely remember listening to the Queen album and in particular the song *Too Much Love Will Kill You,* which is a very sad ballad, written when Freddie Mercury was coming to the end of his life! For some reason it made me think of Rachel and I held an image of her in my mind.

The next thing I knew, I was up at the Culloden battlefield site near Inverness, where I parked and let Tina out for a run. Now I don't know whether it was my darkening mood or whether that there is an atmosphere of sadness about the place but I broke down in tears!

I got Tina back into the car and drove on eastwards to the village of Portknockie, where I parked the car and went for a pint in the local pub.

I knew the place because I had enjoyed a wonderful week's holiday in the area with my best mate Andrew, back in August 1997. It had been largely a golfing trip but it also involved a lot of drinking; not only did we go to that pub but we also consumed vast amounts of beer we had brought with us from the supermarket. We had stayed in a cottage belonging to friends of Andrew's parents and one night, we drank so many cans of Stella Artois that we were able to make a pyramid about a metre high out of the empties and then we went to the pub to play the locals at pool after that. The golf had been great (for me anyway). We had bought a ticket each for fifty pounds, which entitled us to play ten courses in the local area. I particularly remember playing the Dufftown course, which looks down on the Glenfiddich distillery!

I think we got through eight courses, by which time Andrew admitted defeat. We were playing each other as well as the course and me being off a fourteen handicap as opposed to Andrew's seven meant that I had a distinct advantage!

That trip had gone without a hitch and there had been no sign of the weirdness I had experienced on the preceding holidays, but now here I was entering another episode. This time, though, it was happening to me inside Britain and it had come upon me more suddenly. It was as if I were looking in on myself from a parallel universe. At the time, taking off to drive to Scotland with no luggage or without any plans for somewhere to stay once I got there seemed normal!

I only had one drink in the pub at Portknockie and then I drove back towards Inverness. It was a fine clear night and a bright full moon hung in the sky. As I entered the city, I encountered large groups of people and I seemed to be the only person driving. I drove slowly through the throng, careful not to run over anyone; they all seemed to be well oiled and I wondered what might be going on. Just then somebody tapped on my driver's window.

I rolled the window down and a guy reached into the car, saying, "Happy new year, mate."

I shook his hand and wished him the same back. It was past midnight obviously and we were into 1998; for some reason it had come as a bit of a surprise to me!

The revellers were now completely blocking the road ahead so I turned the car around and drove back out of the city, heading for the A9 south. The big Capri ate up the miles and before I knew it I was approaching Kingussie. I turned off here and took the road to Spean Bridge and then onto Fort William, where I was flagged down by a young woman. I pulled over and reached across to open the passenger side door; she got into the car and then asked me where I was going.

I said, "I'm heading back to Cumbria."

She said that she lived on the southern end of town and then she asked me if I could run her home. She had obviously had a fair bit to drink and it was well into the early hours of the morning so I said, "Yeah, sure, I'm heading your way, it's no trouble."

At this point, Tina roused herself from her doggy sleep in the back of the car and crept through to nuzzle the young woman, who let out a bit of a squeak. "Shit, what was that?"

I said, "Don't worry, it's only the dog!"

There was little conversation as I drove her home. I pulled up outside a house on the outskirts of town as directed and the woman got out, said, "Goodbye and a happy new year to you," and she was gone.

I drove on, leaving Fort William behind me and over the Ballachullish Bridge into Glencoe. The moon had vanished, to be replaced by snow clouds and the weather began to worsen as I reached the gorge section of the valley. Snow was falling as I approached a particularly bad right hand bend. Suddenly a snow plough/gritter came hurtling round the bend towards me, right at its apex! The raised blade of the machine was halfway across my side of the road and I just had time to swing the Capri left to avoid it. I got by with my left hand wheels off the tarmac and let out a sigh of relief, thinking, shit, that was a close call!

I was pretty tired by now, as you can imagine but the scare had revived me somewhat and I drove on over Rannoch Moor with renewed focus. It was somewhere south of Tyndrum where I pulled into a layby to stretch my legs and let Tina out for a run and a pee. She jumped out of the car and sauntered over to the verge for a sniff. Whether she got a piss or not I can't say because just then she began to growl. The weather had cleared again and the low moon cast enough light for me to see that there were dark conifers next to the road and Tina was staring fixedly at these, with the hackles standing up on the back of her neck. Her growling began to intensify and it scared me – was there some wild beast lurking in the edge of the trees? I knew there were wolves in Scotland but they were surely in fenced enclosures, or were they? In my fevered, deteriorating state of mind I thought that somehow they were running free and were now stalking Tina and me! I grabbed Tina, bundled her back into the car, climbed back into the driver's seat and drove off at speed!

I suppose I must have returned home but things are a bit vague about the rest of the journey back. The next thing I remember is setting off in the car, again with Tina, in daylight and driving over the back road from Whitbarrow to Greystoke. It is a narrow road and I was forced onto the grass several times by oncoming vehicles, this annoyed me intensely! From here I drove to Askham, where I met a car on the narrow bridge over the river Lowther. I had to reverse and give way to the vehicle. I thought I recognised the occupants of the car as previous workmates but I was becoming delusional and that may not have been the case.

I drove on and headed down the A6 in the direction of Kendal. I was a few miles off the town when I noticed a pickup truck racing down a farm lane towards the road on which I was driving. I passed the lane end and looking in the mirror, I saw the truck pull out and follow me. I rounded a left hand bend and spotted a Renault car parked in a long layby on the left. I slowed down and upon reaching the car, I saw that the front right hand wing was heavily damaged and the wheel was missing. I pulled into the layby in front of the damaged car, just as the pickup truck drew up level with me.

There were two mean-looking men in the truck and the passenger side one rolled his window down and shouted, "What the fuck do you think you're doing?"

I did not answer back but simply rammed the Capri into first gear and took off with a squeal of tyres! The truck driver must have anticipated this because he came hurtling after me and there followed a high speed car chase, during which both my car and the truck occupied both lanes of the road! It was a bendy section of road for about a couple of miles and poor Tina was tossed about in the back as I flung the powerful Capri into the bends! The truck was alongside me when I spotted another big layby, separated from the main road by an island. I glanced across at the truck to see the passenger shaking his fist at me. I swung the Capri into the layby at the last second and screeched to a halt, with the trees on the island screening me from the road. Before the driver of the pickup had time to turn around I turned my car around and set off back north up the main road. Seeing a side road on the right, signposted Tebay, I swung the Capri into it. As I drove up the road, I kept my eye on the rear view mirror but there was no sign of the truck – I had lost it!

I drove much more steadily along over the fells towards the M6 and Tebay. As I went, my mind whirled as I tried to get to grips with what had just happened. Who were the men in the truck and why had they chased me like that? The conclusion I came to was somewhat fanciful; perhaps they were fox hunters, out to get me for past misdemeanours!

Back in 1993 we had terrible trouble on the farm with foxes – my dad had shot one dead climbing up the holly bush in the front garden of the farmhouse. It was trying to get at the bird feeders; and then he got a shot off at another in the field at the back of the house. Then our laying hens started to disappear, one going every day until we only had about three left! We knew it was a fox that was doing the damage and that it was taking the hens in the middle of the day, so dad and I organised a rota by which one of us would stand guard with the shotgun near the hen house while the other ate his lunch. I was on guard duty when I heard the baying of the local foxhound pack, coming from up on the fell. I was actually having a pee when I spotted a fox running at the bottom of the front field, south west of the farmstead. I quickly tidied myself up and set off to run with the shotgun in a northerly direction. I thought if I could just get around to the bottom of the field, two down from where the fox was currently running, I might just have a chance! I ran like the wind and got into position behind the end of a dry stone wall just in time, with the gun barrel levelled over a post and rail section of fence. It was perfect timing, the fox ran straight onto the gun, I pulled the trigger and dropped it with a single shot, using a heavy gauge Eley Maximum cartridge! I got over the fence and ran to where the fox lay dead. Examining it quickly I found where my shot had hit it in the head and also, older pellet wounds across its back, which probably meant it was the animal that dad had shot at a few days earlier. The sound of the pursuing pack of hounds was much closer now and I felt the need to get the dead fox out of sight, so I carried it up to the farm and hid it in the barn.

A few days later there was another hunt and I shot another fox round the back of the house! I was aware that the sound of the shot would be heard by the hunt followers but at the time I did not think it would make much difference.

Dad said that the foxes seemed unafraid of people and seemed to be comfortable coming close to buildings. Indeed, there was a rumour flying around at the time that the authorities had gathered together a truckload of trapped urban foxes and let them loose on the top of Shap summit! I don't know about this but there were a hell of a lot of foxes around at that time. Anyway our hens stopped disappearing and I buried the dead foxes in soft ground near the farmstead. All would have been well except for the fact that a few weeks later and under the influence of drink I bragged to one of my mates, who was a keen hunt follower, that I had shot two foxes that were being hunted. His reaction to this revelation was one of hostility towards me. Apparently my opinion of who killed the fox and how, during a hunt, did not matter but seemingly it did, and I had been much out of order!

A bit later on that year I was playing in an eight ball pool match at our local pub and enjoying a very good night indeed, I was winning on the table and the ale was flowing freely! In between games I got talking to a chap who lived about a mile away from me, just off the back road to the pub. I knew he was a keen hunt follower and was careful not to mention my antics with shooting the foxes!

With the guy was a bloke I had never seen before and this fellow pressed me for information on where I lived and what time I would be leaving for home that night. This had made me a bit suspicious and when, having won the pool match in fine style, I left the pub; I kept my eye out for the police. I had travelled to the pub in the Capri that night and was aware that I was now over the drink-driving limit. I had parked the car in a layby down the back road and walked the last few hundred metres to the pub. As I now made the return walk to the car, I was passed by what looked like a police car (it was difficult to tell in the darkness) coming from where I had parked. Walking on quickly I got to my car and drove off towards home, but I had not got far when I came up behind the van belonging to the hunt follower and his mate. I had not seen them leave the pub but here they were blocking the single track road and moving very slowly at that. Just then I looked in the rear view mirror and saw the glow of headlights coming down the road behind me. Becoming agitated, I flashed my headlights at the vehicle in front, trying to get the driver to speed up but it only served to cause him to go more slowly. Instinct told me it was the police coming behind but there was little I could do, I was trapped. The car behind closed the gap and it was soon right up behind me. The van in front got to where its driver lived and turned off to the right, leaving the road ahead open. Suddenly the blue lights began to flash behind me and I panicked. I floored the big Capri and the engine roared. I took off like a bat out of hell! It was towards midnight and there was nobody else on the road at that time of night and knowing the road like the back of my hand, I gave the Capri its head. The police car behind kept pace for about half a mile and then began to fall away. I flew down the road, completely missing the left hand turn that led to our farm and headed on towards the neighbouring farm. Ahead there was a bad right-hander and I dropped the motor a couple of gears as I entered it, causing the back end to swing out. Regaining control, I charged on to where the road passed through our neighbour's farm and took a left turn leading to his caravan site. The side turning swung immediately right and I skidded on the slippery road, causing the back end to flip out again. I lost control and ran headlong into an electricity pole forming the corner of a shed! I was out of the car before you could say 'knife', leaving the keys in the ignition. I vaulted over the car bonnet and ran in the near total darkness along the road to the place where I knew there was a bridge over the Mosedale beck. I never looked back as I crossed the bridge into open country and I kept on running in a southerly direction, through one field after another until I reached the open fell, where I stopped to regain my breath.

    I continued on south at a fast walk up the fell for maybe a mile in a parallel course with the beck before fording it. This was a dangerous thing to do because there was half a flood running! I made it across though, into the big piece of rough grazing that formed part of our own land and then made my way to the Lobbs (our other farm), where I crept into the barn and snuggled down in some hay bales. Fortunately the weather had been fair and although I was only in my 'going out' gear I was dry and relatively comfortable.

    I stayed in the barn until dawn and then I made my way down the track to our main farm (Highgate Close), where I had breakfast and went about explaining the events of the previous night to my parents. They were much annoyed at my behaviour and particularly about abandoning my car where it blocked the entrance to the caravan site. Our neighbour, who is a mild mannered fellow, had phoned up to say he had moved my partially wrecked car to enable him to go about his business!

    The phone rang after breakfast and it was the police, saying they wanted me to present myself at the police station in Penrith with my documents within twenty-four hours! This is where I thought I would get clever and tell them that my car had been stolen, but later that day, after my dad had run me into town, when I went to the police station I soon found myself in the interview room facing a couple of mean coppers with the tape running! I was shitting myself and soon found myself unable to uphold the lie under close questioning by the good cop, bad cop system. They soon broke down my story and having got me to admit to being behind the wheel of the Capri; I was charged with dangerous driving.

When the case went to court, I was found guilty of the charge, banned from driving for a year and fined five hundred pounds. I also had to take my driving test again and this cost me another three hundred and fifty pounds in driving lessons. In the end, I was off the road for about eighteen months by the time the driving test came around, but this I passed first time in the little Citroen AX belonging to the driving instructor. The Capri was repaired and spent the period of my ban under a sheet in the back of the silage clamp at the farm.

I was very bitter about the whole affair and am still convinced to this day that the whole thing had been a set-up and the slowly moving van on the back road had been there to deliberately stall me so that the police could catch up!

During the period of the ban, any contracting work I had on was accessed by pushbike and I also went to the pub on the bike, at least for a while until I shouted my mouth off one night, accusing those people who were still drink driving of setting me up to save their own skins, at which point the landlord showed me the door and I never went in the place again.

All this went through my mind as I approached the M6. I passed over the motorway, through Tebay, onto Kirkby Stephen and onto the A66, where I headed for Scotch Corner and there took the A1(M) south. I stopped briefly for fuel and was so tired by then that I nearly put diesel in the Capri instead of four star petrol. Just after the fuel stop, a police patrol car came up behind the Capri and followed me for a bit; however, there were no blue lights on this occasion and the copper overtook me and went about his business.

I ended up in Ripon. What I did there I can't say, but eventually I made my way back home and put Tina back into her kennel. At this point things took a turn for the worst and I took my shotgun from the farmhouse and set off once more in the car. What I intended to do with it I can't say. Looking back, I suppose I thought I could use it to shoot something to eat! I was tired and had gone several days without anything to eat. Even in my upset state of mind I knew taking the gun was wrong and would have repercussions but I did it anyway. A few days earlier, back before I had taken off for Scotland, I had got Tina into the farmhouse kitchen in the middle of the night and got the shotgun out. I was convinced that burglars were going to break into the house and I was going to be ready for them with the dog and the gun. I had sat for quite some time in the armchair, with the gun across my lap and with Tina whimpering and crouching on the hearthrug. She was frightened of the gun at the best of times! My state of mind had obviously been deteriorating then, too, because after I was satisfied that the break-in was not going to happen I took Tina back out to her kennel, then returned to the kitchen and took all the medicines out of the cupboards to examine their ingredients and side effects. I also examined the label details on a full bottle of wine and then emptied the contents down the sink – I must have become convinced that there was poison in these items!

As I left the farm again and was approaching the lonnen gate, I was confronted by a man who I had not seen before. He was getting out of his car to open the gate and to come into the farm. I pulled over in front of the cattle shed to let him past and shouted to him to leave the gate for me.

Now, I have since found out that this man was the doctor, coming to see me and that he had experienced quite a bit of trouble finding our farm! My parents had obviously become very worried about me as I was behaving irrationally and secretly arranged for the doctor to make a call on me. Because he had never seen or treated me before, we passed at the farm gate with barely a word. Had he been able to find the farm earlier he may have been able to circumvent what was to follow!

The man drove past and on into the farmyard, while I continued on out, shutting the gate behind me. It must have been getting towards evening as I drove up to Rookin House Quarry on the Troutbeck to Ullswater road where I parked up, got the shotgun and full cartridge belt out of the boot, and climbed over the fence bordering the quarry. Carrying the gun and belt I walked for maybe fifty metres and then laid them on the ground, next to another fence bordering some forestry. The shotgun was in its leather case and would be protected from the elements as I covered it and the cartridge belt with loose rushes, so that I could, I suppose, recover them at a later stage.

I then went back to the car and took off to drive around, I know not where, for a few hours.

Eventually I found myself now in total darkness at the crossroads above Dockray. One road led back to the village, another to Dowthwaite Head, yet another back to Troutbeck and the last one to St John's in the Vale via the old coach road. I took the last turning, having to get out to open a gate to access the road. This route is only used by four-wheel drive vehicles, off road motor cycles, horses and hill walkers. It is certainly not suitable for low slung Ford Capris and I was soon catching the underside of my car on the raised middle of the gravel track as I made my way westwards through the pot-holed surface.

I had fought my way about a mile and a half along the difficult broken surface when I came to the sheep fold named Barbery Rigg. I turned off onto the grass here and switched the engine and headlights off.

As I sat back in the bucket seat, memories flowed back to me of an occasion years previously, when a group of us had brought our cars out here for a midnight party. Back then, the road had been in better condition and we had been able to make our way much more quickly to the rigg from the pub at Dockray. That had been a happy occasion but now, here I was, dog tired and literally at the end of my road, all the images of the previous episodes fell in on me. The world was ending, people were out to get me and basically everything had gone to shit! Even the music I had been playing on the C.D. player had seemed to send me down even further. I reached behind the seat for another disc to play but I could not find one in the melee; the inside of my car must have looked like a bomb-site with the back seats folded down and my possessions strewn about everywhere!

I had reached rock bottom! What the hell was I supposed to do now? Die? But as I sat there for hours, hovering on the edge of sleep or whatever, I did not die or even sleep. Instead I got out of the car, locked it and set off to walk home. Although it was pitch dark I knew the lie of the land like the back of my hand because this was the open fell where our sheep grazed. The route home of approximately two and a half miles, although boggy, was level, with only one or two small streams to cross and the last mile was all downhill.

An hour or so later I entered our farmyard and was greeted by a scene of high activity. The yard seemed to be full of cars, some of them belonging to the police! The back door of the farmhouse stood open, streaming light out onto the yard. As I walked towards the house, I could see many figures bustling about inside. A part of me was aware that this must all be the result of me taking off with the shotgun and I quietly stepped forward to accept my fate. Policemen surrounded me and probed me with questions about the whereabouts of the gun and a young woman doctor spoke to me in reassuring tones, telling me that once the gun had been recovered the police would take me to the hospital, where there was a bed waiting for me. I was tired of running from I don't know what and went meekly to one of the police cars, accompanied by the doctor. I gave the officers directions on how to get to the quarry where I had parked to go on and hide the gun, then I was driven there.

Upon reaching the quarry, the officers escorted me under my direction to the place where the gun and cartridge belt were concealed. The police were very nervous and one of them kept hold of me while another moved ahead, waving a torch. Even with my instructions, the officer with the torch had some difficulty in finding the weapon as I had hidden it so well! It was found, though and we returned to the car, whereupon I was driven to the hospital in Penrith. During the journey the young doctor kept muttering on about a date that she was late for (it being now about ten p.m.), and having got to the doors of the mental health ward (the Beacon Unit); she just palmed me off into the care of the staff there and disappeared. I would have liked her to have gone into this strange and somewhat unnerving place with me and sat with me for a while, but she was gone!

I was escorted past a glassed central office station that looked like something out of a prison block, to a little room containing only a bed and a little set of drawers. The night staff never spoke to me as they closed the door, leaving me alone. I lay on the bed and tried to sleep, but I could not and hours seemed to go by, during which time I grew more and more agitated. Nobody came to see to me. Terrible thoughts whirled round in my head; what were they going to do to me? Was I going to be given electric shock treatment or perhaps injected with drugs? Finally I had had enough and I got up, put on my waterproof coat, went to the door of my room, finding it unlocked and made my way towards the doors that led out of the ward.

What followed was terrible and I will never forget it!

Upon reaching the way out, I tried the doors and they were locked!

One of the night staff had followed me from the office and she said, "Where do you think you're going?" I replied, "Please let me out, I just want to go home."

"You're not going anywhere, now get back to your room," she said.

I took hold of the doors and tried to force them. The nurse grabbed me and forced me into the little kitchenette next to the way out. She held me with one hand and using the other, tried to stuff some pink pills into my mouth! I was terrified, I was being assaulted and suddenly something snapped inside me! Finding a strength I didn't know I had I threw the woman off me, hit her a couple of times and then dragged her to her feet.

Holding her in front of me, I threatened her with a kitchen knife that I had picked up off the work surface and dragged her to the exit doors, where I screamed at the other staff, who had been drawn by the commotion.

"Open the fucking doors," I said.

They obeyed instantly and stood back as I dragged the nurse to the head of the stairs, where I released her and then turned to run down the stairs out onto the car park at the back of the hospital. As I went, the staff shouted after me, imploring me not to go!

Police cars started arriving almost instantly as I ran, doubled up, round the side of the hospital and across the main road into town. I crossed the B&Q car park and scaled the high wooden fence to get onto the school playing fields. I was running on pure adrenalin. From here I crossed the A66 and ran on to reach the M6, where fortunately there was not much traffic as I ran across first one carriageway and then the other.

Now I was into open country and I made my way, more slowly now in the near total darkness, along the edge of the fast flowing river Eamont, where I got a drink and passed under the bridge carrying the west coast railway line.

In the past, I had run from imaginary scenarios but now I really was on the run. I had done something awful and I had to get back home to try and find a way out of the situation. This time the hunted feeling was real and it galvanised me in ways that did not seem possible, considering my level of fatigue!

From the river I turned west, fighting my way through woods and fields for hours, at one point taking a turnip from a field and gnawing on it. Rain began to fall and I thanked God for the marvellous old Karrimor coat that kept my top half dry. However I only had a pair of jeans on my bottom half and with the rising wind and the rain that was almost sleet, I was soon soaked from the waist down, indeed my legs went numb!

The last mile or so of the hike home was completed on the back road, me being almost past caring if the police picked me up! It was still dark and must have been around five thirty a.m. when I lurched into our farmyard. There were no police waiting but I thought better of going into the house, at least for the time being, so I headed for the Dutch barn, where I climbed up onto the stack of hay bales. I used the kitchen knife that I still had on me from the Beacon Unit to cut the strings on a few bales and then made a nest into which I snuggled. I tried to get some rest but sleep eluded me.

I was aware that the police would soon work out where I had run to and come looking, so I got out of my hiding place, made my way to the house and entered, using the spare key from the byre. The first thing I did was rip the phone wires out of the junction box on the window bottom. Then I went upstairs and, careful not to wake my parents, I quietly packed my dad's old rucksack (the one that had been a friend to me on many past occasions) with hiking provisions, put on my ski salopettes and went back downstairs, where I put on my hiking boots and left the house to head for Tina's kennel. She was very pleased to see me and seemed to sense there was an adventure in the offing. I let her out and then we set off, away from the farm. I had put my skiing gloves on but they were bright yellow and I was suddenly conscious of the fact that they would be easily seen, so I took them off and stuffed them into a wall end. It was now almost full daylight as I headed due north through the fields across the valley with Tina running ahead in fine spirits.

I had still not had anything to eat and virtually no rest but I felt strangely energised. Perhaps it was simply the fact that a new day had dawned. I had brought Tina's dog chain with me and soon had to use it as we climbed the northern side of the valley to cross the A66. I lifted Tina over the fences and held on to her chain as I got over myself. There was very little traffic about and we were soon across the road and heading up into Mousethwaite Combe on the lower slopes of Blencathra. The overnight rain had cleared and the new day was cold but quite fine as we climbed the back slope of the Combe. From there we headed over and down to the young Glenderramackin beck, then striking out along its banks up the valley to the col where the beck has its source. It was at this point that we were hit by a squall; a vicious north west wind got up, blowing wet hail into our faces as we went. It was like being sand blasted! The weather cleared up again quickly, though, as we struggled over the col and onto the boggy and featureless Mungrisdale common. Visibility was good and we made good progress, soon arriving down into the valley of the river Caldew. As I approached the river, I could see that it was running high and there were no bridges anywhere in sight. If we wanted to continue in a northerly direction, we would have to ford the Caldew!

On this occasion, I had not fashioned a staff to help me through such obstacles and now as I faced the river, I regretted not having procured one when back at the woods near the A66. There was another problem as well. I knew the water would be well over the tops of my boots and if I wanted to keep my feet dry I would somehow have to stop the water coming in. I sat down on a rock to think and Tina fussed about me, nuzzling my hand. It was great to have her company but she was also an extra worry, I had to keep her safe too! I felt around in the pockets of my coat and found a couple of lengths of baler twine. This was a surprise; I suppose force of habit must have made me put them in my pocket after cutting the bale strings back in the Dutch barn. The idea came to me to tie the bottoms of the legs of my salopettes tightly around the upper parts of my boots, therefore forming a seal that if I was quick enough in crossing the river, would not leak. The salopettes were waterproof and of the dungaree type so I knew they would be able to handle quite a depth of water. I tied the legs of the salopettes in the said fashion, cutting the string with the somewhat blunt kitchen knife and entered the river. Tina paced back and forward on the bank. I knew she would have to take her chance. She had crossed many becks in her time and I felt confident that she would manage this one. The river was maybe six or seven metres wide at the point I had chosen to cross but it was quite swollen, the dark brown peaty water churned and broiled and my courage almost deserted me as I forged into the flow. Unseen slippery rocks rolled beneath my feet, threatening to unbalance me. I heard a splash and, turning, saw Tina had entered the river and was following me. From the bank the water had not appeared to be very deep but I was soon up to my knees and then my waist. The current threatened to sweep me away mid-stream and I forged on more quickly to reach the far bank before I was swept away. Tina swam bravely after me but was swept downstream for maybe fifty metres before she was able to make the far bank. We both scrambled out and I breathed a sigh of relief – that had been a scary experience!

After the river crossing we headed off up Wiley Gill and round the side of Great Calva, before coming down out of the fells to Orthwaite. On we went without encountering another soul, past Overwater, over a low hill, where I picked up some windblown crab apples and ate them, (they gave me indigestion) and on to Ruthwaite. As far as possible, I tried to stay clear of the roads and just use footpaths and not even these in places. I had no map with me at the time, I have traced some of the route taken since and filled in the place names. I distinctly remember stopping at a barn by the side of the river Ellen and trying to get some sleep on some hay bales but Tina was running loose and I did not stop long for fear of discovery.

We walked on to enter Ireby, where I entered the back kitchen of somebody's house through an open door and snaffled a few newly made scones off a worktop – nobody saw me! I gave one of the scones to Tina and we continued on our way, always northwards.

Dusk was drawing in and I now continued on my way on the road, with Tina on the chain. Few vehicles passed us and nobody seemed to pay us any heed; indeed I suppose it just looked like somebody out walking his dog. I followed the signs towards Mealsgate, now in total darkness and began to feel more and more fatigued. Presently we came to a farm entrance and for some reason I took Tina down the lonnen. We had only gone about fifty metres when the farm buildings appeared out of the darkness and on going in to the farmyard, the lights of the farmhouse and a cottage across the yard shone out. I let Tina off the chain, half expecting the farm dogs to set up a clamour but there was silence. Tina snuffled around the yard while I went to the cottage door and knocked. Nobody came so I tried the door. It was unlocked so I went in and into a well-lit living room. There was nobody about; the only sign that there had been anybody there recently was a pair of work jeans, lying on the hearthrug in such a position to suggest somebody had just stepped out of them. I went back outside and explored the farmyard. There were several vehicles parked, one of which was an old Austin Maestro car. It was unlocked and the keys were in the ignition. It would have been a piece of cake to get myself and Tina into the car, steal it and head for the Scottish border (this now had become my goal) but something stopped me. Instead I investigated the main farmhouse where although the lights burned, there did not seem to be anyone around. It was as if everyone had left in a hurry! I tried the back door of the house and it also was unlocked, so I went in and Tina, who had now tired of her investigation of the yard, went in with me. We went through several brightly-lit rooms on the ground floor before coming to a door behind which I could hear voices and the sounds of some sort of celebration. I quickly and quietly retreated to the kitchen with Tina and then, for the first time I noticed all the buffet food lying on the worktops. Then it dawned on me; there had been a party or wedding going on and the guests had retreated to the front room for a singsong! All that food was just lying there and both Tina and I were hungry so what the hell, why let it all go to waste? I wolfed down sandwiches, sausage rolls and cakes. Tina did the same and then we went quietly back out into the night, leaving the unsuspecting revellers to their celebrations.

    I can't remember any more place names we passed through on our way towards the border, but there were several occurrences of note.

    Shortly after we left the farm, a tremendous thirst overtook me. It was all right for Tina, she could get a drink anywhere she wanted but all I could find in the dark was a cattle trough next to the road, a few miles further on. I instinctively knew that drinking the standing water out of the trough would be bad for me but I had difficulty getting even a cup full of fresh water from the ball valve of the trough (I had brought a Thermos flask with me). Just after the trough episode a barn loomed up out of the darkness next to the road. There were young cattle in a pen on the ground floor and upon finding a fixed ladder; I discovered that there was a hayloft above. I let Tina do her own thing round the barn while I climbed to the hayloft to try and get some rest but fate conspired against me. The young cattle thought they were going to be fed and set up a bawling racket. I was forced to retreat from the loft for fear of attracting attention and gathered Tina up to continue on our way.

We wandered on for hours and finally reached the A595, somewhere southwest of Wigton. It was in the early hours of the morning that after walking some distance on the roadside, we came to a large private house just off the road. My raging thirst was back and I headed into the garden of the house, letting Tina off the chain to roam around. I was becoming almost delirious with fatigue as I struggled round the garden, looking for a source of water. Finally I found a hosepipe and turning on the tap there, I was able to get a good long drink and fill my flask. There were several sheds in the garden and I investigated these, careful not to make much noise and awaken whoever might be in the house. There was electricity in one of the sheds and I took a chance in switching on a light. Against the wall of the shed was an old mattress and I laid it down on the floor. I curled up on it and tried to sleep but I was aware that Tina was roaming loose outside, so I couldn't settle. I got up wearily and was about to go back outside when I spied the ground sheet of a tent lying on a shelf. I took it and stuffed it in my rucksack, thinking that it might come in useful later on.

I turned off the shed light, shut the door and quietly called Tina to me. We left the property and continued north east, keeping to the fields on a parallel course with the A595. I was fearful that we would either get run over or be discovered, by walking on the main road. It was more difficult in the fields though, with only starlight to see by and fence after fence, which had to be overcome. Tina tried to jump some of them and I was afraid she would hang herself up on one, like she had done one time back on the farm, resulting in her tearing a large gash on the inside of her back leg (she had needed stitches to repair the damage). Where possible I found places for her to get underneath the fences or alternatively, lifted her over, but although she was not a big dog this extra exertion left me feeling even more drained. At one point in particular, while crossing a large field I remember looking up at the night sky and seeing a large ring of stars which I took in a fanciful way as to represent the outline of a huge spacecraft. At that point I would have quite welcomed being abducted by aliens or beamed up by Scotty, I was so tired!

Things took a darker turn when, having had my fill of the fields, I got Tina back on the chain and took to a side road I had found. It was now coming daylight when I came across a large bungalow. We went down the drive into the back yard, where there was a blue Fiat Panda parked. My mind went back to the Austin Maestro I had seen back at that farm and how, although the keys had been in the ignition, I had not stolen it. Now, though, my inhibitions slipped away and picking up a stone, I broke the window of the little car to get at the door handle. Once inside I looked around for keys but there were none and lacking the knowledge to 'hot wire' the car, I was forced to abandon my idea of stealing the car, taking the weight off my feet and making a break for the Scottish border. Instead I set about investigating a nearby shed, resulting in me knocking over a stack of boxes. This made quite a racket, causing the awakening of the occupants of the house. A voice rang out from one of the windows.

"What the bloody hell do you think you're doing? I'm going to come out there with the shotgun if you don't get the hell off my property."

I quickly gathered Tina up, chucked her over the back fence, climbing it myself and ran off down an open field towards a large stand of Scotch fir trees.

There was an air of unreality about my circumstances, right from the time I had entered the house in Ireby I had been under some sort of delusion that most of the houses and farms on my route had been empty and that the residents had, for some reason of natural disaster, abandoned their properties. Now with me being openly challenged, reality came crashing back in on me!

Once safely into the stand of trees, I spread the ground sheet I had stolen on the ground and using some matches I had brought from our farm, I tried to get a fire started nearby, but the lichen and twigs I gathered were wet and would not ignite. I lay down wearily on the sheet and tried again to sleep. Tina snuggled up to me and licked my face; she seemed to sense that I was in distress and therefore sought to comfort me!

We rested for a while and then left the wood to travel once more through open country. However, in the distance I could see the outskirts of some large conurbation and as we drew closer, I could see that it was indeed probably the city of Carlisle. I got Tina back on the lead as we came out through a gate onto a road that led into the city. As we made our way into the outskirts, any residents we encountered seemed to give us a wide berth!

It was as we approached the centre of the city that the events of a few days ago really caught up with me. I had made up my mind to head for the railway station and I was just crossing the large bridge over the railway, with Tina going merrily along on her chain, when I was jumped by two police officers! They seemed to come out of nowhere and one of them grabbed hold of me while the other asked me if I was still carrying the knife. I fished it out of my inside pocket and the copper snatched it off me before getting on his radio. In no time at all, a large police van appeared and I was cuffed and then bundled into the back along with Tina. My initial calmness about being taken soon wore off as the van rushed through the streets. I became extremely angry and started to throw myself from one side of the van to the other, swearing at the coppers in the front as I did so. I hurt my shoulders on the sides of the van but the police kept going, even though the van must have been swaying! The van came to an abrupt halt after what seemed like only a very short journey and I made myself ready for the officers opening the back doors. When they did so, I launched myself at them out of the back of the van and hit the ground running. However, my hands were clasped together in front of me by the handcuffs and my legs were weak from fatigue.

I went down heavily on my face at the same time screaming to Tina to, "Fly away home."

It was a last cry of defiance as the officers picked me up. The fall had caused the self-tightening handcuffs to grip my wrists in a vice-like embrace and I screamed in pain, imploring the officers to take them off me, but it was in vain as they bundled me towards the glass door of a nearby building. The door opened automatically and the police dragged me through into a kind of airlock; the door then closed behind us and another one opened in front to admit us to a kind of foyer, off which led several corridors. I was dragged down one of these and lowered down onto a mattress in a padded cell. Several people came into the cell as the police released the agonising handcuffs. The coppers left the cell, leaving the door open and I made a vain attempt to rise from the mattress and escape the cell, but the other people around me held me down. I was terrified; I pleaded with them to let me go and then started to cry. Soothing hands attempted to comfort me and soft voices issued comforting words. One man in particular was obviously in charge and he told me he was a psychiatrist and that I was in Rowanwood, the special care unit of the Carleton Clinic, and that I would be well cared for.

I stayed in that cell for a couple of hours, during which a small crowd of what I assumed to be other patients gathered in the cell doorway. They eyed me in a curious fashion. The staff stayed with me until I had calmed down and then I was moved to a private room with a viewing window in the door. It was very similar to the room I had been put into several days earlier at the Beacon Unit, but this time the door was locked. I examined the window, through which I could see open country but there was no escape there – it was screwed shut!

I lay on the bed, wondering what had happened to Tina. Perhaps she was at this moment being taken away by the police to be put down! The day wore on and at intervals somebody came to check on me, but this did not prevent me from sinking into the darkest place I have ever been in my life. I had almost abandoned all hope; only one thing prevented me from falling into total insanity and that was the thought of Rachel, the gypsy girl whom I barely knew, she was my light in that dark place!

In the evening, some food and drink was brought to me and afterwards I slept properly for the first time in ages.

During the next week I fell into the routine of the ward. There were nine other patients and we were awoken at eight a.m. and went to bed around ten p.m., depending on what was on the telly in the common room. Meals were regular and of good quality. The other patients were mainly male but there were a couple of women. It was a locked ward and you were only allowed outside in the central courtyard, where even the brick windowsills were sloped so that you could not climb up them to escape over the roof!

I slowly began to feel better and my desire to escape diminished, I soon struck up a good banter with the other patients and two in particular; one a young bloke who had a Playstation (which I became addicted to) and the other, a girl of perhaps seventeen years old, who had drug problems. There were several heavy smokers amongst the other patients and there was a room set aside for them. I often frequented this room because that's where the best crack was, although I am an ex-smoker myself, and I suppose there was a certain amount of temptation to start again! Every evening the patients gathered at the medical room for their respective doses of medication. I was not given anything; this was, I suppose, because at that point I had not been given an official diagnosis. I did however have a blood test and several days later the staff told me the results and that I had liver damage! This was a surprise to me because I felt fine. I supposed at the time they assumed that excessive drinking had led to my condition and that they would frighten me into giving up the drink by telling me I had a liver condition! I was of the opinion that I was not that heavy a drinker and that if I did indeed have liver damage, it was being caused by something else!

My diary was up and running again by now and on Monday the twelfth of January 1998, I attended the first of several big assessments during which I was told I had been put on a Section 3, meaning that I would be detained for a minimum of twenty-eight days. The rest of the meeting was taken up by the professionals there present, discussing with me the events in the Beacon Unit, which proved a very distressing experience for me!

After the meeting I was called into another room to meet two social workers, whom we shall call John and Mike. They wanted to know all about me, in particular about my private life and this part I found very stressful. They meant well though and I would come to hold them in high regard.

Following this examination of my life, I felt the need for some kind of release and having seen some exercising machines in one of the recreation rooms I asked the head nurse (we shall call him James) if I could have a go on them and he said, "Yes, I will show you how to use the machines right now if you like!" Now James was a rugby player and therefore a pretty fit guy and he soon had me going through my paces on the stepper. Although I had been through a traumatic mental and physical experience I had had a week to recover. Aerobically I was in good shape and I soon impressed James by climbing the equivalent height of the Empire State Building on the stepper! This physical exercise served to ease the memory of the traumatic earlier events of the day.

There was also a pool table, which was in excellent condition and I soon proved to be one of the best players in the unit, enjoying many hours of tactical battles with my fellow patients.

My parents came to see me during the following week and they assured me that the police had returned Tina to the farm and that she was well.

The young guy with the Playstation (who shall be known as David) showed me how to play the Lara Croft, Tomb Raider game and I became fascinated by it, spending many hours playing it alongside David. David also had an excellent selection of videos, which we watched on the communal telly every evening.

On Saturday the seventeenth of January, I was allowed outside the unit for the first time. One of the female nurses took me out through the airlock and across to the shop in the main hospital building, where I bought a few sweets with money my parents had given me. It was great to experience the sense of freedom, because although I was enjoying my time in Rowanwood it was a locked ward, meaning you were virtually imprisoned!

The following day the peace of the ward was shattered when the young girl with drug problems (Lucy) became drunk after some arsehole visitor had smuggled alcohol into the building! Poor Lucy was off her head and smashed the remote control for the telly. She also entered my room and took my electric shaver to bits (which fortunately still worked when I got it put back together). She also messed up a jigsaw of the Jungfrau Region that I had been making. I had a lot of time for Lucy though and I soon forgave her. She was a good kid who had been led astray by a lot of bastards! (I often wonder to this day what became of her.)

On Monday the nineteenth, I attended the second assessment meeting and did quite well. There was also another session with the social workers, John and Mike, which went much better than the previous one. My solicitor phoned to tell me I had to attend an interview (accompanied by him) with the police at Hunter Lane police station in Penrith the following day. I had been warned by the unit's chief psychiatrist that I may be held to account for the Beacon Unit incident!

That afternoon I was let out of the unit on my own for the first time, during which I went to the hospital bank where I withdrew some money. The weather was very cold, with a fresh north wind and snow flurries. At six thirty p.m. my brother Angus and my sister-in-law Anne came to see me and they told me about the skiing holiday that they had been on with my sister Heather, her partner Allan and Ken (a good friend of all of us). I had been booked to go on the trip too but it had come while I was in hospital. I had held out hopes that I might have been allowed out to go on the trip but there was no chance of that happening. (I was able to reclaim much of the holiday cost on medical grounds at a later date.) The trip had gone very well and all concerned had enjoyed a good time!

On Tuesday the twentieth, the social worker, John, came to the unit and took me to Penrith to be interviewed by the police. My solicitor was there and he gave me reassurance as we entered the interview room. I was shitting myself as the recording machine was switched on. There was little point in denying any of the events at the Beacon Unit and I answered all of the questions truthfully. I was then, to my horror, charged with actual bodily harm! And then wheeled out to be fingerprinted and DNA swabbed, during which I said to John (who had also been in the interview room), "I hope you never have to go through this, mate!" he gave me a sympathetic look and then took me back to Carlisle, it was all over, at least for the time being, but being charged with ABH had left me in a very low way!

The following evening Ken visited me and he was much intrigued by the details of the running of a psychiatric facility. He was a fellow farmer and he filled me in on events on his own farm and then cheered me up no end by relating various hilarious tales from the recent skiing holiday.

The period up to Saturday the twenty-fourth was pretty much routine. I did a lot of work on the step machine, played pool and Tomb Raider! Then all hell broke loose; a new patient was admitted and I could see instantly that he was a dangerous sort! Later that day, Lucy claimed to the staff that this new guy had tried to rape her in her room and then she had gone outside, down to the old Garlands Hospital buildings, broken some windows and cut her wrists badly! We were all locked in our rooms until the incident was investigated properly. I wanted to punch the new guy's lights out but that would have done me no good, seeing I had been doing so well. In the evening, the police came and arrested the new patient on the charge of attempted rape and he was taken away to the police station, thank God!

On Sunday the twenty-fifth, my folks came again to visit, this time bringing Tina in the Maestro van and I gave her a run down the field next to Rowanwood, across to the bridge over the M6, where I was told a patient from the unit had been recaptured after escaping a few years previously! Later in the day I walked down to the old Garlands with Lucy, who was in a fragile state. She trusted me, though, as we walked to the old buildings. On the way, she gave me a Carpenters CD, saying it was a present for being a good friend (I still have that disc and it means a lot to me). We went up into the old theatre, where we should not have been actually, because the building was being decommissioned! Sitting alone together we talked about our lives. Hers had barely begun and she was already heavily damaged! I felt honoured to be trusted to be alone with her, considering what she had just been through with that new patient and the alcohol incident!

On Monday the twenty-sixth, I had the usual assessment, where I was told I would be moved to the Hadrian Unit, which was an open ward. This I was pleased about because it was a step nearer to getting out. However, I was not prepared for the conditions I would experience in the Hadrian. I had been somewhat cosseted in Rowanwood and come three p.m. that afternoon I had my eyes opened! The first thing that happened after I moved my stuff across to the Hadrian was that I was put in a dormitory with about six other patients. There was no security for my belongings and the guy in the next bed had the worst case of foot odour you can imagine! It was so bad I actually gagged!

The good news was that I would be allowed to go home for a day and a night on Wednesday. I was allowed more or less unlimited access to the grounds around the hospital and it eased my dislike of the Hadrian to take walks down to the old Garlands buildings and also, once, I left the hospital grounds and walked down a side road into the outskirts of Carlisle (you were not supposed to do this). One day, while I was exploring the old Garlands I came upon the biggest horse chestnut tree I have ever seen and I picked up a conker from beneath its branches. In the spring to follow, I planted this conker from the tree (which now does not exist) alongside several other conkers in buckets, in the garden of our farmhouse. They all grew and years later I planted the young trees out along the edge of a wood at the farm, but the deer ate them. One tree had been overlooked in the garden, however, and when we sold up in 2005 and moved to the bungalow in Penrith, the young tree went with us. It was planted out in an old compost heap next to my garage and has grown very quickly into a fine tree. It's a slim chance but I like to think this tree is the offspring of that mighty tree that once grew at Garlands and whenever I look at it, it reminds me of my first time in a mental hospital!

David had been moved to the Hadrian at the same time as me and he still had the Playstation with him. We were able to while away the hours on that to take our minds off the fact that there was only one washbasin on the entire ward that you could safely use because one of the other male patients had the habit of sticking his fingers up his arse, pulling out shit and then smearing it all over the taps!!!

There were no gym facilities in the Hadrian and I missed my regular workouts.

On Wednesday the twenty-eighth, I was allowed to go into Carlisle on the bus and in doing so, I took the opportunity to try and buy a Playstation of my own as I had now superseded David's efforts in the Tomb Raider game and wanted to take myself further into the game. However, PlayStations were the latest thing and they were as rare as rocking horse shit! I came back empty handed, by taxi.

Later on I was visited by a couple from a farm where I trapped their moles. They would not come inside the unit so we just sat in their car and had a good crack. Angus and Anne came in the evening to take me for my short home visit and there was an unfortunate incident on the drive back. In Rowanwood, I had completed a very difficult double-sided jigsaw and I had the idea I would leave it complete and frame it. It was lying on a board on the parcel shelf of Angus's car on the way home when he suddenly braked hard to avoid something in the road. The jigsaw flew forwards, down into the footwell behind the front seats and was broken into pieces. I was gutted. (That jigsaw has never been remade to this day!) That night I enjoyed a good sleep in my own bed, which set me up for the following day.

I was up at a good time on the Thursday and put in a good day's work on the farm, doing one of my favourite jobs – leading muck. This could only be done during hard frost on our farm and the conditions were ideal. I was also able to give Tina a good run out!

Heather took me back to the Hadrian Unit that evening and it was a wrench, having enjoyed the brief few hours at home. I had a poor sleep that night because not only did the guy in the next bed have smelly feet but he snored loudly too!

On Friday the thirtieth, I complained to the staff about my conditions, stating that if they did not change I would stand a fair chance of becoming ill again! I made another trip into the city and this time I was able to purchase a Playstation at the Electronics Boutique shop. I brought it back to the Hadrian Unit via the same taxi as the other visit and was able to lock it away in my bedside drawer. While I was in the city I had a rush of blood and after going to Thomas Cook, booked a walking holiday to Zermatt, Switzerland, scheduled for the July of that year. (Unfortunately events conspired against me and I had to put the trip back a year.) Later in the day I was delighted to be moved into my own private room, which considerably eased some of the difficulties I had been experiencing. I was in the common room that evening when for the first time I heard the Pink Floyd album, *The Division Bell*. I liked it immediately and to this day it is still one of my favourite albums. (My mother hates it!) Also that evening, a young female patient I had got to know gave me a drawing she had done of an androgynous figure sitting in contemplation. It is really rather good and I now have it framed on my sitting room wall.

I was visited by Heather and Allan on the Sunday and we walked and talked, down around the old buildings. There was a church in the grounds and I had tried the door several times but always found it locked, as is the case with most churches today, at least during the week. I started to pray after my first episode in 1994 and have done so every day since. I am not a regular church-goer but rather prefer to worship and believe in my own way! I do like to go in churches wherever I am in the world though, whenever they are open, to say a few words.

In the early hours of Tuesday the third of February, a new girl was brought onto the ward and she screamed the place down, keeping everybody awake! I found out later that she had experienced an adverse reaction to an anti-malaria drug and this had sent her off her head. Hours seemed to go by before she quietened down and the rest of us were able to get some sleep. In the evening of that day, my best mate Andrew came to visit. We enjoyed a good crack and he gave me a framed Vassily Kandinsky painting but because it had glass in it, it had to be stored in reception, where unfortunately the glass got broken.

I had maintained contact with Lucy even though she was still in Rowanwood and later on that day, I was able to meet her and go down to the library in the old buildings for a quiet chat. She was enjoying a more stable period and I was pleased for her.

Also that day, the chief psychiatrist sent word to me that I could go home for four days and I immediately set about ringing home to see if anyone could come and get me. My sister was available later in the day and I got myself packed ready for her coming for me in the evening.

Having got home, the next four days went by quickly with me doing about five hours of work on the farm each day. John and Mike, the social workers, came to visit me at home for the first time and we had quite a constructive meeting.

I returned to the Hadrian unit on the evening of Sunday the eighth of February and then stayed there until Wednesday the eleventh of February, whereupon I was released from the Carleton Clinic after various advisory sessions with nurses and drugs/alcohol advisors. Heather came to collect me and during the journey home, she told me of her rather harrowing experience of getting my car back along the Old Coach Road and back to the farm! The following day I met with John and Mike at Penrith Hospital, whereupon they took me through to the Beacon Unit. Of course it was the first time that I had been back there since that terrible night and as I went through the doors to the bottom of the flight of stairs that I had dragged the nurse down, I experienced mixed feelings of fear and shame. I faced them though and in the years that would follow I would come to hold the Beacon Unit in high regard!

From here I went through to Keswick, to meet with my solicitor to discuss the forthcoming court case. He warned me that I would very probably be found guilty of the charges, in spite of not being in my right mind when I committed the offence. (I still had no official diagnosis of my condition.) He did not know what the punishment was likely to be if I was found guilty but the meeting certainly put the wind up me!

The weeks that followed went pretty much to my usual self-employed routine, with me working part time on our farm and away, trapping moles for the farmer who had come to see me at the Carleton Clinic. There were regular meetings with the social workers at our farm and I also had to go through to Carlisle to meet with the drugs/alcohol people. This I found difficult because I did not think I had a problem. Surely if I did have one I would have gone and got pissed in Carlisle the first time I was let out of Rowanwood; indeed some of the other patients had done just that! Just after this, Heather phoned me to ask me if I wanted to go skiing with her in Scotland. I jumped at the chance, seeing as I had missed out on the France trip earlier in the year! On Saturday the seventh of March, Heather drove us both up to Glencoe, where we checked out the lift opening times at the ski centre and then we drove on to Newtonmore, where we overnighted at a B&B. The following day we drove back southwest to the Nevis Range ski area, where we enjoyed a great day's skiing in challenging conditions.

We returned to our B&B and then on the Monday we returned to the Glencoe Ski Centre and skied the area there. It was enjoyable but more difficult than Nevis Range, with you having to look out for large rocks hidden in dips in the middle of the piste. They say skiing in Scotland is for the purist! At the end of the day we were able to ski right back to the bottom of the lifts, even though there was not much snow. As we were coming off the slope, we met a young couple we knew very well, who lived just a few miles away from us and I thought, *it's a small world!* Heather drove us home right after we had finished skiing, to complete an excellent mini break. On Wednesday the eleventh of March, I appeared in court for the first time and it was a very stressful experience. My solicitor was by my side the whole time, though, as well as John and Mike's support in the ante-room, they were a great help. The case was adjourned for one month, pending psychiatric reports.

On Friday the twentieth of March, I went to Carlisle to meet a psychologist for the first time (we shall call him Richard) and this proved to be an interesting experience. The first thing he did was get me to remove my spectacles so that the reflection in them would not hide my eyes. I liked him instantly, even though some of the stuff we talked about was extremely personal and after several meetings I decided that if we had met under any other circumstances, we would have become close friends. Indeed, we once met on the streets of Carlisle, completely by accident and instead of blanking me like some other health professionals would have done, he struck up a lively conversation with me! He was a rugby player and also much travelled, impressing me with an account of a horse riding holiday to the high plains of Utah, U.S.A.

Friday the twenty-seventh of March came and I went to my favourite hairdressers at Ambleside, which was a treat before a very difficult meeting with my solicitor in Keswick, where I was informed that the head psychiatrist at the Carleton Clinic had wrote a very damning report about me. I was distraught by this news, knowing full well how the report would look when I came up in court!

To this day I do not fully understand why my character was so badly blackened by the psychiatrist.

The weeks went by and lambing time commenced on the farm. This is always a very tiring period and with the added worry of the coming court appearance, I was exhausted! Also at this time of year there is the added worry of attack by foxes and crows on the young lambs but with the exception of getting the foxhounds in, we had no means of defending our flock because the police had removed all guns from our property and my shotgun licence had been revoked!

On Wednesday the eighth of April, I appeared in court again, and again the case was adjourned, prolonging the agony. I had obtained several good character references from local farmers and dignitaries, though and these seemed to serve me well when before the bench!

I still was able to fit in the occasional round of golf in spite of all the work and worry. Indeed, this activity helped me take my mind off my plight! There was the regular, pain in the arse meetings with the drugs and alcohol people, (I had virtually stopped drinking anyway, for fuck's sake!) and the psychiatrist, of course, the same man who had written that awful report about me! The only bright spot in my contacts with the health professionals was my monthly meetings with Richard, the psychologist. On one occasion, he used his story-board to make a diagram to describe his view of my condition. On the board, he drew a picture of an empty glass and then he proceeded to add items to depict rising levels in the glass. These comprised extreme physical exercise, stress, lack of sleep, poor eating and lastly, excessive alcohol. This last item caused the glass to overflow, resulting in me experiencing a full blown psychotic episode. It was the best thing any of them ever came up with and I could relate to it really well.

Most of the next month was taken up doing work on our farm and around the neighbouring ones, meaning my days were pretty full, leaving me little time to ponder the Sword of Damocles that was the court case, hanging over my head. However, on Wednesday the sixth of May I attended court again, accompanied as ever by my solicitor and John and Mike. This time the case was tried, after they had changed the line-up of the magistrates due to one of them knowing me. I stood nervously in the dock with as much remorse as I could muster while I was found guilty of actual bodily harm and affray. The last part of the conviction was a real body blow because I had been told that affray was a very serious charge indeed! I stood there swaying slightly under the impact and noticed the reporters scribbling away frantically at the back of the court. Sentencing came and I steeled myself to receive my punishment. I was given one year's probation, fined eight hundred pounds with fifty-four pounds costs and also given sixty hours' community service!

I was dismissed and left court feeling limp, but I cheered up somewhat when John and Mike told me I had got off fairly lightly and that there had been a possibility that I could have gone to Broadmoor for what I did!

I left the building, thanking my solicitor and John and Mike for their services and support and then went to meet my sister for lunch at the local Italian restaurant. We discussed the court case and she asked me if I had enough money to pay the fine. I told her I had arranged with the court clerk to pay the fine off in instalments. She then put forward the question of paying the solicitor and I was able to tell her that the cost of that had been taken care of by legal aid.

After this I met the drug and alcohol advisor and he asked me if I would agree to giving up drink for a trial period of one year. I did so, thinking that I had not had much alcohol recently anyway and it should not prove much of a problem.

On Friday the eighth of May, I had a very tough meeting with Richard at Carlisle, with him being in possession of the results of the court case. I saw a different side to him with the criminal psychologist facet coming out, making me feel the impact of my convictions even more keenly.

The following day I experienced my first taste of community service. I went to Warcop (a village at the foot of the Pennines) with a bunch of other offenders to scrape and paint the iron railings next to the stream in the village. It was a fine day and I was not frightened of work anyway (unlike some of the others) and found the session quite enjoyable, which I suppose does not constitute feeling the effects of the punishment!

During the coming weeks I worked hard, most of the time away with my mole trapping, to earn money to pay the court fine. The difficulty was fitting in work with the blizzard of appointments I had to attend; there was at least one a week. If it wasn't the psychologist, it was the psychiatrist, or the social workers or the drug and alcohol people, or the community service and finally the probation centre, where I had to show up every month for the duration of the probation period.

My first visit to the probation centre at Clint Mill in Penrith was quite a scary experience. There were several other offenders in the waiting room and some of them were obviously violent – literally bouncing off the walls! I was relieved to get out of the waiting area to meet with a probation officer.

I had three different ones in my time and they were all good people doing a very difficult job. One of the officers used to take me to a café regularly for a brew while we discussed things. They did, however, prick my balloon somewhat by telling me I could not go abroad while on probation!

Of course, during this period the details of my offence and convictions came out in the local papers and I heard a rumour that the Beacon Unit incident had been on Channel 4 news. This all served to blacken my reputation and was particularly noticeable at the golf club, where I received sidelong glances and in some cases outright shunning. This began to destroy my social life and I went to the club less and less.

A good thing that happened around this time, though, was that my community service was cancelled and in its place, I got an extra probation period.

Part 5

England and Scotland, June 1998 to December 2001.

I had bought a forty-five litre Karrimor rucksack and a pair of walking trousers at Fisher's outdoor shop in Keswick early in June 1998, with the prospect of putting them to good use on a walking trip to Scotland later in the month. I had told my various health professionals and the probation service that I intended to go walking in Scotland and they seemed to be okay with it, provided that I went accompanied by others.

We were preparing for haymaking on the farm on the twenty-third of June and with the Scotland trip scheduled for the twenty-sixth, I hoped in a way that the next few days would not be the start of a fine spell, therefore rendering me unable to go on the trip! I popped into town on the afternoon of the twenty-third to pay my car insurance and to buy some camping equipment for what would be my first ever camping trip.

The weather up to the twenty-sixth stayed mixed and I was able to go ahead with my plans. I would be going on the trip with Angus, Anne and my best mate Andrew. They had all been camping before so they knew the ropes, so to speak. I, however, being a greenhorn, had some difficulty preparing all the right stuff for camping. I managed, though and early on the morning of the twenty-sixth Andrew arrived at the farm. We transferred all his gear into my Capri and together we had quite a load! Angus and Anne were travelling in their own car and we had arranged to meet them at the campsite Angus had chosen in Glencoe.

We set off but had not gone far when I took a detour through the village of Motherby to get filled up with petrol. We could have come back to the A66 but I decided to carry on on the B5288, with disastrous consequences. We had just entered the village of Greystoke and were keeping to the speed limit when a milk float shot out of a turning on the right, ploughing right into us! I hit the van just behind his front wheel with the right front wing of the Capri and we both came to a jarring standstill. I sat for a moment with my hands over my eyes. Neither Andrew nor I was hurt but it had been a considerable impact.

Andrew said, "Fucking hell, that's a great start!"

And I agreed. I was furious as I got out to confront the other driver. He was an older guy and was very apologetic, admitting full responsibility for the crash and this defused me somewhat, enabling us to go about exchanging insurance details. I looked at the damage, the milkman's van only had a bulge in the bodywork but my front wing was severely crumpled and the outside headlight was broken. I was still pretty mad but there was no point getting into a fracas, being mindful of my criminal record and my situation with the probation order, so we got our details exchanged and went on our separate ways, both vehicles being drivable.

I decided to strike while the iron was hot and carry straight on to visit my insurance broker in Penrith before we went any further. This proved to be a fairly straightforward affair because of the other driver admitting responsibility and plans were laid to get my car repaired when we got back from the trip. However, it had delayed us quite a bit and with the Capri's handling being unaffected, I drove quite fast up into Scotland to make up for lost time.

The weather made it hard work, though, with heavy showers and I was quite tired by the time we rolled onto the campsite at Glencoe. Angus and Anne were already at the campsite and we made camp next to them.

I made short work of pitching my tent, having practised back home on the farm and was soon cooking my evening meal inside the tent as it was raining outside. Andrew had his own one-man tent and Angus and Anne had one between them. We were all pitched pretty close together and were able to talk to each other through the tent walls. The others were having a few beers but I was unable to enjoy this luxury, so I got ready for bed and was soon asleep.

Saturday the twenty-seventh. We were all up and about early, having planned the previous evening to try to do the Aonach Eagach ridge. The morning was reasonably fine, overcast with a quite high cloud base and most importantly, it was dry. The midges were biting so we didn't hang around long getting our breakfasts and preparing our lunches. We packed our gear and then set off in both cars, first leaving my car at the western end of the planned hike at the Clachaig Inn and then piling into Angus's car to drive eastwards up the A82 to the Meeting of Three Waters, where there was a lay-by.

We donned our gear and struck off away from the road up the steep, grassy south-facing slope.

At the same time that I bought my Karrimor rucksack I had bought a pair of new boots. They were Zamberlans and although I had broken them in a bit at home, this was their first real test! I had been sad to take the old Scarpas out of front line action but their tread was becoming very worn and they weren't turning the water very well any more either.

We climbed quite quickly in the good conditions, discussing the likely terrain ahead at rest stops. Angus obviously knew quite a bit about what we were likely to expect but he was sparing with the details, I would soon find out the reason for this! We approached what was obviously the beginning of the ridge and as we did so a view opened up down a scree slope to the right. A hundred feet or so down the scree I spotted something red lying among the rocks and upon a whim I decided to investigate. Before any of the others could challenge me, I set off down the steep slope, slipping and sliding on the loose terrain. When I got to the object I had spotted, it turned out to be a rather battered Siggi water bottle that somebody who had maybe fallen from higher up had lost. I thought about leaving it but I had lost a lot of height to reach it so I gathered it up and put it in my rucksack, thinking it might come in useful for something.

I scrambled back up the steep slope to rejoin the others, where I was harangued by my brother for wasting energy on a silly excursion. As I struggled to regain my breath, I thought to myself that he was probably correct in bollocking me!

We continued on along the path, now on more level going and we soon came to the first real obstacle of the hike. The ground in front of us dropped away into an abyss and at first glance there seemed to be no way down. We had no rope for safety, but Angus assured us that it was not as difficult as it looked and taking the lead, he set off over the edge, down a narrow cleft. We followed one by one and when it came to Andrew's turn I saw him blanch and I suddenly remembered that this was his first real hill walking trip and that therefore, this must be a very scary experience, but here he was and it was in at the deep end. He girded his loins and set off over the edge. I went last and although the way down was vertical, there were plenty of good holds and after about twenty metres (sixty-five feet) of descent we were at the bottom of the cliff.

We regained our composure and struck out once more along the ridge, which was at first broad but soon narrowed to a knife edge. The main path ran along level, just below the apex of the ridge on the south side but at certain points you could walk on the top. Angus tried this a few times but the rest of us stuck to the main path.

We soon approached the peak of Meall Dearg at nine hundred and fifty-three metres (three thousand one hundred and twenty-six feet) – the first of the two Munros on the ridge and here we had lunch. There were quite a few patches of mist floating about so the views were often obscured.

After the brief lunch stop we continued along the ridge. There was a lot of exposure with the ground falling away, often vertically, off the side of the path. Presently we came to a place they call the Crazy Pinnacles. This was a very difficult section and it was the place where we first encountered the two young ladies. They were having difficulties and we teamed up with them to get over the tough section. Andrew seemed to get on particularly well with them and he learned that one of them was a scuba diver. They were obviously pretty fit (in more ways than one) but were not that experienced in scrambling. They stayed with us as we continued on to reach the second Munro of Sgorr nam Fiannaidh at nine hundred and sixty-seven metres (three thousand one hundred and seventy-two feet) and then we descended together to the Clachaig Inn.

The traverse of the ridge had taken about six hours and while we were enjoying a drink in the inn, which is a popular climber's haunt, Angus told us we had just done the most difficult ridge walk in mainland Britain! I felt a great sense of achievement at this revelation and we were all impressed with the way Andrew had handled the task. My new boots had performed well but a problem had developed with the insoles; on coming down off the ridge to the inn they had begun to slip down over my toes, which was an uncomfortable sensation. There wasn't much I could do about it at the time but I do remember gluing the insoles into my boots when I got home.

The two girls bought us a drink for helping them and after we had enjoyed a few (non-alcoholic, in my case) we left the inn and drove back up the A82 to retrieve the other car.

When we got back to the campsite, we cooked ourselves the evening meal in the outside cooking area, at the same time trying to swat the pesky midges, and then took a shower in the excellent toilet block.

After this I drove us into Glencoe village, where we parked and then sought out the nearest hostelry, which was the Glencoe Hotel. As we entered the crowded bar, we noticed that the television was showing a football match and it turned out to be England playing Columbia in the World Cup. It soon became obvious that the Scottish contingent in the bar were supporting the Columbians. This was slightly annoying but they were soon silenced when England scored! Our team went on to score again, winning the match two-nil and we left the bar later with a very satisfied feeling! We went back to the campsite and turned in. The others had enjoyed quite a few drinks and were able to get off to sleep right away but I found getting off slightly more difficult, having no alcohol on board!

Sunday the twenty-eighth. We were up, breakfasted and away in good time again. The weather was overcast but dry for the moment. Over the morning meal we discussed what walk to take on that day. We were all feeling fairly well rested and Angus put it to us that he would like to try and scale Bidean nam Bian, the highest mountain in the district of Argyll at one thousand one hundred and fifty metres (three thousand seven hundred and seventy-three feet), so this is what we set out to do. We took both cars to almost the same point that we had started the previous day's walk from and then parked, donned our gear, which, as it was now coming on to rain, was full wet weather tackle and then struck out southwards, across one of the few bridges in the River Coe. We had only walked a mile or so up the steepening lower slopes of Bidean nam Bian when Andrew began to complain of a sharp pain in his knee. He struggled on for a bit but it soon became obvious that he couldn't continue. We stopped and considered a course of action. It was decided that Andrew would go back and take my car back to the Clachaig Inn, where he said he would while away the time until we got back, in other words he was going to go 'on the sesh' (get drunk). So he shouldered his rucksack, took my car keys and set off back down the path. The remaining three of us continued up into the mist and had gone some distance before I remembered that Andrew had put his wallet in my rucksack to keep it dry (him not having a waterproof lining in his). However, he was long gone and there was nothing else to do but continue upwards.

Most of the rest of the hike is a blur but I am fairly sure we summitted the two Munros of the peak of Bidean nam Bian itself and the neighbouring peak of Stob Coire Sgreamhach at one thousand and seventy-two metres (three thousand five hundred and seventeen feet), stopping somewhere for a wet lunch and then returning via the impressive Lost Valley to the remaining car after seven hours' walking. We were soaked and our spirits were somewhat quelled as we took off our wet coats and waterproof trousers to get into Angus's car. Andrew had obviously taken my car and I wondered how he would be able to pay for his drink in the inn. I would soon find out! We drove to the Clachaig and entered the bar to find a very inebriated Andrew playing pool with the two young ladies of the previous day's acquaintance. They were obviously well oiled too and were enjoying Andrew's company.

I asked him how he had paid for his drink, seeing as I had his wallet and he laughed and said, "It was simple, mate, I just used your car as collateral."

I said, "Fucking hell, the management can't have been out to look at the car then, or they would have seen it had a bent wing!" We all laughed and then Angus, Anne and I joined the other three in a drink.

It had been a good day and we had all tackled the hikes over both days with energy and competence. Anne and Andrew had done particularly well, even though Andrew had done some of his hiking in the bar!

We were all pretty worn out and didn't fancy cooking when we got back to the campsite so we ate in the pub, with the two young ladies joining us. After the meal Andrew exchanged names and addresses with the girls and we parted company with them and went back to the campsite, showered and then turned in.

The following day, we packed up all our gear in the thankfully drying conditions and made preparations for the journey home. We decided to go to the visitor's centre in Glencoe on the way back to buy some presents for our families. Having got there and bought the said presents, we saw that there was a documentary film showing about the infamous Glencoe massacre and we went to see it. It proved to be a moving experience and it also left us feeling a bit guilty being English, about the role of the Redcoats in the affair! After this we drove home to complete a very satisfying trip.

The following week, I got word from the insurance brokers that my car would be repaired at the expense of the other party's insurance company and shortly afterwards I took the Capri in to a local bodyworks, where they made a good job of putting it to rights.

Haymaking took place on our farm shortly after the Scotland trip and then during the coming months life continued as normal. I worked hard at my various different types of occupation for a variety of different clients and I felt pretty normal in my state of mind. The Scotland trip had been good and an excellent strenuous physical workout, there had been no re-emergence of my paranoid, delusional behaviour, which I had been told by my various counsellors could be brought on by such a demanding experience. I continued to stay off alcohol but was still able to enjoy a good social life with my many friends, who had stuck by me in spite of my criminal convictions.

It must have been during August when I went to see the psychiatrist for one of my regular monitoring appointments and on this occasion he gave me the diagnosis that I have carried with me to the present day. My condition would be called, 'Mania with mood incongruent psychotic symptoms.' This is a bit of a mouthful but it seems to fit my behaviour well while ill. However, a label had now been officially attached to me and it made me become more aware of the way people may regard me! My name had been splashed over the papers, along with what I had done in the Beacon Unit and I began to wonder how it would affect my chances of meeting and forming relationships with women. Indeed, I was out in Penrith one night shortly following the diagnosis and I encountered the beautiful gypsy girl Rachel, the memory of whom had given me hope in the dark times in Rowanwood. I had an opportunity to speak to her during the evening but I shied away from it! I now had two reasons for not getting involved with her: 1. she was too young and 2. how could she possibly be interested in me? I was that sod that had done that awful thing in the Beacon Unit, that NUTTER! After this I went home in a rather despondent mood.

Something happened though in the weeks following this night out which served to lighten my mood a bit. I was mole trapping for a regular customer on the old rifle range at Troutbeck, when upon beginning to lift one of my special hair trigger traps; I observed something light coloured in the trap as I was pulling it clear of the ground. At first I thought I had caught a stoat, which was quite a regular occurrence, but as I got a better look at it I was astonished to see that it was a white mole. I could hardly believe it; I had no idea such a creature existed, let alone that I would be lucky enough to catch one! I put the animal in my pocket, finished checking my traps and raced back to the farm in a state of high excitement to show my employer what I had caught. The farmer's wife was just as astonished at the sight of the white mole as I had been. I asked her if I could keep it with the idea of getting it stuffed and she said that I could, so I took it home and put it in the deep freeze, along with a normal black coated mole that I had also caught that day. I would keep the animals in cold storage until I could find a taxidermist to stuff and mount them for me. I had asked around a few people I knew who had a good knowledge of animals and they all said that an albino mole was a very rare occurrence! Indeed, one of them said it would be a chance in a million! This all served to encourage me to go to the expense of the taxidermist, which I had been informed could be substantial!

I looked through the yellow pages and found a taxidermist operating out of Staveley, in the south of the county and I phoned him. The guy was extremely interested to hear that I had a white mole and was keen to take on the task of stuffing it, along with the normal mole I had. He said that if I agreed he would mount the moles on a bed of moss (because soil would be too messy), and surround them with a glass case. I agreed to this, giving him more or less carte blanche and within a few days he showed up at the farm to pick up the animals. He told me that the job would take a week or so and that the majority of the time would be taken up in building the glass display case.

A couple of weeks later the taxidermist phoned to say he had the stuffed moles ready for delivery and asked would it be okay if he brought them up to the farm later that day. I said that I would be about and that would be great. He arrived mid-afternoon and opened the back of his estate car, whereupon I saw the fruits of his labour. The glass case was bigger than I had expected, being forty-five centimetres (eighteen inches) long by thirty centimetres (twelve inches) wide by fifteen centimetres (six inches) high and stood on four legs. The frame, base and feet were made out of wood. Inside the case, the two moles were resting on their bed of moss, displayed facing each other as if about to fight! I was delighted with the whole presentation and thanked the taxidermist for his excellent work. Next came the difficult bit as he told me how much it had all cost. I swallowed hard as he told me it was a hundred and fifty-five pounds! However he had done a good job and I wrote him a cheque out. He went away satisfied and I carried the glass case carefully into the house.

As I am writing this now, I can look up and see the case containing the stuffed moles sitting on my chest of drawers. Many people have seen them over the years and marvelled at them! As it turned out, the white mole is not as rare as I had been led to believe because I have caught six more since that first one, some of which I gave away to the people I was working for and the others I buried. In recent years, I have begun using the nickname 'White Mole' and a lot of my friends know me by this title. I also sign off my mobile phone texts with the initials W.M. My pool playing friends and colleagues say that after they have been beaten by me they have been 'molinated'. This often causes me great amusement.

During the late summer and autumn of 1998 I went on many memorable hikes around the Lake District with members of my family and friends and nearly always accompanied by my faithful canine friend, Tina.

In late September, I accompanied my brother and sister to the travel agents in Penrith and having cleared it with the probation service (who gave me special dispensation to go), we booked a skiing holiday to Risoul in the French Alps. Also in the party would be my sister-in-law, Anne and my sister's partner, Allan. This meant, as the date for the holiday was the eighteenth of January 1999, that I only had about three months to save up for it, so I set about taking on as much work as I could manage in between my various appointments with my counsellors. There was quite a bit of pressure on me but I was able to cope.

In mid-October, upon a whim I decided to take off to Scotland on a Munro bagging trip on my own. I should not have done this but knowing the probation service would prevent me from going, I only told my parents what I intended doing. So leaving Tina at home, I headed for the Highlands and in particular, Shiel Bridge on the north west coast, just beneath the Five Sisters of Kintail, where I stayed in a B&B. On the morning of Saturday the seventeenth, I drove back up Glen Shiel on the A87 and parked at the Cluanie Inn. I donned my winter gear as, although it was a reasonable day, the snow was on the higher slopes. I set off, away from the inn and climbed out northwest up the shoulder of Sgurr An Fhuarail over grass and heather. At about five hundred and seventy-nine metres (one thousand nine hundred feet) I hit the snow line and the going became more difficult. The snow quickly deepened and became crusted over with a layer of ice. I had no crampons or ice axe and became afraid. The ground sloped away steeply beneath me and I knew that one slip could send me skittering into the corrie below! I forged on bravely though, kicking steps into the crust as I went and reached the summit of the aforementioned mountain at nine hundred and eighty-six metres (three thousand two hundred and thirty-eight feet). I ate the packed lunch I had prepared back at home in a sheltered place just off the top. I didn't dally long, however, as you soon lose body heat on the lunch stop. The weather worsened as I continued on to the summit of the Munro of Aonach Meadhoin at one thousand and one metres (three thousand two hundred and eighty-four feet). It was a fairly straightforward task to get to this top but it had begun to snow and the wind was also getting up. By the time I started to descend, I was in a blizzard. Visibility was poor until I dropped below the snowline but as I did so, the weather rapidly improved with even a little watery afternoon sun breaking through. I made my way down off the hill and in doing so encountered a herd of red deer. There were stags with the herd and the mountainside echoed with their roars, this being the rutting season. The herd moved off as I approached and shortly afterwards I saw a golden eagle soaring overhead. The sight of these creatures filled my heart with song and I struck into the Eagles number, *Take It To The Limit*. I made my way back down to the A87 and walked back alongside the road to the Cluanie Inn and my car. I went into the inn after I had got my walking gear off and enquired if they had a room for the night and they did, it was a cancellation so I got it cheap!

There is nowhere else for miles around so I had dinner in the inn and then spent an hour in the bar, eavesdropping on the conversation of a group of walkers who had done the south Cluanie ridge that day. While I made do with my alcohol free beer, I listened as the group described how there were seven Munros on the ridge! The ridge forms the south side of Glen Shiel and is the opposite side of the valley from where I had walked that day. I thought that one day I would like to come back and try that walk, maybe with my brother. Having heard my fill, I turned in early.

I returned home the next day via Spean Bridge, across to Dalwhinnie and Pitlochry on the A9, where I took a look at the fish ladder on the River Tay. The ladder has glass sides in the chambers so that you can watch the salmon swimming through and I saw several large fish pass as I watched, this being the main salmon run season. That evening I went to my brother's house at Culgaith for supper and I received a telling off for going up to Scotland, not necessarily because I had gone without the probation service's permission but more because I had gone walking on my own, this being against Angus's view of safe procedure!

The following weeks were filled with work and appointments, one of which involved going through to a clinic at Carlisle for an E.E.G. test to examine my brain. This involves having a strobe light strapped to your face and flashing light blasted into your eyes for a period of about a minute. This is a very disconcerting experience and it left me with blotches on my vision for a short while following. The clinician told me that the equipment showed that I had an abnormality in the right side of my brain and that I may have a form of epilepsy. I was quite sceptical about this revelation because I thought that this would mean that I had epileptic fits and I had never before or since had such an experience! Anyway, for a while nothing more came of this and I continued to live my life medication free.

During December I went to the dry ski slope at Kendal for some practice sessions to limber up for the forthcoming holiday and on the afternoon of Sunday the thirteenth I was just setting off from home on one of these trips. I drove up to Troutbeck and I was just passing the old sheep loading area of the old auction market when I noticed a grey Rover saloon parked. As I turned out onto the A66, the vehicle followed me. I was running a bit late and I pushed the Capri hard as I drove through to Penrith. The grey Rover soon disappeared in my wake as I made my way towards town. I had just passed through the M6 motorway roundabout at Skirsgill and was accelerating towards the A6 roundabout at Kemplay when I noticed in the rear view mirror a police motorcycle coming up fast behind me with the blue lights flashing! I slowed down and pulled over into a layby and the copper pulled in, in front of me. As he did so, the grey Rover I had seen earlier pulled in behind me and two men in suits got out and approached my car. The police motorcyclist parked his machine and also approached the Capri. I rolled down the side window and one of the suited guys asked me to come with him. The guy was obviously a copper in plain clothes so I did as I was asked. I got into the back seat of the Rover and the two plain coppers got in the front while the motorcyclist started going through the contents of my car! I was subjected to a barrage of questions about my whereabouts on a given day and I was told that a man answering my description, e.g. with a moustache, had robbed two shops in Penrith a couple of days earlier and that this was just a routine enquiry. I was somewhat outraged that I had been thought of as being a thief but having answered their questions truthfully; they decided that they could not feel my collar for the crimes and they let me go.

As I returned to my car, the police motorcyclist said, "I have been looking at your music C.D.s, mate – you have a good taste!"

I smiled and said, "Thanks mate," and then got into the Capri to continue my journey. How the police knew that I was making that journey that day and following that route I will never know, but they must have been acting on a tip-off!

During the weeks following this incident I went to work on the deer farm near Penruddock, where I encountered red deer which had been partly domesticated. There were also fallow deer and the rare Père David's deer on the farm. Some of the animals grazed the surrounding fields but a lot were kept inside in big sheds, where they were fed on silage and concentrates. It was quite a stressful experience, getting used to handling unfamiliar machinery and new feeding systems. The animals were very skittish and great care had to be taken when entering or leaving a shed, because they were ever watchful for an escape avenue. It could also be quite dangerous, particularly with the red deer stags who although de-antlered, could rush at you when your back was turned and give you a nasty poke with their stumps!

I got used to the new ways of operating though and became a trusted employee, to such an extent that I was left in charge of the farm while the owners went skiing (although under partial supervision by the farmer's father-in-law). I travelled the few miles from our farm every day during my period in charge of the deer farm. In the mornings and evenings, I would feed and see to the deers' needs and in between, I would trap the moles on the surrounding fields.

One day, however, everything went a bit pear shaped, because one of the Père David's became very ill. There were only five of these rare beasts and they were kept outside in a field down by the river. The animals had huge antlers which were covered in velvet and the beast that was suffering, which was the size of a cow, had gone down off its feet and got its antlers stuck in the ground! I was able to free the antlers from the cloying earth (the winter weather was wet and cold at the time), but there was obviously something more serious wrong with the animal. Now I, being a worrier anyway, quickly got myself into a bit of a state over what to do! I resolved to bring some bales of straw from the buildings to prop the animal up and also to spread some straw round it to try to keep it warm. I then reluctantly phoned the owners up in Italy to tell them what had happened and to seek advice as the father-in-law had no more idea what to do than I had. Over the phone the owners told me that the Père David's had a tendency to up and die! They did not advise bringing the vet in but rather to just try and do the best I could, and that was it! The beast lived for a couple of days but it would not eat and it finally expired. I was able to bring its carcase out of the field, away from the other animals in the carrying box on the back of the tractor with the help of the father-in-law. It was a distressing ordeal, which was followed shortly afterwards by two bad experiences with the farm machinery, leading to my stress levels being raised and I was advised by my counsellors to quit the deer farm before I suffered another episode! I did however manage to see out my overseeing period while the owners were away on holiday.

It was about this time that I joined a dating agency after much prompting from my social worker. The agency was based in Carlisle and the joining fee was fifty pounds, for which you received portfolios of prospective partners based upon matches with details supplied about yourself. It was then up to you to make contact with the said people to arrange meetings. I attended a sort of screening meeting at Carlisle, but I did not tell the lady interviewing me that I had experienced mental health problems and this would eventually come back to haunt me!

Having got the details of several women, I embarked upon a series of blind dates. I met the ladies, who were of varying age groups, at a variety of different locations (one of which was a car park in Penrith). The dates went fairly well on the whole but all of the women, to be honest, were a little boring and there was certainly no spark or chemistry there!

On New Year's Eve, I drove Andrew and a couple of my other male friends out to the Herdwick Inn at Penruddock, where we had a nice meal and then went on to sample the nightlife in Penrith. I was of course still off the drink and did not mind driving. Andrew lived at Keswick but he was staying over that night at ours. We did the usual round of pubs and then finished off the night in Toppers Nightclub, where I got dancing next to a couple of luscious girls, but that was as far as it went and I came away empty handed as usual. My friends had got quite a skinful and it was a merry ride home! We had seen the New Year in with fine style.

The first few weeks of 1999 leading up to the ski holiday on the seventeenth of January sped by, during which I had a meeting with my alcohol counsellor, where after a bit of prompting on my part it was decided that I could have some alcohol on the forthcoming holiday, providing that I didn't overdo it!

Sunday the seventeenth arrived. Heather picked me up late morning and then we went on and picked her partner, Allan, up at Threlkeld and then went on to meet Angus and Anne at Penrith before we drove on in two cars to Newcastle Airport. The flight to Grenoble was good and also the coach transfer to the French ski resort of Risoul, though a little long. It was ten fifteen p.m. when we were dropped off outside our apartment building and it was snowing. There was no holiday rep to meet us and any staff that were on duty seemed reluctant to check us in. After a hasty phone call to the holiday company office, a bleary eyed rep turned up and she was able to check us in and get the staff of the bar on the ground floor to rustle us up some food and also some beer, which I guzzled with great relish, being the first drinks I had enjoyed in over six months! Things had improved after a shaky start and after being shown into our two apartments, we unpacked and went to bed in better form.

I shared one apartment with Heather and Allan, while Angus and Anne occupied the other.

During the following days Angus, Anne and Allan had ski school in the mornings while Heather and I explored the ski area, which extended over a ridge to the neighbouring resort of Vars. In the afternoons we all skied together. There was not much snow but the weather was great. The pistes were good but on one red run, there were rocks showing through the thin snow cover and I severely damaged the edge of one of my skis and was forced to get them repaired, during which time I hired a pair of the latest skis and liking them so much I bought a new pair of the same type when I got back to the ski shop. The technician there told me that my old skis would only be reliable from then on to use on very good pistes; this information forced my hand in making the decision to buy the new pair.

We did our shopping for the apartment meals at the nearby supermarket, making our breakfasts and evening meals and eating out on the slopes at lunch time. We bought wine to drink with our evening meals and I consumed three glasses of red on the first evening, followed by a few beers later. This was probably too much and by mid-week I was feeling the effects of my over indulgence, leading to the re-emergence of some of my old symptoms. I became a bit aggressive and a certain amount of paranoia showed its face, particularly on the evening of Thursday the twenty-first, when I forgot to pick up my ski gloves in the ski room of our apartment building and on returning to the room, found that someone had taken them! For some reason I thought Heather had picked them up and I needlessly blamed her, after which there was a bit of a row! They were a brand new pair of good quality gloves but I never saw them again. Luckily I had a pair of thinner walking gloves with me, and these I used to see out the holiday.

There were several very memorable events during the week, the first of which were Allan's number of attempts to board an extremely vicious ski lift! It was a drag lift of the long aluminium pole type, the pole having a telescopic section, which gave you a couple of seconds after taking the pole from the loading rack to put the button on the end of the pole between your legs before take-off, and what a take-off it was! When the pole engaged, Allan was launched into the air, spun through 180 degrees and dumped in a heap. This happened about half a dozen times before Allan gave up on this beast and retired to an easier lift. It must have been hellish embarrassing and annoying for him, but it was amusing for the rest of us!

We went sledging one evening, on plastic bags on the slope outside the apartment building and on another evening Anne and I went Ski-Dooing, with me in the driving seat. We had a kind of race around the lower slopes with several other machines and it was great fun.

The wobbles in my mood seemed to come under control even though I continued to drink, but there was one final experience of the holiday to come that would test me to the limit!

Saturday the twenty-third was the last day's skiing of the holiday before we returned home but a couple of days earlier, I had made arrangements to spend some of this day on an activity that I had never engaged in before; I had booked and paid for a parapenting flight with an instructor. So on the morning of this day I met the said instructor at the bottom of the main ski lift. He had on the biggest rucksack I had ever seen, which I assumed contained the parachute. We went up the lift with our skis on and the large sack on the chair between us. I had my sticks with me but the instructor (whose name I forget) left his at the bottom. At the top of the lift, which was the highest point around, we skied across to the top of a steep slope where we took our skis off. The instructor sidestepped down the slope some distance and found a place where he could build a small level platform in the snow. He then beckoned me down to him and we set about unpacking the rucksack, taking out the parachute and spreading it out on the slope above the platform, then we carried our skis down and set them out on the platform. We then got into the harnesses attached to the parachute strings, clipped our skis back on and then, standing together with me in front, the instructor said in his good English, "When I say go, we slide over the edge of the platform and go straight ahead. The parachute will fill with air and we will soon be airborne."

I said, "Okay."

He gave the command and we were off. As we left the platform, we picked up speed quickly on the steep slope and I felt a jerk from behind as the parachute inflated. Suddenly we began to veer to the left and the instructor cried out, "There is a problem. STOP!"

Somehow we managed to put our skis into a parallel stop to the left and came to a halt. I looked behind in time to see the parachute sinking to the ground with a strange twist in it. Some of the lines had obviously got tangled, causing the parachute to fail to inflate properly. The instructor was not amused and said something in French, which I took to be a curse, he was also somewhat embarrassed and apologised, whereupon we took off our gear and with the guy saying, "We try again," we bundled up the parachute and carried it back up to the starting point with the rest of the stuff. Strangely, I was not unnerved by this aborted take-off; rather I was even more excited by it. We got everything ready again and set off once more. This time after about fifty metres of hair-raising plunge down the slope the parachute inflated correctly and it pulled us clear of the ground. We floated out over the valley in the clear crisp air. It was a wonderful feeling as we looked down to the ant-like skiers on the slopes below. We flew straight and level for a distance of perhaps a couple of miles. I looked up at the large red canopy of the 'chute above us and then down at our skis dangling beneath and thought it was a great feeling to be free of the earth.

I shouted back to the instructor, "Where do we land?" He pointed straight down. I was slightly confused by this signal, thinking, we must be two thousand feet (six hundred and ten metres) up, how do we lose height so quickly? Then I received the answer. The guy said, "Are you ready?"

I thought, *for what?* And said, "Yes, I suppose so."

Suddenly the guy pulled sharply down on the left hand parachute straps and we veered around to the left, into a tight circular flight that quickly became a 'death spiral'. We were flung out, round like a pendulum, losing height quickly and I experienced an incredible rush of adrenalin, I had never felt anything like it before (or since) and I was euphoric! As we approached the ground, the instructor pulled on the right hand straps and we came out of our plunge, to float once more levelly above a straight, nearly flat stretch of ski piste. After a bit more tweaking and fine manoeuvring, we came in to land in an uphill direction with our skis pointing straight ahead. Any skiers there were on the slope in our path scattered and we touched down gently on the snow and slid to a halt. The instructor told me I would have to go back up the lift and get my sticks, so I shook his hand and thanked him for a great flight (which had cost eighty pounds, but it had been worth it) and then we parted company. I had about half a mile to ski to get back to the bottom of the main ski lift and I had never skied without sticks before, but I was buzzing and felt completely invincible! I set off and soon became used to the strange sensation of being without the sticks, quickly making it down to the lift, where I went up it and retrieved my sticks.

I did a few runs and then felt the overwhelming desire to celebrate with a drink, so I skied back to Risoul, entered the nearest bar and ordered a massive stein of beer. Now, these glasses hold two litres but I quickly slurped that one and ordered another! This was all on an empty stomach and I quickly became pissed! I staggered back to our apartment building, almost knocking a few people over with my skis and arrived just as the other members of our party got back from their day's skiing. I gibbered and jabbered to them about my experience and they looked at me as though I was insane and then became worried that I was entering another episode. They set about trying to pump some black coffee into me to sober me up and generally trying to calm me down. Eventually they succeeded but it was a worrying time, even for me, who realised that I was teetering on the edge of the abyss!

That was the highest feeling I have ever experienced and if it happened now, when in my middle age, I would probably have a heart attack!

The others got me to bed eventually, where I slept fitfully under the influence of the alcohol and coffee.

The next day I awoke feeling groggy but managed to get myself sorted out and packed up ready for the journey home.

We returned home from the crisp clear skies of the French Alps to the pissing wet of an English winter and life once more returned to its usual routines. I was feeling all right again but upon attending a meeting with my social worker, John, and my probation officer in the days following the holiday I received a bollocking for starting to drink again. Apparently the alcohol counsellor had not told the other members of the team that he had given his permission for me to drink on the holiday!

During the following weeks I began to work on several contracts for the national park with Thomas, with whom I had worked on the big Swart Beck job at Glenridding. I have got Angus to thank for getting us this work and the jobs were priced, resulting in their being the best paid I have ever done! The jobs involved repairing and rebuilding the collapsed walls of old buildings and lime kilns around the Caldbeck and Ireby areas, using local stone and traditional lime mortar. Thomas is one of the nicest people I have ever met and he is by far the best and most knowledgeable workmate I have ever had! The work was interesting and rewarding and I enjoyed this period immensely.

In late March, I managed to get permission from my counsellors to take a trip to Aviemore in Scotland on my own and I enjoyed a couple of days skiing on the slopes there. I skied the well-known piste called the White Lady, which runs down next to the main chairlift. My final night's hotel accommodation in the town proved to be a bad choice, when I was given a room above the bar and the noise was horrendous. Even though I had quite a bit to drink myself, it was a long time before I got to sleep and even then I slept poorly. I returned home and set about earning money for my forthcoming Swiss summer holiday. I had to endure the usual round of meetings with the professionals and in one of them, the psychiatrist tried to get me to start on medication but I refused, being worried about what the side effects would do to me!

In early April, lambing started on our farm and much of my time was taken up with that. I had given up my membership of the golf club, having not played for some time.

In May, I bought a Honda 300cc quad bike and a sheep trailer from Lloyds in Carlisle. I had tried to get dad to buy one for the farm many times but he had refused, so I had used my money, earned from my national park contracts, to buy the machinery for my own contracting use and also to use on the farm. I also bought a trailer that was big enough to carry the quad bike and tow behind the Capri, from a firm in Newton Reigny. Just after this Andrew, Heather and I went on a hike around the Langdale Pikes and early on in the walk, before we had left the valley floor, I spotted a lone Herdwick ewe on its back next to the river and I ran across to see if I could help it. When I got to the animal, I found that it was trying to push its lamb out, which was coming with a leg back, so I restrained the ewe with one hand, pushed the lamb back in with the other hand, brought the offending leg forward and then pulled the lamb out. Andrew and Heather must have thought I had taken leave of my senses when I ran across to the sheep but I had no doubt I had done the right thing, because it could have been hours before the farmer had found the ewe and the crows would have found it before then! It was my good deed for the day!

It was a good day out on the fells, in which we climbed the notorious Jack's Rake – a narrow ledge scramble up the front of Pavey Ark. When we got back to the Dungeon Gill Hotel, we enjoyed a well-earned pint in the bar.

On the fourteenth and fifteenth of the month, I did a job for the national park that will live long in my memory! Early in the morning I met a group of national park workers at their depot at Threlkeld and we travelled to Swirls car park, just off the A591 near Thirlmere, where we awaited the arrival of a flight of army helicopters. Two of the machines (whose type I forget) arrived from the north at nine a.m. and landed in a cloud of flying grass on a level area at the side of the car park, drawing a crowd of onlookers! As the rotors of the machines came to a standstill, our group of workers were loaded into the passenger sections, along with our lunch bags. The helicopters started up again and we took off to fly up onto the shoulder of Helvellyn, where the machines descended and hovered just above the ground next to the main footpath and we jumped out with our kit. It was an exciting experience but not the first time I had flown in a helicopter, having flown in one between the French ski resorts of Les

Deux Alpes and Alpe Duez in the winter holiday of 1995. The two helicopters flew off to join two more at the base of Goat Crag, north of the Thirlmere dam. Here, another group of park workers loaded large rope nets with a sheet of terram fabric in the centre, with large rocks from a scree slope. The loaded nets were then hooked onto the carrying attachments of the hovering helicopters and flown across the valleys to our position on Helvellyn. When each machine arrived, it lowered its load of rocks, (about two hundred and fifty kilograms) to the ground, where it was unhooked and then when the helicopter left, it was our job to run in each time and roll the rocks out of the net into a position alongside the footpath. The empty nets were then bundled up and every so often a helicopter would take a load of empties back to the loading site.

It was a great job and exciting, too, especially when one rock escaped the net as it neared the ground and went bouncing off down the fellside!

Obviously any walkers that were on the footpath had to be kept away from the unloading site. The weather was fine and dry and each day culminated in us being flown back down to the car park, where we arrived under the envious gaze of the inevitable crowd of onlookers.

At the end of the second day's work all of us, including the pilots of the helicopters, agreed to celebrate the completion of the job with a night out in Keswick. Heather joined us and we spent much of the evening in the Golden Lion pub, breaking off briefly for a trip across the street, to see a couple who Heather knew performing musically in the Oddfellows Arms, where the guitarist of the couple performed his excellent rendition of the Dire Straits hit, *Brothers In Arms*. It was a great night and I got a shed load of drink down me! There were no ill effects from this session and in the period following this job, I helped on another national park contract, restoring an old lime kiln at Caldbeck and also doing my regular mole trapping, plus working on the farm. I was a very busy person in those days!

Over the previous winter I had got to know a whole new bunch of people who have become good friends. This started when Ken (my friend who farmed across the valley) asked me if I would like to play eight ball pool for the Mill Inn at Mungrisdale in the Castle Sowerby League, so I went along one Tuesday night in late 1998 for a try out in a home match against a team from the village of Welton. Our team, The Mill Inn 'A', had been struggling for a few weeks to get enough players and I filled in a gap. It had been several years since I had played competitively, having fallen out with my previous team's captain at the Troutbeck Hotel!

There was myself, Ken, Bob, Nick, Stan, the two Rogers and another Steve in the team but not all were available to play each week. We needed six to make up a team and we played six single frames and three doubles frames in the match. This particular match was won eight-four by our team (one point for a single and two for a double). I had played pretty well, though a little rusty at first, but the main thing was that the crack was excellent. I immediately hit it off with Bob, who is a keen fell walker and also got to know our captain, Roger Bucknall, who owns Fylde Guitars in Penrith and also used to make pool/snooker cues for the top players, as well as his high quality musical instruments. He has also made cues for some of our team, but not me as I had owned one I had bought in a sports shop in Penrith many years earlier. After the match, Roger B pointed out to me that he had watched me play a shot in my single which had required backspin or 'screw' and I had failed to apply it. He was amazed when I told him I didn't know how to play this shot, in spite of all my previous years of experience! So he set about showing me the shot on the table and from then on my positional play improved markedly!

I drove to the match on this particular night but over the season, Ken and Bob shared the driving with me, coming to pick me up at the farm when it was their turn. This meant that I was able to have some good nights out on the drink, even being able to play well under the influence.

There were some quite long journeys to some of the matches, particularly to the Red Dial pub on the Cockermouth to Carlisle road, which was a twenty mile round trip. The Red Dial had a very good team and we had some great matches against them. I often played late on in the order of play, meaning that I often had to produce the goods at an important moment, leading to my trade mark 'fist pump' after potting the deciding black ball. Other teams picked up on this and their players would also indulge in fist pumps to take the piss out of me if they beat me! Over the winter my quality of play became higher and higher and I overheard the other Steve in our team (Steve Butcher – a Londoner by birth) say during one match, "I will put my house on Steve Titt potting this black," which I then went on and did, resulting in the quotation becoming a catch phrase! The pool season finished in April, with our team finishing high up in the first of the two divisions and there was no summer league, but my social circle had increased and the emphasis of it had moved from golf onto pool.

Coming back to May 1999, I went on a hike on the thirtieth with Heather, Ken, Andrew and his girlfriend Tracy, up Great Gable from Wasdale. The plan was for Heather, Ken and me to travel around to

Wasdale in my car and meet Andrew and Tracy there; this was so that I could do a bit of mole trapping at a farm near the Ravenglass Estuary on the way. I was almost finished the job, but just needed to set another half dozen traps in the last field to see the contract out and, the job being a hundred mile round trip from home, I thought I could save on a trip by setting the last traps on the hike day. So this is what I did and setting the traps was not a long job, meaning we were able to make it to the rendezvous at Wasdale Head more or less on time. Having met up we donned our gear and set off for Great Gable in fine dry conditions, we took the path across the southern-facing shoulder of Gable on the route to Styhead Tarn and when we were about halfway around the flank of the mountain I said to the others, "Who fancies taking a look at Napes Needle?" Heather and Ken voiced their interest in the idea but Andrew and Tracy said they would rather head on for the tarn and take the easier main path on, up to the summit of Gable. So agreeing on trying to meet up at the summit, we separated at a place where a faint climber's path struck off left from the main path, steeply upwards towards the crags where I knew Napes Needle lay hidden against the towering shoulder of Gable. The three of us were soon panting as we ascended this challenging route but we were all pretty fit and were soon scrambling up into the base of the crags.

Heather said to me, "Where is the Needle?"

Now, I had been here before so with certain knowledge I replied, "It's up there, about a hundred feet above and to the left!" She looked but couldn't see it, which was not surprising because Napes Needle is well camouflaged against the rock face behind and only reveals its secret location when you get in close. The Needle is a narrow pinnacle of granite about eighteen metres (sixty feet) high, separated from the main rock face by a narrow cleft and is a famous magnet for rock climbers and photographers.

We climbed on up the rough path and suddenly Ken cried out, "I see it!" We all looked up to see the Needle almost magically appearing like a giant fang from the background rock face! We fought our way up to the base of the tower of rock and stopped for a drink and a rest. Now I had no intention of trying to climb the Needle, for this is a serious undertaking and only the domain of experienced rock climbers, but there is a scramble up into the cleft behind the fang and this is called 'threading the Needle!'

After we were rested, I broached the subject of threading the Needle and the other two expressed their desire to give it a try, so we started up the scramble to the right side of the Needle. The route quickly narrowed and steepened as we entered a crack which was only just wide enough to admit us and our rucksacks. There were plenty of good holds though and we were soon struggling up into the narrow cleft between the Needle and the rock face.

Here we rested a while before making the more difficult descent down the other side, to the base of the pinnacle. From here, we struck off up to the right, scrambling up steep rock and up a gully to emerge on a more level rock-strewn area which led on up to the summit of Great Gable at eight hundred and ninety-nine metres (two thousand nine hundred and forty-nine feet). There is a plaque at the summit which commemorates the local war dead and we visited this. There was no sign of Andrew and Tracy so we waited around for a bit, but with none of us having a mobile phone at that time there was no way to contact them, so after about ten minutes we set off down the western flank of the mountain, down a well-used route, soon coming across the other two of our group sitting on a rock. We joined up and made the return to Wasdale Head, sharing stories of our climbs as we went. We had a nice pint in the hotel at the end of our walk and then returned home to end another memorable hike.

It was not long before I was walking again, though, having already planned another trip to Scotland with Angus and Anne with a view to getting myself as fit as possible for the forthcoming Swiss trip. So on Friday the fourth of June we set off in two cars and taking the tents, headed for the campsite at Glencoe once more, arriving there at four p.m. after a lunch stop at Stirling Services on the way. We pitched the two tents with the midges biting savagely, managing to pick a drier period on an otherwise showery day. We cooked our suppers, had a few beers and midges and weather allowing, had a bit of a crack about the hike on the next day. Now, Angus is brilliant at organising these trips and he has all the relevant routes planned and printed off from his Munro books, so all Anne and I have to do is sweat it out on the mountain and follow him! We turned in early to try and get enough rest for the expected exertions of the morrow.

I had experienced little difficulty in getting the okay for the trip from my counsellors. It helped that John, the social worker, held Angus in high regard!

On Saturday morning, we awoke, after a reasonable sleep on my part, although I had to put earplugs in due to the noise from neighbouring tents. The weather was still showery and the midges were worse than ever, forcing us to eat our breakfasts inside our tents. The previous evening we had gone over Angus's plan to climb the Munros on Buachaille Etive Mor and Buachaille Etive Beag on the south side of Glencoe, so now on the appointed day we prepared our walking gear, loaded my car with it and then set off up the A82 to the same place where we had parked to do the Aonach Eagach the previous year.

Having parked, we donned our wet weather gear and rucksacks, crossed the River Coupall and struck off up the northern prow of Buachaille Etive Mor. There was intermittent light rain but it was reasonably warm and the visibility was quite good, with only patchy mist. We made good progress up a wide stony gully to make the summit of the first Munro of the day; Stob Dearg at one thousand and twenty-two metres (three thousand three hundred and fifty-three feet) in quick time. Then we traversed the long spine ridge of Buachaille Etive Mor to arrive on the second Munro of Stob Na Broige at nine hundred and fifty-six metres (three thousand one hundred and fifty-seven feet), where we had lunch.

Just after as we set off walking again with the mist down, two ghostly figures appeared out of the gloom. They materialised into two young sheep. One was obviously a ram, having a fine spread of horn and the other a gimmer shearling, perhaps his sister. They regarded us haughtily and they were the only sheep we saw all day and were of the Scottish Blackface breed. They appeared to have several years' fleece growth on them so had obviously not been shepherded for some considerable time! Angus led the way as we descended steep grassy slopes on a faint path to the col at Allt Gartain. We had dropped almost four hundred and fifty-seven metres (one thousand five hundred feet) and we looked up the other side of the col with dismay, knowing we had to go back up the same distance to summit the next Munro. For a few moments we considered baling out down the long valley floor to our north and back to the car, but we girded our loins and attacked the steep slopes of Buachaille Etive Beag.

It was an exhausting ascent but we made it eventually, with a few rest stops, out onto the summit of our third Munro; Stob Dubh at nine hundred and fifty-seven metres (three thousand one hundred and forty-three feet). We then traversed the spine of the mountain back in a north easterly direction to the fourth and final Munro of our hike; Stob Coire Raineach at nine hundred and twenty-four metres (three thousand and thirty-four feet) and then we descended into the valley off the north east shoulder of the mountain, making it back to the car at five forty-five p.m. and in a relatively dry state. The hike had taken nine and a half hours and it had been a hard day! I drove us to the Clachaig Inn and we had a couple of well-earned pints before returning to the campsite, to shower and make supper amid the midges. We turned in early after a brief discussion about the itinerary for the following day.

I was up at five a.m. on Sunday the sixth and breakfasted long before Angus and Anne. Although a bit stiff from the day before, I was raring to go and my feet were not too sore either! The other two quickly caught up in their preparations and we were soon out on the road, on our way out to South Ballachulish on the entrance to Loch Leven. This time we went in Angus's Volkswagen Golf, leaving my Capri on the site. It was a very different kind of day to the previous one, with a cold northerly wind but much drier. My diary information about this day is a bit patchy, meaning I must have been more tired than I realised at the time but I know we did the two Munros to the south of Ballachulish; Sgorr Dhonuill at a thousand and one metres (three thousand two hundred and eighty-four feet) and Sgorr Dhearg at a thousand and twenty-four metres (three thousand three hundred and sixty feet).

We started off up forestry tracks, through a pine forest and then out up steep grassy slopes onto the first Munro. Contrary to the previous day, there were many more walkers out on the hill and feeling strangely energised; I felt an overwhelming desire to overtake everybody in sight to get to the top of our first objective. I left Angus and Anne some distance behind and they were not amused when they caught up with me, no doubt thinking I was behaving irresponsibly.

We continued on towards the second Munro with a bit of a cloud hanging over our group and also, the physical weather had worsened slightly, with the occasional wintry shower and a biting wind chill from the strong northerly air stream. We were making our way over the very light coloured stony ground towards the second top when suddenly Anne tripped and fell quite heavily. She got up again almost immediately but had skinned her knees slightly and was a bit shaken. She had a pronounced limp for a bit as we continued, but it slowly wore off and we were able to bag the second Munro and descend back to the car. From the summit of Sgorr Dhearg we had been able to get a good view northwards towards Ben Nevis and there was new snow on it!

After we had stowed our gear in the car, we drove down to a local hotel where we had our supper and a couple of beers. While we ate we discussed the events of the day, noting that we had walked about ten miles in roughly six and a half hours, which was pretty good going! The next day, Monday the seventh, was due to be the day we would return home and Angus asked me if I was going straight home. I ummed and ahhd for a bit and then announced that because there was only one Munro left in

Glencoe that I hadn't climbed, I would like to try and bag that one to finish off the trip! Angus said, "Don't you think you've done enough?" in a concerned fashion. I replied, "I think I still have enough left in the tank to do it!"

Anne spoke up then saying, "Oh, well, suit yourself then, but we won't be coming with you, my leg is still sore so we are going straight home!"

From the hotel we drove back to the campsite, had a few more beers and then turned in. I was more tired than I had admitted to the other two but I was determined to get out early the next morning and do the final top. I dropped off to sleep almost instantly!

I awoke early, feeling that I had not slept very well. It had been very cold in the night and I reminded myself that I needed to buy a new, warmer sleeping bag!

I ate my breakfast in the tent to avoid the pesky midges and then broke camp. Angus and Anne were up and about but were a bit grumpy so I quickly bade them goodbye, wished them a safe journey home, loaded my gear into the Capri and set off, firstly in the direction of Glencoe village to fuel up my motor and then back up the A82 to a place where the road turns a sharp left hand bend. Here there is a small car park. I pulled in to find that mine was the only vehicle there. I donned my gear, locked the car and then set off in the favourable conditions up the glen, following the Allt na Muidhe river. After a short walk I reached the farmhouse of Gleann Leac na Muidhe and I could see that the path continued up the floor of the glen near the river, but feeling bullish, I decided to tackle the steep prow of Aonach Dubh a' Ghlinne! It was good to be out on my own again on the hills, not having done so since the trip in the previous October. I set myself at the steep slope, moving quickly, but the exertions of the preceding days soon came to tell on me. My breathing became ragged and my legs began to burn. I flogged on doggedly though on the mainly grassy incline and soon reached the ridge, then continuing on over more level ground, I made my way to the minor top of Stob an Fhuarain at nine hundred and sixty-eight metres (three thousand one hundred and seventy-six feet). I then dropped down some hundred metres to a col and then climbed on up to the other side over rocky ground to emerge on the summit of the Munro; Sgor nah-Ulaidh at nine hundred and ninety-four metres (three thousand two hundred and sixty-one feet). Here I took what is now known as a 'selfie' with my camera, pointing down a gully with my face in the foreground. There was a passing light shower and the picture came out showing a rainbow in the background. Shame I can't find that photo to show the reader.

I sat down on my rucksack and ate my lunch, at the same time admiring the view northwards towards Ben Nevis. I was alone at the summit and in fact, it turned out that I never met another soul on that walk! Although I had been pushing myself pretty hard and was tired, my state of mind was good and there were no signs at this point of the re-emergence of my mental symptoms that would herald the beginning of another episode.

I finished my lunch as fast as I could, having become chilled in the cold conditions and then made my way off the western shoulder of the mountain, back down into the glen to strike the headwaters of the Allt na Muidhe river. From here I walked out down the glen, past the farm and back to my car. I have not made a note of the time taken or the distance walked in my diary but my Munro book shows it as thirteen kilometres (eight and a half miles) and seven hours. I was probably over this time because of the number of stops I made.

I stowed my gear in the car and then set off home up the A82. It was probably one of the most difficult return journeys from Scotland I have ever made due to my level of fatigue. It took four and a half hours to get back to Cumbria and I had to make regular stops for caffeine and toilet breaks. I made it back okay, though and felt a great sense of achievement.

You would have thought I would have needed a holiday to get over that trip but no, I was straight back into work the next day, plunging into four separate mole trapping contracts. One of these involved setting my traps in a field right by the side of the A591 at the King's Head Inn, Thirlspot. The field, which is called the King Meadow, had been put by for silage making and the grass was very long, making it difficult to work out where the mole runs were located and also their direction of travel. I managed to fight my way through the grass though and soon had the required number of traps set. Now, I always level out the molehills by kicking them over, mainly to show the customer that I have caught the moles by there being no new hills appearing; but also, if the hills remain standing the mower will cut into them and throw the soil into the cut grass when the field is cropped. This then ends up in the silage and can cause a nasty condition called Listeriosis, which affects the animals that eat the silage! However, in this case, there being so much grass and the mole hills being so big – approximately two feet (sixty centimetres) across – I had sought another solution. Having brought a couple of large plastic buckets, I set about clearing the hills off the field and dumping the soil behind the low wall next to the road. It was a fine hot day and I was soon stripped to the waist and sweating profusely. I had to make many trips with the heavy buckets and I had attracted the attention of the inn customers, who were sipping their cold drinks at the outside tables. They were only a few yards away, across the road, but I could see that there were no nubile young females I could show off my muscles to, so that was a bit disappointing! The work took a lot out of me, which was not good following so quickly in the wake of my mountain climbing trip, but I was more resilient in those days!

I continued with my trapping work for the rest of the week and then on the twelfth of June, having made plans a couple of weeks before, I set out on my next adventure, this time with Andrew. The plan was to walk the Ennerdale Horseshoe. It is more commonly done as a fell race but neither Andrew nor I are runners. We planned to do the walk over two days and take our camping gear, hopefully finding a place to pitch our tents out on one of the fells on the route.

I was up very early on the twelfth and spent quite a bit of time getting my rucksack packed. There was a lot of gear and the sack being only forty-five litres in capacity meant that I had to strap some of the camping equipment on the outside. I got managed though, even finding room for four cans of beer. The whole lot weighed nearly twenty kilograms (forty-four pounds) and was by some degree the heaviest load in a rucksack I had ever shouldered!

At the last minute I decided to take my dog, Tina, who seemed to sense an adventure was afoot, causing her to dance around the Capri as I loaded up. Of course, I had to take food and some water for her as well, which was an extra burden, but I didn't mind as I knew she would be good company.

Andrew had taken his car to a garage in Penrith for repairs and I had agreed to pick him up there with his gear before heading back and on round to Ennerdale. However, when I had got ready, with all my gear loaded plus Tina, and had travelled through to pick him up he told me that something had broken on his rucksack, meaning that he would have to buy a new one. Of course, this meant a lengthy delay as we travelled back to Keswick to visit an outdoor shop and buy a new sack. Now Andrew is a big bloke, standing six foot four inches tall and he chose a rucksack to suit his stature. It was a massive ninety-litre one and stood at almost a metre tall! Having made the purchase, we then had to transfer all his gear into the new sack and I noticed with delight that he had brought some beer too. Of course, his burden was even heavier than mine and we exchanged worried glances and words about whether we would be able to carry such weights over the horseshoe, which we knew to be over thirty-five and a half kilometres (twenty-two miles) in length and involved two thousand one hundred and thirty-three metres (seven thousand feet) of ascent! We agreed that the rucksacks would get lighter as we used up our supplies, so that eased our worries.

Finally we were off, but we had not gone far when we encountered an accident on the A66, in the dual carriageway section next to Bassenthwaite Lake. The road was blocked and the traffic was at a standstill. As we sat there, growing more impatient by the minute, the driver of a cattle wagon a few vehicles ahead of us got out of his cab and walked back along the line of traffic. I recognised him instantly as one of the farmers I had just been working for. I hailed him and he came over smiling and told us that a car had gone off the road a few hundred metres ahead, but that the emergency services had almost got it cleared up. We had a short crack and then he went back to his wagon.

Soon we were able to proceed and went on round to Ennerdale. It was around eleven a.m. by the time we had got parked at the end of Ennerdale Lake and got our gear ready to start the walk. The weather was dry, fine and warm as we started off along the forestry road on the northern side of the lake. Tina skipped along beside us as we went. I was relishing the opportunity to spend some quality time with my best mate, whom I had come to know when joining Keswick Golf Club in 1986 and we had grown close.

We left the road at High Gillerthwaite at a place where a well-worn path headed off up the fellside.

We had only gone a few yards when Andrew said, "Bugger this. I'm not carrying all my beer up there; I'm going to have some of it here to give myself a boost! Are you joining me?"

I replied, "Yeah, sure, you're right."

So we took our packs off, sat down and cracked open a couple of cans, much to the amusement and also the consternation of other passing walkers.

One woman said, "Goodness me, I thought you would be drinking at the end of your walk, not at the start!"

We finished our beers and then shouldered our packs before putting ourselves at the steep slope facing us. I was feeling a bit squiffy from the beer as we toiled up the lower slopes of Red Pike. We were soon blowing hard and feeling the full weight of our packs.

Andrew gasped out, "What the fuck are we doing?"

And I responded, "Hell's teeth, I don't know, but I hope there are some good-looking women up there to spur us on!"

Finally we reached the summit of Red Pike at seven hundred and fifty-five metres (two thousand four hundred and seventy-seven feet). We threw our packs off and sat down for a rest and a drink of water. In those days, I only had water bottles, which meant you either had to stop and take your pack off to get a drink, or you got your mate to get a water bottle out for you. This was a pain in the arse until the invention of the 'camel back' system of a plastic reservoir in your pack, with a gravity fed pipe round to where you can suck water out of it. I now have one of these and it has been one of the best purchases I have ever made.

The day was still fine and we were able to get good views out over Ennerdale Lake to the mountains at the other side, which formed the other half of the horseshoe.

It was a daunting sight and I said to Andrew, "Bloody hell, we have a long way to go!"

He agreed and then said, "The day is getting on a bit, where shall we have lunch?"

I replied, "How about when we have gone a bit further along towards High Crag?" He came back, "Yeah, that sounds good."

I looked towards the east and could see that the way we would go was up a bit to the summit of High Stile and then down a bit to High Crag.

By the way, there were no bonny women in sight to encourage us!

We set off once more, with Tina taking the lead. There was no need to leash her because she was aloof to the few Herdwick sheep out on the tops, although I knew that if I gave the command she would be off to round them up! It did not take long to get up to High Stile at eight hundred and six metres (two thousand six hundred and forty-four feet) as our pace had quickened due to the easier gradient. From here we carried on down slightly to High Crag at seven hundred and forty-four (two thousand four hundred and forty-one feet), where we ate our lunches.

After the break we continued over Seat Fell and then dropped down steeply on a pitched, paved path down Gamblin End to Scarth Gap, which is a large col where the path comes over from Buttermere to the Black Sail Youth Hostel in the top end of Ennerdale. Gamblin End is a steep drop of some maybe ninety-one metres (three hundred feet) and I was glad we were doing the horseshoe clockwise, therefore going down it. (At a later date I would do the horseshoe again, but in the opposite direction, which meant going up Gamblin End and it would prove a tortuous ascent!)

From Scarth Gap we climbed steeply on up to the multi-summitted top of Haystacks at five hundred and ninety-seven metres (one thousand nine hundred and fifty-eight feet). By now, the afternoon was wearing on and we started to look for a place to camp.

After walking on eastwards we came to Innominate Tarn where, upon getting to the east end of it, we found a grassy area just big enough to accommodate two tents. We made camp, got our stoves out and I prepared some beans for myself (not being much of a cook, these are one of my favourite foods). After our suppers we enjoyed the last of our beer supplies, drinking while perched on the rocks near our camp. Tina had eaten her supper of flaked maize mash and was sitting near us. Suddenly her attention peaked and a small family of Greylag geese came marching up the path, past our tents and then launched themselves onto the waters of the tarn. It was a charming sight.

By this time, it was coming in dusk and there was the odd midge biting, so we decided we should get into our tents.

Just then Andrew said, "Have you noticed that guy sitting on that rock at the top end of the tarn?"

I replied, "Oh yes, I see him. Do you think he is lost?"

Andrew retorted, "I guess he must be, I don't see a tent!"

We moved on down to our tents, got inside and I climbed into my sleeping bag.

I had not been long laid down when Andrew said from his tent in a low voice, "Do you think that guy is still there? What if he's an axe murderer and comes over in the night and kills us?"

I laughed and said, "Don't be daft, he's probably gone now."

I settled down again and tried to sleep but I could not. Andrew's comments had got me thinking, and so finally I got up, went outside and looked up towards the head of the tarn. Even though it was nearly dark I could see that the guy had gone, so I told Andrew, who it transpired was still awake also and then we both settled down again, feeling relieved. Tina came into my tent with me and after she spent a bit of time fussing about, I realised that she was cold so I opened my sleeping bag and she climbed in with me. It was a bit of a tight fit but we managed and she actually made a bit of a hot water bottle!

The following morning I awoke feeling a bit groggy, having not slept particularly well; Andrew was the same. We discussed the events of the previous evening over breakfast, in particular the strange, lonely figure that had been perched on the rock. Years later I learned that Haystacks had been the great fell walker, Alfred Wainwright's favourite mountain and that his ashes had been scattered around Innominate Tarn. This has led to my fanciful theory that the figure we saw on that evening was the ghost of Wainwright himself!

We broke camp and shouldered our rucksacks, which were a bit lighter now and then headed off eastwards to Blackbeck Tarn, where we filled our water bottles from the stream that fed the tarn. From here we struck out south-eastwards towards Green Gable. Tina gambolled along happily by our sides. We passed round the side of Green Gable and into the col known as Windy Gap, before climbing steeply over more rugged ground up to the summit of Great Gable at eight hundred and ninety-nine metres (two thousand nine hundred and forty-nine feet).

The day had started off quite fine, but by now the weather was closing in. It was cold at this altitude and we did not hang around long after we visited the war memorial plaque at the summit. We dropped down steeply north westwards on a zigzagging path to the col at Beckhead Tarn and then back up westwards, to the summit of Kirk Fell at eight hundred and two metres (two thousand six hundred and thirty-one feet), where we ate a bite of lunch just before it started to rain.

One and a half days' walking with heavy packs were beginning to tell on us and being as the weather looked set in, I broached the subject to Andrew of bailing out after the next fell, Pillar, and heading back down into Ennerdale, to the car. He agreed to my plan and after donning our wet weather gear, we strode off across the broad top of Kirk Fell north westwards and then dropped down steeply into the Black Sail Pass col. From here we climbed more gently westwards on a long incline to the summit of Pillar at eight hundred and ninety-two metres (two thousand nine hundred and twenty-six feet). The rain had become heavier and Tina was now looking miserable, so we made the final decision to bail out. It would mean that we would not complete the horseshoe but I'm sure none of the three of us minded at that point!

We dropped off the top of Pillar in a north westerly direction, down a long steepish path into Ennerdale, entering the conifer forest near the valley floor before making our way out on flat going to the forestry track that we had started the walk on.

Having got back to the car after eight hours' slog we quickly loaded our gear and then I drove us back to Andrew's house at Workington, where his girlfriend, Tracy, made us a nice meal. We were pretty tired after eating but I would not be able to rest long, because after the meal we all went outside and Andrew managed to somehow lock us out of the house, meaning that I had to drive us through to Silloth to get his spare house keys from his parents' house!

It was getting dark by the time I got us back to Workington with the spare set and I was keen to get home as Tina had been in the car a long time. I shook hands with my friends on their doorstep and we parted, declaring that it had been a good weekend and that we would have to do it again sometime. It was a tiring drive home and both Tina and I were glad when we pulled into the farmyard.

As before, it was straight back into work the next day and during the following week I pursued my usual working activities, which included doing a bit of house painting for my workmate Thomas, from the national park jobs. Since the Ennerdale trip, Andrew and I had discussed over the phone plans to climb Helvellyn for the summer solstice celebrations, so on the twenty-first of June I got an early start with my work, starting with cleaning out the muck spreader on our farm ready for its summer lay-off and then travelling to nearby Mungrisdale village to pick up a hired strimmer from a farm there that I had done work for. I then set about carrying out the first part of my contract for the parish council, to cut down the vegetation on the roadside verges through the village. I worked for seven hours in hot sticky conditions, which was exhausting and dehydrating due to having to wear protective clothing. Bits of grass, slugs and the occasional bit of dog shit flew up around my head from the whirling strimmer head and I was bitten by the midges disturbed from the foliage by my activities!

I finished the shift at five p.m. and drove to the petrol station at Motherby, where I had an account, and filled my gallon container with unleaded fuel. Then I went home and set about my preparations for my trip up Helvellyn. Now, I had only told Andrew that I would meet him on the summit of the mountain and had said nothing about how I intended to get there! Although tired from my day's work, I was energised and excited by the plan that I had formed on how to get to Helvellyn – I had decided to go on my quad bike! So having made plans to camp somewhere on the mountain that night, I loaded the carrying racks on the quad with camping gear, food, beer and the spare petrol I had bought, and then got Tina from her kennel and set off up the track to our top farm of Lobbs. Tina seemed excited about the prospect of another adventure so soon after the last one but she was nervous of the quad. I had tried to get her to ride on the machine with me several times but unlike most other farm dogs I had seen doing so, she refused outright to have anything to do with it! This was unfortunate because it would have saved her a lot of energy, particularly when I was shepherding!

Our farm lies about nine miles (fourteen and a half kilometres) due north of Helvellyn and we had grazing rights on Matterdale Common, which lies on my planned route, so I knew the lie of the land well, but I had only ventured out there once before on the quad.

From Lobbs I rode my machine south up the hundred acre (forty and a half hectares) enclosure of rough grazing owned by us, to the gate that opened onto the common. There were few obstacles and the going was good; also it was a fine evening. Tina ran alongside quite happily but I knew we had a long way to go and I had brought extra food for her too. Immediately beyond the common boundary there is a stream, which runs through a deep gully, making it impassable for quad bikes at that point. This forced me to have to ride east for about half a mile to a place where I could safely cross.

The land heading south from here is flat for about a mile and I was able to push on quite fast. Very quickly I reached the old coach road, which crosses the common from the Dockray area in the east to St John's in the vale to the west. This is no more than a gravel track with grass growing in the middle, but is quite heavily used by four-wheel drive vehicles.

Due south from the road lies the impressive Wolf Crags and I knew this was going to be one of the greatest obstacles on my journey! There is a possible route up the western end of the crags, though, where the steep rocky edifices give way to fairly steep grassy slopes.

I rode west along the coach road for roughly half a mile, before turning off it and riding up the lower slopes of the western end of the crags. I engaged my lowest gear as the ground before me steepened and then stood up on the footrests, leaning forward into the hill as I went. This was the steepest incline I had ever been up on the quad and my heart was in my mouth as I went up! There was a rocky outcrop near the top of the slope, which I had to negotiate my way round, but I made it and then there was only one small, less steep slope to overcome and then I was up it! Tina and I were panting hard – her with exertion and me with fear!

From the top of Wolf Crags the route was a gradual incline over grassy slopes, dotted with peat hags. I made good progress up the shoulder of Great Dodd, passing between the twin-nippled rocky outcrops of the Knotts. The final pitch to the summit of Great Dodd was steeper, but nothing compared to the end of Wolf Crags. I stopped at the top to give Tina a rest and to admire the view in all directions from eight hundred and fifty-six metres (two thousand eight hundred and eight feet). I have been up here many times on foot, mainly in times gone by to gather the sheep but more recently, hiking.

We set off again down the nice smooth grassy gradient, south west to Watson's Dodd at seven hundred and eighty-nine metres (two thousand five hundred and sixty-eight feet) and then east, back up to Stybarrow Dodd at eight hundred and forty-three metres (two thousand seven hundred and sixty-five feet). From here we headed down the now broad, smooth path, steeply to Sticks Pass at seven hundred and fifty metres (two thousand four hundred and sixty feet). Here my route was crossed by the big path coming up from the Thirlmere valley over to the Glenridding and Glencoyne valleys.

From this major crossroads we headed on south up to Raise at eight hundred and eighty-three metres (two thousand eight hundred and ninety-seven feet) and then on over White Side at twenty metres lower. As we approached the brooding bulk of Helvellyn, I began to think about somewhere to leave the quad and pitch my tent, as I knew the final pitch up the northern prow of my objective peak was too steep to allow passage for my machine. I stopped to take in my surroundings and give Tina another well-earned rest. To the south west I could see Browncove Crags and at the base of these was a level grassy area. The ground between this point and where I sat on my machine sloped down gradually and was largely rock free. I decided that the Browncove area looked like the ideal campsite and turned the quad down the slope to ride to my objective.

It must have been around eight p.m. as I avoided the last of a series of peat hags to reach my goal. I offloaded the quad on a flat grassy area and then rode it up into a concealed place between several large boulders, where I parked it and removed the keys.

All the way from the farm I had not met another soul and there was nobody about at my chosen campsite either, but I was taking no chances with the security of my valuable machine! Satisfied with my parking arrangements, I then pitched my tent and put all the other gear inside it. Being in the days before I had a mobile phone, there was no way of contacting Andrew to tell him where I had camped or of knowing whether he and Tracy, plus their friends, were even on the mountain at this point!

Having got the camp set up I shouldered my rucksack, which contained a few provisions for the last part of my journey to the top of Helvellyn. As I stood and looked up towards the summit area, I realised that I had lost quite a bit of height by descending to the base of Browncove Crags and I quailed slightly at the prospect of the steep, rock strewn ascent of roughly two hundred metres (six hundred and fifty-six feet) that faced me. Suddenly I became aware of how tired I was and I thought how good it would be to just creep into my tent and sleeping bag and forget about doing anything else! But I gave myself a talking to and set off up the steep slope, with Tina trotting happily beside me.

After about half an hour's stiff climbing, I emerged on the summit of Lower Man on the northern end of the Helvellyn massif at nine hundred and twenty-five metres (three thousand and thirty-four feet) and then made my way south to the main summit of Helvellyn at nine hundred and fifty metres (three thousand one hundred and sixteen feet), where to my amazement I found Andrew, Tracy and the others waiting for me! They had all come up from Swirls car park in Thirlmere and were in merry mood. (I think a bottle of some sort of alcoholic brew had already been passed round!) Andrew had on his large rucksack, containing his camping gear and Tracy had on a smaller sack with the other stuff they would need. The other members of the group informed me that they would not be joining Andrew, Tracy and me to spend the night out, rather saying that they would be descending again shortly! Up until that point the evening had been fine and we had seen the sun about to set in the west, but just then the mist rolled in, obscuring everything.

There were few other people about on the summit and I asked Andrew why he thought this was and he said, "That's because we have got the wrong bloody night, mate. We should have been up here last night!"

"Bollocks," I said and then continued, "Oh, well, we shall just have to make the most of it then, won't we?"

"Yes, absolutely, mate. I have brought plenty of booze and anyway, where's your tent?"

I then went on to tell them where I had made camp and Tracy said, "We will have to get moving, then, if we are going to get our tent pitched next to yours before darkness falls!"

I agreed but I was thirsty and announced that I was going to crack open the one can of beer I had brought up from camp. I did so and Andrew opened a bottle of wine and dug out a couple of glasses and the three of us drank a toast to our endeavours. The other members of the group were leaving, so we all shook hands and shortly Andrew, Tracy, Tina and I were the only ones left standing at the Trig point on the summit. The alcohol went straight to my head and I was feeling decidedly squiffy as we made our way back north to Lower Man in the by now chilly conditions. We dropped down out of the mist from Lower Man, retracing my earlier route in the failing light and got back to my campsite with only just enough daylight left to enable Andrew and Tracy to set up their tent.

When they had got organised, we ate a light supper and then got stuck into our booze supplies. As the alcohol flowed, the crack became very good indeed; it was not completely dark and although we had no torches, we were able to see each other as we perched on the rocks surrounding our campsite.

It must have been after midnight when we finally turned in, feeling quite pissed! Once again, Tina worked her way into my sleeping bag just before I went out like a light.

We were supposed to be up there to see the sun up on the solstice but of course we had got the wrong night and also, we overslept on the morning of the twenty-second. Plus there was the additional factor that just above us to the east was the bulk of the Helvellyn range, which would have hidden the rising sun from us anyway!

We emerged bleary-eyed from our tents around six a.m. and Tracy announced that she had hardly slept at all and had been very cold – they had packed the wrong sleeping bag for her! We all had a bit of a hangover and were all a bit grumpy with each other as we ate a cold breakfast and then broke camp.

It was a fine morning, which was fortunate considering our mood. Having got ready to depart, we shook hands and then the two of them said goodbye and headed off westwards, towards the lip of the Thirlmere valley. I had gathered up our empty booze containers and loaded them onto the quad, leaving the campsite looking as though nobody had been there, which is how it should be!

Tina was in fine fettle, being the only one not hung over and she rushed around merrily as I started the quad and then rode back out to the spine of the range. I retraced my route of the previous evening with one exception – from the summit of Great Dodd I descended north west down the other shoulder of the mountain, on grassy slopes to the Mosedale sheepfold and then out down the valley parallel with the Mosedale Beck to the old coach road, thereby avoiding the steep, perilous descent down the end of Wolf Crags!

I got back to the farm at nine a.m. and put Tina away in her kennel to get some much needed rest, but there would be no rest for me because I had to go and finish the strimming job in Mungrisdale! So I offloaded the quad, put it away, quickly ate another breakfast, got my work gear on and drove to the farm at Mungrisdale where I had left the strimmer.

I put in nine and a half hours' exhausting work in hot conditions, at one point throwing off my protective gear and sagging to my knees next to the village hall. I thought I was going down with heat exhaustion but I recovered to continue and finish the job at eight fifteen p.m. I took the strimmer back to the farm and got my pay off the farmer, who was chairman of the parish council. I was home by nine p.m. and I enjoyed my supper and a nice bath.

The following day – the twenty-third of June – I was up at seven thirty a.m. to get ready for one of my regular psychiatrist's appointments at nine thirty a.m. in Penrith. I was not in the best of moods as I sat in the waiting room of the hospital; I was tired from my recent activities and also, I found these appointments stressful and intimidating. I was particularly annoyed when an Indian psychiatrist called out my name and when I entered the consulting room he informed me that my usual psychiatrist was off sick. (I later found out that she had experienced a nervous breakdown!) I had never seen this chap before and although he was nice enough, he made me tell him everything that had happened to me and then went on to do his best to shoehorn me into taking medication! I held my own, though, countering his efforts by pointing out that I had a busy working and social life, and stating that I felt the medication would destroy these! I was in there about an hour before I was finally able to make my escape and go about my business. I paid the money from the strimming job into the bank and then returned home, where I flung myself into the start of haymaking on the farm.

During the following days the weather proved unsuitable to make hay and we had to get the contractors in to make the crop into big bale silage. Over this period I also did a spell of mole trapping at various locations along the length of Ullswater.

On the evening of the twenty-sixth of June, I telephoned one of my blind date candidates and after a promising conversation, I arranged to meet the lady on the following day at Southend Road Car Park, Penrith.

I enjoyed a lie-in on the morning of the twenty-seventh before helping Dad with a few small jobs on the farm. I had lunch and took a bath before setting off for Penrith in the Capri. I entered Southend Road Car Park shortly before the arranged meeting time of two thirty p.m. and looked out for the blue Ford Escort that the lady drove (we shall call the lady Jane). There weren't a large number of cars on the park and I soon spied Jane's vehicle. I parked near her, got out and approached the Escort. Jane saw me coming and got out of her car, I noticed, with some difficulty! She limped towards me, supported by a walking stick and said, "Are you Stephen?"

I replied, "Yes. You must be Jane?"

She nodded and then I asked her if she would like to go for a drive. She said that would be good because she found walking any distance difficult! I had been able to make a brief appraisal of Jane as we met and although she was a rather large lady, she was not unattractive. The information from the dating agency had informed me that Jane was twenty-six years old and I felt that this was not too much of an age gap from my thirty-eight years!

We got into my Capri and I drove us out of town to Ullswater, right up the length of the lake and then out over Kirkstone pass to drop down the Struggle (which is a very steep hill) to Ambleside. During the journey, conversation had flowed quite freely, with me finding Jane easy to talk to and really quite fun to be with! From Ambleside, I drove on out up Great Langdale and that is where disaster struck! I was just heading out steadily to the farthest point you can drive up the valley before the road bears sharp left to head over the pass into Little Langdale, when there was a loud twang from the engine compartment. I instinctively depressed the clutch pedal and it went straight to the floor with no resistance. I knew a moment of panic then and I realised what had happened – the clutch cable had snapped! I pulled on the gear lever but the car would not come out of gear. Jane, who realised something had broken, cried, "Oh, God, are we going to crash?"

I had no time to respond. Just ahead of us a farm track left the main road at the sharp left hand bend. Luckily the gate was open and I was able to drive through. My mind whirled as I sought an escape from our plight and of course it came to me quite simply and quickly – turn off the engine! So I turned the car off the track onto the level field at the side and switched off the ignition. We came to a standstill and I sat quietly for a short while, breathing a sigh of relief!

I turned to look at Jane and she was staring straight ahead, her face had drained of all colour!

I said, "Hell's teeth, that was a scary moment!"

Jane turned to look at me and just nodded. At that time I was not a member of a motoring organisation and I knew we were consequently in a spot of bother. I sat for a minute, thinking, and then I came to the conclusion that I would have to try to contact my mechanic in the village of Threlkeld. I had no mobile phone and even if I had had one there would probably have been no signal, given our location!

We were not far from the Dungeon Ghyll hotel and I said to Jane, "You stay put, I am going to try to find a pay phone."

The day was fine but I didn't seem to notice at the time, being preoccupied with our plight. I got out of the car and walked back to the main road and then on the quarter of a mile or so to the Dungeon Ghyll Hotel, where I quickly found a pay phone, got some change from the bar and made two calls, first to home to get my mechanic's number and then to the man himself. It being a Sunday, I was loath to trouble him but I had no choice. On the phone, I apologised for bothering him and went on to explain what had happened. I asked him if there was any possibility of him coming to sort out the problem, but he explained that the replacement of the broken cable would have to be carried out in the garage and that he had no trailer with which to recover my stranded vehicle. His advice was to get the car in second gear, with the engine off, and then start it in gear and drive it back to his garage without the clutch. He went on to tell me that I could change gear by varying the throttle and that it should not prove too much of a problem, apart from the fact that I wouldn't be able to stop unless I switched the engine off! I thought he was being a bit flippant and was maybe slightly amused about the whole episode. I was anything but amused, I had never driven any vehicle without a clutch before and I quailed at the prospect!

I rang off, telling the mechanic I would give it my best shot and then walked back to my car. I got in and explained to Jane what I was going to try to do. She seemed nervous about the whole idea but we had no choice but to try. I was able to get the gear lever into second with the engine off and then I turned the ignition key. The car lurched forward on the starter, fired and then started and we were off. I swung the Capri round on the grass and headed back onto the track and then onto the valley road. I knew the big Capri would do forty m.p.h. quite comfortably in second gear and I resolved to keep it in that gear, and not to try any fancy gear changing manoeuvres! We had a straight run back to Ambleside but I was very tense as I drove steadily down the narrow road. The first big test came as we entered the town. There was a 'give way' junction where our road joined the road coming from Coniston. I approached this with my heart in my mouth. I thought if I turned off the engine at the junction I might not be able to get it started again, so on reaching the stop line I looked to the right and the gods smiled on us; there was nothing coming and I was able to go straight out and on into the town. I knew the route through the town and on out towards Threlkeld on the A591 very well and I knew there were no more junctions until we had to turn right onto the B5322 at

Stybeck farm to head down St John's in the Vale, which meant an unhindered run of maybe eleven miles (seventeen and a half kilometres).

I negotiated my way through the town quite comfortably. Fortunately nobody ran out in front of us, thank God and we made our way out towards Grasmere. As we went, though, I became more and more worried and stressed. Suddenly I found myself talking about my past. At the time, I thought Jane would understand as I related the whole torrid tale about my numerous breakdowns; after all, she did have a disability, but I have learned over the years that there is a big difference between a physical disability and a mental one! At first, she had talked to me to encourage me in my driving efforts but also, to bolster her own confidence with the prospect of impending doom hanging over us! She must have thought she was not going to get home in one piece and that this was the worst date she had ever been on! As my tale unravelled, she became very quiet indeed and although I must have realised I was scaring her, I could not just seem to shut up! I drove on through Grasmere and up over Dunmail Raise, still gabbling away. The temperature gauge of the Capri rose as we climbed over the pass; the engine was revving quite hard as I pushed the car as hard as I dared. We dropped down to Thirlmere and the car cooled down again.

I drove the remaining few miles to the afore mentioned junction, which is a sort of fork off to the right and there is a pull in lane in the middle of the road. Fortunately the gods smiled on us again and there was nothing coming in the opposite direction. I made the turn and then continued on down St John's in the Vale to cover the last few miles to my mechanic's garage at Threlkeld quarry. There was one last right hand turn to make before we reached our objective but once again we prevailed and I was lucky; there was nothing coming and I turned up the lane to the garage, pulled over onto the roadside and turned the engine off. I collapsed in my seat and breathed a sigh of relief. I looked across at Jane and she was staring straight ahead with a nondescript expression on her face.

"Come along, it's all right now. Let's go up to the garage and see if we can get a ride home for both of us," I said.

She got out of the car stiffly, which suggested there was more bothering her than her physical disability, and said nothing.

Up at the garage my mechanic was working on a car and he came out from underneath it as we approached.

He was grinning as he said, "I see you made it then!"

I nodded and then asked him if I could phone my brother to ask him if he could come and collect us.

The mechanic said, "Yeah, no problem. Just go in the house and my wife will fix you up."

Jane and I did so. I made the call and then the kind lady made us a cup of tea. I could have used something stronger but I made do.

When my brother came to pick us up, he thought the whole episode was hilarious – bloody sod! He drove us through to Penrith and back to Jane's car in Southend Road. She jumped out as if bitten by a flea and almost ran across to her car – I guess she couldn't get out of there fast enough!

I shouted, "Goodbye, Jane," as she fled but she did not seem to hear me and there was no reply!

I must just say that if that lady ever reads this she will recognise herself in the narrative and can I say, "I apologise to you in the most humble way, for frightening you that day!"

I must also add that if I have learned anything from that experience, it would be that you don't start talking about your mental health problems on a first date!

That turned out to be my last blind date and therefore the end of my association with that particular dating agency. Jane must have reported back to the agency that they had a complete nutcase on their books, resulting in me not receiving any more information from them!

Something about the whole episode must have made me make the decision to change my appearance, because shortly afterwards I shaved off my bushy moustache and Angus did the same with his, perhaps for the matter of association!

After Jane had made her hurried escape I went through to Culgaith village with Angus, accompanied by the fish and chips we had bought in the town, to eat them at his house there. We enjoyed our suppers and had a convivial evening, at the end of which Angus offered me the use of his Vauxhall Carlton for a few days while my Capri was being repaired. I accepted gratefully and drove his roomy saloon home.

I used my brother's car over the next week, to get to various locations to clear out undergrowth on several footpaths and bridleways for the National Park Authority. Again I was using a hired strimmer, but this one had an optional circular steel blade for dealing with stubborn vegetation. The weather was hot and humid, which made the work taxing. I was heavily under pressure at this time from a large number of customers requiring me to do a variety of different jobs and looking back, I don't know how I coped!

While I was clearing out one of the bridleways at Helton, a couple came through on horseback and I stopped my machine for the horses' benefit. The couple had a stable complex nearby and they asked me if I would clear a bit of undergrowth for them in amongst hands (as well as). I told them I would come round later and that is what I did; putting another four hours onto what had already been a long day. I finished at the horse people's place at nine p.m. and I was rewarded with the treat of a bottle of Old Speckled Hen (real ale) and at 6.2% alcohol it went right to my head, but went down without touching the sides!

On Thursday the first of July, I had a doctor's appointment to see about my knees, which had been aching for some time but the G.P. had little constructive advice for me, which was not what I wanted to hear with the walking holiday fast approaching. While I was in town I ordered four hundred and fifty pounds' worth of traveller's cheques and fifty pounds' worth of Swiss Francs at my building society for my holiday.

The period up to the thirteenth of July was spent doing more mole trapping up Ullswater and haymaking back on our home farm. I had the Capri back by now but was grateful to my brother for the loan of the Carlton – without it I would have been stuck! On the twelfth of July, something unfortunate occurred; I was trapping up the Greenside valley from Glenridding, when I spied a small gap in a dry stone wall and decided to repair it. As I finished it, I was just replacing the last heavy top stone when I felt a stab of pain in the back of my right shoulder. This had occurred once or twice before in my working life and I knew I was in for a spell of suffering! I had finished my work by lunch time and with the pain increasing I sought out the services of an osteopath in Penrith but he was unable to fit me in at such short notice and I had to return home untreated. I had a neck bracing collar at home, which I had used before and I put this on and it eased my suffering somewhat but I knew the pain from the muscle spasm would not go away until I received some sort of manipulation on the shoulder. However, time had run out to get anything done about the ailment because the very next day I set off on my holiday, still wearing the neck brace!

At two a.m. on the thirteenth of July I got up and made my final preparations for my trip. My shoulder pain had spread up into my neck and I had difficulty turning my head. I loaded my gear, which included my skis (I was heading for Zermatt, where there is summer skiing) into the car and at three thirty a.m. I set off for Manchester Airport. I arrived at Ringway Airparks at four fifty-five a.m. after a trouble free drive, parked my car and got the transfer to the airport. Check-in and security went smoothly, although I did receive some funny looks from other passengers, who on spying my ski bag no doubt thought it was a strange time of year to be going skiing!

At six fifty-five a.m. I flew out on a small Lear-type jet to Geneva. My luggage had entered the Swiss fly/rail luggage system so I knew I would not see it again until I got to Zermatt. There were quite a few empty seats on the plane and the flight was nice and relaxing, which was just what I needed, considering my shoulder injury and the recent pace of my life! The holiday had of course been cleared with my various counsellors but I had encountered some opposition, especially from the probation people. I was away now, though, free and clear of all of them! I did however feel a bit apprehensive about the holiday; after all, three out of my last five trips abroad had gone wrong and the fifth one had involved some shaky spells. Andrew had told me that going away on my own was not conducive to my mental health but here I was, doing it again! Although I was not on any prescription medication, I had sought out the advice of the local health food shop in Penrith to see if they could recommend a herbal product that might be useful in times of stress and they had sold me a small bottle of Rescue Remedy, which I was told to use in emergencies.

I landed in Geneva and quickly made my way to the train station, which was situated under the airport. I was unencumbered by luggage apart from my flight bag, so I was able to move about freely. The price of my holiday included the train transfer and I already had the tickets I needed. I sought out the platform for trains to Lausanne and having found it I only had to wait a few minutes for the required train to arrive. I boarded and settled down for the journey to Lausanne.

In Lausanne, I changed for the train to Brig at eleven thirty a.m. and on this leg of the journey I went through Montreux, where Freddie Mercury from Queen recorded his last songs and indeed, where he ended his days!

I was pretty tired on the train transfer, but was careful not to fall asleep and miss the vital stop and change at Visp. Here I caught the train on the rack and pinion railway up to Zermatt but by mistake I boarded a reserved train! It had begun to move out of the station before I realised so there was little I could do but try and blag my way through. I moved through the nearly full carriages and spied an empty seat. I asked the people sitting adjacent if the seat was taken; they eyed me suspiciously and then replied in English that I could sit there. I sat down and explained to the people how I had got on the wrong train. They turned out to be a German family on holiday and proved to be very nice, with good conversation skills!

It was now about three p.m. as the train made its way up the narrow valley to Zermatt. There is also a road up the valley but the public can only use it as far as the village of Tasch, where there is a big covered car park.

As the train approached a steeper section of track near Tasch, there was a clunk from underneath as the cog pinion engaged with the rack between the rails. At this point I was looking out of the window on the right side and I saw where what seemed like a whole cliff face had avalanched into the valley bottom. There were boulders the size of a house in the debris and it was an awesome sight.

I found out later that the huge rockfall was thought to have been caused by the permafrost melting due to global warming! Apparently the rockfall had obliterated the railway and road causing both routes to have to be moved across the valley. Luckily the fall had occurred at night, resulting in there being no injuries, but had of course led to severe disruption in the higher parts of the valley until the authorities had got the transport links sorted out!

As the train pulled into the town of Zermatt, I caught a glimpse of the mighty Matterhorn, which had emerged from behind the foothills up to the right. It was a fine afternoon and this famous mountain was revealed in all its splendour. There was new snow on its flanks, blanketing its pyramid form almost down to its base!

I got off the train in the station, saying goodbye to the German family as I did so and then consulted the little diagram of the town that the travel agent had given me. I would be staying in the Excelsior Hotel and having worked out how to find it, I made my way through the bustling traffic free town. Now 'traffic free' means there are no cars allowed, but it does not mean there are no vehicles because there are plenty of electric taxis and delivery vans, which you have to watch out for because you can't hear them! There are also horse drawn carriages and you have to watch out you don't tread in the horse shit!

I had visited the town once before in the early '80s, when I had skied over on a winter holiday from the linked Italian resort of Cervinia. It had been a brief stay though and I had not had time to explore the town properly; also, it being summer now, there was no snow and things looked completely different. The town lies at one thousand five hundred and ninety-three metres (five thousand two hundred and twenty-six feet) and in summer the snowline rarely drops below three thousand two hundred and sixty metres (ten thousand six hundred and ninety-six feet).

As I made my way towards the Excelsior, I took in my surroundings and noted that the town lay at the head of the valley, hemmed in by the partially forested lower slopes of the foothills of the larger mountain ranges all around. There seemed to be little agricultural land around the town, the terrain being largely too steep for it. I took notice of the architecture, it being a mixture of large modern hotels and apartment buildings alongside more traditional Alpine style houses.

I found the Excelsior and upon entering I spied my suitcase at reception. Somehow, amazingly, it had arrived before me but there was no sign of my skis. I checked in with the rather dour receptionist, got my room key and went upstairs, accompanied by the hotel porter who carried my heavy suitcase. I slipped the guy a couple of francs after he had showed me round my room and then unpacked. The Excelsior was a three-star hotel but my room proved to be more like one out of a four-star, with lovely furnishings, en-suite facilities, television, balcony and best of all – a mini-bar! At reception they had told me that my skis would probably be on a later train and would therefore not arrive until late evening.

Having got my gear stowed away in the drawers and wardrobe, I raided the mini-bar for a beer and then checked out the balcony, which, although small, had a table and chair plus a nice view out across the adjacent beck to the eastern side of town. I sat down at the table with my cold beer and the book I had brought with me – it was a novel by Wilbur Smith and was called *A Time To Die*, and of course, although this holiday was likely to involve certain dangers, given what I planned to do, the title of the book did not give me cause for concern! I am a huge fan of Wilbur Smith and now in 2014 I have every book he ever wrote!

I read until I finished my beer, took a shower and then had a short nap before going down to dinner in a fresh set of clothes at seven p.m.

I enjoyed an excellent meal, during which I eyed up a couple of beautiful Japanese women who unfortunately, turned out to be attached!

After dinner I walked up town to do a bit more exploring, finding the Alpine Centre on the main street, from where I needed to get my lift passes for skiing in the coming days and also where I would need to enquire about guided hikes or mountain climbs! Also, I found the main church, which was open and upon entering I found it to be beautifully decorated and ornamented. I spent a moment in quiet prayer here before looking around the churchyard, where I found the well-marked graves of many climbers who had died on the Matterhorn!

Thunderclouds had gathered around the valley and rain was threatening so I made my way back to the Excelsior. I went into the main bar and ordered a half litre of beer which, having had a couple with my dinner, was proving to be an excellent brew. As I sat enjoying my drink at one of the tables, I became aware of the pain in my shoulder and neck, I had not experienced much discomfort from the injury during the day and had dispensed with the services of the neck brace but the pain had now returned! I thought to myself that I had better try to get something done about my shoulder, and fast, because otherwise it was going to ruin my holiday, so upon finishing my drink I went to reception and enquired about local physiotherapy practices. I was given the location of a practice nearby and I resolved to get an appointment there the following day. I then went back to my room and turned in at ten p.m.

Wednesday the fourteenth of July. I was up at seven thirty a.m. and upon looking out of my window I saw that it was a fine clear day, there had obviously been a little rain the previous evening and I could see that the nearby beck, enclosed by its concrete embankments, was in spate (the larger watercourses in the Alps are often in spate in summer, even on fine days, due to the meltwater from the high glaciers and snows). I put on the clothes from the previous evening and my everyday shoes and went down to enjoy an excellent buffet breakfast (I was staying on half board, which meant I only had to find my midday meal) before walking out to the little nearby supermarket to get some provisions to see me through the middle of the coming days.

Having left the shopping back in my hotel room, I went for a walk up by the side of the beck, towards the head of the valley. On the way, I passed the main gondola ski-lift station, which takes you up to the Trockener Steg Glacier. The path took me up to the place where the beck exits a spectacular gorge right at the head of the valley. There is a walkway built up the side of the gorge, much in the same fashion as the one in Grindelwald and I explored this before returning to the town and making my way to the physiotherapy practice I had been told about. To my surprise, on entering the practice I was told by the receptionist that they could give me some treatment right away and I was admitted to a treatment room where a rather attractive young Swiss woman told me to remove my shirt and lie face down on the couch. After asking me some questions on my injury, she then began to give me the best sports massage I have ever had. She was very strong and was able to get her fingers under my shoulder blade somehow and work on the knot of muscle that she told me was present there. The treatment was somewhat uncomfortable but I could feel the manipulation working. I enjoyed a good conversation with the lady as she worked, during which she told me that she had been born and raised in Zermatt. I asked her if climbing the Matterhorn was as difficult as I had heard it was, and she said it was and that you were strongly advised to hire a guide! At the time I had no intention of climbing such a difficult mountain, but I did have aspirations to attempt to scale some of the lesser peaks, availability of guides and money permitting!

The massage lasted half an hour, after which I was told I could resume my normal activities. I paid the fee, which was forty-eight francs (approximately twenty-six pounds), said goodbye and thank you to my masseuse before returning to my room at the Excelsior and getting my hiking gear on. Upon leaving my room and passing reception, I was hailed by one of the staff and the lady told me my skis had finally arrived, which was a good job because I was starting to worry that they had got lost in the system.

The day was growing hot as I left the hotel in my shorts and carrying my big rucksack to head for the Sunnegga funicular railway station, across on the base of the eastern side of the valley. Here I bought a ticket and boarded the train, which whisked me up steeply underground to the top station at two thousand two hundred and eighty-eight metres (seven thousand five hundred and six feet). Upon leaving the station I headed out up the steep, well-used path under the gondola lift (that was not working) to Blauherd at two thousand five hundred and seventy-one metres (eight thousand four hundred and thirty-five feet) where I caught the cable car to Unterotthorn at three thousand one hundred and three metres (ten thousand one hundred and eighty feet). I had got warm and somewhat out of breath on my hike up underneath the gondola and it was good to have a breather in the large un-crowded cable car. My shoulder felt fine as I stood looking out of the windows at the unfolding spectacular panorama. At the top station I exited the cable car and moved out onto the viewing platform. It was now around four forty-five p.m. and the sun was lowering in the west. Although the sun was well past its zenith and casting shadows into the east faces of the mountains, to the west the panorama was still impressive and worthy of a few photos. I had brought two cameras on the holiday – my old Minolta semi-automatic and my Olympus auto-wind with zoom lens.

Both cameras took very good pictures and I had both of them with me every day, mainly because the batteries in the Minolta were always expiring and were hard to come by!

The Matterhorn stood proud across the valley, slightly to my left, standing at four thousand four hundred and seventy-eight metres (fourteen thousand six hundred and ninety-two feet). While panning round to the right I could see the Ober Gabelhorn, the Zinalrothorn and the Weisshorn, all of which are over four thousand metres (thirteen thousand one hundred and twenty-four feet). I took several photos and then turned around slowly to my left to take in to the south, fine views of the Breithorn at four thousand one hundred and fifty-nine metres (thirteen thousand six hundred and forty-five feet) and ranging from its left – the Pollux at four thousand and ninety-two metres (thirteen thousand four hundred and twenty-five feet), then Castor at four thousand two hundred and twenty-three metres (thirteen thousand eight hundred and eighty-five feet) and in the south east – the Monte Rosa at four thousand six hundred and nine metres (fifteen thousand one hundred and twenty-two feet). This last great peak is the highest mountain in Switzerland, straddling the border with Italy. I took some shots of these peaks and then turned further round to look to the east. There were several more four thousand metre peaks shown on my map in this direction but they were hidden behind a ridge just behind the cable car station. To the north, the valley stretched back down towards Visp, where I had changed trains for Zermatt.

Time was getting on and I realised I had quite a hike to get back to Zermatt and that it would take at least a couple of hours, judging by the times shown on the signpost positioned just outside the cable car station. It was all downhill, though and I set off at a brisk pace down the Tufterchumm valley in a northerly direction. The terrain was quite smooth and I realised that this was a ski piste in the winter.

I made good time down this valley on good, well-marked paths. It had been cool at Unterrothorn but it now began to grow very warm again as I decreased in altitude. At two thousand five hundred metres (eight thousand two hundred feet) this side valley opened out as the path descended into the main valley to the north of Zermatt. As I reached this point, I disturbed a small herd of what looked like red deer. I quickly raised the Olympus and got off a snapshot on zoom, but they were a distance off and when I got the film developed at home the herd was virtually indistinguishable from the background in the photo.

Further down the mountainside, I entered the small hamlet of Tufteren and there was a small restaurant right next to the path. I stopped here for a quick beer; it was ice cold and was a bottle of Beck's. From here it was plain sailing back to Zermatt, with me feeling buoyed up from the effects of the beer. I had walked fast and made it down the four point three four miles (seven kilometres) in only two hours!

It was hot and humid as I made my way through the eastern side of town, back to the Excelsior and I was somewhat sweaty but it was seven p.m. and dinner time, so I had no time for the much-needed shower. I left my rucksack at the dining room door and made my way to my table, whereupon I found that it was fondue night in the Chinoise style. I had never attempted to tackle such a meal before and I looked around to other guests in a clueless fashion, to see what they were doing with their food. A young Japanese couple saw that I was in a state of confusion and kindly came across to show me what to do with the unfamiliar utensils and the strange food. The girl was beautiful and she melted my heart, as well as the cheese in the fondue!

I finished the meal and went up to my room for a shave and shower before returning to the main bar for a few well-earned beers.

It had been an excellent start to my holiday and I was feeling good, but I turned in at eleven p.m., after drawing a blank with my socializing attempts to make new friends in the bar!

Thursday the fifteenth of July. I was up at six forty-five a.m. after a good sleep and I made my mind up that today I would go skiing, so I got my gear sorted out but did not yet don my ski clothes. Instead I went down for breakfast in my everyday clothes and then I walked to the Alpine Centre on the main street, where I bought a day ski pass for fifty-eight francs (thirty pounds). I then returned to my hotel and changed into my skiing attire, which included the boots I had bought in Canada and brought with me. (These items had put me slightly over the luggage weight limit on the plane!) As I was passing through the hotel foyer, I noticed there was a new receptionist on duty; she was very attractive and she gave me a nice smile as I went past, which got the day off to a good start! I made my way to the ski room where the porter had left my skis, got them out of their bag and then carried them outside.

It was a ten minute walk up to the gondola station and I was glad it was early morning and therefore cool as I clumped up the tarmac road in my ungainly boots and several layers of clothing, plus carrying the skis. The day had dawned fine and clear and promised to be a stunner.

As I was nearing the gondola station, I heard someone behind me say, "It's a good day for it, isn't it?"

I turned to find, to my surprise, the receptionist from the Excelsior approaching. She was all decked out in her skiing gear and must have left the hotel just after me.

I said, "Hi, yes, it looks like it's going to be a super day, is it your day off?"

"Yes, I get two mornings off each week to go skiing if I want to."

Her English was very good and we soon struck up a good crack. I told her my first name and she gave me hers, which was Rita. On entering the gondola station, we quite naturally boarded the same cabin, placing our skis in the little buckets on the outside as we did so. We were the only occupants of our particular cabin as it trundled out of the station and up towards the first stage terminus at Furi – one thousand eight hundred and sixty-seven metres (six thousand one hundred and twenty-five feet). I am not normally very good at talking to women but on that fine morning I was on particularly good form and I regaled Rita with stories of my past skiing exploits; in particular the tale about the time I had skied over to Zermatt in the early '80s from Cervinia and included the bit about how the top stage of the lift we were on, the Klein Matterhorn cable car, had been closed, meaning that in order to get back to the ridge to ski back over into Cervinia I had to take the notorious 'T-bar' drag lift up the Oberer Theodul glacier! I was with a group guided by the Horizon Holidays rep and there was quite a large queue for the lift, it being late in the day. The lift operator was organising the queue into pairs to speed up the process and I was paired with the Horizon rep, whose name I forget. Now, she was much shorter than me, meaning that when our turn to catch the lift came and the T-bar was positioned on our bums, it was at an uncomfortable angle. All the drag lifts in Cervinia were single person buttons and I had never been on a T-bar before. The experience proved to be a harrowing and exhausting one. The lift, although not up a steep gradient, was very long, encompassing the entire length of the Oberer Theodul glacier! My partner on the lift was a good skier but it transpired that this was also her first time on a T-bar. Instead of just relaxing and going with the flow, we pulled against each other side by side all the way up, how we didn't fall off the bloody thing I will never know and I had cramp in my left leg after exiting the lift at the top.

Rita was much amused by my tales and she entertained me with a few of her own before we changed to the next stage of the lift at Furi – a cable car to Trockener Steg. There was quite a load in this cabin and I was pressed up tightly against Rita, which was an enjoyable sensation! The cabin passed over several pylons on its journey and as it did so it made a sudden dip and swoop causing us occupants to cry out, "Whoosh!"

We docked at Trockener Steg at two thousand nine hundred and thirty-nine metres (nine thousand six hundred and forty-two feet) and here we changed to the spectacular Klein Matterhorn cable car, which is an impressive engineering achievement! This cabin was about the same size as the last one and in it, amongst the recreational skiers, were downhill racers and slalom skiers, who were catching the lift back to the top to begin another training run for their winter FIS season. Zermatt has one of highest summer skiing areas in the Alps and is therefore a popular proving ground for the professionals.

Once again, I was crammed in close to the lovely Rita and thinking things were going really well! The cabin swung out of the station to head up on its unsupported cable to the top station. It was a steep ascent and my ears popped. Beneath us the rocky slopes had given way to snow and ice. The views out of the cabin windows were spectacular. To the west was the perfect pyramid profile of the Matterhorn, now showing fully its almost perpendicular east face, which fell, snow covered, to the ice shelves at its base.

This grand mountain was first climbed by the Englishman, Edward Whymper, in 1865, by way of the north eastern Hornligrat ridge. He was part of an international group and they were in competition with a group of climbers coming up from the Italian side of the mountain. It was rumoured that the Whymper party got to the top first and then threw rocks down at the approaching Italian party! They paid for this disgraceful behaviour in full on the way down, because while they were descending a particularly difficult section just below the summit, the leading climbers fell! The party was roped together and in order to stop the whole party being dragged over the edge of the north face, Whymper, who was second off the back of the group cut, the hemp rope (it was rumoured) and the leaders fell to their certain deaths on the ice sheet far below! Whymper and the surviving member of their group returned to Zermatt to tell the awful tale. It took the search parties several days to find the bodies of the dead climbers.

You can learn about the mountain and the people that have climbed it in the museum in Zermatt.

Looking out to the east side of the cabin, you could see the mountain range stretching towards the sprawling bulk of the Monte Rosa. Rita and I were close to the front of the cabin and by craning your neck, you could see up to where the cables entered a concrete bunker in a small rocky peak. Afterwards I read that the concrete used to form the top station structure had to be flown up by helicopter and had to have special additives in it to stop it freezing!

We docked at the top station in the Klein Matterhorn at three thousand eight hundred and seventeen metres (twelve thousand five hundred and twenty-three feet). The doors opened and we were greeted by an icy blast, which immediately made me grateful for the extra layers I was wearing. Rita and I were carried along on the tide of skiers into a level tunnel, which bored through the peak to exit onto a high frozen plateau. Along the way, she asked me if I wanted to take the lift to the very summit of the Klein Matterhorn and I said I would, so that is what we did. The lift was just like a hotel one and you emerged onto a metal viewing platform at three thousand eight hundred and eighty-three metres (twelve thousand seven hundred and forty feet). The views were fantastic, with a three hundred and sixty degree panorama. I got my Minolta out from beneath my coat to take some shots but I had to remove my ski gloves to operate the camera; it was bitterly cold and I had to hurry my photo session. You could see all the mountains around that I described earlier, but now you could also see the great peaks to the east of Zermatt that had been hidden from me the day before. These included the Taschhorn at four thousand four hundred and ninety metres (fourteen thousand seven hundred and thirty-one feet) and the Dom – the highest mountain wholly inside Switzerland at four thousand five hundred and forty-five metres (fourteen thousand nine hundred and twelve feet).

My spirits soared as I took in this breathtaking vista and I turned to Rita and said, "Wow, what a magnificent view!" and she just smiled and nodded. We returned via the lift to the tunnel and then made our way out onto the snow covered plateau. After clipping on our skis we set off on the crisp level surface, using the skating technique to cover the three hundred or so metres to access the main ski piste. There were vast ice sheets beneath us and crevasses everywhere, meaning you had to keep to the marked runs! The beginning of the piste, which was at the head of the Oberer Theodul glacier, led off to the west and it was an easy blue run. It only took a couple of turns to get into my stride and then I was away. Rita was an expert skier and was soon taking the lead over the superbly conditioned snow surface. The piste formed a wide road across a steeper slope and as we went we encountered the racing skiers getting ready for their practice runs. The run soon opened out onto a huge, wide skiing area that stretched down to the north in the direction of Trockener Steg. Ahead of us to the west was the cable car station at Testa Grigia at three thousand four hundred and seventy-nine metres (eleven thousand four hundred and fourteen feet) on the Italian border and further over out of sight was the resort of Cervinia, where I had stayed on three consecutive winter holidays in the early '80s.

We tore down the run down the glacier and I was soon breathing hard with the exertion and the altitude. I was making some excellent big carving turns and feeling euphoric, while Rita made pretty short, rapid turns. The medium steep first section of the glacier gave way to a more gentle stretch and then became almost flat for a bit and we had to get into the 'tuck' position to maintain momentum. The piste ended rather abruptly in a slushy area near the cable car station at Trockener Steg and we had to unclip our skis and walk the last hundred metres to the station over rocky ground.

We went back up the cable car to the Klein Matterhorn, but this time on exiting the tunnel we took a virtually level drag lift (a button) from the tunnel in a southerly direction to the ice dome of Gobba di Rollin at three thousand eight hundred and ninety-nine metres (twelve thousand seven hundred and ninety-two feet) again on the Italian border and skied a gentle run westward to link back in with the main glacier piste. I had not asked Rita if she wanted to ski with me; rather it had just seemed like a natural progression from taking the lifts together!

We stayed together for almost three hours, skiing down and taking the lifts back up several times before she departed back for the Excelsior to resume her duties and I took one last run down the glacier. As I exited the tunnel at the Klein Matterhorn for the last time that day, I paid a visit to the ice grotto there, which I had noticed earlier in the day. A tunnel led down inside the ice sheet; it was lit by a vivid blue natural colour near the entrance and then further in by artificial light. There was a rubber mat on the floor to stop you slipping. The tunnel ended in a large, well-lit chamber and in this there were many impressive ice carvings of such things as animals, pagodas and even a horse drawn carriage. I had a good look round amongst the display and took a few photos on flash and then went back out into the open air.

It was now nearing midday and I was getting tired. The skiing had taken a lot out of me and I was realizing that I had not done enough preparatory exercises to ready myself for it. I had enough left in the tank for one last run down, though and I set off down the piste to Trockener Steg. The slopes were due to close at two p.m. anyway, because by that time the day had warmed to such an extent that the snow had become slushy and further activity would damage the pistes. Having done the run with my legs aching I retired to the restaurant at the Trockener Steg complex, where I enjoyed a nice, reasonably priced meal of bratwurst with rosti (sausage and fried potatoes) and a beer. The day before, while walking, I had just had a quick lunch 'on the hoof,' of a banana and some chocolate.

After I had eaten I returned down the cable car and gondola to the town. Just as I was approaching the second last stop at Furi I noticed that there was after all some farmable land near the town, because beneath the cable car a couple of farm hands were busy mowing grass for hay with their Allan Scythes. I had not noticed these high pastures on the way up because I had been too busy trying to work my charms on the beautiful Rita!

Having returned to Zermatt, I was walking down the road towards my hotel when I noticed a nice bar right beside my route and I left my skis on the rack outside, then took off my jacket and sat at one of the outside tables. The day had grown very hot down here in the town and I was grateful for the cooling shade of the parasol above the table. Presently an attractive waitress approached and I ordered a large beer. The outside sitting area was un-crowded and I quickly relaxed, almost to the point of falling asleep. I was roused from my reverie by the arrival of my beer. As the waitress placed the drink on my table, she must have noticed that I had been nearly nodding off because she said, "You must have had a tough morning on the slopes, sir?"

I replied, "Yes I have and may I say what I nice bar you have here. You may be seeing quite a bit of me!"

She laughed and said, "It's nice to have good customers."

The girl was done out in Swiss national dress and she looked a picture. We exchanged a bit more small talk before she went off to serve other customers in a swirl of skirts. The beer she had brought was of the Feldschlossen label and was very good. I sat back and took a long swig of the cold foaming brew and looked up at the Matterhorn, standing proud above the valley and tried to imagine myself climbing it!

I was thirsty and my glass was soon dry. I ordered another and sat enjoying it lazily – this was utopia! I almost nodded off again and jerked myself awake to finish my drink, gather up my gear and head off down the road.

When I got back to the Excelsior, Rita was on duty at reception and she greeted me with a rather guarded smile. This, as I quickly learned, was probably because standing beside her at the desk was a strapping fellow of about six foot four inches, whom she introduced to me as her boyfriend, Carl. I was gutted. I thought I'd been making good progress with Rita and now suddenly but as usual, par for the course for me, the rug had been pulled from under me. That was the end of my romantic ambitions in that direction but Rita remained friendly and helpful. I guess the morning's skiing with me had just been good customer relations.

I spent the rest of the afternoon by going to the little supermarket for more midday provisions and then continuing to read my Wilbur Smith book on my balcony. It was a real page turner in Wilbur's usual fashion. I raided the mini-bar a few times for beer and spirits as I read, but on my last visit to it of the afternoon I noticed the little price list rather obscurely placed inside and on reading it I was astonished at the price of the alcohol contained within! I thought, *shit, I'm going to run up a hell of a bill if I continue to use the mini-bar*, so that was the last time I used it!

At about six p.m. I shaved, showered and then went down for my evening meal. I was seated at a table on my own, being the occupant of a single room and although there were other English couples nearby I was too far away to engage in conversation, so I kept my own counsel.

After dinner I went out to reception and asked Rita, who was still on duty, if there was a popular bar nearby where everybody gathered in the evenings. She told me that the Matterhorn bar just up the street was well frequented but mainly by locals. I thought, *that will do for me*, and I set off up town to find it. On locating it and entering, I decided that it was a bit like entering a country pub back home; everyone went quiet and looked at you as if to say, 'What the hell are you doing here?' There were pictures all around the rather pokey room of climbers on the Matterhorn and I studied these.

I was interrupted from my observation by a voice saying in broken English, "You here to climb that?"

I turned to locate the speaker and saw a swarthy-looking bloke eying me. I went across to his table and asked him if I could sit down. He indicated a vacant chair and then asked me if I wanted a drink.

I said, "Yeah, a beer would be great, thanks," and he shouted across to the barman to bring one over. The guy at the table repeated the question about me climbing the Matterhorn and I told him I didn't think I was up to it, but that I was interested in hiring a guide to climb a couple of the lesser peaks. Communication was a bit difficult with his poor English but it was better than my German and we managed. The barman brought my beer over and I continued my discussion with the swarthy bloke who, it transpired, worked at a local quarry. He told me that the Breithorn and the

Pollux were popular climbs for tourists and that the hire of a guide was not too expensive! I drank my beer and then bought my companion one back. He was particularly interested to learn that I worked on the land and told me that he hadn't come across any other farmers holidaying in Zermatt! As the evening wore on, we were joined by other locals, some of whom were just coming off duty from their various professions. The crack was great and the beer was going down a pace. I really felt rather at home and by the end of my time in the bar I had re-thought my earlier opinion of the place.

I was quite pissed when closing time came and I said goodbye to my new found friends to waddle rather unsteadily back, to fall into my bed at the Excelsior.

Friday the sixteenth of July. I got up about six forty-five a.m. feeling a bit rough but was soon getting myself organised. I had slept well and decided that this day I would go for another hike, but where to? There were so many possibilities. I looked at my map and made my mind up to try and hike to the Gorner Glacier, out to the south east of town.

I breakfasted, packed my big rucksack and headed out. Rita was on reception again and I left details with her of the route I intended to take. I made my way across to the east side of town and set off up the well-marked path to the Gorner Glacier. The weather was again glorious but the Matterhorn was shrouded in mist in the morning as I made my way up the wide stony path through the conifers. The path ran alongside the Gornergrat cog railway and I could have taken a train, but I was in need of some exercise to work off my beer from the previous evening.

It was a long way up to the top station of the railway and it must have been early afternoon by the time I reached it. There were hundreds of other tourists milling about at the Gornergrat station at three thousand and ninety metres (ten thousand one hundred and thirty-eight feet). It turned out that I did not have to climb to this station to access the glacier, but I was glad of the opportunity to view the great mountains to the south from the station's viewing platform, which was perched right on the edge of a precipice, falling away to the Gorner Glacier below. From left to right was the Monte Rosa, Castor, Pollux, Breithorn, Klein Matterhorn and, sitting mightily in the west, the Matterhorn.

I backtracked down a couple of hundred metres, to where a path signposted Monte Rosa hut branched off and then set off on a long slight decline eastward into the Gorner Glacier valley. After about three and a half kilometres (two point seven miles) of fast walking, I came to the edge of the glacier, where the path just continued out onto the ice to head across towards the Monte Rosa hut. Looking out across the shimmering surface I could see markers placed on the ice to keep the climbers out of the crevasses. There were several groups of climbers out on the ice, bound for the hut, which you could see, perched on a rocky shoulder a mile or so away at the other side of the glacier. I had no crampons at that point so I could not venture any further. The glacier was fairly flat at this point and you could hear the ice squeaking and popping as it moved! I sat down on a rock, which was surprisingly warm from the sun, and ate a quick, late lunch from my banana and chocolate supplies. Several groups of climbers passed on their way to the hut and nodded to me as they did so. There were also quite a few ordinary hikers milling about too, who like me, probably did not have crampons to enable them to cross the glacier.

After I had fed and watered myself I retraced my route back to the valley rim and then took a path heading down westwards, parallel to the glacier valley, to a place where the route took me over the edge and very steeply down grassy slopes to the valley floor. On the way, I had taken a photo of myself with the self-timer on the Olympus by standing it up on a rock (I had no tripod). The picture has me standing, looking away towards the Matterhorn in the background and the mountain was now virtually cloud free. The picture came out very well and I have it framed on my bedroom wall. At that point there had been no other walkers on that path but further on, I encountered an American couple who took a couple of photos of me with my camera, with the summit of the Breithorn in the background. I returned the favour for them.

The path I was on was smooth and had a hard packed clay-like surface; it was very steep and descended to the valley floor in a series of switchbacks. It was an exhilarating descent of about two hundred and ninety metres (nine hundred and fifty feet). At the bottom I was beyond the snout of the glacier and here the valley floor was strewn with gravel and boulders, some quite large. A large beck, which was the same one that ran through Zermatt, thundered down the centre of the plain of debris and you could hear the churning water moving the boulders on the river bed.

The path continued down the side of the valley floor, parallel to the beck and eventually turned right to become a well-maintained gravel road, leading down past the gorge I had visited on my first day and went on towards Zermatt. I entered the tree line and the track became a tarmac road. As I was passing some buildings, I was startled by three girls, about five years old, who jumped out at me from behind a wall. They rushed up to me with handfuls of pretty rocks and although they only had a few words of English, it was plain that they were trying to flog the rocks to me. I laughed and dug some loose change out of my pockets, which amounted to about five francs (two pounds fifty) and made the exchange. The girls ran off laughing, no doubt thinking they had ripped off another unsuspecting tourist but I was quite happy, I had got some nice rocks and it had been a charming moment!

When I got back to town, I had a couple of beers at the nice bar I had found on my way back from skiing and then returned to my hotel, got ready for dinner, read a bit and then headed down for my meal. Afterwards I mooched about a bit round the hotel and then turned in about ten thirty p.m.

Saturday the seventeenth of July. The morning of this day was spent skiing again and I did the same runs as the previous occasion, plus a tough black run off the western flank of the Klein Matterhorn. This run, I learned, was one of the speed skiers' pistes; at certain times of year competitors would dress up in Lycra suits, don streamlined helmets and plunge straight down the slope against the clock, reaching incredible speeds!

The weather was again superb and I forgot to put sun cream on my face, resulting in me getting burnt by the hot sun and also, the reflection from the snow.

In the afternoon, I went shopping round town for postcards and visited the bank to get a substantial number of traveller's cheques changed into cash. I also visited the Alpine Centre, where I got booked into a group to climb the Breithorn with a guide on the coming Monday and I paid the guide's fee, which was about a hundred and seventy francs (eighty-five pounds). I was told by the staff at the centre that I would need to hire crampons, a rope harness and an ice axe for the climb, so I went straight from the centre to an outdoor shop and hired the required items for the duration of a week.

The holiday company rep was visiting my hotel when I got back and she seemed impressed when I told her about the coming climb on the Breithorn!

The rest of the day went by in a blur, but I spent some of it planning the walk for the next day. I would attempt the hike to the Schonbeil Hut, far up the Zmutt Valley to the north side of the Matterhorn.

Sunday the eighteenth of July. I was up at six thirty a.m. and quickly readied myself for what I knew would be a long day. I packed extra provisions for the hike, breakfasted and then visited a small kiosk just up the street, where I bought a map of the area to the north of the Matterhorn. I then shouldered my rucksack and set off up and out of the southern end of town. Just as I was clearing the last of the buildings, I met a large herd of shaggy brown goats, being driven down the road by a couple of young goatherds dressed in traditional outfits. It was a fine sight and I took a couple of photos. The weather was again very good, with only a little high cirrus cloud in the west and although it was early morning it was already growing warm in the valley. I did not need my map at this early stage, but rather just followed the signs for the Zmutt Valley. I headed out on a good, wide gravel path in a south westerly direction, straight towards the Matterhorn, which stood proud in the early morning sun. My Zamberlan boots were now well and truly broken in and there had been no more trouble with the insoles, they fit me like a glove! Also my previously injured shoulder was perfectly fine; all in all I was in great form!

There were quite a lot of other walkers on the same route and I passed the time of day with them as I overtook them.

The incline of the path was fairly slight and I soon reached the point where the Zmutt Valley joined the main one. Here there was a huge boulder, a glacial erratic, which had a kind of stone-walled garden built on top of it.

Shortly afterwards, I entered the little hamlet of Zmutt at one thousand nine hundred and thirty-six metres (six thousand three hundred and fifty-two feet) and I stopped to admire the very old traditional wooden buildings with their colourful, flower-decked window boxes. I also noticed that there was some farmable land around the hamlet and some of the buildings were therefore barns, which were built on stilts atop large flat stones, presumably to stop vermin getting up into the stored crop and damaging it. To the south of Zmutt, the land dropped away into the narrow valley gorge where the meltwater from the high glaciers thundered down towards Zermatt.

From Zmutt I turned westwards, following the right hand side of the widening valley and immediately became aware that this was a great place for a photo. There were no other walkers near to take one of me, so I did the same as the other day and set my Olympus up on a rock, set the self-timer and ran ahead to climb onto a large boulder and look back at the camera just as it went off. The shot came out great, showing me on the boulder in the right hand side of the picture and the Matterhorn in the left hand side – I have an enlargement of this photo on my bedroom wall too!

The Wetterhorn, Grindelwald, Switzerland

My Capri 2.8I special

Rock lifting, Greenside Mines

Lifting rocks, Greenside Mines, Lake District

Angus in the barrow lift at Greenside Mines

Trowel, caught mole, trap that caught it and overhead view of the mole tunnel

Trapping in progress

The white mole and its normal black cousin

Another angle on the white mole

Scissor mole traps ageing from bottom 2 years to top over 100 years!

The retaining wall at Mungrisdale limekiln

Napes Needle, Lake District

On the summit of the Pollux near Zermatt

Pond building contract, Southerfell, Lake District

Army helicopter delivering stone above Castle Rock, Lake District

The rebuilt bee-boles at Uldale

My faithful canine friend, Tina

I walked on steadily up the valley with the Matterhorn on my left. It changed shape as I gradually passed it and I got the full view of its great north face, down which some of the members of the Whymper party had plunged to their deaths all those years ago.

From the lower gorge area, the Zmutt valley widened out and the floor of it became strewn with glacial debris. There were signs of man's hand in amongst the plain of gravel and rocks, with concrete structures built here and there and I vowed to investigate these on my way back.

Gradually the debris-strewn area gave way to the snout of the Zmutt Glacier and the path I was on began to climb more steeply, up along the edge of a large lateral glacial moraine. At certain places, you could stand with the toes of your boots in fresh air above a gut-swooping drop to the ice below!

At one point a large side valley came in from the right and framed in the end of it was the impressive peak of the Ober Gabelhorn at four thousand and sixty-three metres (thirteen thousand three hundred and thirty feet) and I took a photo of it.

Finally the path left the moraine and zigzagged up a steep rock-strewn slope towards the Schonbeil Hut. On the zigzags, I took another memorable photo, of a bunch of pretty flowers with glaciers in the backdrop (this now adorns the wall of the spare room). I reached the hut at two thousand six hundred and ninety-four metres (eight thousand eight hundred and forty feet) and found it to be a fairly modern stone-built structure with a large sun terrace. I learned later that the Schonbeil Hut is on the Haute Route – the high mountain trek from Chamonix in France to Zermatt.

I wearily took off my pack and sat down at a table on the sun terrace. There were several mountain climbers and long distance hikers coming and going in and out of the hut. Some were hanging washing out to dry!

A young lad who was obviously waiting on approached me and spoke to me in German and I said, "Sprecken Sie English?" ("Do you speak English?")

His face split into a broad smile and he said, "Yes of course. Can I get you something to eat and drink, sir?"

I smiled back and then ordered a gulash soup and a large beer, if he had one. I had a monster thirst on me but did not know if they would have beer at this place, it being the only hostelry for miles around! I need not have worried though, because the young lad nodded, rushed off and was soon back with a large foaming glass of the 'amber nectar.'

It was by now early afternoon and although I had eaten on the way, from my rucksack, I was hungry. I tucked into the delicious soup, accompanied by the ubiquitous black bread when it arrived and drew deeply on my excellent Feldschlossen beer. The view from the sun terrace was awesome. The Matterhorn was now to my south east across the Zmutt glacier and looked completely different from this angle. It was easy to see why the mountain was so difficult to climb; it was well defended from all sides. Even the Zmuttgrat ridge, nearest to me, looked a tough challenge! Stretching round to the right from the Matterhorn was a wide arc of mountains beginning with the Dent d'Herens at four thousand one hundred and seventy-one metres (thirteen thousand six hundred and eighty-five feet) ranging to a series of lesser (but still over three thousand metres – nine thousand eight hundred and forty-three feet) peaks with great glaciers nestling at their bases. Behind the hut the terrain rose up in great rocky shoulders hiding even bigger peaks behind.

The sun was still out but the high cloud in the west was starting to thicken up. Although I was high up, there was little wind and it was warm on the terrace. I quickly finished my beer and ordered another one off the attendant young waiter, who was obviously pleased for the opportunity to practise his English! I finished my soup and studied my map; I had walked approximately twelve kilometres (seven and a half miles) from Zermatt and I had the same to do in the opposite direction. There being no transport of any kind, the hut must be supplied by helicopter! It was time I got moving, the day was wearing on and I had a feeling that the weather was going to change, so I glugged the rest of my beer, paid the young waiter, shook his hand and thanked him for his excellent service, then donned my rucksack, staggering slightly from the effects of the beer as I did so and then set off back down the path. I was feeling decidedly squiffy and took extra care on the steep descent back to the edge of the glacier.

As I made my way back down the valley, thunderclouds formed in the west and slowly built up to start to obscure the sun. I reached the place where I had seen the concrete ground-works on the way up. A path led out across the debris-strewn valley floor to the structures and I took it. On inspection, the man-made features turned out to be part of a hydro-electric scheme, which as I got further down led to a large dam in the gorge, which had not been visible from the other side of the valley.

The weather closed in quickly, as it has a habit of doing in the mountains and with it my mood began to darken. I had pushed myself pretty hard on the outward journey and then overindulged on the alcohol and suddenly, out of nowhere, signs of my psychosis had returned! I tried to think positive but it was no good, I could feel myself slipping into the abyss. Then I remembered the Rescue Remedy and I quickly fished it out of the top compartment of my rucksack. I unscrewed the top of the little bottle, squeezed the rubber end of the dropper and filled the little glass tube. You are only supposed to put a couple of drops of the fluid on the back of your tongue at a time, but this was an emergency and I squirted the entire contents of the tube into my mouth and swallowed. I don't know for sure if it was the Rescue Remedy that worked or what, but I soon began to feel better as I made my way across the dam and back onto the north side of the Zmutt valley to descend towards Zermatt. Just then there was a loud crack of thunder and it began to rain. I pulled my waterproof trousers over my shorts and donned my favoured Karrimor coat. Looking back towards the Matterhorn, I could see that the rain was falling as snow on the higher elevations.

I was still in a slightly fragile mental state as I entered the town and vowed to take it easy for the rest of the day. The rain was still falling as I made my way back to the Excelsior for a shave and shower.

I had a glass of wine with my dinner and then retired to my room to read my Wilbur Smith book for an hour, before turning in early. I knew I would need as much rest as I could get to prepare for what would undoubtedly be an exciting and taxing climb on the morrow.

Monday the nineteenth of July. I was up early after a rather patchy sleep and got my equipment ready for the coming climb. I looked out of my room window and saw that it was a fine, clear morning; the thunder must have cleared the air! I was first down to breakfast at seven and quickly ate it before returning to my room to gather my gear and then leave the hotel, to head for the gondola station to meet the climbing group at the appointed time of eight a.m.

When I got to the gondola, I found that there were a number of groups gathered there waiting for their guides. I had been told at the Alpine Centre that my group included three Japanese men and a Swiss chap. I identified my fellow climbers in the throng and headed over to them. Introductions were made, which was a little difficult because the Japanese guys had little English. However, the Swiss chap spoke good English and his name was Arnold. I fixed his name in my memory by thinking about Arnold Schwarzenegger, who is of course Austrian by birth and of much greater physical stature than this Arnold! Because communication was good with Arnold we immediately struck up a rapport. He was busy telling me about his life as a city banker when he was interrupted by a tall guy, carrying a rope and wearing a baseball cap with Zermatt Alpine Centre printed on it. This, then, was our guide, Richard Andenmatten and he shook hands with each of us warmly. He then gave us a brief rundown in English of the order of the day and at the same time checked that we all had the required items of climbing equipment. I could feel the excitement starting to build in me and I sensed this was going to be a memorable experience!

The price of the gondola and cable car lifts was included in the cost of the climb, and our group was waved through onto the gondola lift by the lift operator.

The six of us boarded two separate cabins and we were whisked away, up two Furi and then up the two cable cars to the Klein Matterhorn. There was little conversation on the way up; I suppose we were all feeling a bit nervous, except of course Mr Andenmatten. As we approached the top station, I looked out of the left hand window of the un-crowded cable car at the great ice-domed peak of the Breithorn and I was filled with more than a little trepidation!

We exited the top station into dazzling sunlight and I was glad of my Reactolite spectacles, which immediately darkened in the bright light. It was bone-crunchingly cold and I was glad of the extra layers I had donned back in the town. Across to our left was the shining targeted peak of the Breithorn and from this angle it did not look too much of a climb, but it turned out that the mountain was further away than it looked!

Our guide assembled us in a line on the snow and then unfurled his rope. The rest of us were then told to get our rope harnesses out and put them on; you did this by stepping through the leg loops and pulling the harness up to tighten it round your waist. He then roped us all together through the special loop in the harness, about five metres (sixteen feet) apart. I was at the back, the anchorman position (I had heard this was an important station and felt the weight of its responsibility). Mr Andenmatten then reiterated the importance of following exactly in his footsteps as he led us away southwards, across the Breithorn Plateau. He had rather put the wind up me and I guess the others too, with the tale of a climber disappearing into a crevasse that had suddenly opened up right beside the path near this very spot!

Fortunately all the members of our party were in good physical shape and we made good time across the level plateau, turning eastwards to the start of the steep snow slope pitch that would lead us to the summit of the mountain. At this point – three thousand eight hundred and twenty-four metres (twelve thousand five hundred and forty-six feet) – we were told to stop and get out our crampons. Now, I had never used these awkward looking devices before and to start with, I tried to put them on the soles of my boots upside down! Arnold, who was just in front of me, saw that I was struggling and came to my aid, showing me how to step into the devices and then tie the attached cords round my boots. My crampons were twelve pointers, specifically designed for ice climbing with ten sharp spikes underneath and two sticking straight out front on each boot. We also unstrapped our ice axes from our packs and holding them by the head, placed them in our favoured hands with the shafts pointing towards the snow, so that we could arrest ourselves in the event of a fall.

When we had all got ourselves prepared, we set off up the incline at a reasonable pace. However, I was feeling bullish and kept catching Arnold up in front of me. For this I received a bollocking from Mr Andenmatten; he said, "Englishman at the back, slow down and pace yourself!"

I was suitably chastised and did as I was told. As it was, the steepness of the slope forced me to pull in my horns anyway and I was soon breathing hard in the thin air.

After about one and a half hours' hard climbing over soft new snow, we emerged onto the summit ridge. The weather was still superb and the view to the north, although the same one I had seen from the Klein Matterhorn, was breathtaking! Then I looked down at my feet and my guts gave a swooping lurch. I was standing atop a ridge that was only a foot wide and the ground fell away from it vertically, some six hundred metres (one thousand nine hundred and seventy feet) to the glacier below! Until that moment I had never really experienced vertigo but I felt it then on that ridge. For a moment I felt giddy and for the first time ever on a mountain, I was afraid!

It took a few moments to gather up my courage and move off westwards with the rest of the group towards the summit. As we did so, we met another group of climbers coming the other way and they proved to be a pack of rude, bolshey bastards who literally forced our group off the ridge – fortunately to the less steep south side – in order to get past!

We reached the summit after this inconvenience at about midday and went round shaking hands with each other and smiling. We stood at four thousand one hundred and sixty-five metres (thirteen thousand six hundred and sixty-five feet), the highest I had yet climbed and it felt wonderful! We sat down in the snow to eat a bit of lunch and Mr Andenmatten singled me out for special praise for my efforts. I swelled with pride and felt rather big-headed!

After the brief lunch stop we re-packed our gear and then Mr Andenmatten changed the batting order for the coming descent back to the plateau. I was put in the lead position and I led the group away down the mountain. I had not had such a euphoric, adrenalin-fuelled feeling since the parapenting flight in the French Alps and now once more I was as high as a kite. My heart filled with song and before I knew what I was doing I had broken into the first lines of the Eagles hit, *Take It To The Limit*. In those days, I considered myself to have quite a good singing voice and I let rip in the clear mountain air as we walked. I remembered all the words of the song perfectly and as I finished, I can say that I thought it was a good rendition, which was proven by the fact that I received a round of applause from my companions!

I set a fast pace down the steep snow slope but there was no more singing as we made it back to the plateau and then on back to the cable car at the Klein Matterhorn.

On the way down in the cable car, Mr Andenmatten told us the story about the two American extreme skiers who had been killed while trying to ski the precipitous east face of the Matterhorn. Looking out of the cabin window, across to this awesome face, it was difficult to imagine how anybody had been able to pluck up enough courage to attempt to descend such a difficult face. We were told how one of the skiers had never been found. I suppose, like in other parts of the Alps, the glacier at the foot of the Matterhorn would give up its dead in a hundred years or so!

I asked Mr Andenmatten what it was like to climb the Matterhorn, having assumed he had done so. He had and he told me that the Hornligrat Ridge was not too difficult and then he added, "You could do it, Steve, and if you would like, and are able to come back here again in the next few years, I could take you up it." I was gob-smacked that he had that much faith in my abilities and his comments planted a seed in my mind!

The rest of the group were still with us in the cable car and Mr Andenmatten announced that we would all receive a diploma for climbing the Breithorn and that we could pick them up at the Alpine Centre later that day.

Arnold asked me if I wanted to have a drink to celebrate the climb and I said I would love one, so when we got back to the lift station at Furi he and I said goodbye to and shook hands with Mr Andenmatten and the Japanese guys before heading to the nearest bar, where we ordered a couple of large beers.

As we sat on the sun terrace of the bar, sipping our cold beers in the glorious sunshine, we discussed the climb and also the possibility of getting another peak done in the next few days. Arnold was staying in Zermatt for a little while longer and I thought we had made a good team, so why not try and do it again? He agreed and we made plans to meet at the Alpine Centre at four thirty p.m. that day to see what was available.

Furi was of course the place where I'd seen the farmers cutting the grass for hay and now, a few days later, due to the hot sun, the crop was ready to be gathered in. There seemed to be an army of people of all ages at work on the pastures near where we sat, some raking the hay into rows with hand tools and others driving the little motorised wagons that picked up the hay and transported it to the barns on the hillside, where it was forked into power driven blowers to be blown up onto the lofts.

As I sat taking in the rural scene, I reflected on the events of the day and of the previous afternoon. After I had got up, there had been little time to worry about my mood swing the day before and I had launched myself into the climbing experience with gusto. I now felt fine again and I put the episode down as a minor wobble and tried to put it behind me, at the same time exercising a certain amount of caution concerning my activities. I was determined that this holiday was not going to go south like so many of my previous ones!

Arnold brought me out of my contemplation and I realized he had been talking all the time, so I cleared my throat and said, "Yes I agree with you," hoping that would cover my lapse in attention. It did and I began to concentrate once more on what he was saying. He really was quite a fascinating guy, being of a similar age to me. His working life had involved a lot of brain work, whereas mine had contained a lot of hard physical graft!

We finished our beers and then took the gondola back down to Zermatt, where we parted company until later.

I went back to the Excelsior for a shower and then read for a bit on my room balcony before making my way to the Alpine Centre for four thirty. Arnold was already there and we went to one of the desks together to ask about available guided climbs. The lady there told us there was a German gentleman trying to get a group together to climb the Pollux on Wednesday the twenty-first. We jumped at the chance, even though it seemed quite expensive at two hundred francs (a hundred pounds). The lady said she would contact the German chap and okay things with him. She went on to say that the climb would be confirmed on the following afternoon. We were about to leave the desk when I suddenly remembered the diplomas and I asked the lady about them. She checked her list of names and then sorted through a small pile of A4 size sheets. She presented us with the relevant documents and I was impressed with mine; it was thick card with a photo of the Breithorn at the top, the height of the mountain beneath and then my name, plus the name of the guide and the date. It was also embossed with an official stamp. I have the diploma proudly displayed on my bedroom wall today.

Arnold and I parted company as we came out of the centre, agreeing to meet there again at the same time the following day.

I went back to my hotel and read until dinner. Afterwards, I was regaling the barmaid with the story of my climb and upon mentioning my guide's name; she told me that Richard Andenmatten was eating outside in the hotel's terrace area. I immediately went out and found him having supper with a woman who I presumed to be his wife. He was pleased to see me and then even more so when I offered to buy him and his companion a drink. The waitress took the order and I paid her when she brought the drinks over. Mr Andenmatten had achieved something of a hero status with me and I would have liked to stay and talk with him, but he was busy eating and conversing with his partner so I shook his hand and then departed back inside the hotel, where I had another beer on my own and then went to bed.

Tuesday the twentieth of July – my birthday! On this day, I had planned to ski again but when I got up to the Klein Matterhorn cable car, I found it was not running, meaning there was no other way up, so I left my skis in a locker at the Trockener Steg station and returned to Zermatt, where I got changed into my walking gear, packed my rucksack and then set off on my decided hike to the Hornli Hut on the north east ridge of the Matterhorn! Although I was trying to take it easier for a bit, here I was, off again. My tail was up and I was on a roll! Just looking on the map I could see it was a long way, but I committed myself and I was off.

The weather was reasonably good, it was dry with patchy cloud but there was mist around the Matterhorn. I made my way out of town southwards and up past Furi on well-marked, good-surfaced paths towards Schroarzee at two thousand five hundred and eighty-three metres (eight thousand four hundred and seventy-four feet). It was a long grind. At first I was in the trees and then I entered high mountain pastures, where I could hear the distinctive squeaking calls of the marmots (an alpine creature similar-looking to an otter, but land bound). There were several burrows belonging to these animals near the path but on this occasion, I did not catch sight of one.

At Schroarzee, I grabbed a bit of lunch from my pack and ate it sitting on a rock near the pretty little glacial lake there. From here I headed on south west, upwards into high mountain terrain. The path zigzagged up past buttresses and over ridges. At one point there was a steel ramp and steps up a cliff face. Higher still, there were tricky sections with steel rungs leaded into the rock and I slipped on one of these and nearly broke my ankle! Finally I reached a rock-strewn slope that led steeply up to the large Hornli Hut, nestling just below the apex of the Hornligrat Ridge at three thousand two hundred and sixty metres (ten thousand six hundred and ninety-six feet).

I had passed many hikers and climbers on the way up, for this is the most popular route up the Matterhorn. The hike had taken me four and a half hours and I was pretty tired. The mist was now swirling all around and there were only brief glimpses of the great mountain, but you could sense its power; it seemed to exude a kind of menace and I felt very small in its presence! It was a rather desolate and unwelcoming place; there was a little new snow on the ground and no greenery and even the people seemed melancholy. I suppose some of the climbers were contemplating their coming ascent of the mountain and the risks contained therein. I quickly ate some food from my pack and drank some water at an outside table before hightailing it out of there.

The return journey to Schroarzee was largely uneventful, apart from me finding a pedometer that somebody had dropped, or rather thrown away because later I found that it didn't seem to work right!

By the time I got to Schroarzee, I was pretty knackered and there being a gondola from there back to Furi, I bought a ticket and took it, grateful for a sit down in the cabin. The mist had descended even further now so there was no view on the way down.

At Furi I took the main gondola back to town and got there with just enough time left to get to the Alpine Centre to meet Arnold at the appointed time. He asked me what I had been doing that day and was rather impressed with my efforts. The climb was on for the following day and from what I could gather from the centre, that there was just myself, Arnold and the German in the group. Also, it was an early start, with the rendezvous at the gondola being at seven a.m.

Arnold and I parted company again and agreed that we would need plenty of rest to prepare for the coming effort, so I went back to the Excelsior and took it easy, turning in early almost right after dinner.

Wednesday the twenty-first of July. I was up at five forty-five a.m. and soon had my climbing gear packed. After an early breakfast, I picked up the packed lunch that the hotel had prepared for me the previous evening and left with my gear for the gondola station. I got there a few minutes before the arranged meeting time and found Arnold already there. With him was a gentleman of maybe sixty-five years of age and I was introduced to the other member of our group, Rudolph. This, then, was the German guy who had got the ball rolling. I eyed him up and decided that although he was a fair age, he looked fit enough. His English was very good but he was slightly aloof and I made a quiet vow to myself not to mention the war! Just then the guide appeared, noticeable by the ubiquitous baseball cap. His name was Ricky and like Mr Andenmatten, he was Swiss, but unlike our previous guide he was rather surly and gave the impression that he didn't want to be bothered with us that morning. Maybe he had been out on the piss the night before! We all shook hands and then headed into the lift for the journey up to the Klein Matterhorn.

There was little banter on the way up after Ricky had explained some of the safety issues to us. There were quite a few FIS racers in the last cable car to the top but I didn't recognise any famous faces. The weather was superb once more on the way up and it was virtually clear as we exited the tunnel at Klein Matterhorn. There was no wind but it was bitterly cold as we made the same preparations as for the previous climb.

We left for the walk across the Breithorn Plateau at eight a.m., with the guide leading, of course, and me in the rear. We trekked on a more or less level route for about five kilometres (three point one miles), passing very near several yawning crevasses on the way, quite close to the route. The shadows in their depths were a deep blue and the sight of them gave me a chill in my soul. At one point I had to stop for a pee and it meant that we all had to stop because we were roped together. I stepped off the well-trodden route into soft snow and immediately received a bollocking off Ricky for risking stepping into a crevasse. The earlier chill had dispelled and the sun blazed down, reflecting strongly off the snow. It became quite warm and we were forced to shed a layer of clothing. There was little conversation on this snow walk to the start of the climb. I tried but with no success to get a singsong going!

We eventually reached the base of the pyramid of rock, ice and snow that formed the peak of the Pollux. Here we all strapped on the crampons and then set off steeply up a frozen gully. Even this early section of the climb was more difficult than anything on the Breithorn trip and I found the rope a hindrance at times. We were all puffing hard in the thin air but going well; then the going got even tougher, with a scrambling section. Ricky issued words of encouragement to us and our efforts were rewarded by a certain thawing of his attitude towards us. We entered a sort of sideways channel between two walls of rock, which opened out onto a vertical face across which there seemed no way forward! Then I noticed there were chains bolted to the rock face and there was a narrow ledge – and I mean narrow! – About five centimetres (two inches) wide situated about a metre and a half (five feet) below the chains. It was maybe ten metres (thirty-two and a half feet) to the snow slope at the other side of this daunting obstacle and we gathered round Ricky as he instructed us in the technique we would have to use to cross the face. He led us out onto the face and we observed how he held onto the chains while using the toe points of his crampons to grip the narrow ledge. We copied his example and one by one we followed him across. There was a hell of a drop below us, and I tried to ignore the sucking feeling it applied to me. Having conquered this difficult challenge, it was only a simple walk up a snow ridge to the summit. On the last pitch, we overtook another guided group and Ricky stopped to talk to the other guide. Although he was speaking German, I grasped that he was impressing on the other leader how well we had done in crossing the face and I felt my heart swelling with pride!

Once at the summit of the Pollux at four thousand and ninety-two metres (thirteen thousand four hundred and twenty-five feet), we sat down in the snow to eat our lunch. We were all on a bit of a high, including Ricky and we held an animated discussion. He told us how well we had done and that it had been a pleasure to guide us. Some groups, it transpired were not as competent as us and the guides had to work a lot harder. I felt really good about this and I'm sure Arnold and Rudolph shared my feelings. Once again, I was singled out for special praise and it lifted me even higher. This mountain is not as high as the Breithorn but the route we took was much more difficult than the one we did on the Breithorn!

Photographs were taken and Ricky took one of me with my Minolta, sitting on my rucksack with Arnold and another approaching group in the background. I have this one developed from a slide and blown up into a print of fifty centimetres (twenty inches) by forty centimetres (sixteen inches) mounted in the hallway.

The actual climb from the glacier had only been about five hundred metres (one thousand six hundred and forty feet) and had only taken about two hours, resulting in it being only early afternoon as we finished our lunches. I took a few moments to admire the view towards Castor at four thousand two hundred and twenty-three metres (thirteen thousand eight hundred and fifty-five feet) and the Liskamm at four thousand five hundred and twenty-seven metres (fourteen thousand eight hundred and fifty-three feet) before getting my gear re-packed to begin the descent with the others. We came back down on a slightly different route, avoiding the rock face with the chains and with few other difficulties. I felt really good but again my attempts at encouraging the others into song failed and we made our way down and back over the Breithorn Plateau with only sporadic conversation.

Ricky left us at the Klein Matterhorn, saying he had another group to meet to take up the Breithorn later on that afternoon.

Arnold, Rudolph and I retired back down to Furi for a drink at the bar there, where I was not satisfied with the one, feeling a need to celebrate but lacking enough money to push the boat out and encountering a certain reluctance from the others to pay to do so, I was forced to go without until I got back to Zermatt! We parted company after that, with a rather frosty glance from Rudolph, but we all shook hands and agreed that it had been a very satisfying day.

On getting back to town, I visited the bank for some more cash and then went back to the outdoor shop, intending to hand back my hired equipment, but I only returned the ice axe. I decided to buy the crampons and the harness because I thought I would need them in the future and they were in good order. I can't remember what I paid for them but I think I got a good deal! I also bought a pair of Leki walking poles, on account that they were supposed to help pressure on your knees when coming downhill; I had started to experience a bit of pain in my knee joints by the end of the holiday.

I went back to the Excelsior after that, shaved, showered and rested before dinner.

After I had eaten I went up to the Matterhorn bar for a few beers, but it was full of brash English folk bragging about their exploits, none of which I believed to be true. I didn't stay long and retired to finish the day off in my room, reading.

Thursday the twenty-second of July, up at six forty-five a.m. It was the last day of my holiday so I decided to go skiing. I sort of had to anyway, because my skis were still in the locker up at Trockener Steg. After I had breakfasted and sorted my gear I headed up the lifts to the Klein Matterhorn, picking up my skis on the way. I had one long run back to Trockener Steg and while I was waiting there for the cable car back to the top, I was approached by a young chap who turned out to be Canadian, and we got talking. He was not a very experienced skier and somewhat nervous of the high mountain terrain, so he asked me if I would show him around the slopes. I agreed and we skied all morning together. I had to wait for him some of the time but it was not an inconvenience and the crack going back up in the cable car each time was brilliant.

During this downtime in the skiing, I regaled him with tales of my exploits in Cervinia during the ski holidays of '83, '84 and '85, particularly of the time when I was staying in the Hotel President and I met a young English guy staying in the same hotel but was part of a bigger group staying in the Hotel Mignon. Early on in the holiday I was introduced to this group and they turned out to be members of the pop group, The Barron Knights, and their entourage of attendant wives and girlfriends. We hit it off immediately, skiing together and carousing the nightspots of the small town. It was tremendous fun; they were great skiers, hard drinkers and smokers. I also smoked in those days and I'm sure some of the stuff we smoked was barely legal! We played strip poker one night in the Mignon bar and I was winning for a long while and then I suddenly had a few bad hands and I was down to my underpants in no time. I don't think we got all our kit off but I can't be sure; the memories are a bit hazy. There was one particularly fit girl playing, but she gave up and went to bed before she could lose any of her kit and I could catch a glimpse of her curves!

They took me to a nightclub one evening and what I did there or how long I stayed is a total blank, but I woke up in my own hotel bed the following morning with a hell of a hangover!

Then there was the occasion at the mid-station area of Plan Maison, above Cervinia, when I was taking a break from skiing and visiting the little café there. I was in the queue behind a fairly short lady with long blonde hair. She got served and then turned around and started talking to me, then she suddenly stopped talking, put her hand to her mouth and said, "Oh I'm sorry. I thought you were someone else!" She had a distinctive, gravelly tone of voice and she looked familiar. I was about to say something back to her when a huge guy appeared out of nowhere and stepped between me and the woman. I immediately backed off and put two and two together; this guy was a 'heavy' and the woman must be somebody famous! The pair moved off and I never saw them again but later that day I was telling my holiday rep about the incident and she said, "Oh, yes, the woman you met was probably Bonnie Tyler, the singer, she is skiing here this week!" And of course, she was correct. The penny dropped fully with me, realising that was why the woman looked familiar to me.

My new Canadian friend had not heard of The Barron Knights but he was very familiar with the work of Bonnie Tyler!

In 1985, the last time I was skiing in Cervinia, it started to snow midway through my two-week holiday. In Britain we do not see snow so often and I have never before or since seen snow like I experienced on that trip. It began one morning with darkening skies; there was no wind but there was a sense of pregnancy about the weather. A veil of snow began to fall around the upper reaches of the Matterhorn, or Mt Cervino as they call it on the Italian side. It took all morning for the veil of snow to descend to Cervinia, but then it all closed in. It snowed solidly for three days and three nights and then the wind got up and it became a howling blizzard. The ski-lifts were closed and you could hardly get out of the hotel door. It must have put down a hell of a depth of snow but when it finally did clear up you couldn't tell, because the wind had blown it all away!

Also on that trip the 'Chinook' wind came to the resort, bringing warm air from North Africa and depositing a layer of fine brown sand on the snow. The snow began to melt in the warming conditions and skiing became difficult until the weather changed.

I was enjoying my reminiscing. The young Canadian guy was very impressionable and I took full advantage of this, finishing my tale telling with the occasion when Ken Ostle and I were skiing in 1995 in the French resort of Les Deux Alpes. We took a day trip to the neighbouring resort of Alpe Duez but we did not go by road – we went in a helicopter! There was a group of five of us and it cost about forty pounds per person. The other resort was only a ten-minute flight away but it was my first trip in a whirlybird and was very exciting. Our skis were carried in pods on the skids of the machine. It was the best 'pose' I have ever had, arriving in Alpe Duez in a whirling cloud of snow; I felt like royalty!

Having landed in front of a crowd of curious onlookers, I quickly got my skis and then separated myself from the group. I was the best skier and I wanted to make full use of my one day in the resort by covering as much ground as possible. I headed off from the heliport, got a piste map from the nearest lift station and then took the cable car to Pic Blanc, the highest point in the resort at over three thousand and forty-seven metres (ten thousand feet). There was only one piste off the top and it was a black run; and what a black it turned out to be! The mist was down and there were few other skiers about, or indeed anything by which you could judge distance. I set off down the very steep run very carefully but my heart was soon in my mouth; the piste rapidly transformed into a mogul field, and what moguls they were! On such a steep slope, they just seemed to form a series of massive steps and as I picked my way down in the near whiteout conditions I kind of dropped from one bump to the next at about two metres (six feet) each time. It was frightening but I made it to a place where the piste levelled out and narrowed into a steel-lined tunnel through a ridge. There was snow in the tunnel and I skied through it to emerge on a narrow snow ledge, which led to the next section of piste. The run became less steep and the visibility improved, resulting in me being able to increase the pace.

There were no other recreational skiers on the slope and I thought it was odd and then I found out why. I was hailed by a piste control guy standing at the edge of the slope. He waved me over and then proceeded to harangue me in French. I shouted back, "Parlez-vous Anglais?" (Do you speak English?). He said, "Monsieur, what the hell do you think you're doing? The piste is closed!"

I had not seen any signs to substantiate this claim and so I just laughed at him, waved and skied off down the slope.

I managed to explore nearly all the pistes in the resort during the day, after those early, heart-stopping moments and returned to the heliport with enough time to grab a beer before rejoining my group and catching the return helicopter flight to Les Deux Alpes. It was a grand day out!

Getting back to my time with the Canadian guy; we finished our time on the slopes when they closed for the day and I asked the guy (whose name I forget) if he would take lunch with me but he declined, saying he had to get off, so we shook hands, parted and I never saw him again.

When I got back to town, I packed my skis away in the Excelsior ski room, ready for the journey home and then changed before going to shop for a few presents for the folks back home. The rest of the day was largely uneventful and I retired about ten fifteen to prepare for the trip home.

Friday the twenty-third of July. I was up at six forty-five a.m. having slept well. I packed my suitcase and then got it and the skis sent from reception to enter the fly-rail luggage system. I had my breakfast and then went for a last walk round the town, visiting the church to say a short prayer to give thanks for a safe holiday and to wish for a safe trip home. Back at the Excelsior I said goodbye to Rita on reception and she shook my hand. I had left a nice tip in my room for the very efficient maids, and paid my bill.

I departed Zermatt on the ten a.m. train down to Visp, taking a last long look at the Matterhorn before I entered the station, thinking, I will be back and then we will see about you!

The journey home involved a three hour wait at Geneva airport before I could check in and then a two hour wait at Manchester airport, to catch the shuttle bus to the airpark before I could pick up my car. My luggage got through the system okay though and I got home about twelve forty-five a.m.

There was little time after I got back from Switzerland to rest, because I had arranged before the holiday to help out at Ken Ostle's farm across the valley with an organised shearing day on Sunday the twenty-fifth of July. I was up at seven a.m., breakfasted and then across to Ken's for eight thirty a.m. I took Tina over with me to help gather the sheep in and then battle commenced. The shearers were New Zealanders and there were three of them. There were seven hundred sheep to shear and each man sheared a sheep every minute! I worked alongside Ken and his brother Geoff, doing all sorts of jobs, such as bringing the sheep in from the nearby fields, using Tina; rolling up fleeces, packing them into wool sheets and generally cleaning up as we went. I put in six and a half hours of hectic work but it was good crack, as is the case on such a social occasion.

That evening I went to see my grandmother, who was in a residential home at Cockermouth and we had quite a good crack.

Haymaking recommenced on our farm right after the holiday and I threw myself into this. I had to break off though, for one of my regular psychiatrist appointments and it proved to be yet another disappointing, almost pointless visit. I loved visiting the psychologist, Richard, but frankly in that period I found the psychiatrist a waste of time! He wanted to know how the holiday had gone and I told him it had been brilliant, but at the same time omitting the part about the slight wobble I had experienced

I had a good night out on Saturday the thirty-first of July with Ken and my other Mungrisdale friends. We toured the pubs in Penrith and ended up in Toppers Nightclub where I saw my favourite girl, Rachel, who was also having a good time, it seemed. I was not driving and got quite a skinfull, meaning that I had a hangover on the following morning. I did not have to get up very early though, which was a good job because I had arranged to meet Andrew, Tracy and their friend Tom for a hike at lunch time. Tina would go with us too, but she was a bit smelly and I had to bath her.

From our farm we drove to Hartsop village, south of Ullswater and hiked up onto High Street and back round in a horseshoe, to drop down to the Hayeswater reservoir. Early on the weather was fine and hot, but in the late afternoon a few thunderheads built up and there was the occasional rumble. This caused Tom, who was afraid of thunder and lightning, to flee back towards the car. The rest of us found this slightly amusing.

During the hike, Andrew and I reminisced about a trip we took in August 1997, when we took a holiday cottage in Portknockie on the Moray Firth coast in Scotland for a week. (I have already mentioned this holiday earlier in the narrative, but here are some more details of the trip). We travelled up in my Capri and we had quite a carload of gear, including our golf clubs. I had decided to do the journey up the long way by going up the west side and then coming across eastwards to Inverness and along to Portknockie. It was a long journey and took all day. We had an interesting occurrence on the way; just out of Invergarry we came across two gorgeous blonde girls hitchhiking. They had large rucksacks on and I nearly stopped to pick them up, but it was impossible; my car was already rammed with our own stuff! I had to drive on with great disappointment; it was just my bloody luck!

It was evening time before we arrived in Portknockie and it is a small place, so we had little difficulty in locating our cottage.

The holiday was ostensibly a golfing trip but it also turned into a hard drinking one as well! We got a golf ticket, which allowed us to play ten courses in the area for fifty pounds for each of us. We played Cullen, Keith, Dufftown, above the Glenfiddich distillery; and Lossiemouth, that I can remember. I played well but Andrew, who is a big hitter, had trouble with his direction and on one memorable occasion, while teeing off on a hole at Lossiemouth, he was distracted by one of the Torndado jets taking off from the adjacent airbase and he hit his ball three hundred yards forwards but also hooked it a hundred yards left, right into the middle of a caravan park! We did not hear any cries of pain so that was okay, but he never got the ball back. I hope he doesn't mind, but to me it was a very funny incident

We had some right old sessions on the drink. We had bought several large packs of the 5.2 per cent Stella Artois lager cans at Fort William on the way up and on the Sunday afternoon we got stuck into these. I can't remember how many cans we slurped but there were enough empties to build a pyramid a metre high! Then afterwards when went to the pub and played pool against the locals, at the same time getting even more drink down us!

Angus and Anne, who were newly married at the time, were staying at Fraserburgh with their kids at the same time and they joined us for a day on the beach at Cullen. The kids were playing in the surf while we sunbathed above the tide line. Suddenly there was a shout from my nephew, Paul, who had kicked a football out into the waves. He was just a young lad and became distressed by the fact that his ball was being carried out to sea. I got up and ran into the waves after it. I was soon having to swim and there was a strong undertow, causing me to be carried further out. I reached the ball and grabbed it, turned and started back for shore. I was well out of my depth and am not a very strong swimmer, so I had to give it everything I'd got to get back to shore. I made it but it scared me a lot and I haven't been back in the sea since. All in all it was a good trip; the golf had been very competitive and I came out on top most of the time.

Back on the hike; we got back to the car and found Tom waiting for us, looking a bit nervous. When we had stowed our walking gear, we drove to the Patterdale hotel for a delicious pint and then moved onto the hotel at Dockray and enjoyed another one there. I left Tina in the car; she had enjoyed her day and had not been frightened by the thunder. While we were drinking at an outside table, I told my companions about my Zermatt holiday and particularly the bit about the guide being willing to take me up the Matterhorn. I was aiming my attention at Andrew in particular and asked him if he fancied going with me in a few years' time and tackling the beast.

He rather blanched and said, "Hell's teeth, mate, I don't think I will be up to anything as difficult as that!"

I was slightly disappointed but his reaction did not shake my growing seed of an idea to climb the mountain. After we left Dockray we headed home to finish another good day.

A few days later, I was mole trapping down at the Old Church Hotel on the western shore of Ullswater. There were several of the 'black coated gentlemen' working on the main lawn of the hotel and they were making a real mess. It is a beautiful place and if anybody ever wanted to look at the owner's motivations for hiring me to catch his moles they should have seen that lawn – it was like a ploughed field! At the end of the contract I had caught four moles and I was just putting my traps away in the car when I noticed a sheet of paper on the windscreen. On inspection, I found it to be a typed menu for dinner that night in the hotel. I was curious as I read down the list of courses and then laughed out loud when I came to the main courses. One of them read, 'Fricasse of Wild Mole à la

Titterington'. The owner must have spied me looking at the menu and came out to see me with a broad grin on his face.

I matched his grin and said, "You're not seriously going to put this on the tables, are you?"

And he replied, "Yes, of course, but if anybody asks for that course I am just going to say it's unavailable!"

We both laughed and then I made a bill out for him, got my pay and then the owner said, "There are a couple of old traps in the shed at the back, similar to the type you use. Do you want them?"

I said, "Yeah, great. I'm sure they will add to my arsenal."

He got me the traps and I still have them today; one of them is a very good trap. I kept my copy of the menu and have it framed and displayed. I have never trapped at that location again and it is now a private house.

From the third to the tenth of August I did a big walling job with my workmate Thomas, at Caldbeck. It was a contract for the national park, to take down and re-build approximately fifty-five metres of retaining wall on the roadside in the middle of the village. The weather was red hot and I had only a pair of shorts on. The stone was good to build with and the crack was great with Thomas, as always. I had trouble concentrating from time to time as several attractive women walked by, admiring our work. It was a good advertisement and we got several more jobs out of it in the village. I had hoped those women were admiring me, all bared out in the sun but they did not seem to notice me, which is par for the course.

I was still on probation at this time and I had to report to the office once a month. The meetings nearly always went well and I didn't mind having to attend them. Sometimes the probation officer and I would even go for a coffee at a nearby café. I liked to think I was somewhat different to the other punters they had to deal with!

Around this time, I had several good nights out in Carlisle with the Mungrisdale gang but we all remained single after them and only managed to come away with a hangover each!

During late August I did a lot of wire fencing at Ken Ostle's farm and although it was hard work, we had a good crack as we worked.

On the seventh of September, I helped Ken and some other farmers to gather the sheep in off Southerfell. We used our dogs, of course, and our quad bikes. It was a difficult fell to gather because there is so much bracken on its slopes; the sheep have a habit of hiding in it and you can start at one end of the fell with a good number of sheep but by the time you get to the other end, half of them have dodged into the bracken and disappeared. The day fell apart for me when disaster struck on the shoulder of the fell. I was riding my Honda across a steep slope when the front wheel dropped into a hole hidden beneath the bracken. I lost control and the machine rolled, throwing me off on the downhill side. The quad rolled over me and then went cart-wheeling down the fellside. I picked myself up and was uninjured but I watched with horror as the quad rolled towards the edge of a steep ravine. Then, to my amazement, it came to a standstill on a small level area of ground, right at the edge of the drop-off. I made my way down the thirty metres or so to it and saw it was upright. On inspection, I found that the only damage was a slightly bent handlebar; it must have been cushioned on its tumble by the deep bracken. I was immensely relieved and realized how lucky I had been, but I still had to get the machine back out to safe ground. Fortunately Ken was nearby and he came to my aid. He was much more experienced at riding quads over steep ground than me and he rode my machine out of its predicament for me with ease. The incident had shaken me up quite a bit though and fortunately we were at the end of the gather and I was able to take over from Ken and finish the job; it had not been a very good day!

This episode reminded me of another one a few years earlier that had occurred only about half a mile away. Ken and I were putting up a new wire fence for his neighbour, alongside the same ravine that my quad had nearly disappeared into. We were using Ken's 4WD Subaru pickup to transport fencing materials up the fellside to the job. On one particularly damp morning, we were coming back down the steep shoulder of Southerfell in the pickup in first gear.

I said to Ken, "We won't lose traction going down here, will we?"

He replied, "No, this motor can handle any slope!"

With that, he immediately changed up into second gear. Suddenly the vehicle seemed to go light and our forward speed increased. I shouted, "Shit, we are in a slide." The Subaru took off down the fellside. Ken desperately tried to regain control but the slide was unstoppable. There was a little wooden sheep shed about fifty metres dead ahead. My heart was in my mouth; surely we were going to pile straight into it. At the last moment, the pickup hit a small hump on the slope and it was enough to turn the careering vehicle out of direct contact with the shed but we caught it a glancing blow on the corner, causing the pickup to spin sideways. Our momentum had barely been slowed by the impact and we slid on, picking up speed again. Further down the slope there was a wire fence, with a number of large beech trees dotted along its length. Still sliding sideways, the pickup slammed into one of these tree trunks! Ken's sheepdog was in the Subaru with us and the impact threw her on top of me. We had come to a standstill, thank God.

Ken looked at me with a kind of quirky grin on his face and said in a trembling voice, "Well, that was fun, wasn't it?"

It took me a second to find my voice and then I uttered, "Thank Christ we hit this tree, we could have gone a lot further and been killed!"

We got out of the vehicle shakily and inspected the damage. Contact with the tree had occurred in the back wheel area and the wheel was bent under slightly, making the vehicle undrivable. I can't remember how we got the pickup out from the side of the tree and back to the farm, but we did and it was repaired. I don't think Ken went up that slope again in it though. There is a kind of green algae that grows in the grass on those slopes at certain times of year, making conditions very slippery; perhaps the algae had been responsible for the accident?

Getting back to September 1999; on the morning of Friday the seventeenth I had one of my regular appointments with my probation officer, which went well and then I departed for Scotland on a camping/walking trip that would include Angus, Anne and their friend Alex Driver, whom I had never met before. I had loaded all my gear before I left for my probation meeting in Penrith and I drove from there up to Stirling Services; where I was due to meet the others around two p.m. They were late and I had time to eat my lunch. I was then introduced to Alex. The others had a bite to eat also, then we continued on up in convoy to Fort William and on into Glen Nevis, where we set up camp at the big site there. After we had got sorted we had a couple of cans of beer and then headed into Fort William for our suppers. When we had eaten, we headed to one of the popular pubs where there was live music playing. There was a young guy singing and he performed rather a good rendition of Robbie William's *Angels*. It was a good night and we got quite a few beers down us, apart from the driver, of course.

The weather had been showery, windy and cool on the way up but our first night in the tents was dry and quiet, resulting in a good sleep.

Saturday the eighteenth. We were all up around seven a.m. and I cooked my breakfast in the boot of the Capri, put some lunch and a flask of coffee ready before we headed out in Angus's VW Golf GTI to Spean Bridge, where we took the A86 towards Newtonmore. We turned off near Tulloch onto a forestry track, which terminated after about three miles at a little car park at the northern end of Loch Treig. We donned our walking gear and then set off at nine forty-five a.m. in dry but windy conditions up grassy, wet slopes onto Stob a' Choire Mheadhoin at a thousand one hundred and five metres (three thousand six hundred and twenty-five feet). We were all going well and we headed onto the second Munro of Stob' Coire Easain at a thousand one hundred and fifteen metres (three thousand six hundred and fifty-eight feet). In a way, I found it quite easy after my recent Swiss trip. We came back down to the car for five p.m. by a slightly different route; the hike had been about fifteen kilometres (nine point three miles) and the crack had been excellent – especially with Alex, who I was quickly coming to like. We then headed back into Fort William to visit one of the outdoor shops, where Alex bought some new boots. His feet had blistered early on in the hike due to badly fitting boots. He got fixed up but I wondered how he would come on the following day, because he would have to break the new boots in on an even bigger hike that Angus had got planned!

We ate fish and chips from a nearby chippy and then returned to the campsite, showered, changed and then walked the five hundred yards up the road for a few drinks at the bar/restaurant there. I didn't stay long though, because I suffered an allergic reaction, I think from the air freshener in the campsite toilet block. My nose was streaming and I was sneezing quite uncontrollably! I went to bed, tossed and turned and sort of sweated the thing out of myself. By morning, I felt a lot better. The weather overnight had been wild, rough and damp but it was improving.

Sunday the nineteenth. We had a little lie-in until seven thirty a.m. and then had breakfast, put our lunches together, loaded both cars with our gear and then drove them up Glen Nevis. We parked one car at Achriabhach and then all continued on in the other car, to park it at the end of the road. We donned our gear in the rather damp, windy conditions and then headed up the level path into the gorge encompassing the Water of Nevis River. After about a mile we came to the only crossing on the river for miles, the Steall Bridge. This is a wire rope bridge and not for the faint hearted. It consists of three cables about an inch thick (two and a half centimetres), one to walk on and the other two about shoulder height to hold on to. The cables are suspended in a single span over a length of about twenty metres and roughly two metres above the water. I had never crossed one of these constructions before and was nervous. Angus went first, followed by Anne and Alex, then it was my turn. The others seemed to be going okay but they were wobbling about a bit. I stepped onto the foot cable, grabbed hold of the hand cables and shuffled across, one foot in front of the other, trying not to be influenced by the disorientating effect of the swirling brown water beneath. I was across in no time and had wobbled a bit but it had been okay.

Once on the other side of the river, we continued along the western bank until we found a rough path heading up steeply beside a tributary waterfall in a southerly direction. We climbed steadily up this "stalker's" path to eventually reach the summit of the first of five planned Munros – An Gearanach at nine hundred and eighty-two metres (three thousand two hundred and twenty-one feet). From here we continued on in a southerly direction over the satellite top of An Garbhanach to Stob Coire a' Chairn at nine hundred and eighty-one metres (three thousand two hundred and eighteen feet) where we had lunch behind a few rocks, which were the only shelter nearby from the rising wind.

Once we had recharged our batteries, we headed on south west towards Am Bodach. As we made our way across the exposed, broken ground, the wind, which was blowing from the south west, increased into a howling gale. The air was already cool and the wind chill increased. The gale tore at us, pushing us one way and then the other and it became quite scary. At one point we were literally forced to crawl across a particularly exposed section. We struggled up onto Am Bodach at a thousand and thirty-two metres (three thousand three hundred and eighty-five feet) and the wind began to ease. It was dry by now and the cloud level was above the summits.

Along the way I had been eating dried apricots to keep up my energy levels. They had been in my rucksack for quite some time and must have been past their eat by date. I began to get a churning sensation in my tummy and became slightly concerned that I would have to try and find a place to move my bowels. Alex had been eating some of my apricots too and I asked him if he was feeling okay, and he said, "Actually, I am feeling a bit off colour." I told him I thought I was going to get the 'runs' shortly and he gave me a rather quizzical look.

I was suddenly reminded of the time I was skiing in Les Arcs in the French Alps in 1986. I was on a self-catering holiday with a friend and my sister Heather and one morning, I must have eaten something bad because I was just starting to ski the piste from the top of the Aguille Rouge, the highest point at over three thousand and forty-seven metres (ten thousand feet) and suddenly I felt a violent cramp in my guts. I thought, *shit, I'm going to have to GO!* I knew a moment of panic. There was no toilet anywhere near, I was at the top of a mountain and there was only rock, ice and snow. There was also no privacy; the piste ran across the edge of a yawning chasm and there were only a few feet of soft snow separating the piste from the edge of the drop. I desperately unclipped my skis, fumbling with the binding levers and stepped into the soft snow. I pulled my salopettes down and squatted just in time before I voided my bowels! At first there had been no other skiers in sight but now, suddenly the slope was filled with people, passing only a few metres away. I was in full view and the skiers pointed and laughed. Some of them even stopped to gawk, my face must have gone as red as a beetroot and it was and still is my most embarrassing moment! Having eased the pressure on my guts, I used the snow to clean myself – I had nothing else! Then I covered myself, put my skis back on and headed on down the slope. I knew however that I was not out of the woods yet, because already I could feel the pressure and pain starting to build again. It was a long way back to Les Arcs and I had to descend a steep slope, go up a chairlift and then ski down another piste to the town before I would reach the nearest toilet. I tore off down and skied the fastest and probably the most recklessly I have ever done and made it to the chairlift. It felt better going up the lift seated because it meant I was sitting on my problem; the pressure was on again on the return run to the town, but I made it back to our apartment just in time before the next attack! When I had 'been' a few more times, I sought medical help and the doctor prescribed some tablets, which cost twenty-two pounds and that was a lot in those days! They worked though, drying me up. I was weak for a few days afterwards but I was soon back to my normal self.

Back on Am Bodach, I contemplated my situation and told Angus and Anne of my stomach ache, too. They said to try and hold on until we got a bit lower down. So I steeled myself and we continued on down and back up westwards to Sgorr an Lubhair at a thousand and one metres (three thousand two hundred and eighty-four feet.) Then we walked north down and back up to the fifth Munro – the highest one, Sgurr a Mhaim at a thousand and ninety-nine metres (three thousand six hundred and five feet.) I was holding on to my guts for all I was worth but we had done five of the eleven Munros in the Mamores range and it was all downhill from there to the car. Just off the summit, I found a sheltered place with a bit of moss about and I could not hold myself any longer. Unlike the French incident, there was nobody else about and I was able to void my bowels in peace. I used the moss to clean up and then continued down. I had to go four more times on the way back to the car at Achreabhach and each time I did so, my companions walked on respectfully but with, I suspect, a certain amount of amusement!

We had started walking at nine forty-five a.m. and it was six forty-five p.m. when we got back to the car. We had done approximately eight miles (twelve point nine kilometres) and it had been a good hike, with good crack and somewhat eventful with my attack of the runs. Alex had managed to hold onto his bowels and also had broken in his new boots with very few problems. We retrieved the other car and returned to the campsite, showered, had a couple of cans and then drove into Fort William, where we had a poor meal at a restaurant before returning to our tents and collapsing into our sleeping bags.

Monday the twentieth, I was up around eight a.m. and cooked a couple of boiled eggs, my favourite food. I also had some soup, which might seem a strange thing to have for breakfast to some people. We then broke camp, packed all our gear away and headed into Fort William to do a spot of shopping. I bought a Scottish dance music C.D. for Dad and a headscarf for Mam. We had lunch at a chippy at one p.m. and then started the drive home. We broke our journey at the Glencoe ski centre, where I checked out the price of the lifts, and again at Stirling Services for a bite to eat. We had driven in convoy until that point but we soon became separated on the M80 and M74 and I stopped a further twice to avoid getting overtired; the driving conditions were difficult, with wind and rain. It had dried up by the time I got home at six thirty p.m. and I unpacked my gear, presented Mam and Dad with their presents, then let Tina out for a run.

It had been a great trip and I had got to know Alex quite well. There had been talk on the trip about him joining a big group of us on a ski holiday in the coming winter and I looked forward to that.

It was straight back into work the next day, grafting alongside Thomas as we tried to put Bob Ridehalgh's sewage system to rights at his house in Mungrisdale. We put in a few hard days on it and it was unpleasant work, as you can imagine.

On the twenty-third of September, I had a big meeting with my counsellors at Elmwood house in Penrith. They grilled me about my activities in the past months and there was a new psychiatrist present, who was of the opinion that I was slightly manic. He suggested that I go on medication, namely Carbamazapine. I was not happy about this development and I felt intimidated at the meeting and somewhat afraid of this new psychiatrist, so I agreed to try the drug. I had, however, taken an instant dislike to this new counsellor and in the future this would grow! I was given a prescription and then the meeting broke up. The upside of it had been that there was a very attractive student nurse present, wearing very revealing clothing. I went directly from the meeting to the pharmacy and got the prescribed course of pills. I tried the medication for a week, but the information leaflet with the drug warned you about operating machinery while taking it and these activities were a big part of my livelihood; plus it made me feel like shit so I stopped taking it.

Ken Ostle and his parents had decided to give up farming for various reasons and I spent the twenty-fourth of September helping them prepare for their farm sale the following day. There was much to do and it was a busy day. On the sale day, my main duty was marshalling the traffic in the car parking field across from the end of their farm lane. There were hundreds of people at the sale and it was a long day. At the end of it Mr and Mrs Ostle, Ken, his brothers and I were exhausted and also there was a certain amount of emotion involved. They had been farming a long time and it was going to be a wrench being away from it.

My hectic life continued in spite of the effects of the Carbamazapine I was taking for a time. I did a spell of dry stone walling with Thomas, repairing the walls on our neighbouring farm and also another national park contract, helping to repair the old coach road up on Matterdale Common, using diggers and dumpers to move gravel around. I threw the track off a mini-digger one day and I was not popular!

On the twelfth of October, Thomas and I started one of our most interesting and difficult contracts ever, at a house on the back road along the bottom of Southerfell. The plan was to build three ponds in the back garden of the house. The lawn area in which we were to construct the ponds was on a bank and each pond was to be linked by a little stream running down from the fence at the top. We started by excavating three holes of different sizes and worked with hand tools because the slope was too steep for a mini-digger. There was a lot of soil and we carted it away into a nearby field, using my quad bike and big trailer. Then we had to build up walls inside the holes using sand, cement and stone from a ruined barn nearby. The channels linking each hole were then constructed in a similar fashion and a pipe dug in to take the outfall water from the ponds away from a drain at the base of the lower pond. Rubber liners were then cut from sheets and placed over the stonework in each hole. More stonework was erected to hold down the overlaps of the liners and therefore form the rim of each pond. It was a big job and at the end of it we had a ceremony to mark the switching on of the water. It was a very satisfying feeling to see the water spill down to flow into each pond in turn and fill them. It was one of the best jobs Thomas and I had done and it was worth almost a thousand pounds each to us! We were both entering a very lucrative period in our working lives, buying our own cement mixer, which we looked after with great care. There were several contracts repairing lime kilns in the area and also St Patrick's Well at Glenridding for the national park.

Socially, I enjoyed an evening showing slides of my Swiss trip to Andrew and Tracy at their house in Workington. Quite a bit of beer was supped and I stayed over. Also there were several nights out in Penrith with my Mungrisdale friends.

My back was playing up again. The muscles in it had all become tensed up and I went for a back massage from a very attractive young lady at the North Lakes Spa. She was a farmer's daughter from out at Mauld's Meaburn and we got on very well; I even had a couple of dances with her one night at Toppers Nightclub shortly afterwards.

The winter season of the Castle Sowerby pool league had started again on Tuesday nights and we had a great win on the twenty-third of November, beating the Snooty Fox at Uldale six-three. I played particularly well, making an excellent clearance in one frame. Bob drove that night and I got a large skinful of beer.

For home matches at the Mill Inn I went on my push-bike with the lights and got pissed. It was a hard ride home and one night I almost ran into the pack of semi-wild horses that roamed the area; they were black ones and difficult to pick out in the beam of the bike headlight. I almost hit one and just avoided going over the handlebars!

The weeks went by, during which I did some mole trapping and worked on lime kilns with Thomas at Aughertree near Uldale. I took Tina with me on dry days and she enjoyed ratching about while we worked. Each day I took my quad in the trailer behind the Capri and we used it and the trailer to ferry materials across from the road over the fell to the site of the kilns.

By the fourteenth of December, we were close to finishing these kilns. Angus had told us that he would buy us and his other national park workers a Christmas drink at the Mill Inn at approximately three p.m. so we tried to organise our day around that. Unfortunately the weather closed in mid-morning and it started to snow. By the time we finished work and were leaving for the rendezvous at the Mill Inn, it had put three inches down. The snow was lying thickly on the roads and they were treacherous. I was towing the trailer carrying the quad behind the Capri and although it was a powerful car, it was poor on the snow, with its wide tyres. I managed to get as far as Millhouse Village with little difficulty, but then I was faced with a moderately steep hill to get to my turn off to Mungrisdale and the Mill Inn. I put the car in second gear and set off up the hill. I soon began to lose traction and the trailer's inside wheel began to drag against the banking at the roadside. Somehow the car managed to keep going, although the wheels were slipping and spinning out. The engine was almost stalling and the car was sort of juddering. It must have put enormous strain on the gearbox because I had to have it replaced shortly afterwards. I made it to the turn off though and took the Mungrisdale Road. I had gone on another couple of miles and then I came to the long straight known as Mellfell. It is on a slight gradient, but not as steep as the hill I had just struggled up. This made no difference, however, because the wheels started to slip and I slowly came to a skidding standstill. The roads were the most slippery I had ever known them to be.

I was flummoxed. What was I going to do now? If I unhitched the trailer and tried to go on to the Mill Inn in the car alone, somebody might steal the quad and trailer. I had managed to get my inside wheels onto the verge and the road was fairly wide so I decided to offload the quad, unhitch the trailer and then hitch the quad to the trailer to go on to the pub with that outfit. I did this, leaving the Capri partly on the road, but there was enough room for other vehicles to get past my stranded motor.

I was counting on Angus having the park Land Rover at the pub and maybe he would give me a tow. I rode the quad with trailer to the pub in the freezing conditions; it was three miles and I was shivering by the time I got there. I was nearly on time though and parked my outfit before going into the hostelry to meet the others. I was pretty stressed out and in need of a drink, a strong one at that, so when Angus asked me what I wanted I ordered a pint of the 5.2 per cent Stella Artois!

I glugged the pint down, had a short crack with the others and then Angus said, "We had better get your tackle sorted out, hadn't we?"

I agreed. It was starting to get dark so Angus and I left the others and we went out to hitch my trailer to the park Land Rover, load my quad and then we took the outfit back to our farm. After we unhitched the trailer and quad he drove me back to where I had left my car. On the way, he towed out another stranded motorist and she was very attractive, which brightened the day somewhat. The strong drink had gone to my head and I was feeling flakey and somewhat manic with the combination of the alcohol and the stress. Angus towed me back onto the road with the Land Rover and I set off to follow him back home. The Capri travelled fine, unencumbered by the trailer and quad and I got home okay, but it had been an exhausting time and it took me the rest of the day to calm down.

Just after this, I went mole trapping out at Whitehaven Golf Club. The course had been built fairly recently on the site of an old open cast mine that had been refilled. There were few moles on the fairways because the soil was of a poor quality; it was wet, dank and smelled bad. The greens were a different kettle of fish though, having been constructed with good quality, sandy topsoil. Here the moles had gone to town; the molehills looked like a severe outbreak of acne on the smooth surfaces. It was a tiring job, being a sixty-six mile (a hundred and six kilometres) round trip from our farm and I had to make seven visits.

It proved to be expensive in more ways than one, because halfway through the contract I had ten traps stolen off the course. I was livid. The course was close to a housing estate and anybody could have taken them! I caught nearly eighty moles on the course though, even with the weather being frosty some of the time, causing me to have to put dead grass instead of soil around the necks of the traps, to allow them to release easily when sprung by the moles.

It was quite a difficult, tiring time for me and I got myself upset over a few things including the wheel bearings on my trailer failing; one of the grease nipples did not work properly, causing part of the problem. I tried to complain to the firm that sold me the trailer but they told me I had overloaded the trailer, causing the bearings to fail. I'm afraid I lost my temper with them! When I had quietened myself, I asked them if they would put new bearings in for me, and they agreed but said I would have to pay for them. I got the bearings replaced but I was not happy; I felt I had been treated poorly by that firm and never did any more business with them.

Christmas came and went. I got a few nice presents and had a few good nights out with my mates.

On the twenty-seventh of December, Andrew and I took Tina and hiked up Blencathra. We skirted the bottom of Sharp Edge, contouring round to Horsehead Brow and back up around to the summit. The weather was glorious but there was about six inches of snow lying, making it difficult going in places. We got back to our cars at four fifteen p.m. It had been a good day's walk and Tina had enjoyed it particularly; she loved the snow. That evening I went out to Andrew's for supper and wine. The crack was good as always and I stayed over.

I decided on a sudden impulse that I would see the new millennium in on a Scotland trip, so early on the twenty-ninth of December, without notifying the probation service, I loaded my skiing and hiking gear into the Capri and set off for Fort William.

The drive up was difficult. There were snow showers over Rannoch Moor, causing a lot of spray from the heavily salted roads. It was dark by the time I reached Fort William and I had noticed my headlights had become dimmer. I thought something had gone wrong with the electrics but when I stopped to examine the lights I found that they were caked over with a thick crust of salt from the road. The car's gearbox was also starting to make quite a bit of noise and I went to a garage, where the mechanic took the Capri for a test drive. When he came back, he told me the bearings on the lay shaft were shot. This, then, was the damage from the recent slippery hill climb while towing the trailer. The mechanic told me the problem would not render the car undrivable but I would need to get it fixed soon.

I found a hotel down near the town's waterfront where there was a room available, got checked in, and then, after I had settled into my room, went down to the restaurant, where I enjoyed some of the nicest fish and chips I have ever had. Then I went into the public bar, where I put my money on the pool table to reserve a game. There were several locals playing and while I quaffed my beer I studied the form; there were a couple of decent players. My turn came and in the first frame I took my opponent to the cleaners! Then I was beaten in the next and had to put my money on again. I went on to win several more frames, drink several pints and generally enjoy the crack. The pool rules there were slightly different to ours but I soon got used to them. I left the bar and turned in about eleven p.m.

Thursday the thirtieth of December. I was up at seven thirty a.m. after quite a good sleep; the room was very comfortable. I packed up, had a nice breakfast, paid the bill and then loaded my car and set off out of town on the A82 towards Spean Bridge. Although there was no snow lying down in the glens, there was plenty high up and I thought I would see what the skiing was like on the Nevis Range slopes, so I turned off right for the ski centre. When I got there, I bought a day lift pass, donned my ski gear, boarded the gondola and travelled up onto the higher slopes of Aonach Mor. I then took a drag-lift to near the summit. There was loads of snow but it was quite warm and thawing slightly, making the conditions a bit sticky. There were loads of other skiers and even a few snow boarders on the mountain. From the top of the lift it was only a short climb to the summit of Aonach Mor, so I took my skis off and carried them to the top at a thousand two hundred and twenty-one metres (four thousand and six feet). It was quite a fine day and the view to Carn Mor Dearg at a thousand two hundred and twenty metres (four thousand and two feet) and then the mighty Ben Nevis at a thousand three hundred and forty-four metres (four thousand four hundred and nine feet) was spectacular. Aonach Mor is of course a Munro and I took the opportunity to bag it, although whether it counted, doing it from the ski-lift, I don't know, but I didn't really care.

I spent a few moments on the summit and then skied back down over the smooth snow to the main pistes, where I explored the different runs available. I never stopped for a proper lunch, rather opting to replenish my energy with chocolate from my small rucksack in between runs. The skiing, although not particularly challenging, was difficult in the warming conditions.

I skied until about two thirty p.m. and then took the gondola back to the bottom. It would have been difficult to ski all the way down because there was little snow on the lower slopes and the terrain was quite rough (there is an excellent mountain bike track down this slope where they hold international races at certain times of year).

When I had packed my gear away, I drove to Spean Bridge and then took the A86 to Newtonmore and then onto Kingussie, where I booked into the Duke of Gordon Hotel for one night. I got a single room and being a four-star I thought it would be quite expensive, but it turned out to be very reasonable at twenty-eight pounds for bed and breakfast. I booked and paid for dinner and then had a couple of pints of Tennants lager in the bar – it was good taking! There were several coachloads of mainly older people staying in the hotel, making for quite an interesting atmosphere. This was particularly good when later, after I had shaved and showered, I entered the large lavishly decorated dining room. Before entering, the guests kind of queued up and waited for a piper, whom I assumed was part of the clan Macpherson, who have their clan gathering in the Duke Of Gordon, piping us in for dinner. There were (and still are) several large interesting oil paintings adorning the walls of the dining room and they depict a sort of mountain/woodland scene with archers partly hidden in the undergrowth. They made me think of *The Lord Of The Rings* but were probably meant to show scenes from the Highland uprisings!

Dinner was made up of four courses, the content of which I can't remember but I do know I had a small bottle of Chablis white wine with the meal and it was delicious. The dining room was packed and a lot of the other guests appeared to be English, but I never managed to engage any of them in conversation, being sat at a table on my own. Afterwards I had a few more beers in the bar and then went to bed.

Friday the thirty-first. I was up and down for breakfast at eight thirty a.m. after a good night's sleep. The morning meal was a hot Scottish breakfast but served buffet style, with tea/coffee and cereal to start. I had made plans the previous evening to go skiing on Cairngorm, so I had dressed in my ski clothes for breakfast. The meal was lovely and afterwards I packed my gear, paid the bill and checked out.

Having loaded the Capri I headed out onto the A9 and drove to Aviemore and then across east to the Cairngorm ski centre. It was dry, with patchy cloud and sunny intervals but also quite windy. I got my ski boots on in the big car park, shouldered my skis and headed up to the ticket office, where I bought a day pass. It was then on through the building to board the main chairlift.

This has now been replaced by a controversial funicular railway!

The ride to the Ptarmigan Centre at the top was somewhat hair-raising due to the strong south west wind causing the chair to swing quite violently at times. Once at the top station, I skied out on fairly good snow to explore the runs. I had of course been here before and I knew my way about. I skied for about four hours, doing the White Lady run to the bottom a couple of times. There are snow fences down the side of this run, to hold the drifting snow on the piste.

At two thirty p.m. I packed in for the day and returned to Aviemore, where I got fuel and was annoyed by an ignorant bastard who sounded his horn at me to hurry up at the petrol pump!

I had set myself to return to Kingussie to bring in the New Year so I returned there and thence to the Duke of Gordon, where luckily I found the room I had vacated that morning still available. I booked it but had to pay more this time, probably because it was a special night. After I had left my stuff in my room, shaved and showered, I had a couple of pints in the bar, during which I decided that I had no suitable clothes to wear to celebrate Hogmanay. I had never been in Scotland for New Year and this was a special one, being the dawn of a new millennium and I determined that I would walk down town and see if I could pick myself a suitable outfit for the occasion.

There had been much talk in the media about massive worldwide communication breakdown due to the Y2K scenario and of course I was a little worried about this, as were I'm sure a lot of other people!

So when I had finished my drink I went out, down the street and found a general purpose store. I told the guy in charge there what I was about and he fixed me up with a pair of olive green moleskin trousers -- very appropriate – a collared shirt in green check and a pair of strong brown walking shoes. I spent over a hundred pounds and for my custom I was awarded with a glass of Scotch whisky! On the way back up the street, I caught sight of a couple walking behind a line of parked cars at the other side of the road. The guy looked very like Prince Edward – perhaps it was indeed him! I found out later that he was often in the small town.

Once back at the Duke, I phoned home, and Andrew, using the payphone to let them know I was staying up for the New Year and then I went in for dinner, again to a tune from the ubiquitous piper. I was dressed in my new outfit and the colours matched those of the piper. The dining room was once more packed and it looked as though every room in the hotel must surely be taken.

After another excellent meal I donned my fleece and then went out on the town. At first I explored several bars down the main street, enjoying a drink in each. There were many revellers out and about but I was unable to find anyone playing pool. I came back up to the Duke and just opposite it was the road that ran down to the railway station. I hadn't been down here so I set off to explore and found the Silver Fijord – a small hotel with public bar. I entered the small public bar and felt immediately at home; it was like stepping back twenty years in time! I was regarded with a certain amount of suspicion by the locals at first, who probably thought I had strayed out of the tourist part of town, but I marched up to the bar confidently, bolstered by the Dutch courage from the drink I had already consumed and ordered a pint of Tennants lager.

There was a group of four old guys standing at the bar and one of them said, "Where are you from, then, mate?"

I told him, and then I was asked what I did for a living, I said, "I'm in farming," and that broke the ice – I had stumbled upon the mother lode. These guys were all local farmers and I soon had a great conversation going. The drink started to go down well and I was soon joining the gang on the whisky. Now, whisky is not my normal tipple, rather preferring something like Bacardi or Pernod but this night I really pushed the boat out! The rounds of drinks kept coming and these farmers were not getting their liquor from the optics in set measures, they were drinking the stuff by the finger measure and I had to keep up. Those guys could hold their drink as I thought, *could I?* but I was never in their league.

Midnight was approaching and we moved through into the main bar, where there was a bit of a dance going on. I was really quite pissed but I remember several complete strangers coming up to me and shaking my hand; one of them had a particularly unusual handshake. At midnight we all joined hands and sang *Auld Lang Syne* and I got kisses off several nice women, one of whom was especially pretty and singled me out for special attention. Perhaps, due to the colour of my new outfit, she thought I was some kind of long lost member of the Macpherson clan.

After we had seen the new millennium in, we all piled out and up the road to the large car park behind the Duke, where a firework display was put in motion. The cold air had got to me and suddenly I was completely bluted (drunk). I only saw half the display – I was nearly blacking out and just managed to make it back to my room in the Duke, I almost had to crawl the last bit! It was one of the best nights out I have ever had, but it was one of those where the room spins when you get into bed!

On Saturday the first of January 2000, I awoke at eight a.m. to find that the world had not gone to hell in a hand cart. Presumably the computer and communication systems had not crashed and I was obviously still alive, but suffering from quite a hangover. I felt quite driven, however, and decided that for the new millennium I would climb Cairngorm, seeing as I had not done it from the Ptarmigan restaurant on the previous day. Even when I have had a lot of drink I am nearly always able to face breakfast the following morning and this day was no exception. I had a slap-up feed in the dining room and then packed my gear, paid the bill and went out to my car. Just as I was about to drive out of the hotel car park, I spied a police car idling at the end of the road up from the station. I was still feeling groggy and was aware that I must surely still be over the drink drive limit, considering the amount of whisky I had put away the previous evening, so I waited for a few moments and shortly the police car turned out onto the main street, luckily towards Newtonmore, which was the opposite direction from which I intended to take. I let the copper get some distance down the street before I pulled out and drove north, out of Kingussie and onto the A9. During the journey to the Cairngorm Ski Centre I moderated my speed and kept a careful eye out for other police vehicles; fortunately there weren't any.

When I had parked, I got my hiking gear on, and it was a full winter outfit – the weather, although reasonably fine and dry, was colder and there was once again a strong wind blowing from the southwest. I locked the Capri, shouldered my rucksack and headed up past the buildings of the centre in a southerly direction. I set off at first on a well-made path where the wind had scoured the snow off down to the bare ground, but I was soon having to walk across snow fields. Luckily the snow had a firm crust on it and I was able to proceed without leaving a mark. As I made my way towards Coire an t-Sneachda, the gradient was fairly gentle and I did not need to put my crampons on. After about half an hour I entered the bowl of the aforementioned Coire and up on the western side of it was a huge snow bank. On this great drift, I spied a figure, kind of sliding down the slope, running back up and then sliding down again. The person repeated this action a few times and I thought it was rather odd behaviour, so I decided to investigate. I walked up to where the person was now sitting down, resting and it turned out to be a bloke, maybe in his forties.

I went up to him and said, "Are you all right, mate?"

He grinned and replied, "Yeah, sure. I'm fine, thanks, pal. I'm just enjoying the fine weather."

I noticed he had a Yorkshire accent and that he had obviously not cleaned his teeth for some time.

I offered him my hand and said, "Happy New Year, mate, what are you doing here?"

He shook my hand and returned the greeting, at the same time looking somewhat confused – perhaps he didn't know what day it was! He told me he was in the Coire doing a bit of snow holing. I had never heard of this activity and frankly I had decided that the guy was slightly nuts. Huh, I am a fine one to talk!

I wished the guy all the best and then struck off eastwards across the frozen floor of the Coire. Just as I reached the middle I stopped to adjust my clothing and I had to put my walking poles down. This was the first time I had used them and they had been useful for stability in the gusty conditions. Suddenly a vicious whirlwind sprung up out of nowhere and nearly carried my poles away; I just managed to grab them in time.

I continued out of the Coire and climbed steeply over clean, scoured stony ground up the west-facing slope of Cairngorm and onto the summit at one thousand two hundred and forty-five metres (four thousand and eighty-four feet). There is a small weather station on the summit but not much else. I gazed southwards to where Ben Macdui sat in the bright sunshine. This is Britain's second highest mountain at one thousand three hundred and nine metres (four thousand two hundred and ninety-four feet) and I would have liked to have gone on and climbed it, but it was miles away and time was going on, plus the wind was tearing at me – it must have been gusting to over seventy mph! I turned away from this tempting proposition and walked north, off the summit and down to the Ptarmigan restaurant, where I got a bite to eat before walking down the side of the White Lady ski piste. As I was nearing the bottom of the piste, I met a group of what were obviously R.A.F. mountain rescue personnel out on an exercise. I stopped and told the lead chap about the guy I had encountered in the Coire an t-Sneachda and he just said, "Oh, don't worry about him, mate. We are keeping an eye on him. He's been up there for about a week, kipping in his snow hole!"

I grinned and returned, "Oh, that's okay then. I was just a bit worried about him, that's all."

I left the R.A.F. guys and went on down to the ski centre and back to my car. When I had off-loaded my gear, I set off on the long drive home, going via Fort William and Rannoch Moor. I stopped a few times on the way and also ate a whole bag of dried apricots while I was driving, to keep me going.

When I got back to Carlisle, I turned off the M6, and on an impulse headed through the city, on out and down the A595 towards Cockermouth. I thought I would pay Andrew a surprise visit and wish him and Tracy a happy new year. Just as I was passing through Wigton I came up behind a slower vehicle. I got stuck behind it for a short distance until I came to a floodlit straight section of road (it was now dark). I dropped the powerful Capri into third gear and accelerated to overtake the slower vehicle, exceeding the speed limit as I did so. After I had successfully made the manoeuvre I slowed down again, but noticed a police car parked on the roadside. I thought, *shit, I wonder if that cop clocked my speed?* As I drove on, I looked in the mirror to see if the police car was coming after me, but it hadn't moved.

I relaxed, and for a couple of miles nothing happened. Then suddenly a vehicle came racing up behind me and blue lights began to flash, sirens were sounded and I was pulled over somewhere to the south of Wigton. Other police vehicles appeared out of nowhere and I was surrounded – it was like something out of a movie. Several coppers approached my car and I half expected them to be brandishing firearms, but they were not, thank God! I was tired and now also somewhat scared; surely all this palaver could not be concerned with a speeding offence?

I wound my car window down and said to the officers, "Can I help you?"

One of the cops replied, "Can you please come with us, sir?" So I did as I was asked and I was taken into one of the cop cars and grilled about my recent whereabouts and activities. I was also asked if I was taking my medication. I told the officers that I was not on any medication, but they did not seem to believe me.

I was held for about half an hour while the cops made a few more enquiries and then they let me go. I was quite shaken up as I drove on past Cockermouth onto the A66 and on to Andrew's house in Workington. As I went, I kept one eye on the mirror and I'm sure I was followed for the rest of the journey!

I parked up outside Andrew's house and went up to knock on his door. When he came to the door, he did not seem surprised to see me. I shook his hand and wished him a happy new year and I was invited in. Tracy was there and I gave her a hug. We had a good crack and a couple of drinks, during which I told them of my brush with the police. They were somewhat concerned and thought maybe I had been stopped because I had gone to Scotland without clearing it with probation. We talked for a while longer and then I went home.

I spent a couple of days working on our farm and tried to get back into my normal routine, but I was very tired from my activities in Scotland and I began to feel my mood changing to one of a darker nature. The gearbox on my car was starting to worry me even more due to the noise it was making, so on the fourth of January I drove into Penrith and got quotes from two garages for repairing the gearbox, I had also had a quote from my regular mechanic and all three were of a similar amount. I was looking at quite a bit of money! All this was stressing me out and it had been a difficult day.

Things all came to a head the following day. Relations with my parents had been deteriorating for a few weeks and I had the biggest fall out with my mam ever, after which she told me to get out and never come back! That afternoon I had a probation meeting and I poured my heart out to the officer. She was very concerned about me and told me not to do anything silly. But that is exactly what I did. I drove home, packed some gear and then high-tailed it for Scotland once more.

I ended up at Newtonmore about nine p.m. after driving up the A9. I managed to get a room at a small hotel on the junction with the Spean Bridge road. I had cried in the car on the way up and I was feeling like my life was beginning to fall apart once more. I had three pints of lager in the hotel bar; I should probably not have done this but I was desperate to console myself. I had said some awful things to my mother, who I am very close to. I still deeply regret what was said but I can never change it. I went to bed feeling very low.

Thursday the sixth of January. I was up at seven thirty after a poor sleep. I had a good breakfast though, during which I asked the staff if there was a decent garage in the village. They said there was a garage but having heard the nature of my problem with the Capri; they advised me to try Inverness, where there were bigger garages. So I settled up with the hotel after packing my gear and drove up to Inverness on the A9. Once there, I located a big Ford garage on the outskirts and having got a reasonable quote from them I booked the Capri in for a gearbox and clutch replacement the following day. I then thought, *what to do now?* I could have explored the city but instead I got in my car and drove all the way out to Ullapool, then on up to Lochinver and finally across to Lairg where I booked into a B&B.

The following morning, having enjoyed a better sleep I breakfasted, settled my account, loaded my gear and set off back home via the route I had taken on the previous day, but instead of heading back to keep my appointment with the garage at Inverness, I kept to the west coast, down to the Kyle of Lochalsh, inland to Invergarry, Fort William and on down over Rannoch Moor to Stirling, where I had a bite to eat at the services and phoned Andrew to ask him if I could stay the night. He said it was okay but he also told me that my dad, my sister and my brother had all been in touch with him trying to ascertain my whereabouts. They were all really worried!

When I got back to Andrew's, I was exhausted and tried to resuscitate myself with alcohol. This only made me manic and Andrew and Tracy had a job quietening me down, but they finally got me to bed at eleven p.m.

I had forgotten all about my appointment with the Ford garage at Inverness and I never went back there to get those repairs done!

Saturday the eighth of January. I was up by seven a.m. and had a much needed shower, followed by a little breakfast with Andrew and Tracy. They were both really worried about me, especially when I told them I had not slept well and that I had more or less done a runner up to Scotland without telling the probation officer what I intended. They advised me to get home as soon as I could to patch things up with the probation service and put my family's minds at rest, so I got my gear back into the Capri, wished them both goodbye and headed off home. However, I made a detour to the nearest supermarket on the way to buy a few groceries, as during the last couple of days I had been hatching a plan to move into the granny flat at our farmhouse, so that I could experience having to fend for myself. The intense argument with my folks had rattled me and I felt I needed time to recuperate on my own and also, in my fragile state of mind, to avoid any more confrontations.

Looking back now I can see that this move was just another way of running away from it all, in a similar vein to the examples of trying to escape in the episodes of the preceding years.

When I got home, I was able to speak to Dad because he had not got as heavily involved in the recent argument as my mam. I quickly patched things up with him, as was in fact essential because there was much work to be done alongside him on the farm. However, I could not face my mam at all and quickly offloaded the car and took the groceries up into the granny flat. I spent the rest of the morning cleaning up an old kitchen cabinet out in the yard and then getting Dad to give me a lift up the stairs with it into the flat. I now had most of what I needed to live in the flat. There was a double bed in there, too, but I opted to keep my bedroom occupied also, which was just across the landing. Just after I had got most of the stuff sorted out, my sister arrived and she was furious with me for upsetting everyone and taking off like I did. I stood my corner with her and countered with the question, "What about people upsetting me?" Another argument then ensued and I stormed out of the house, let Tina out of her kennel and went for a walk down the wood, towards the viaduct over Mosedale Beck.

When I got back, I put Tina back in her kennel and then phoned my workmate, Thomas, to arrange to drop a cheque round to him, which was his half share for one of the recent national park contracts. Heather had left by this time, thank God. Then, still feeling somewhat upset, I drove round to Thomas's house, dropped the cheque off, had a short crack and then drove up Ullswater and back. On the way, I passed several police cars and I sensed they were looking out for me; I was soon to be proved correct!

Having got home, I did the usual round of animal feeding and mucking out, before getting a small fridge set up in the granny flat to complete my living arrangements. Andrew phoned shortly afterwards to invite me on a hike the following day. God bless him, he was trying his best to help me in any way he could and I, of course, took him up on his offer. We arranged to meet the following morning at the top of Dunmail

Raise between Thirlmere and Grasmere at ten a.m. I cooked a simple meal in the flat and then turned in.

Sunday the ninth of January. I was up at seven twenty a.m., grabbed a quick coffee, then bullocked (fed and mucked out the cattle) before breakfasting in the flat and putting my lunchbox together. I was still avoiding my mother! I packed my big rucksack and grabbed my boots, shouted a quick message to Dad to tell him where I was going, loaded the gear and Tina into the Capri and took off for Dunmail Raise. On this day, I saw no cops!

The weather was dry with sunny intervals, but very cold as I arrived at the summit of Dunmail Raise at two hundred and thirty-eight metres (seven hundred and eighty-one feet) and sat in the car for a short while to wait for Andrew. When he arrived, we shook hands and got our gear on. At the same time I chained Tina up to the fence to stop her running into the road.

Andrew studied me critically and said, "Are you sure you are well enough to do a hike, you daft sod you?"

And I responded with, "Yeah, sure. I'm feeling much better today."

And yes I was. I had slept better than I had for a while and I was raring to go. We agreed on the route, which was up by the beck to Grisedale Tarn, then up onto Dollywagon Pike. We set off along the side of the A591, with Tina pulling hard on the lead and quickly covered the short distance to the stile over the fence onto the open fell. Having got over onto the fell I let Tina off the lead and she bounced away ahead. We quickly climbed to the tarn, talking as we went. Andrew was quick to point out that I could be in a spot of bother, having possibly broken the terms of my probation agreement and he also thought that the authorities would be keeping an eye out for me through the cops!

From Grisedale tarn we climbed up the steep zigzagging path to the summit of Dollywagon Pike at eight hundred and fifty-eight metres (two thousand eight hundred and fifteen feet), where we had a quick lunch. It had to be quick because we soon became chilled in the bitter conditions (there was icing from seven hundred and sixty metres (two thousand five hundred feet).

Andrew said, "We are a fair height up here, why don't we go on over Nethermost Pike and onto Helvellyn?"

I replied, "Yeah, sure, why not? We still have plenty of daylight."

So this is what we did after I'd given Tina her well-earned tin of cat meat that I had lugged up. Although it was very cold, the cloud base was above the summits and the views were great as we made our way to the summit of Nethermost Pike at eight hundred and ninety-one metres (two thousand nine hundred and twenty-three feet) and then along to Helvellyn. Along the way there were ice climbers at work on the huge frozen snow cornices at the edges of the east facing corries.

At the Trig-point on Helvellyn I shook hands with Andrew and thanked him for being such a good mate and then we retraced our steps down towards Grisedale Tarn. On the way, a straggler attached himself to our party. He was a young guy from Scotch Corner who had no map and had got slightly lost trying to find his way back down to Patterdale. We soon put him right and for a while enjoyed each other's company until we parted at the tarn – him for Patterdale and us for Dunmail Raise.

When we got back to the cars at four forty-five p.m., it was almost dark and we quickly stowed our gear and Tina, before driving back to the King's Head Inn at Thirlspot for a quick pint to top off a cracking day!

I had the usual bullocking to do when I got home and then I cooked a simple meal in the granny flat. The groceries I had bought recently included the mandatory tins of beans, spaghetti and ravioli, accompanied by the usual eggs (we no longer had our own hens after a badger had ripped the back out of the henhouse and killed all of the last ones). My cooking skills were limited then and still are now; to be honest, I hate the task. After the meal I watched a bit of telly and fell asleep in the armchair. I must have been out for the count for a couple of hours; it had been a tiring day. Eventually I returned to my bedroom and rolled into bed.

The following day I did my usual early work on the farm and then went mole trapping up at Patterdale. It was a cold, raw day with a vicious south west wind and I had a hell of a time keeping warm. I packed in at lunch time and the farmer's wife made me a nice meal, plus I was given a whisky to warm me up. In the afternoon I went into Penrith to pay a couple of cheques into the bank and then got some more supplies at the supermarket. It was amazing how fast I was getting through the food and consequently, how much it was costing me, setting up on my own. The rest of the day was largely uneventful; I had seen no police and I did my usual routines before turning in about ten thirty p.m.

Tuesday the eleventh of January. I breakfasted after bullocking and then went trapping again at the same farm, aware that I had to get home for three thirty p.m. to attend a regular meeting with my social worker, John. I finished trapping at two thirty p.m. and returned home. John turned up at our place at the appointed time but I quickly realized to my horror that he was not alone; the farmyard seemed to fill with cars, as first one lot, then another, of the authorities arrived. There was a police car containing two burly officers, and a car, out of which stepped my doctor and the psychiatrist. The cavalry had arrived! Everybody piled into the house and my living arrangements were inspected. All the time, the two coppers kept an eye on me in case I bolted. I was interrogated by all concerned, to ascertain whether I was in such a state as to be taken from the farm and admitted to the looney bin once more. During all this my dad hung around, trying to give me moral support. The psychiatrist informed – or rather should I say threatened – me, that if I did not immediately agree to take medication I would be sectioned and taken to the Carleton Clinic there and then, so I was forced down the medication avenue. The fat shit then made out a prescription, shoved it at me and literally said, "Once this stuff hits you, you won't feel like doing a FUCKING thing!!"

A fine bedside manner, don't you think?

The handing over of the prescription seemed to bring matters to a close and they all left. I promptly burst into tears and then suddenly my mam was there, holding me! I blubbered into her shoulder and apologised for the awful things I had said recently and she said, "It's all right, I forgive you. Now are you going to stop this silliness and give up the granny flat idea?"

I thought for a moment and then replied, "No, not just yet. I want to give it a bit longer and see how it turns out."

Dad had tried his best to stick up for me during the interrogation and even challenged the fat bastard of a psychiatrist for using bad language against me.

I was shaken by the whole experience but there was no time to sit and dwell too much on the events, I had a pool match to go to. Dad did the bullocking and I got a bath, had something to eat and then drove out to Mungrisdale, to pick Bob Ridehalgh up and then continue on to the Old Crown pub at Hesket New Market for the match. I was already very tired and although the weather earlier in the day had been fine, dry and quiet it was now blowing a gale and pissing down, making the driving very taxing. Bob was by now aware of my mental health history and as I told him the events of the day on the drive, he was a source of great comfort to me.

Now, the Old Crown is a difficult place to play pool. The table, although a good one, is shoehorned into a small room with the bar in one corner. Any shots you have to play from the bar corner you have to execute with the butt of your cue up amongst the beer pump handles. It was a tight match and we lost it five-four. I could really have used a skinful of beer to drown my sorrows after the defeat and the trying day, but it had been my turn to drive and consequently I had to stay sober. On the drive home, Bob and I talked more about my day and like Andrew, he thought that there would still be repercussions from my wild probation-breaking trip to Scotland. He was not wrong!

Wednesday the twelfth of January. I was up at six thirty a.m. after a reasonable, if short, sleep. I had a coffee, then let Tina out for a run as I did twice every day; bullocked, breakfasted, changed into my town gear and then headed into Penrith to do some bank transactions. I also had a back massage appointment at the North Lakes Spa at one thirty p.m., which I was looking forward to, with the anticipation of having one of the pretty masseuses rub me down. I also got my prescribed medication; Risperidone (a mood stabilizer and anti-psychotic) at the health centre pharmacy.

On the way into town, I was followed by a police car but they did not pull me in. However, having driven up out of town to the North Lakes Hotel on the outskirts and parked, being early for my massage appointment, I was just walking across to see my sister, who worked in the hotel office, when a police van screeched into the car park and two officers jumped out, ran across to me and virtually dragged me into the cage in the back of the van. I did not resist but before I was shoved in the cage, I was read my rights and then told I was being arrested for a suspected change of address, which almost seems laughable now when I think back. On the journey down to Hunter Lane Police Station, I did not charge about in the cage like I had done that other time in Carlisle; rather I tried to keep calm. At Hunter Lane I was searched and given the opportunity to make a phone call, which I did, phoning my dad to tell him what had happened. Dad said he would come into town right away and see what he could do to get me out. I was put in a cell, wearing only a shirt, jeans (my belt had been removed) and socks. I was told that a duty solicitor would come and see me shortly.

I sat in that cell, fretting, for three hours with only a glass of water to drink before the duty solicitor turned up and interviewed me. Half an hour later I was handcuffed to a Group 4 security officer and taken before the magistrate's court, where I was charged by a judge who knew me (which must have been inappropriate) with breaking the conditions of my probation by travelling to a foreign country without permission. The case was adjourned for two weeks and I was granted unconditional bail.

I found out later that the probation officer who was in charge of me had been rumoured to have had a nervous breakdown and I hoped to God that I had not been responsible for contributing towards her condition!

As I left the court, the security guy released me from my handcuffs and I was aware of how much of a flight risk I was regarded at the time. I was escorted back to Hunter Lane, where my dad was waiting for me. I was released from custody and dad took me up to the North Lakes Hotel for my car. Before I drove home, I went into the hotel to see Heather and tell her what had happened. She was a bit frosty after the recent argument but at the same time, concerned for me. We had a short crack, during which we healed the rift and then I drove home via the petrol station at Motherby, where I paid my monthly bill.

At home, I got changed into my working gear and then let Tina out for a run in the wet, cold conditions before doing the bullocking. I was pretty tired by now, as you can imagine and I was also stressed and somewhat paranoid. I had really been put through the wringer and was of the opinion that the authorities had been very heavy handed with me, almost using a sledgehammer to crack a nut!

Work was finished for the day and I made myself a meal, had a bath and then tried to relax in front of the telly. Just then there was a knock on my door and Dad came in and we had a crack. We discussed the forthcoming court appearance. Obviously I would need a solicitor, so he advised me to get in touch with the family law firm in Keswick first thing in the morning. We talked for a bit longer and then I went to bed.

Thursday the thirteenth of January. I was up by six thirty a.m. And had grabbed a quick coffee and bullocked before breakfasting. My head was feeling woolly but I was managing to control my paranoia. I phoned the solicitors and they were able to give me an appointment, later that morning, to see the solicitor who had represented me at court in 1998. I was pleased about this because I genuinely liked the guy.

I made my way down to Keswick where I met with my solicitor, but he told me that he was not in the best of mental health himself and intended to come out of criminal law, therefore he was unable to represent me. This seemed like the last straw to me and I promptly broke down in tears in front of him. After a good cry I felt better and when I had pulled myself together again, he told me to go and see a law firm in Penrith that he had heard good reports about.

I returned home and made a spot of lunch in the flat before asking Dad if he would go to Penrith with me to see this new firm of solicitors. He agreed and got changed into his jacket and tie (my dad always dresses well when going into town, especially when seeing professional people). We travelled into Penrith in Dad's Austin Maestro van and after parking, made our way to the law firm premises. I had neglected to phone for an appointment, rather opting to just drop on them cold. This proved to be a poor decision. At reception, the secretary ummed and ahhed about whether there were any solicitors available to see us and we were told to take a seat and wait for an available slot. After a lengthy wait, we were ushered in to see a tall, lean guy who upon hearing the details of my case agreed to represent me, at a price of course. Legal aid had stopped for me by this time and I was somewhat worried what the final bill would be. I must admit my first impression of this new solicitor was not good. He seemed to have a greedy air about him and this was borne out in the following weeks. We left the solicitors, having made an appointment to see my new representative again on the twenty-fifth of January, the day before my court appearance, then we returned home to do the bullocking and I finished off the day with the usual cooking, washing up and watching telly before turning in.

It was around this time that I was engaged in a plan to continue to keep the farm going after my dad retired, which was fairly imminent. The previous summer I had gone to visit Business Link near Penrith to get advice on putting the farm into an Environmentally Sensitive Area (E.S.A.) scheme, whereby the government paid you to farm in an environmentally sensitive way. This scheme was essential if I was going to raise enough funds to keep the farm going. Business Link had sent an agricultural advisor out to the farm; this turned out to be my workmate Thomas's son, Paul Arkle. Paul is a really nice bloke and he, Heather and I had walked the farm so that details of flora and fauna could be taken to decide which bracket of the E.S.A. scheme the farm could be put into. It had been a fine day and a very enjoyable, interesting and also revealing walk around our land. There were some very encouraging findings; some of the rough grazing contained rare plants and also, some of the hayfields had similar rare species so if managed in a particular way, would yield substantial E.S.A. payments. At that stage the future looked rosy, but unfortunately in early 2000 my plans all fell apart. There were several reasons for this: firstly, my grandmother owned the farm and did not agree to changing things; secondly, my dad was tenant and refused to sign over the tenancy of the farm to me, which was one of the prerequisites of the E.S.A. Agreement; and thirdly, my family thought that I was not in a stable enough state of mind to take on such a large responsibility! So I had to abandon the idea and it was probably for the best.

Getting back again, on Friday the fourteenth of January I did my usual morning routine before going to Patterdale to take out all my mole traps to finish that particular job. I got my pay off the farmer there and returned home in time for a meeting with the social worker, John, at one p.m. My parents were present at the meeting but all I have documented about it was that John was very unsympathetic towards me all of a sudden. Perhaps he had been under the sway of the psychiatrist. Anyway, the meeting had not gone well. After John had gone I went over to Ken Ostle's farm where I had a crack with his parents and seeing I was in a state of woe, they came up with a wonderful idea. They were selling up and moving to High Hesket soon and they thought that their gorgeous, huge grey and white tom cat (whose name was Tiny!) would get run over on the A6, which ran right past High Hesket, so they asked me if we would like him up at Highgate Close. I was delighted by the prospect, having fallen in love with Tiny at first sight a few years earlier. Tiny had been found as a kitten, wandering the pencil factory at Keswick and somehow or another Ken's younger brother Stephen had taken possession of the young cat and brought him up to their farm. I told Ken's parents I would ask my own folks if we could have Tiny and raced home to do so. When I got home and broached the idea, my dad wasn't keen, but my mam jumped at the chance. Our own much loved old cat Sandy had died recently and I had buried him with full honours in the wood behind the farmhouse. A special sandstone headstone, engraved with his name, was set in concrete atop the grave and adorned with various attractive rocks brought from Scotland and the like. Sandy had been a great cat and he had come up from my grandmother's when she became unable to look after him anymore. He had had one fault though, which was that he had a habit of getting up and lying on your face when you were sprawled asleep in the armchair. This was not too much of a problem, apart from you having to pick his ginger hairs out of your mouth when you woke up, but it could have been disastrous if there had been babies or young children about – they could have been smothered!

Anyway, it was decided that we would take on Tiny and I was delighted. All that remained now was how to get him over to our farm. Neither we nor Ken's folks had a cat box, so either we had to borrow one, or buy one. Bob Ridehalgh had cats and I would be seeing him later that day at a rearranged pool match fixture, so I would ask him then if he had a box.

After bullocking, suppering, shaving and bathing I drove out to Mungrisdale to pick Bob up. I asked him about the cat box and he had one that I could borrow, so I made arrangements to pick it up from him in a few days' time. We continued on to the match, which was away at Hutton Roof pub. We lost the match five-four and I played poorly, which was not surprising considering the pressure I had been under recently. Both Bob and I were a bit dispirited on the way home, but he offered me words of encouragement in dealing with the new solicitor. I dropped him off, returned home and went to bed.

On Saturday the fifteenth of January, I started to take the Risperidone medication and almost immediately started to feel the side effects. Yes, it quietened me down, but also made me slightly disorientated and I had the sense that I was looking at the world through a thick pane of glass. I spent the day doing jobs around the farm, but also took Tina down to the beck with ten new mole traps. I found a quiet backwater and put the traps in a pool, making sure they were completely immersed. I would leave the traps like this for at least a month to allow the fresh water to remove the smell of the galvanising from them. You can also bury the traps but this tends to make them rust faster. Sadly, modern steel is of a much poorer quality than in earlier days – I have several traps over a hundred years old which are in better condition than those just a few years of age. Moles have a very keen sense of smell and you need to take several precautions to prevent these wily creatures from detecting the traps in their tunnels. These include rubbing your hands in soil before you start to trap, to mask scents such as soap and cigarette smoke. I have been a much more successful trapper since I gave up smoking!

That evening I drove the Mungrisdale gang into Penrith for a night out. We had quite a good time but as usual, nothing happened that was likely to change our bachelor status. I was tired but the medication did not affect my ability to drive. It was not a late session and I was home and in bed by eleven thirty p.m.

Sunday the sixteenth of January. A few nights earlier Andrew had phoned me to broach the idea of hiking up Scafell Pike, seeing as the weather forecast had been quite good. I had thought it a good plan. I was a little worried how I would perform on this lengthy expedition, due to the effect of the medication, but agreed to go nonetheless, so I was up a good time after a reasonable sleep, although the medication seemed to have stopped me from dreaming, which you could say diminishes the quality of your life somewhat! I did my usual farm jobs before breakfasting, preparing my lunch, packing my rucksack and loading it, my boots and Tina into the car. It was a cold, dry day but the cloud base was fairly low as I drove to Seathwaite farm in Borrowdale, where I got a park on the roadside – this is a very popular starting point for climbing Scafell Pike (England's highest mountain) and it is sometimes difficult to find a parking place.

Andrew had mentioned on the phone that his cousin Harvey was likely to be coming on the hike and Harvey also owned a border collie, which accompanied him on his walks.

Having got parked I spied Andrew and a guy who was about the same age but of a smaller build, getting their gear out of their car about twenty-five metres further up the roadside. A magnificent black and white collie was bouncing around them.

I got out of my motor and shouted a greeting to them. They waved and Andrew shouted back, "There you are, you daft bugger."

I opened the back of the Capri and Tina jumped out and ran over to Andrew and Harvey and promptly started smelling the bottom of Harvey's dog (whose name I forget). For a second or two I thought the two animals were going to fight, but it soon became obvious that they were going to become the best of friends. I donned my gear, locked the car and then joined the others. I was introduced to Harvey and we shook hands. He had a good grip and also, I sensed that he had an outgoing nature.

We started off up the road at eleven a.m., which is probably a bit late for the Scafell Pike excursion on a winter's morning. We passed through the yard of Seathwaite farm, with our dogs on their leads to rule out the chance of a fight with the local farm dogs. From the farm we took the level, broad path to Stockley Bridge, which is a stone arched one spanning the beck at the bottom of Grains Gill. We crossed it and then took the main path up towards Great End. It is a long, gradual climb on a partially pitched path and there are a few tricky, rocky, slippery sections. The cloud base was still low and there was no wind, making it warm work. I was feeling the effect of the medication – it was as if I had had the brakes put on me and I seemed to be having to work harder than the other two. The crack was brilliant though and Harvey was turning out to be as daft as a brush. The two dogs, who were now off their leads, were also having a good get-together, bouncing around, running about and playing with each other.

When we got near the base of the great crag of Great End, our route took us south east, up to the path crossroads of Esk Hause and we took the right hand path westwards towards the back of Great End Fell. We had entered the cloud now and it was very cold, with snow on the ground. The gradient of the path was gradual to begin with but after we had passed the back of Great End we reached a kind of notch in the route between the shrouded tops of Ill Crag and Broad Crag. We stood on the edge of a steep slope, covered in snow; it looked slippery and having brought my crampons, I decided to put them on. Andrew and Harvey had none, so as something of a laugh really I offered Andrew one of mine to put on. He took it seriously and tried to fix the crampon to the base of one of his boots. However, his boots were not compatible with the spiked device and he abandoned the idea. I put both crampons on and then we set off down the slope. The other two slipped about a bit and I found that I had more grip but the crampons got clogged up by the soft snow and did not work to their full potential. We reached the bottom of the notch and climbed the other side, to enter an area where the path became obscured by boulders of varying size. These, being partially covered in snow, were a challenging obstacle and we had to be careful to avoid putting our feet into the gaps between the rocks and risking a broken ankle.

The terrain had levelled out at this point and the route was marked by a series of small cairns. We picked our way gingerly across the boulder field and then dropped down into another notch before climbing out on what proved to be the final pitch to the summit of Scafell Pike. Suddenly we emerged out of the cloud and before us stood the huge, stone built summit cairn, which is in the shape of a turret. We climbed up the kind of ramp on the northwest side of the cairn and stood on the top at nine hundred and seventy-seven metres (three thousand two hundred and five feet), mingling with the many other walkers up there. The view was extraordinary; I had never before or have since seen anything like it. Above us was clear blue sky but all around was a flat plain of white cloud with only our summit, the nearby nine hundred and sixty-four metres (three thousand one hundred and sixty-two feet) summit of Scafell itself, the nine hundred and thirty-one metres (three thousand and fifty-four feet) summit of Skiddaw, the nine hundred and fifty metres (three thousand one hundred and sixteen feet) summit of Helvellyn and far away to the east, the summit of Crossfell at just under nine hundred and fourteen metres (three thousand feet), the highest point of the Pennine range, sticking up through the cloud layer. This phenomenon is called a 'cloud inversion' and it is a rare and beautiful occurrence!

We had reached the summit at one thirty p.m. in only two and a half hours, which is quite a quick ascent, I think. After we had admired the view we sat down amongst the rocks near the cairn to eat a late lunch. I opened a large tin of cat meat for Tina and emptied it out on a flat rock. She wolfed it down, but not before Harvey's dog had managed to steal some of it. We didn't hang around long in the freezing conditions and were soon packed up and on our way down off the north west shoulder of the mountain, towards what is called the Corridor Route. This took us down into the valley on the northern side of Scafell Pike and eventually on towards Styhead Tarn, passing the notorious Piers Gill, a deep chasm slashing the western side of the valley, into which several people have slipped and died over the years!

The path is a good one and well used, but there is one tricky scrambly section, about two thirds of the way back to Styhead Tarn. From the tarn we walked out through the hanging valley between Seathwaite Fell and Great Gable before dropping back out down to Stockley Bridge once more and making our way back to the cars below Seathwaite Farm. It was five fifteen p.m. when we loaded our gear and the dogs back into the cars and we had walked approximately ten miles (sixteen kilometres).

We drove to the Scafell Hotel in Rosthwaite where Andrew once worked as a chef and had a quick but enjoyable pint before going our separate ways and heading home.

Once home, although tired, I still had to help with the bullocking and then afterwards make myself something to eat. It was pretty late by the time I had done all this and had a bath but it had all been worth it. It had been a brilliant day and the crack had been great. Meeting Harvey had been enjoyable and sometimes hilarious. It had all served to take my mind off the forthcoming court appearance.

The next few days went by quickly, with me doing work on our farm and also on a lime kiln at Aughertree Fell, between Caldbeck and Uldale with Thomas. He came round by our place one day and took my trailer to the job on the back of his Ford Mondeo. We went via Bassenthwaite village, where I dropped my car off to be tuned at a garage there and then continued round to Aughertree with Thomas.

After the day's work we went back to the garage and picked up the Capri. I could tell on the drive home that she was running better, even though I was pulling the trailer, but the gearbox was still rattling away and I knew I would have to get it fixed soon.

During this time I had a meeting with the social worker, John, at home, which went much better than the last one and also a meeting with the psychiatrist in Penrith, which also went better. Both of them were probably in clover due to getting me onto medication! I saw my own doctor too, to consult him about a bad stomach I had been getting and he told me it could be a side effect of the Risperidone pills, leading to him prescribing some more medication to help with that problem. Also around this time, the powers that be decided that I also had slight epilepsy, which had been diagnosed from the E.E.G. scan I had had done at Carlisle a while ago. Consequently I was prescribed the drug Epilem, which contains sodium valproate and I started taking these pills. I seemed to be on so many pills all of a sudden that I was positively rattling.

On the evening of Wednesday the nineteenth of January, I went to Bob's and picked up the cat box. I then called in at Ken's farm on the way back and we set about getting Tiny into the box. It proved to be quite a difficult task; he seemed to sense something was afoot and rushed around the living room, trying to hide. We finally caught him running up the curtains and got him into the box. When I got him home, I let him out in the un-lived in back kitchen of the farmhouse where, once released from the box, he shot off into the corner of the room and into the ash box hole under the old set-pot boiler. It was two days before we saw him come out and take some food! Gradually, though, he got used to his new situation and his new family and was allowed through into the main living area, but not upstairs. After about a week of him using the cat litter box he was allowed outside where he met and seemed to get on with the two farmyard cats, who were called Larl Blacky and Rearing Up – so named for the habit of rising up on his back legs to be stroked. They were both males, we thought, and were rampantly gay. They had free range of all the farm buildings and were fed once a day on bread and milk to supplement their diet of any mice they could find. We rarely had rats, which would have required the services of a large farmyard tom cat as I don't think Tiny was capable of dealing with these vermin.

On Friday the twenty-first of January, I had an excellent meeting with my psychologist, Richard, in Carlisle early, and then in the afternoon the probation officer came out to the farm and I also had a good meeting with her.

The following day I began to take a double dose of the Respiridone, after being broken in to the drug. I hated having to do this but I was doing my best to comply with the psychiatrist's instructions. Tina was getting a bit stinky so I bathed her and she came up smelling like a bed of roses. I had done this to offset my embarrassment of her stinking up the place on the next hike, which had been arranged for the next day.

Sunday the twenty-third of January. After getting up early, at five thirty a.m., I did the bullocking, breakfasted and then Heather's partner, Allan, came with his shotgun and positioned himself in the wood below the farm while I roamed the nearby fields to try to disturb any carrion crows into the range of Allan's gun. These bastards were on the increase again after our period without any guns to deal with them. We never got anything though and gave up after an hour or so. After this I got changed, packed my rucksack, loaded it and the sweet-smelling Tina into the Capri and drove down to the Coledale Inn at Braithwaite, where I met Andrew and Tracy at eleven a.m.

We donned our gear and then set off up the footpath out of the village, heading south west. The crack was limited because none of us were on top form. I had been up in the night checking on a heifer that had been newly tied up and kept getting loose. (All our cows were tied up with rope or chain bands round their necks to make them more manageable – this was the traditional way of doing things. Nowadays the cattle are loose housed, which makes them more difficult to handle.) Tracy was complaining of a sore hip and I think Andrew had a hangover.

There are two fairly low tops, which bisect the area of the two valleys between Grisedale Pike and Causey Pike to the west of Braithwaite.

I told the other two that I intended to climb these two fells and Andrew said, "We will just take the main easier path up the valley and meet you further on, mate."

I agreed and struck off to the right, heading up onto Stile End at four hundred and forty-seven metres (one thousand four hundred and sixty-six feet) and then on a gradual rise to Outerside at five hundred and sixty-eight metres (one thousand eight hundred and sixty-three feet). I was tired already and feeling the effect of the double dose of medication even more.

I suppose I was trying not to let the drugs I was on rule my life and to some extent, I was fighting against them.

The only one of the group who was in fine form was Tina, who was bouncing along. Every now and then I caught a whiff of her dog shampoo, declaring that it was much preferable to the previous odour!

From Outerside I dropped down south west to rejoin the main path and soon caught up with my friends. The summits I had just done were fairly featureless, grassy affairs and I told the others that they had not missed anything up there. As we began to climb the steepening path towards the col between Scar Crags and Sail, it became obvious that Tracy was starting to struggle, so I declared that we would have the lunch break at the col. We reached this gap between the two fells, which stood at approximately six hundred metres (one thousand nine hundred and sixty-eight feet) and sat down for lunch. It was a gorgeous sunny day with only light winds, but cold as we sat eating our sandwiches, admiring the view towards Grisedale Pike. We had intended to walk on up over the next two tops to the highest fell in that particular range; Grasmoor at eight hundred and fifty-two metres (two thousand seven hundred and ninety-five feet), but it soon became plain as we talked that Tracy was unable to go any further and that the main objective now was to get her down.

So after the break we shouldered our rucksacks and dropped off down the south facing slope, more or less on unbroken ground into the valley between Scar Crags and Rigg Screes. Tracy was really hobbling along now and she was obviously in pain from her hip and I began to wonder if we were going to have to get the mountain rescue out! She kept going though and we made the valley bottom, striking a good path out by Rigg Beck to head eastwards. The going became easier and Tracy made better progress. We exited the valley at the well-known purple house, which is a wooden two-storey construction that a previous owner painted purple (it is up for sale as I write this). The purple house sits next to the Braithwaite to Newlands Hause Road and I knew we just had to walk back along the road to get to the cars

If we had been in better order, one of us should have gone ahead for a car to shorten the journey, but we were not, so we fought our way as a group along the fairly level road back to Braithwaite. It seemed to take for ever and the tarmac is always harder to walk on after you have been on the hill. We all became exhausted and somewhat snappy with each other before we finally made it back to the Coledale Inn. We put our gear away and went into the pub, accompanied by Tina as I had seen a sign that dogs were allowed. After ordering a pint each we collapsed into the easy chairs and our mood began to improve. Tracy was in a lot of pain though and following this difficult day, she had a lot of treatment on the hip.

When we had resuscitated ourselves, we left the pub, said our goodbyes and went home, where I had to strike in and help with the bullocking once more. I then had to drag myself round the flat to prepare a meal, shave, bathe and then fall into bed.

The following day was the one on which Thomas and I finished off renovating the last lime kiln at Aughertree. I had my usual bullocking to do before making my way with the car and trailer, containing the quad bike, to meet Thomas at the place where we left our cars to take the bike and trailer across the fell to the work site. On the way to Aughertree, I had phoned the solicitor from the phone box at Hesket New Market to ask for an appointment for the next day, I had heard nothing from him since the initial meeting and the court appearance being only two days away, I was worried that there had not been enough discussion to prepare for it! I got the required appointment and continued on my way.

Thomas and I spent the morning ferrying tools from the work site back to the road using the bike and trailer, and generally tidying up the site.

We had eaten our packed lunches sitting on the top of the newly repaired kiln and just as Thomas got up to put his things away I said, "Wait a minute, mate. I have a surprise for you."

I rummaged around in my bait bag and dug out a half bottle of Chablis white wine and a couple of glasses.

"I've brought this to celebrate the completion of the job," I remarked.

Thomas's face split into a broad grin and he said, "What a novel idea."

I poured the wine and we tucked into it. There were two glasses each and it was delicious. I felt quite squiffy afterwards as I rode the quad back to the road.

We had to drop some scaffolding off at the national park depot at Threlkeld after driving back round by Bassenthwaite, where I paid the garage there for their recent good work on my Capri. After leaving the scaffolding, Thomas and I parted company, but it would not be for long because we had pencilled in the commencement of our next big job together for the following morning – phew! There was no let-up and although the medication was slowing me down a bit, I was able to keep going at about three quarter's throttle.

Although it was only January, the weather was almost spring-like and it really had been quite balmy for our lime kiln celebrations. These favourable conditions continued for Tuesday the twenty-fifth, upon which Thomas and I took the quad and trailer plus our wire fencing tools across the valley, to start a contract to take down an old wire fence and erect a new one on the steep slopes of Southerfell. We parked our cars at Southerfell farm and then began ferrying equipment and materials up to the fencing site with the quad and trailer. Now, the trailer being big enough to hold the quad is okay when being towed by the quad on level ground, but when engaged in the transport of material up a steep slope the trailer can prove heavy and ungainly. This scenario almost proved disastrous for me on my first trip up the steep grassy slope, which lead from the road near the farm up to the work site. I loaded the trailer with a couple of heavy straining posts, a couple of rolls of wire netting and a few other bits and bobs before setting off up the slope. Of course I had engaged four-wheel drive on the quad and things were going great until I got halfway up the slope. At this point there was a small spring that oozed water out onto the grass. I rode the quad and trailer up into this area and almost immediately realized that the ground was somewhat soft and certainly slippery, but it was too late. Suddenly all four wheels of the quad began to slip and spin and I lost traction and therefore forward motion. The outfit began to slide backwards and I knew a moment of panic! The rearward slide picked up momentum and although I had every brake on the machine engaged I was unable to slow the outfit. Just when it seemed that disaster was imminent a minor miracle occurred; the trailer jack-knifed across the slope and brought the slide to a halt. My heart was hammering in my chest and I sat for a few moments to quieten myself. I engaged forward gear again and straightened the outfit out before riding it back down to the road, where I lightened the load somewhat before putting the quad back at the slope for another attempt. This time I avoided the slippery spring area and made it up to the work site. However, near the top of the slope my route took me between two outcrops of rock and the trailer was a tight fit so I only used it for this one trip, instead opting to use my much smaller sheep-carrying trailer and indeed, just the quad on its own, by carrying materials on its racks.

    We continued to work on the fencing job on and off over the next week and it was during this period that I experienced a one-off occasion in which I had difficulty operating machinery while under the influence of medication. It did state on the packaging of the drug that I was taking that you were advised not to operate machinery, but how the hell was I to continue my type of work without doing so?

    I had the sheep trailer on the back of the quad and I was trying to get through the gate, off the road, to start one of the many ascents to the fencing job. I had got the approach to the gateway wrong and I had to reverse the outfit for another attempt. Somehow I got the trailer jack-knifed and I experienced a total mental block on how to extricate the outfit from this position. I sat on the quad in a state of total confusion for what must have been over a minute. Thomas was with me and he asked me if I was all right. His intervention seemed to galvanise me into action and I shook my head to clear it of the fog that had descended on me, straightened the outfit up and rode it through the gate. Later on during that trip up to the work site something else strange happened; Thomas was riding on the rack of the quad as we approached the working area and we had just passed through the two outcrops of rock and I had got the line of approach wrong. Having passed the outcrops I shouted to Thomas over the sound of the engine, "It's a good job we haven't got the trailer on, I could have turned it over coming through there!"

"Hell's teeth, you daft bugger, the trailer is on!" he replied.

I stopped and turned round to find the trailer was indeed on; I had had a complete blank about it being there. I was somewhat embarrassed by the occurrence. Fortunately I have not had such an experience again!

Getting back a bit again, my court appearance was at ten a.m. on Wednesday the twenty-sixth of January and I had got myself up early, done my farm work, got myself clean and smart and to the court building in good time for the hearing. As it turned out, I needn't have rushed because the cases had backed up and the powers that be were running behind schedule. My solicitor, with whom I had had my preparatory meeting on the previous day, and my probation officer were waiting in the anteroom. When I was finally called into court, these two associates went with me and proceedings advanced very quickly. My solicitor got up and uttered a brief statement, which I considered to be a load of bollocks. I thought then and still do now that I could have made a far better job of defending myself; also my pockets would have been fuller as the solicitor's fees turned out to be in excess of three hundred and fifty pounds! Anyway, the judgement of the court was that for the offence of travelling to Scotland without prior permission I was to be given an extra year's probation period. I was much relieved by this outcome because in a strange kind of way, I enjoyed going to the probation office. (I'm sure there are many who would totally disagree with this statement). There turned out to be another reason why I liked going to probation, because housed in the same building as the probation office was a small gym and it was around the time of my court hearing that I joined this gym for a period of three months. I had to go through the induction process by having my vital signs checked and the like. It transpired that I was in very good shape and I was soon raising a sweat on the many different pieces of apparatus.

There was another very good reason for attending the gym and that was that my favourite gypsy princess was a regular visitor there. She did not work out on the machines, but rather just hung around the fringe of the workout area. Of course this made me work harder on the machines, especially the rower. I guess I was kind of showing off and it must have worked to some extent, because I caught her watching me a couple of times.

Time went by and I booked the Capri into Newlands Close Garage (now Cowperthwaites Garage) on the first of February to get a new gearbox and clutch fitted. The car was also due for a service so I got that done as well. Brian Cowperthwaite kindly gave me the use of a courtesy car while my own was being repaired; it was a little Peugeot and it ran like a sewing machine!

I had booked a table for six at the Italian restaurant in Penrith for the evening of Saturday the fifth of February after taking the Capri in. There was to be me, two of my Mungrisdale friends and three women who were known to my friends, on this so-called date. As it turned out on the night, us three blokes were stood up by the three women, but we were used to getting knocked back and we had a great night anyway.

I had picked the Capri up from the garage the day before and Brian's men seemed to have made a good job of it. The rattles from the gearbox had certainly disappeared. I drove on the night of the meal and we ended up in Toppers Nightclub, which is now a Wetherspoons. We had a real carful on the way back, with the cousin of one of my friends and his wife cadging a lift back to Mungrisdale with us in the early hours of the next morning.

Talking of my Mungrisdale friends, it was at this time that Ken Ostle was doing the full length of Africa trek/excursion and he had his wallet and passport stolen from a bus, which of course created horrendous difficulties for him, as you can imagine. He managed to get things sorted out eventually and continued on to finish the journey. He had become a very adventurous person indeed after his early skiing holidays with me, going on to do the Machu Picchu trail in Peru. He now lives in Australia!

On the evening of Saturday the twelfth of February, one of my Mungrisdale friends picked me up and we went out in Penrith. I had a Valentine's card with me which I intended to give to Rachel – the gypsy princess. I had seen her numerous times at the gym and out in town; the flame was burning brightly inside me. Written on the card were some of the lyrics from the Bon Jovi songs, *In These Arms* and *Bed Of Roses*. These are two of my favourite ballads and the lyrics really put across the strength of my love for Rachel at the time.

We were in the Gloucester Arms when I spied Rachel and after a bit of faffing around, I managed to pluck up courage to give her the card, but she was leaving. I made to follow her out of the pub but suddenly a young guy barred my way and said to me, "Where the hell do you think you're going?" I stared at him and made to push past him, he grabbed hold of my shirt and for a moment I thought he was going to hit me!

I said, "Get your bloody hands off me, I only want to go and have a word with Rachel."

By now, of course, I had realized that this guy was some friend or relation of the girl and was just trying to protect her so I quickly added, "Easy, mate. I mean her no harm."

He released me but the moment to give Rachel the card had passed and she had disappeared. I never got another opportunity that night and I still have the card to this day, unopened in its red envelope.

The following day I met Andrew at Crummock Water and we hiked up the side of a gill to the col known as Coledale Hause. Tina was with us and she was in fine form, she loved the walking days. As we walked, I discussed the events of the previous evening with Andrew and he was of the opinion that I had been lucky not to get into a bit of serious bother and he said there is no future in pursuing this girl, so forget about her. He was right of course and I tried to take notice of his advice.

From the Hause, we struck up south west in the mainly dry but cold/raw conditions. Suddenly the mist descended on us and we changed our minds away from the desired objective of Grasmoor and returned to the Hause before climbing out northwards onto Hopegill Head at seven hundred and seventy metres (two thousand five hundred and twenty-six feet). From there we returned to the cars via a ridge walk, which took us over Gasgale Crags. I had enjoyed a small lie-in that morning and we had not started walking until eleven forty-five a.m. we were back at the cars at four thirty p.m. and then went for a pint in the Bridge Hotel at Buttermere before returning home.

On Friday the eighteenth of February, I asked permission from probation to go to Scotland again and they gave it. Things had been going well in that department and I had loaded the Capri with skiing/hiking gear before meeting with probation on the presumption that I would be given the go-ahead for the trip.

At three p.m. I departed Penrith and drove up to Kingussie, arriving there at seven forty-five p.m. after stopping at Stirling Services for tea on the way. I got a room at the Duke Of Gordon, had a couple of pints in the bar and then went to bed. Unfortunately my room was the one next to the lift, which meant there was disturbance, seemingly throughout the night. Also, there was a waste pipe in the corner of the room, which rattled every time someone went to the toilet. Consequently I did not sleep well!

Saturday the nineteenth. I was up by six thirty a.m. and down for a delicious breakfast at seven thirty a.m. Afterwards I picked up a packed lunch and then re-booked the hotel for the next night, making sure I got a different room.

From Kingussie I drove south down the A9 and pulled off near the Balsporran Cottages, near the summit of Drumochter Pass. There is a good car park here and this day there was plenty of available space. It was a lovely fine, clear day but very cold and the snow was quite deep as I left the car with my big rucksack and my full winter gear. From the car park I struck out westwards at nine thirty a.m., past the cottages and over the railway tracks. There was a good track winding through the low glacial drumlins and although there was six inches of snow on it, the going was good. It did not last though and my objective being the Munro of Geal Charn meant that I soon had to leave the track and climb steep heathery slopes. Heather is quite difficult to walk through in summer but now, at this time of year, with the added snow it was gruelling work. I fought my way up the south east facing flank of the mountain and reached the round-topped summit at nine hundred and seventeen metres (three thousand and eight feet) by midday. The views were amazing in all directions and I wished I had had the company of Tina, but there were difficulties in housing her during the nights on these trips. Not every form of accommodation caters for dogs and cooping her up in the car for the night seemed unfair. (Not to say I've not done this when I was not in my right mind, though!) I had lunch and contemplated the Munro across the valley to the south. It didn't seem too far to go around the head of the valley and bag that one too, so that is what I did. I was soon making good progress over the reasonably level terrain and the wind had scoured the snow into drifts, so the going was easier than it had been lower down. I completed the horseshoe walk round the head of the valley and reached the summit of my objective A'Mharconaich at nine hundred and seventy-five metres (three thousand one hundred and ninety-eight feet) by one forty-five p.m. I set off down the north east facing shoulder of the round-topped Munro and soon entered steep, hard frozen snow slopes so I stopped and put my crampons on, then continued the descent and walked out back to the car for three thirty p.m.

I returned to the Duke and got a shave and bath in my new room, then went down the street to the chippy and got fish and chips. After I had eaten I enjoyed a couple of pints in one of the pubs and then returned to the hotel where I turned in early at seven forty-five p.m. I was pretty tuckered out after my exertions and the previous poor night's sleep.

Sunday the twentieth. I was up at six fifty a.m. having slept much better, and down for another excellent breakfast by seven thirty-five a.m. I then packed my gear, paid the bill, loaded the car and then drove south the couple of miles to Newtonmore, where I took the A86 to Spean Bridge. I drove fast along this road and nearly came to grief a couple of times on the occasional patch of black ice. From Spean Bridge I took the A82 towards Fort William and then turned off to the Nevis Range Ski Centre. It being a Sunday and a fine one, everybody and their grandmother had decided to go skiing so this meant when I had got my gear on, I had to queue for an hour to buy a lift pass. When I had got sorted, I joined the next queue for the gondola. It was all a bit tedious but I finally got up onto the mountain of Aonach Mor.

I skied for four hours or so but it was not very enjoyable. Although cold, the snow conditions were sticky, the lifts were very busy and then the wind got up and sandblasted me with ice crystals. I took the highest drag lift at two p.m. and walked to the summit of Aonach Mor in my ski boots to bag it. I skied back down a hairy black run, close to the edge of a huge cornice, to get back into the area of the top gondola station, where I took the lift back down to the base station, loaded my gear into the Capri and left for home about three p.m. The drive home was pretty straightforward, involving a stop at Stirling Services for tea. The Capri ran like a bird and I was home by eight p.m.

During the following week I continued to work on fencing projects at Southerfell with Thomas and also had a meeting with the psychiatrist, where I tried to get him to reduce the dose of my medication. I felt that the drugs were starting to make me feel depressed. I had little success though. I also had a meeting with probation, who were keen to learn how the Scotland trip had gone. John the social worker came to see me at the farm and he was an hour late, which unfortunately was a regular occurrence!

Tiny, our new house cat, was settling in nicely and becoming an integral part of the family.

I enjoyed the occasional game of ten-pin bowling and I went through to Carlisle with the Mungrisdale lads on the evening of Saturday the twenty-sixth of February for one of these nights out. We had two games. In the first one, I was not particularly good but in the second, I played a blinder, bowling a 'turkey' (three strikes in a row). I wasn't driving, so was able to get quite a few pints down my neck.

My high spirits did not last though and my mood took a severe dive during the following week, I had a hell of a job getting out of bed and my motivation was poor. I hated the medication and I'm sure it was a large contributory factor in my mood. I had rarely been depressed in my life but now it seemed to be a regular occurrence. Work was difficult but I had Thomas to spur me on and we started two new national park contracts, to repair two lime kilns at High Ireby.

My mood picked up a bit for a week or so then began to dive again. On Wednesday the fifteenth of March, I went to see the psychiatrist and it was a new guy. I liked him immediately and he was a great improvement on the previous one. However, I could not move him on the medication issue; he told me I would have to be on medication for the rest of my life! This only served to send me down even further. I had to play in my regular pool matches and my performances were generally poor as you can imagine. On the twenty-second of March, I met with my doctor and broke down in tears in front of him while pleading with him to help me on the medication issue. He was genuinely concerned for me and I came away with his permission to halve my pills. Of course, I could have stopped taking the pills at any time then, but I was anxious to do the right thing by my counsellors and also I did not want a repeat of the Beacon Unit incident!

My mood slowly picked up in the following weeks and I was able to get a lot done. There was the lime kiln work, dry stone walling on a couple of different jobs in Caldbeck (all with Thomas) and regular mole trapping contracts, alongside my routine farm work.

It was a good job I was feeling better, because lambing began on our farm at the beginning of April and I was heavily involved with that. The weather was not particularly kind to us that lambing season and it always makes extra work when it's like that.

Towards the end of April the pressure on our farm eased off a bit and I was able to go trapping again. I went out to the farm that I trapped regularly, near Sellafield on the west coast. Because it was a hundred mile round trip I set every trap I had in my possession, therefore trying to finish the job in as few visits as possible. Here I was, then, when I had another amazing trapping experience. I was just lifting those traps I had set the previous day on the edge of a ditch at the bottom of a field near the farmstead, when I pulled out a white mole. The next three traps I checked also contained white moles! I was astonished; there must have been a whole family of white ones living in that area; or perhaps it was due to the proximity of Sellafield! My mood, which had been flagging again recently, was lifted by this piece of incredible luck. I was too busy to get most of these rare specimens to the taxidermist so I buried three of them, but kept one for the farmer in case he wanted to get it stuffed.

This occurrence makes me remember two other trapping events in the nineties. One was while checking my traps on the edge of the ditch next to the fourth fairway at Keswick Golf Club. I was using a couple of barrel traps at the time, in which you can catch a mole in either end of each device. On this occasion, I did better than that; I caught four animals in one trap at one go, but they were not moles, they were half-grown weasels. They must have been coming down the tunnel en masse and got in the trap. There was a hell of a tangle of bodies and it took me a while to sort it out.

The other occasion was while checking traps on the second hole of the same course when again; I lifted a sprung barrel trap to find, to my astonishment, which quickly changed to slight annoyance, that there was a large pork sausage with four cocktail sticks for legs stuck in it! I took the sausage out and re-set the trap. When I got back to the clubhouse, some of my younger playing partners were waiting for me with broad grins on their faces. It was quite a prank they had played on me and I was not amused, but this faded when the following day I caught a mole I had been having trouble with in the same trap – the sausage must have served to spice up the trap!

On Sunday the thirtieth of April, a week after Easter, Angus, Anne and her two daughters, Katie and Hannah, came up to the farm and also Heather joined us after climbing Clough Head (the mountain just south of Threlkeld village). It was a lovely warm spring day, so we all walked across to the edge of the Top Field, where the land fell away down a steep bank into the Jimmy Bottom (a kind of flat grassy area on the inside of a bend in Mosedale Beck). Anne had brought a basketful of different coloured pace eggs and we had a hell of a laugh rolling these down the bank in the Easter tradition, to see whose could get to the bottom without cracking. Also that day, my grandma was brought to the farm by a friend to pick primroses on the sides of the old Cockermouth to Penrith railway, which ran through our land. These lovely flowers were the favourites of my grandma and she had picked them from the railway sides nearly every year of her long life. Unfortunately, this was to be her last time!

During early May we must have been having trouble with the fox amongst the lambs, because in my diary it states that we were hanging out old coats on gate posts around the lambing fields, to try to make it look like someone was standing in the gateways, thereby deterring the fox.

These coats were brought into the house each night to get them smelling of humans; this was referred to as 'bringing the sentries in'. Of course we no longer had any guns and we could have got the local hunt in to try and get the fox, but Dad was not a fan of this because it caused too much stress amongst the lambing flock. Anyway, I think the sentries must have done some good because the fox trouble slowly petered out.

The workload was easing off at this time and the weather was superb, so on the seventh of May Angus and Anne came to the farm at nine a.m. and we set off, with Tina and our hiking gear in my car, to drive round to Wasdale Head, where we met Andrew at eleven a.m. It was red hot so we all had our shorts on. We set off past the hotel, over the beck by the little hump backed bridge and walked north west up the Mosedale valley on a good, mainly level path. After about a mile we struck off south west and climbed up the exhausting Dorehead Screes, where the path was almost non-existent. It must have been close to three hundred and five metres (a thousand feet) of gruelling ascent to the col at Dorehead and we were knackered when we got to this point. We soon recovered, though and continued north west towards Red Pike. My mood was pretty good at this time, mainly due to the excellent weather and I was enjoying myself once more.

Tina was also having a good time, probably appreciating the opportunity to enjoy a trip out without having to gather any sheep! We reached the summit of Red Pike at eight hundred and twenty six metres (two thousand seven hundred and ten feet), which is on a sort of rocky ridge. Here we had a latish lunch and then continued on north west, through a dip and up to the round-topped summit of Little Scoat Fell at a similar height to Red Pike. Then we crossed the dry stone wall there and descended into the little col to the north before climbing the short distance up onto the notable rocky peak of Steeple at eight hundred and nineteen metres (two thousand six hundred and eighty-seven feet). This was one of the summits Andrew and I had missed when trying to walk the Ennerdale Horseshoe, having bailed out due to bad weather on Pillar, which is the next summit to the east. We returned to Little Scoat Fell and then trekked on over to Pillar before descending eastwards to Black Sail Pass and then back down in a southerly direction, into the Mosedale valley once more. By this time, my bare arms and legs were getting burnt in the strong sun. We made it back to the Wasdale Head Hotel just after five p.m., meaning the hike had taken us about five and a half hours. The crack had been great throughout the walk and it continued as we slurped a couple of pints each in the beer garden. We set off home at six fifteen p.m. and when I got back I still had my routine bullocking to do, making it after ten p.m. when I finally got finished up. However, I didn't have to cook for myself in the flat any more because my self-imposed exile in the granny flat had come to an end at the beginning of lambing time, when my dad told me I would not have enough time to get all the lambing work done and cook for myself, so I went back to the old arrangement and gave up living in the flat for good.

During the week beginning Monday the eighth of May, I went on another national park job, helping to off-load the cargo nets from the army helicopters on Helvellyn, Sticks Pass and at Castle Rock. Once again, our work party got airlifted up to the work sites and it was an exhilarating experience, as before. Even more exciting was the fact that a very attractive student was in our work party. She was a farmer's daughter from Bassenthwaite and because the weather was red hot, she was dressed only in shorts and a tee shirt. Phew, I couldn't keep my eyes off her! She was a very nice young woman and I got many opportunities to chat to her.

At the end of that week I went on another hike, again with Angus and Anne but instead of Andrew, we had Alex for company, along with the ubiquitous Tina, of course. On this occasion, we met at the top of the Carrock Valley, where the Cumbria Way comes through on the east side of the Skiddaw range of fells. I had not been walking with Alex since the Scotland trip where I had got the shits and he said to me before we started walking, "I hope you haven't brought any more of those out of date apricots today?"

I laughed, replying, "No, don't worry, mate. You're safe enough today."

From the cars we struck out westwards, steeply up through deep, difficult heather covered slopes onto the round-topped summit of Knott at seven hundred and ten metres (two thousand three hundred and thirty feet), where we had lunch in the hot, sunny conditions. From Knott we struck off north east over fairly level, heather-free ground to the area of Iron Crag where there are many old mine workings. Here Angus gave us all a lecture on the history of the mines and the work that he and his national park co-workers had done to protect the site.

From here, we hiked out north east again to High Pike at six hundred and fifty-eight metres (two thousand one hundred and fifty-eight feet) and then eastwards over good level going to the summit of Carrock Fell at six hundred and sixty-one metres (two thousand one hundred and sixty-eight feet), before descending steeply south west through heather and rocks, back to the cars. There are several good bathing pools in the river Caldew near to where we parked and these were full of people of all ages, frolicking in the water in the hot conditions. Tina had been in great form throughout the walk as had the rest of us. During the day we had discussed initial plans for a skiing holiday in the coming winter, which would comprise a large group of the family plus a couple of friends. We returned to our respective homes after the walk and as usual I had the bullocking to do. We were still a week or so from turning the cows out to summer pasture but the beasts were becoming restless, I guess they were sensing that turnout was near.

A few days earlier, during one of the pool matches Bob Ridehalgh had asked me if I would go on a cycling trip to Scotland with him and a couple of his other friends and I had jumped at the chance. It was to be a long weekend beginning on Friday the nineteenth of May. Although I had no mountain bike of my own at the time, Bob said I could borrow one belonging to his son.

The day of the trip arrived and I was somewhat apprehensive. I had not been anywhere with any of these people before and especially not on bikes. The itinerary for the trip was somewhat vague, but I had been told to pack my big rucksack with stuff for walking and also my general bits and bobs for spending nights in youth hostels (I had never been hostelling before either!). Any extra gear would go in a couple of panniers fixed to the bike I was going to be riding. Bob came at six p.m. and found me in a state of confusion – I had got packed but was sure I had forgotten something. Bob soon got me organised and encouraged and we loaded my gear into his old Renault estate. I was the first on his list of pick-ups and at this point there was not too much gear in the back of his car, but there were a couple of bikes strapped rather haphazardly to the roof rack. Bob had told me not to worry about food and I observed that there were a few bags of non-perishable goods already in the car. A few days previously I had had a dentist's appointment in Keswick and afterwards, I had bought a new compass and a Swiss Army knife at an outdoor shop in the town. *Up until then I had relied on my pocket knife for use on expeditions but this new experience*, I thought, *called for something a bit special.* My Swiss army knife has many tools on it, including a little saw. These items were amongst the first items I packed; I had an uneasy feeling about this trip and I had tried to prepare for all eventualities.

Having got loaded we set off and Bob drove us to Stoddah, near the village of Penruddock, (I went to primary school there) where we picked Ron up from his house, along with his gear and his bike, which was added to the pile on the roof rack. I had met Ron only once before but he is an amicable kind of bloke and we soon had a good crack going as we drove on into Penrith to pick up the last member of our party – Mac, whom I had never met before.

After we had got Mac's gear loaded we set off for Scotland, the old Renault now heavily laden. The crack was great as we made our way up the M74 at quite a fast pace and there was one memorable incident near Beattock Summit when, travelling in the left hand lane, awaiting our turn to overtake a knot of traffic, we were suddenly overtaken ourselves by a sports car, but it was not the usual overtaking manoeuvre; this guy passed us on the left, therefore on the hard shoulder!

At the time Mac worked as a police patrol driver and he shouted, "Somebody get that bugger's number," as the red car flashed by.

We didn't get the guy's number though and fortunately for him, we never saw his car again.

At Stirling we turned off onto the A82 and drove to Crianlarich, where we pulled in to the youth hostel there at nine forty-five p.m. We had stopped briefly on the way at Callander for fish and chips so we did not have to worry about making our own suppers in the hostel kitchen. We unpacked only what gear we needed for the night, made a brew and then turned in at eleven p.m. The hostel was quite big but was very busy and the six bunk dorm we were in was full. Luckily I was able to bag a bottom bunk, which was important for me, as I always have to get up through the night for a pee! There was bedding provided for the bunks but you had to have your own sheet sleeping bag and Mam had kindly made me one out of a couple of old sheets.

Saturday the twentieth of May. We were all up at seven a.m. and I had slept reasonably well, but had not been prepared for the snoring you get exposed to in those kind of sleeping arrangements. Also I had of course been up through the night for the required pee, but had managed to get out to the toilet and back without disturbing anyone. During the stop at Callander on the way up, Bob had quickly gone to the supermarket and bought some eggs and bacon, plus some gammon with a good shelf life. We all mucked in with cooking and washing up in the large hostel kitchen, enjoying a banquet of scrambled eggs, bacon and beans from the supplies Bob had bought. After the meal we each put our own packed lunches together and I made my flask of coffee, which was to become the source of much comment later in the day!

Afterwards we offloaded the bikes from the roof rack of the Renault and then Bob instructed us to get all of our gear from the car and take it along with the bikes to the railway station, which was only about a hundred yards away. Up until that point I had been somewhat in the dark as to where we were going, but then Bob announced that we would be leaving the car at the youth hostel and getting on the next train north with all the gear, with a view to taking what gear we needed for an overnight stop off the train at the station at Corrour on Rannoch Moor, leaving it there all day with a view to transporting it the mile or so to the youth hostel at the west end of Loch Ossian in the evening. Meanwhile we would get back on the train and continue on with the bikes and our rucksacks to Tulloch Station, where the line comes down off Rannoch Moor to turn west towards Fort William. Here we would leave the train and cycle back through the valley on the eastern end of the Grey Corries mountain range to Corrour. "Simple," Bob said! I thought, *Jesus, this sounds like it's going to be an epic*. It proved to be apt thinking!

So we went to the station and got on the ten a.m. train with our gear, but we had to put our bikes in the freight carriage. The weather was dry and warm, but overcast as the train pulled out of the station to head north.

This is a grand train journey and I would recommend it to anyone.

The train was fairly full, but the four of us managed to find seats and I was soon relaxing, taking in the scenery as we passed Tyndrum and then Bridge Of Orchy, before climbing up onto Rannoch Moor, where the line crosses miles of peat bog. The construction of this line was a huge undertaking, I understand.

When the train stopped at Rannoch station, Bob told us to be ready for the next stop at Corrour, because we would only have a few minutes to offload our gear for the hostel. Corrour arrived and we whirled into action, only just managing to get the gear into a shelter on the platform and get back on before the train started moving again. We settled down again and enjoyed the ten mile ride to Tulloch station, where we got off the train, retrieved our bikes from the freight carriage and then set off to ride west along the A86 towards Spean Bridge.

I had not had the chance to get a practice ride on my unfamiliar steed and I quickly had to stop and adjust the height of the saddle. Also the gears (of which there were eighteen) took a bit of getting used to. I kept changing the range lever instead of the individual gear lever. I was at the back of our little chain of riders and I couldn't help noticing how little gear the other guys had, compared to me with my large rucksack and a pannier either side of my back wheel. I had been prepared for anything but I would soon find out that I had far too much stuff. I had left the mechanical aspect of the bikes up to Bob and I assumed he had all the tools we needed!

We rode for about four miles (six point four kilometres) before Bob shouted back to tell us to turn off to the left down a narrow track. We made the turn and crossed a bridge over the river Spean before climbing uphill out onto an old railway line, which took us westwards. The railway lines were long gone, but the skeletons of the sleepers were still in position across the track. The riding quickly became bumpy and difficult, then we came to an old metal bridge across a nasty little ravine. There were some half rotten sleepers on the bridge, which also had low tree branches hanging over it. Bob and Mac managed to wheel their bikes across but Ron and I baulked at this obstacle, opting to scramble down into the ravine and out the other side. It was a difficult manoeuvre and I was greatly relieved to get through it unscathed! A mile or so further on the line ended abruptly at the entrance to a tunnel and further progress was halted in this direction, by a solid fence across the tunnel mouth.

It was by now about lunch time and I got my provisions out of my panniers and flopped down on the grassy embankment to take the chance to grab a bite while Bob and the others pored over the map.

Bob observed my actions and said, "Oh, well, it looks like we're having lunch then!"

He came across to me and picked up my Thermos flask, which was a one-litre stainless steel one. "What the bloody hell is this? It weighs a ton, are you sure it isn't a nuclear flask?" he commented, laughing. (This has become a standing joke between us ever since!)

It was at this point that the full impact of my amount of gear hit me and I became aware of the fact that although I was the youngest member of the group, I was acting like a drag anchor on proceedings and holding the others up.

I said to Bob, "I'm afraid I've brought too much gear, I've never done anything like this before."

He smiled and said, "Don't worry, I'll take your panniers on my bike and lighten your load."

I was grateful to him and somewhat relieved.

After lunch and having studied the map we struck off south, away from the railway line, over open country. There was little to show anybody had ever been this way before and we had to wheel the bikes through heather, uphill around a plantation of young conifers. It was a tortuous route but eventually we struck a good path, coming out of the Lairig Leacach valley at the eastern end of the Grey Corries.

Unfortunately this is where the shit hit the proverbial fan for me, when suddenly the left hand pedal on my bike, which I was now riding again came loose and I had to stop. I shouted up to Bob ahead, to make him aware of my predicament and he came back with the tool kit. However he didn't have a spanner quite big enough to fit the main pedal nut, which had become unscrewed. We were only able to get the nut tightened so far.

I set off again but the nut came loose again after about five hundred yards and we had to stop again, then again and again to retighten. It was a real pain in the arse and slowed our progress significantly. Fortunately the route became too narrow in places to ride without the pedals catching and we had to push the bikes through these sections. I was worried, though and pretty stressed out as well by the time we had made our way through to the bothy, just beneath the Munro of Stob Ban at the eastern end of the Grey Corries range. I was holding the group up and although we had plenty of daylight, time was moving on.

It would have been a help to me if I'd had Tina along on the trip but the logistics prevented this. Dad always looked after her while I was away, feeding, watering and exercising her. She would have been great company for me under such stressful circumstances!

We rested at the bothy for a short while before heading on south, past the watershed and into the Allt na Lairige valley to trek through to the southern end of Loch Treig. The pedal nut had to be tightened at regular intervals but I was starting to come to terms with the problem. I can't remember seeing another soul outside our group all day, even though it was the weekend. It is a pretty wild, uninhabited area we were trekking through.

At Loch Treig we came across an old shepherd's cottage that had sadly fallen into disrepair. The inside of it was full of rubbish and people had been using it as a toilet!

From the cottage we rode and pushed our bikes eastwards around the end of the loch and up to the side of the railway track we had travelled through on earlier in the day. There was a good path here, which led us south the last couple of miles to Corrour station. In a way, this last stretch was the hardest of the day, with the end being virtually in sight and my exhaustion beginning to tell. At the station we found that there was a café and lo and behold, it had a licence to sell alcohol. We piled into the café and collapsed into the chairs around an available table. A waitress took our order for four pints of her best beer and while doing so, asked us where we had come from. Bob explained to her, and told her of the trouble we'd had with my bike. She said the owner of the café had a good set of tools and that she would ask him if he could fix my bike.

Our beers were brought to us and we all tucked into the foaming lager. I don't think beer has ever tasted so good! The café was surprisingly crowded considering Corrour is in the middle of nowhere, although I suppose if you take into account the railway and the proximity of the Loch Ossian youth hostel, the number of people present was understandable.

While we were quaffing our lager we discussed the events of the day so far, at the same time poring over the map. I think it was about eight p.m. by this time and we measured the distance we had travelled from Tulloch station at about eighteen miles (twenty-nine kilometres). It certainly felt like it, I was knackered! We finished our drinks and the café owner approached with his toolkit. Outside, the friendly proprietor found a spanner to fit my pedal nut and tightened it up good and hard. I thanked him and then our gang went to the shed on the railway platform to pick up the rest of our stuff that we had left there early in the day. We half rode and pushed our bikes, carrying the boxes and bags full of food/beer etc. (Yes, we had beer, I had made certain of that!) Quite how we managed to transport it all the mile or so to the hostel, I'm not sure but we were pumped up on lager. Disappointingly, the tightening of my pedal was not successful and it came slack again before we got to the hostel!

On approach to the hostel, I could see it was built of wood, with a corrugated iron roof. The location was beautiful, though, with the building nestling close to the shore at the head of Loch Ossian, with fine views down the loch towards the massive bulk of the Munro of Ben Alder in the east.

Dusk was closing in as we carried our gear into the hostel. I was somewhat surprised and unnerved to find that the building was packed.

I said to Bob, "Will there be a bed for us all, do you think?"

"Yeah I'm sure there will be, I've booked accommodation for us." He replied.

We set about trying to get ourselves sorted out with a bunk each in the male dormitory, with some difficulty. We managed though and then started to get a meal together in the crowded kitchen. The cooking facilities were extremely limited, with only one four ringed gas cooker and it was a real scrum. Bob was brilliant though and was soon fighting his way to the cooker in amongst the crowd, which seemed to be composed of Belgians mainly. Mac, Ron and I helped as best as we could but it was manic.

Somehow Bob managed to cook the fine pieces of gammon he had bought on the way up, with beans and one or two other bits and bobs and we enjoyed a fine meal in the packed conditions. We got washed up afterwards in the only sink and then I wondered about breaking out the beer. I thought, *it will make me even more likely to get up in the night but what the hell?* So I got us a can of Stella Artois each out of my supplies and we guzzled them before turning in, in the cramped dormitory. Unfortunately, I had the top bunk in a tier of three and it seemed a long way up to it. Before I made the climb to my bunk I tried to find the toilet while the dormitory light was still on (the hostel had only a small generator to power the lights and this was turned off at night). All I could find was a lean-to shack out the back with a metal bin in it and there didn't appear to be a light in this shack! I thought, *Jesus, this is a rum carry on.* I took the opportunity to pee in the bin and then went back into the dormitory, just as the lights went out. I noted from my wristwatch light that it was eleven p.m. I felt for the ladder to my bunk and started to climb; suddenly my right foot slipped off the ladder and I stepped on somebody's face. There was a grunt and then silence, and then, regaining my balance, I struggled on up to my bunk. ~This was accommodation in its most extreme form! I burrowed under my covers and tried to sleep.

As I lay there, with thunderous snoring growling out all around, I pondered the events of the day. Things had been pretty full on and for the first time I began to think that but for the calming effects of my medication, I would probably now have been entering another episode. Physically, I was a bit lacking in energy but in spite of the problems with the bike, I had been more or less able to keep up with the rest of the group. When we had been at the hostel at Crianlarich, I had joined the Scottish Youth Hostels Association and upon paying for my night's stay, I had been presented with a kind of loyalty card, which you got stamped every time you stayed at a hostel in the association. When you had accumulated a certain number of stamps, you got a free night's accommodation. This hostel at Loch Ossian was also in the association so I vowed to get my card stamped the following morning.

I lay for what seemed like an eternity but was probably only about a couple of hours and then the need to pee came upon me once more. *Fuck,* I thought, *why did I have that beer!* I tried to indulge in some fantasy about a beautiful woman to take my mind off my distended bladder but it was no good, I would have to go. I carefully climbed down the ladder and felt my way in the pitch black to the door out to the lean-to.

Suddenly I felt someone moving behind me and I said, "Who's there?"

"It's me, Ron. I'm pissing myself, quick, let me through," a voice said.

Ron pushed past me and out into the shack. There was no door on it and starlight dimly illuminated the interior. I bumbled about a bit in the gloom and found the metal bin but Ron headed outside.

"Are you not going to use the bin?" I asked,

And he replied, "Bollocks to that, I'm going to water the plants!"

As I voided my bladder into the bin, I couldn't help hearing Ron's torrent pouring onto the ground outside and I stifled a laugh. We made our way back to our respective bunks and then I resumed the fight to sleep but it was largely unsuccessful. However, I made it through till morning without having to get up again.

Sunday the twenty-first of May. Everybody seemed to get up at the same time, about eight a.m. and of course, we all clogged up the kitchen at the same time. Where and how everybody got washed remains a mystery to me to this day! Somehow we managed to cook breakfast and do the washing up in the scrum. We then had a team meeting. Mac, Ron and Bob wanted to cycle again, which was fine for them but I had the broken bike. We discussed a bit more and then Bob told me that the mountain across the head of the loch to the north was a Munro and he had not climbed it. I said, "Neither have I." So he suggested that he and I went for that while Mac and Ron cycled down the loch-side and maybe out through the valley from its eastern end, north to Laggan, before taking the A86 back to Tulloch and coming back to Corrour on the train. We all agreed on this plan and then went our separate ways. Bob and I prepared our hiking gear, which included my Zamberlan boots; these were the only footwear I had with me at this stage and they had of course been used for biking the previous day, proving rather numb for the task, but now they would come into their own. We took the two un-needed bikes and all the other spare gear to the station before returning to the hostel and making our final preparations.

The weather was again favourable as Bob and I waved goodbye to Mac and Ron before walking round the head of the loch, to begin climbing the slopes of Beinn na Lap. This mountain is renowned as one of the easiest Munros to climb, isolated apart from access from the train station and perhaps the lodge at the eastern end of the loch. Beinn na Lap is nine hundred and thirty-seven metres (three thousand and seventy-four feet) and you are already three hundred and ninety-one metres (one thousand two hundred and eighty-two feet) up at the loch, so it is not too much of a climb.

The slopes were steep but largely grassy as we climbed in the dry but slightly overcast conditions. There was little wind and it was quite warm.

We reached the summit in under two hours, having enjoyed excellent crack on the way up. At the top I sprang my little surprise on Bob and produced the last two five hundred millilitre cans of the 5.2% Stella Artois that I had brought on the trip. His face lit up as we downed the rather shaken up but cool beer and then had the packed lunch we had prepared earlier. The strong beer went right to our heads and we enjoyed a good giggle.

After lunch we made our way down the steep, heather-covered eastern flank of the mountain and I was surprised at how many times Bob slipped and rolled into the heather. It turned out that he had virtually no tread left on his boots but it was probably also the effects of the beer that caused his antics!

We got back down to the loch in about an hour and a half and then proceeded to walk east along the shore, to inspect the huge construction site at the lodge which was being refurbished at the eastern end of the loch. A new gravel road had been driven in from Laggan and somebody was obviously spending a lot of money on the project, probably foreign money! It being a Sunday, of course there were no workers on the site and we were able to have a good nose around unmolested.

As we continued on round the bottom of the loch, I looked up at Ben Alder but much of its massive bulk was shrouded in mist. Its summit stands at one thousand one hundred and forty-eight metres (three thousand seven hundred and sixty-six feet) and I have not yet climbed it to this day. The view from Beinn na Lap had also been spoiled by some low cloud drifting around.

We walked all the way back to the youth hostel around the southern edge of the loch and as we approached the hostel, the guy who ran it came out with a shirt and asked us if it was one of ours. Bob took it off the guy and said, "Yeah, thanks, it's mine."

At this point I remembered I had not got my loyalty card stamped so I asked the guy if he would do it for me. He nodded and took my card into the hostel to stamp it. When he came back and gave my card back, I shook his hand and said, "Thanks for the stay, maybe we will see you again some time."

"Yes, but things might be a bit different here when you come again, and I mean that in a good way," he replied.

Bob told me some years later that a lot of money had been spent on the hostel and it had been substantially upgraded. I had thought; *oh well, no more pissing in a bin out the back then!*

We said goodbye to the hostel manager and then walked up to Corrour Station to wait for the arrival of Mac and Ron. We sat drinking coffee and eating broth in the station café, discussing the trip, which was now largely over. I rued the fact that I had not brought a camera to record what had truly been a memorable experience.

I don't know how Bob had managed to organise it but when the six thirty p.m. train from Tulloch rolled in, he said, "This is the train we need to get back to Crianlarich."

"What about Mac and Ron?" I asked.

"Oh, don't worry about them, I expect they are on this train," he commented.

Maybe it was just numb luck but he was right, because as we rushed out to the shed on the platform to load the bikes and other stuff, Mac and Ron stepped down from the train to give us a hand. Mac was looking somewhat sheepish for some reason and I soon found out why. We loaded the gear and then Bob and I managed to find seats in the crowded carriage near Mac and Ron. When the train had pulled out of the station, Mac came over to recount the tale of his and Ron's day. It had been a straightforward bike ride out to Laggan on fairly good, level tracks and then a smooth ride back along the A86 to Tulloch, but having got on the train to Corrour an incident had occurred! They had got to their seats only to find that there were a couple of Oriental folks sitting in them. Ron had hoiked these two unfortunates out of these seats and they had disappeared into the next carriage with their tails between their legs. When Ron and Mac had got settled into the vacated seats, they examined their tickets and found that they were in the wrong carriage! Mac was somewhat perturbed by the experience as, I suspect, were the Orientals!

As the train trundled across the barren wastes of Rannoch Moor, I looked across to the west, towards the far distant eastern end of the Glencoe valley, but the weather had closed in a bit and the fine view was slightly obscured. We descended to Bridge of Orchy and Tyndrum and I reflected on the matter of asking the probation people about going on this trip. They had been most impressed that I would be in the company of a policeman, a dentist and a top expert in the field of industrial ceramics; they had given their full support to the endeavour!

When we got our gear off the train at Crianlarich, we took it back to the youth hostel and to the car, where we loaded it up and then set off home at eight thirty p.m. Just after we embarked, Ron sprang a little surprise on us. He had got some beer from somewhere and he handed the cans of Heineken around in the car, but not to Bob, of course, who was driving. The lager, although a little warm, went down extremely well. We returned via Loch Lomond and stopped there to inspect an old castle that had been turned into a youth hostel. It was in the SYHA so we thought it would be worthy of a stay sometime.

We dropped Mac at his house in Penrith, then Ron at Stoddah, shaking hands and exchanging glowing comments about the trip as we did so and then Bob drove me home.

We offloaded my gear and then Bob said, "That was a fantastic trip; we will have to do another one soon."

I agreed. We shook hands and then he went home. I stowed my gear and then went to bed, it was twelve thirty-five a.m. Just before I went to sleep I reflected on the trip. Overall it had been a good one, but there had been bits of it that were extremely stressful and although I didn't like taking the medication, I was forced to agree that it had saved me from going over the edge at times.

I must have been slightly high after the trip because when attending one of my regular meetings shortly afterwards with Richard, the psychologist, he commented on my mood and suggested that I came off caffeine, for a bit anyway. I tried for a while, purchasing decaffeinated coffee and tea but I quickly found that my energy and motivation levels were lowered to the point where I didn't feel like doing anything. Also I had to make a special trip to town for the decaffeinated beverages because Philip Brown, our mobile shop man, didn't have any on the van. Philip is a great guy and very popular with us all. Then, as now, he comes to the house every Saturday afternoon with a wide variety of produce. The crack is always brilliant and at the times when my folks are away, he acts as a pseudo counsellor to me!

I was very tired after the trip and I had a few easier days before throwing myself back into my work.

On Tuesday the twenty-third of May, I had a meeting in the Beacon Unit at Penrith with my social worker, John and an Indian psychiatrist. It only lasted twenty minutes but in that short time it was decided that my risk level should be reduced from high down to medium. As always in those early years following the Beacon Unit incident, I found it quite harrowing having to go there. It always brought the events of that terrible night back to me.

It must have been around this time that my sister bought me my first mobile phone. It was a Phillips and was a real brick of a thing. I wore it on my belt on a kind of hook and used it in late May when trapping at the lower end of Ullswater, to contact the farmer up at Glenridding to tell him about a sickly sheep I had found.

On Sunday the twenty-eighth of May, following a night out in Penrith with Angus, Anne and Alex, having spent the night at Angus and Anne's house at Culgaith I awoke at seven a.m. and got Angus and Anne out of bed, before breakfasting and then loading our hiking gear into Angus's car and setting off down, round into the Kentmere Valley to walk the Kentmere Horseshoe. It was a lovely day as we departed from the car at nine thirty a.m. Tina was not with us, as there would have been problems kennelling her at my brother's house. We struck up westwards out of the Kentmere Valley, on a good path to Garburn Pass and then turned north up over Buck Crag and on to Yoke at seven hundred and six metres (two thousand three hundred and sixteen feet). Then came a series of ups and downs over Ill Bell at seven hundred and fifty-seven metres (two thousand four hundred and eighty-three feet), Frostwick at seven hundred and twenty metres (two thousand three hundred and sixty-two feet) and Thornthwaite Crag at seven hundred and eighty-four metres (two thousand five hundred and seventy-two feet). We had lunch here, along with quite a few other people. There were a number of attractive young women out on our particular walk that day and the fine, hot weather had brought them out in shorts, phew!

From our lofty lunch stop, we turned west across onto Mardale Ill Bell above the pretty tarn of Blea Water and then down south east, quite steeply to Nan Bield Pass before climbing out again onto Harter Fell at seven hundred and seventy-eight metres (two thousand five hundred and fifty-two feet). From here we turned south and enjoyed a comfortable stroll down to Kentmere Pike at seven hundred and thirty metres (two thousand three hundred and ninety-five feet), then on a good path, down a gradual decline back into the Kentmere Valley and back to the car. It had been a long walk measuring some eleven miles (eighteen kilometres) but the terrain had not been difficult, with most of the tops being smooth and the paths good. The crack had been excellent as well, along with the views to the rest of the Lake District Fells. The walk had taken just under seven hours and we were pretty tired as we drove back to Culgaith for supper and a beer before I returned home to unpack my gear and then turn in at ten p.m.

During the following days I continued with my trapping work and also helped dad to turn the cows and calves out. This was always an exciting job as there were usually some high jinks with the beasts. They had been inside for seven months and the calves had been born indoors. It was quite a simple matter to turn out the cows but the calves were a different prospect entirely. They had to be put on the halter and steered out to the little garth (small field) staging area, where they were released to charge around excitedly in the bright, unfamiliar sunshine. They would blunder into the fences until they got their bearings but there were rarely any injuries. When the beasts had settled down, they were moved into bigger pastures.

Early in June I got a call from a lady at Cockermouth, who wanted me to catch the moles that were digging up her fine new lawn. When I got out there, the house turned out to be part of a new row that had been built next to a park, adjacent to the River Cocker. The properties were high value ones and their front lawns had been freshly laid. Once I got started on the job, I quickly attracted the attention of the neighbours and they also had moles, so I ended up trapping three separate gardens with great success. The moles were coming in from the park and their runs were shallow and easy to find. I caught a mole in each garden and then there was a further interesting development. One of the neighbours was a divorced lady and she was very nice. I was encouraged by my main customer lady to get to know the neighbour lady and maybe take her out, so I made a bit of a play for her, but things were slightly complicated by the fact that the lady had two teenage daughters living with her. I kind of made plans to take the lady out ten-pin bowling in Carlisle later in the month but I'm afraid I bottled out and kind of stood her up – apologies to her if she reads this!

Although I had enjoyed the Cockermouth experience as a whole, my mood took a dive again and I had difficulty getting out of bed for a few days afterwards.

My old faithful Karrimor waterproof coat was now beginning to look a bit tatty, so I spent a hundred and seventy pounds on a new Paramo Nikwax technology coat at an outdoor shop in Penrith. This garment, although bulkier than my old one, is an excellent coat. It is royal purple in colour and I still use it today. On the eighteenth of June, I took it for its first outing on a hike in the Langdales. Angus and Anne came to the farm for nine a.m. and I drove us, with Tina, down to the Dungeon Gyhll Hotel in

Great Langdale, where we parked and waited half an hour for Andrew to join us. When he did, we got our gear together and took a rough, very steep path straight up the north side of the valley, right behind the hotel. It is mainly rock climbers that use this route on their way to several notable rock faces there. It was red hot and I was soon rueing packing my new coat as it is quite a weight. I found the going very difficult and I sweated cobs on that first part of the hike. Tina bounded along merrily as usual, though. I had not had her out on the fells for a while.

We got up the steep section out of the valley and joined the good, well used path out between Harrison Stickle and Pike of Stickle. We then headed north west on fairly level going to Martcrag Moor at five hundred and forty-seven metres (one thousand seven hundred and ninety-four feet) and then north down to Stake Pass where the Cumbria Way comes over to the Borrowdale side. There was the usual good crack as we ate our lunch at this point and the usual consternation from the others over how long it took me to eat my sandwiches and various other provisions. (I always like a good lunch stop, if the weather is good anyway.)

From the lunch stop, where the hot weather had again brought out some fine sights wearing shorts, we headed south west up a shallow valley to Angle Tarn, then up steeply north west to climb out onto the rocky summit of Esk Pike at eight hundred and eighty-five metres (two thousand nine hundred and three feet). We dallied here for a few minutes to admire the fine views in all directions and to take a few photos. Tina, who investigated every dog she came across in a friendly way, had enjoyed her large tin of cat meat at lunch time and was firing on all cylinders. From Esk Pike, we headed south east down to Ore Gap and then up again, fairly steeply in a southerly direction, to the rocky summit of Bow Fell at nine hundred and two metres (two thousand nine hundred and fifty-nine feet). There were fine views of the Scafells to the north west from here and we again took photos. From our lofty perch we headed down to Three Tarns, where we took the path east and dropped down the Band, back into Great Langdale and to the Dungeon Ghyll Hotel, where we enjoyed a couple of shandies in the beer garden. The hike had been about ten miles (sixteen kilometres) but I'm not sure how long we were walking. After we had quenched our thirst we parted company from Andrew and made our way home. It was about seven thirty p.m. when we got back to the farm. I checked the temperature at the back of the house and it had been twenty-three degrees centigrade (seventy-seven Fahrenheit) in the shade – no wonder I had found the going tough, but it had been a good day.

There was much less bullocking now the cows were out and Dad had seen to what needed to be done. It had been some years since we dispensed with the services of our milk cow, which had been milked by hand; we now got the milkman to deliver, like most other people. Milking our own cow had tied us up more, with the chore having to be done night and morning, every day.

The day after the Langdales walk, I did my yearly strimming job cutting the grass verges through Mungrisdale village. It was red hot again and I became overheated and a headache came on. One of the kind ladies in the village brought a large glass of iced squash out for me and was a bit concerned when I told her I had a bad head. She promptly brought me a couple of paracetamol and before long I was feeling fine again.

It took me a few days to finish the job and then on Thursday the twenty-second of June I took the day off to relax a bit and pack up my camping gear, ahead of what I expected to be a very strenuous week's walking in the Highlands.

Friday the twenty-third of June. It was the afternoon by the time I had done all my preparations for the trip. The plan was that I would drive up to Glen Nevis campsite and meet Andrew, Tracy and a couple of their friends there later in the day. I drove to Penrith in my laden Capri, bought some provisions at the supermarket and then set off up the M6 at two twenty p.m. I made the usual stop at Stirling Services and then drove on up the A82 to Fort William, arriving there at six twenty p.m. before going on the couple of miles into Glen Nevis, to the campsite there. I pitched my tent in favourable conditions, made a brew and something to eat then relaxed in my camping chair to wait for the arrival of the others. It was ten fifteen p.m. before Andrew and Tracy rolled up and they were without their friends. Angus and Anne would join us there the following day.

I helped Andrew and Tracy make camp and then we cracked open a few beers and sat about talking by the light of my gas lantern until eleven thirty p.m., when we turned in.

Saturday the twenty-fourth of June. We were up at five forty-five a.m. and all of us had slept reasonably well in the benign weather conditions overnight, it seemed. We busied ourselves with breakfast and putting up our packed lunches in our separate tents which, although the campsite was busy, we had been able to pitch side by side. The plan was that Andrew and I would climb Ben Nevis by a roundabout route while Tracy would visit Fort William. Her hips were still giving her problems walking any distance, so she opted for a more relaxing activity. The weather was somewhat marginal for climbing the Ben, with the odd light shower and quite a lot of hill fog drifting around, so obviously it was quite cool. We decided to go for it. I think this would be the first time Andrew had climbed the Ben but it would be my second, having first done it as a teenager.

At eight forty-five a.m. Andrew kissed Tracy goodbye and then he and I set off up the road from the site, to cover the few hundred metres to where a bridge crosses the River Nevis and the main tourist path starts for the Ben. We both had our big rucksacks on with all our gear in them; we were fully aware of the conditions you can find on Britain's highest mountain and had prepared accordingly. I had come out of my recent, slightly depressed mood and was feeling more upbeat, which was good because I knew we had a tough day ahead of us and also in the week to come, because Angus had already outlined plans to climb many of the remaining Munros in the Mamores range to the south east of Ben Nevis, after he and Anne had joined us.

We chatted away as we joined the streams of walkers making the ascent that day. They were dressed in a wide range of clothing and footwear, some of it quite bizarre!

Good progress was made up the steepening path out of Glen Nevis in a north easterly direction and we were soon approaching the shoulder of the Ben, where a path turns off the main route to pass near the waters of the Lochan Meall an t' Suidhe. Andrew and I took this route, thereby separating ourselves from the main flow of traffic.

We contoured round the north west shoulder of the Ben and down into the valley of the Allt a Mhuilinn beck. The weather had cleared a bit by the time we crossed this beck and it had warmed up. We were able to look up to the south and see the great crags which dominate the eastern side of Ben Nevis, they were an impressive sight. From the start, I had intended to include in the roundabout route, the ascent of the Ben's eastern neighbour, Carn Mor Dearg and its famous arête or ridge walk round and back up onto the Ben. I had kind of kept this part of the plan to myself to surprise Andrew. I knew he would be able to make the traverse of the arête because of his confident approach to tackling the Aonach Eagach a couple of years earlier. I quickly realised that my plan had been rumbled though, when Andrew got his map out and worked out our position, stating, "It looks like we are going to do Carn Mor Dearg and its arête then, right?" I grinned and nodded; he punched my arm and called me a sly bugger.

We were now faced with a stiff climb up out of the valley we were in, over patchy scree and rough grass some seven hundred and twenty metres (two thousand three hundred and sixty-two feet) up to the summit of Carn Mor Dearg.

"Right, let's do it," I said and we put ourselves at the gradient.

It was a long hard flog but we made it in under two hours, out onto the rocky summit of Carn Mor Dearg at one thousand two hundred and twenty metres (four thousand and two feet). We flopped down and dug our lunches out of our sacks at one p.m. As we ate, we looked westwards towards the great crags of the Ben, but as we did so the mist began to roll back in to obscure our view. We were the only walkers on that summit at the time but shortly after lunch, as we set off south towards the arête, we encountered a couple of elderly Scottish chaps and we kind of teamed up for the assault on the notorious ridge walk. It turned out to be fairly level scrambling, similar to Striding Edge and Sharp Edge in the Lakes, but there were some sections that were more difficult. The mist was down so we were protected from the sucking/exposure effect of the steep drops to either side. The arête runs round in a horseshoe and it broadens out at its western end to join up with the south eastern shoulder of the Ben. I'm not sure how long it took the four of us to traverse the arête but it is just over a mile long.

After the arête, our party broke up again and Andrew and I were once more alone. We set about tackling the hundred and twenty-two metres (four hundred feet) of steep boulder-strewn slope out up onto the summit of Ben Nevis at one thousand three hundred and forty-four metres (four thousand four hundred and nine feet). It was four p.m. and there were dozens of other people at the summit, some playing in the old snowdrifts. The mist was down, though and we were denied a view. We sat down on a rock on the broad summit plateau and Andrew sprang a nice surprise on me. Handing me a small bottle of beer, he said, "Here, get that down your neck!" I prised the top off with my Swiss Army knife and glugged the hoppy lager down gratefully.

We didn't dally long because the sky had darkened considerably and it soon began to rain. I gave my new coat its baptism of fire and donned my waterproof trousers as well, before we set off down the mountain, on the wide zigzag tourist track off the western side of the summit. The rain became heavier and there was even the odd clap of thunder. The temperature had dropped considerably as well.

The weather cleared up again as we descended and we were able to take our waterproofs off. My new coat had performed well. It was six fifteen p.m. when we got back to the campsite and it had got out into quite a fine evening. Tracy was back from town and we discussed our day's activities over a few beers outside our tents. I reckoned we had done about twelve point four miles (twenty kilometres) and we were pretty knackered, but happy. Tracy had enjoyed her day too, with the trip into town and a short walk up the glen and back.

Angus and Anne arrived just after we had showered in the excellent toilet block, but they couldn't get a pitch near us and had to put their tent up in the next field. They joined us later, though, for supper up at the nearby restaurant and we enjoyed a good crack before returning to the site and going to bed about eleven p.m.

Sunday the twenty-fifth. Angus woke me at seven forty-five a.m. urging me to get moving as we had mountains to climb. I was feeling a bit groggy and didn't feel like doing anything really, but Angus was very persuasive and he soon had me eating a rushed breakfast. Anne put a flask of coffee up for me and made some sandwiches. Andrew and Tracy were breaking camp – they had only really come up for Andrew to climb the Ben and were now getting ready for home. They set off for home just as Angus, Anne and I loaded our walking gear into Angus's car. They bade us goodbye and wished us favourable walking weather for the rest of the week. It was good to start with anyway; it was a dry, warm day with hazy sun and only the odd patch of low cloud.

I don't know whether it was because I was feeling a bit below par that day or what, but my memory and consequently my diary details of the walk that day are a bit sketchy. However, I will give the reader the information I have. We drove up Glen Nevis and parked at Achriabhach, then set about tackling the two Munros at the western end of the Mamores group. Walking out south from the car we climbed first Stob Ban at nine hundred and ninety-nine metres (three thousand two hundred and seventy-seven feet) and then went west onto Mullach nan Coirean at nine hundred and thirty-nine metres (three thousand and eighty feet), before heading out back north to the car. These were fairly straightforward mountains to climb but I was hampered a bit by a sore right shin. We did about nine point three miles (fifteen kilometres) and it took us six and a quarter hours. The crack was good, although there was a bit of grumpiness between us all, early on!

On the way back down the glen, we visited a small stuffed animal exhibition at a museum and then returned to the campsite to find that the police were there, arresting somebody. I moved my tent and things down next to Angus and Anne's, got a shave and shower then joined the others for a barbeque, washed down with a few beers. Afterwards Angus and I went up to the nearby bar for a couple and did a bit of bonding, before returning to our tents and going to bed.

There is no mention of the midge situation in my diary so I assume they were not too much of a problem.

Monday the twenty-sixth. I was up again at five forty-five a.m. and quickly breakfasted, plus put my lunch together in my tent. I could feel that the temperature was low and on unzipping the entrance of my tent I saw in the strengthening light that it was a fine, still, fresh morning. I could hear that Angus and Anne were up and about nearby also. The previous evening Angus had outlined his plan for this day, in that we would tackle the two Munros south of Tulloch, (where our other expedition had got off the train) and east of Loch Treig.

I was feeling more up for it than the previous day and was soon ready to go. When the others had got ready, we set off in my car and I drove up to Spean Bridge and along the A86 almost to Tulloch. I turned off, as instructed by Angus, onto a little side road to the right, then drove on a couple of miles to Fersit at the northern end of Loch Treig, where I parked. Having stopped, I noticed a few wisps of steam drifting up from beneath the Capri's bonnet. I opened the bonnet and saw a thin jet of coolant squirting out of a pinprick hole in the plastic radiator expansion tank. *Great*, I thought, *something else to bother about*, but there was nothing I could do about it there. I would just have to carry some spare water and hope that the leak didn't get any worse till I got home.

We donned our gear in the favourable conditions and left the car at nine fifteen a.m. Again, my details of this day are a bit vague but we would walk south up a steady incline, over soft, grassy terrain and up onto our first Munro of Stob Coire Sgriordain at nine hundred and seventy-nine metres (three thousand two hundred and twelve feet). We then turned east above the waters of the Lochan Coire an Lochain to drop down to a col (or bealach) and then up onto our second objective – Chno Dearg at a thousand and forty-six metres (three thousand four hundred and thirty-one feet). Here we had lunch and admired the views. It had started to cloud over but it remained dry. We set off back off the top of this smooth-topped hill, which matched the nature of the first top and back north west, down a steady decline over increasingly boggy ground and out back to the car for three fifteen p.m. we had done ten and a half miles (seventeen kilometres)

The brief cloudy spell had passed and the sun was out again as I drove us back to Fort William, where we shopped and enjoyed an ice cream before returning to our campsite in Glen Nevis. We had a few beers while Anne cooked us pasta with Ragu sauce. The crack had been good throughout the day and it continued into the evening. After the excellent meal, Angus and I washed up in the communal sinks, then I got a shave, took a shower and then we all went for a 'warm down' walk up the glen and back before bed at ten thirty p.m. It had been a good day and although tired, I had performed well.

Tuesday the twenty-seventh. On this day, Anne's knee was giving her a bit of gyp, so she went shopping in Fort William while Angus and I drove out to Drumsallie on the A830 Mallaig road. We went in my Capri and on the way I put one of my favourite C.D.s on the player, it was AC/DC's *Let There Be Rock*. This is a raunchy album and I turned the volume up, much to the annoyance of Angus, who doesn't like rock music. I sang along and drove quite fast as we made our way to Drumsallie.

The plan was that we would climb Gulvain, an isolated Munro to the north of Drumsallie. We parked just off the main road, donned our gear and set off to walk up the Gleann Fionnlighe. Although level and on good tracks, it was a long way in to the foot of the mountain – approximately four miles (six point four kilometres). Really we should have had mountain bikes, but Angus had left his at home and I did not yet own one. We had departed from the car at nine twenty a.m. and the walk in must have taken about two hours and then we had to start climbing. It was hard work but the ascent was not difficult, being on largely grassy slopes.

Presently we reached a lower un-named top at eight hundred and fifty-five metres (two thousand eight hundred and five feet) and looked on up to what we thought was the summit of Gulvain. We walked on to this summit in the fine, dry and quite quiet conditions, reaching it at one p.m. We sat down on the grassy summit to eat our lunches and looked across a bealach to another summit to the north, about a mile away.

I said to Angus, "Do you think that is the main top there?"

"No, I don't think so. It doesn't look any higher than this one, but I'm not sure because it is off the edge of my map," he replied

The summit we were on was at nine hundred and sixty-one metres (three thousand one hundred and fifty-three feet), which was certainly high enough for a Munro. I was enjoying a hardboiled egg and just then a tiny whirlwind blew up and sucked the eggshell up I had discarded, to carry it away over the hill end. We carried on discussing whether or not to carry on and bag the other top while we ate, but in the end decided not to go for it. We would regret this decision later!

On the return journey, Angus struck off in front and left me far behind. I don't know why he did this; maybe he had got the hump about something. Anyway, he wasn't going anywhere without me – I had the car keys. When I finally made it back to the car at four thirty p.m. with tired legs, he was sitting with his back against the back wheel of the Capri.

"Are you okay?" I asked.

He just shrugged and said, "Let's go home."

Angus must have had some sort of hunch about our choice of summits because he went on about it in the car on the way back. The hunch was borne out when we got back to the campsite and he examined his Munro book to find that we had missed the main summit, mainly because we didn't have the map showing it with us. We were extremely pissed off, but it was a mistake we would never make again. From then on, Angus always made sure we had all the maps and photocopied route finders with us on the hill.

We have since been back and gone on to claim the true summit of Gulvain, which is only twenty-six metres (eighty-five feet) higher than the south top we had been on!

We drowned our sorrows in beer, deciding that the affair should be from then on known as the Gulvain Incident. Anne cooked us a nice meal, which further helped soothe our annoyance. Afterwards I phoned Andrew on my mobile to fill him in on our activities.

Our two tents had a new neighbour; a young English guy had set up his tent next door. He was on an extremely long cycling trip and had all his belongings towed behind the bike in a kind of little trailer. I got talking to this newcomer and during our conversation, his face kept dissolving into a kind of rictus or strange grin. Perhaps this was due to always cycling into the weather and is maybe indicative of all long distance cyclists; I do not mean to be insulting towards them! Anyway, the guy was nice enough and I introduced him to Angus and Anne, and we all enjoyed a good crack before we turned in at ten thirty p.m.

The Gulvain walk had been around thirteen miles (twenty-one kilometres) and the distances we had already walked in the week were really mounting up. The water leak on my car was behaving itself but I made sure to keep topping up the radiator.

Wednesday the twenty-eighth. I was up at five a.m. and went for a walk down the side of the nearby river Nevis after doing my ablutions. During this jaunt, I saw a huge trout in the calm waters and also, a very curious sight; four white rabbits. Perhaps a tame rabbit had escaped and bred with the wild population, I will never know. I mooched back to the campsite, made my breakfast and packed lunch, then waited for Angus and Anne to get ready. It had been discussed that we would try and climb the remaining Munros, at the eastern end of the Mamores range and it would probably prove to be the longest walk of the week.

When the others had got ready, we loaded the gear into Angus's VW Golf and he drove us up to the car park at the top of Glen Nevis. We got our boots and rucksacks on and headed off up the side of the Nevis gorge in warm, dry but slightly overcast conditions.

When we got to the Steall bridge, instead of crossing it we continued on a good path along the northern side of the River Nevis and on for about two and a half miles (four kilometres) to find a place where we could safely ford the river. The water level was low, so we were able to cross quite easily without taking our boots off. After the crossing we struck off south east over quite boggy ground, which firmed up as we began the assault on the north west shoulder of the breast-shaped Munro of Binnein Beag. The crack up to that point had not been very inspiring. I guess we were all tired and feeling a bit ratty from our recent tough days, but things would very shortly get worse!

From the lower slopes the dome-shaped summit of Binnein Beag had been visible but as we climbed the increasingly steep shoulder of the mountain, the mist began to descend. There was little sign of a path, so we decided to tackle the peak by a direct route up a stony gully. I was soon labouring and began to fall behind the other two. They had got about thirty metres ahead of me when they started to disturb small rocks and gravel, which rained down on me. I shouted up to tell them to wait for me, but they either didn't hear or they ignored my plea and the debris continued to fall. I became annoyed and my temper, which had recently been masked by the medication, started to show itself once more. I finally cleared the gully, thankfully unscathed. Looking at my watch, I saw it was lunch time. Angus and Anne were sitting on a rock near the summit at nine hundred and forty-three metres (three thousand and ninety-three feet) and as I approached them I said, "For fuck's sake, did you not hear me shouting? Some of those bloody rocks could have brained me!" They just looked at me and said nothing, for a minute or so anyway and then all hell broke loose and a full scale row started. We railed at one another until we were nearly hoarse. Fortunately we were alone on the summit, saving embarrassment for other walkers.

"It's bloody bait time," I said, getting the last word in and I flopped down on a rock and got my sandwiches out. The other two rather reluctantly followed my example. A stony, pregnant silence fell over our group, which was further exacerbated by the quiet, misty, rather eerie conditions.

After we had eaten we sort of mechanically started out down southwards to a bealach at seven hundred and fifty metres (two thousand four hundred and sixty feet) where there is a small un-named lochan. Any conversation there was limited to only navigational information and even that was strained. The mist was still down as we passed the lochan and started to climb the northern shoulder of Binnein Mor, our next Munro. We seemed to climb for a long time and our group once more became strung out over the increasingly steep and rocky incline. Great buttresses began to appear out of the mist and we were soon scrambling up and around these, but no more rubble fell on me. Eventually we gained the summit cairn of Binnein Mor at one thousand one hundred and thirty metres (three thousand seven hundred and seven feet) and then continued on to the south top at a thousand and sixty-two metres (three thousand four hundred and eighty-four feet) before heading about a mile out onto our third Munro of Na Gruagaichean, at a thousand and fifty-five metres (three thousand four hundred and sixty-one feet). It was here that another disagreement broke out – Angus and Anne wanted to call it a day and go back to the car, but I knew there was still the easternmost Munro – Sgurr Eilde Mor – to do and I was thinking we were pretty close to it. I made plain my intention to go on and climb this other Munro, stating that I would probably never be this close again. The others said they were leaving it to another day, so with that, we parted company and not on very good terms, either!

The mist was still down as I watched Angus and Anne disappear off to the northwest. Suddenly I felt very alone. There was nobody else about, but there was nothing else to do but go for it now; I was committed. I got my compass out and using it and my map, navigated my way back to the south top of Binnein Mor and then southeast down to the summit of Sgurr Eilde Beag at nine hundred and fifty-six metres (three thousand one hundred and thirty-six feet), where I took stock. Visibility was still poor, but a reasonably worn path zigzagged steeply off the eastern shoulder of this peak and I followed it, and my nose, knowing that if I didn't come to the large waters of the Coire an Lochain before long, I had gone wrong. I descended for what seemed like an age, but finally came to the large lochain, whereupon I skirted its southern shore on a rough path. As I made my way round to the east side of the lochain, I began to feel less alone. Physically there was no-one else about but I kind of felt a spiritual presence, perhaps it was my guardian angel! I knew the last Munro was above me in the mist but it took me some time to find a rough path, heading up steeply eastwards into the murk. As I climbed, the mist began to thin and I was able to see ahead towards the summit of Sgurr Eilde Mor, which was still some distance above me. I took off my Paramo coat, which I had donned in the earlier, cooler lunch stop conditions, having now warmed up considerably again. The going was good, if steep, and I was soon approaching the conical summit, which was similar in nature to those of the previous two Munros. At the top at a thousand and eight metres (three thousand three hundred and seven feet) I sat down on a rock and admired the view out between the patches of mist to the north towards the Grey Corries. I took my rucksack off and got out the rest of my supplies. As I ate, I reflected on the earlier arguments. In a way, they had been unavoidable. It was good to be out on my own but I wondered how things would be when I got back to camp!

Having eaten and taken on water, I shouldered my rucksack and set off down the quite easy slope of the northern shoulder of the mountain, which was dotted with quartzite rocks. The slope quickly became grassy as I descended into the glen to follow the stream of Allt Coire a Bhinnein out to a watershed near the little hillock of Tom an Eite at four hundred and one metres (one thousand three hundred and fifteen feet), where the waters of the River Nevis begin. I had to negotiate several peat bogs in this area, but there was no deep water and I soon struck a good path heading from east to west. I set off west at a good pace, I was tired but the day was going on and I was aware that Angus and Anne would be worrying about me, so I made the best speed I could back towards Glen Nevis.

When I got back to the car park at the head of Glen Nevis, I was surprised to see Angus and Anne waiting for me next to their car. As I approached, Angus saw me coming and opened the boot of the car. He took out my training shoes, waited until I got close and then threw them at my head. Luckily I ducked or they would have hit me in the face! He shouted, "Here, get these on and get in the bloody car and don't take off like that again!" They had obviously been fretting about me and I felt somewhat guilty/silly about my behaviour. I took off my walking boots, donned the trainers, put my gear in the car and then we set off down the glen.

There was zero conversation in the car and from then on that evening. Things were very tense between us and I sought out the company of the cyclist we had met recently. He and I went up to the pub later for a couple of pints and I retold the story of my day.

Later, as I went to bed, feeling quite stressed, I tried to form a plan about what to do in the coming days. Arguments in our family always take some time to iron themselves out and I knew that being with Angus and Anne would only lead to further tension, so I made up my mind to go for a drive the next day on my own. I wrote my diary up before I climbed into my sleeping bag and using the map, I measured the distance walked that day at fifteen and a half miles (twenty-five kilometres).

Thursday the twenty-ninth. I was up at seven a.m., having not slept well, which was not surprising given the events of the previous day. Up until that point I had been sleeping fairly well, but now all of a sudden I had cause to worry about my mental health once more. By now, I was fully aware that lack of sleep was one of the main contributory factors towards a breakdown and I knew that the way I was pushing myself, I would have to be careful, or I would fall into the pit once more, medication notwithstanding!

I felt knackered but I busied myself with breakfast in my tent. I could hear there was activity from Angus and Anne's tent and I wondered what they had got planned for the day and whether it would include me. I soon found out when Angus came and announced that he and Anne were going to do the same Ben Nevis walk that Andrew and I had done on the first day. He asked me what I was going to do. Obviously I was not going to repeat that walk, so I had the perfect get out clause. I told him I was going for a drive and he said that it would be good for me to take it easier for a bit, therefore agreeing that we would go our separate ways that day.

As I walked to the toilet block to do my ablutions, I could see that it was a fine clear day all around and that it would be great conditions for doing the Carn Mor Dearg arête and climbing the Ben. I was somewhat envious, considering Andrew's and my walk had been in cloud a lot of the time and we certainly had had no view from the top of the Ben!

Back at the tents I said goodbye to Angus and Anne and also to the cyclist, who was leaving that day, and then I got in my car and drove off down the glen. At Fort William I pondered on where to go and then decided I would drive out to Mallaig on the west coast. I took the A830 and drove out the forty miles (sixty-four point three kilometres) or so to Mallaig in fine settled conditions. It was a funny road back then, with some sections of single-track highway with passing places, interspersed with three lane sections where you could get your foot down.

Once at Mallaig, I parked up and walked round the town for a bit, admiring the view out to the Isle of Skye. My tiredness had ebbed away a bit by this time and I wondered what to do with the rest of my day. On my way through to Mallaig, I had noticed a golf course near the village of Arisaig and so I made up my mind to see if I could get a game. I went back to my car and drove back to the course, which is at a place called Traigh. It is right by the coast and there are lovely white, sandy beaches nearby, where the azure blue sea comes rolling in.

I pulled into the car park next to the little clubhouse and went to enquire about getting a game. There was a little golf shop and the guy in charge told me I could hire clubs for six pounds and play all day for twelve pounds. It sounded pretty reasonable so I paid the guy and he gave me a nearly-new set of clubs, some balls and a scorecard and off I went to find the first tee.

I can't remember very much about the course but I do know that it was only nine holes, hilly in nature and that the opening tee shot from the first hole was uphill to a blind green, so it must have been a par three. It had been some time since I had swung a club and it took me a while to get loosened up and to familiarize myself with the hired set of clubs. There were few other golfers out on the course, though and I was able to play at my own pace. I went round the course three times, losing several balls from my precious supply in the process. It was a very enjoyable day and after I had taken the clubs back to the golf shop on completion of my game, I went down for a stroll on the nearby white, sandy beach. As I walked, I gazed out to the islands of Rhum, Muck and Skye, which seemed to hover on the shimmering blue sea.

Later, I went for a meal and a pint in a pub in Arisaig before driving back to the campsite at Glen Nevis. On the way back, I encountered the cyclist I had befriended from our campsite. As he came struggling up a hill towards me, he displayed his usual kind of rictus grin and waved.

On arrival back at the site, I found that Angus and Anne had returned from their hike up Carn Mor Dearg and the Ben. They were quick to point out to me that they had enjoyed a glorious view from both summits and I tried to compete with my golfing tale, but I didn't get far and with things still being difficult between us, the conversation soon died away and I was left to my own devices. I was soon away to my bed that evening, leaving the others to do their own thing.

Friday the thirtieth of June. I was up at five thirty a.m. and wasted little time in getting ready for a hike that I had planned just before going to sleep. I had slept much better and was feeling energised. I had every intention of going off on my own again, as it was proving to be much better for me in light of the difficult relations with Angus and Anne! I got my gear together and went to the others' tent to quickly tell them where I was going. I didn't give them time to voice any objection or find out what they intended to do this day and rushed off without further ado, up the glen in my car.

My intention was to climb Aonach Mor and then Aonach Beag from the south side, so I drove up to the park at the end of the Glen Nevis road, parked up, donned my gear and then walked up the gorge side towards the Steall Bridge. The weather was again good, with virtually clear skies and little wind. I passed the bridge and continued on alongside the Water of Nevis until I reached the Steall Ruin, which is the remains of some old building, probably a shepherd's hut. From here I struck out northwards, up into the Allt Coire Giubhsachan valley, where I saw some red deer. I followed the stream in the valley out to its source, high up near the bealach between Carn Mor Dearg and Aonach Mor. It was tough going, over grass, heather and then scree. I was blowing hard as I ascended from the bealach, up a final steep slope to make the summit of Aonach Mor at a thousand two hundred and twenty-one metres (four thousand and six feet). I had my lunch here, sitting on a rock and admiring the views all around. I could see all the summits of the Mamores range to the south and was able to appreciate the amount of ground I had covered there just a few days before.

I estimated that in the four days culminating in that Mamores walk, I had walked some forty-five miles (seventy-two and a half kilometres) and then there was this day on top of that!

After lunch, and having not encountered another soul up to that point, I set off, walking south down a ridge into a bealach and then back up steeply over broken ground onto the summit of Aonach Beag at a thousand two hundred and thirty-four metres (four thousand and forty-eight feet). A patch of mist suddenly rolled in and rather spoiled my view from this fine peak, so I wasted little time in descending off it to the south. This route was very steep and tricky, with a very narrow path, which virtually disappeared over some scrambling sections. I scared myself several times on this difficult descent, but I eventually made it down to easier going, whereupon I began to eye up the nearby Munro of Sgurr Choinnich Mor, on the western end of the Grey Corries range. For a while I considered trying to bag this summit as well, but time was going on and I thought better of it.

I continued walking out south over two lower tops, to make my way back to the Water of Nevis. It was by now getting on in the afternoon and the sun was strong, making for warm walking conditions. The terrain was not difficult, though, consisting of grassy slopes with only the occasional boggy area. As I neared the path running down the side of the Water of Nevis, I spied a lone, heavily laden walker coming along the said path from the east. We came together as I joined the path and naturally struck up a conversation. The walker proved to be a young Scottish guy called Carl and he told me he had been walking for days, wild camping as he went, and he had even crossed the wastes of Rannock Moor. Now though he was heading back towards civilization and he was keen to learn of the facilities of our campsite in Glen Nevis. We were both heading in the same direction and we quickly formed a friendship, as lone walkers tend to do in the wild places. However, I had an ulterior motive; a cunning plan was beginning to form in my head. I would attempt to inveigle this poor unfortunate soul into our group at the campsite, thereby using him as a distraction to help me cope better with the current poor relations with Angus and Anne.

I am not prone to this kind of behaviour but I guess at the time, being over tired and a little bit manic, it seemed appropriate!

We talked all the way back to my car and Carl gratefully accepted a lift down to the campsite. As we were stowing our gear in the Capri, I checked the map and measured I had walked about eleven miles (seventeen point seven kilometres).

As I drove us back down to the site, Carl, who was obviously impressed with my chariot, asked me questions on the performance of the Capri. Now I am not that technically minded and I must confess I kind of made up some of the details of the vital statistics of my motor.

It was around five p.m. when we rolled onto the campsite and Angus and Anne were back from whatever they had been doing. I introduced Carl to them and encouraged him to set his tent up adjacent to ours, in the same place where the cyclist had been camped the day before. Carl promptly did so and while he was about it, I did my ablutions in the toilet block. When Carl had got himself set up and showered, I encouraged our group to go up to the pub for a meal and drinks. Once I had a few beers inside me, I feverishly dominated the conversation, anxious to control the situation and thereby ease the tension between Angus and Anne and me. I was positively garrulous, almost to the point of making a fool of myself, but I got through the evening. God knows what time I turned in but I must have been quite pissed!

Saturday the first of July. I awoke at six a.m., feeling rough, but I seemed to have slept well. I opened the tent flap and saw that Carl was up and about too. I told him I was heading home shortly and asked him if he wanted a lift anywhere. He said he would appreciate a ride into Fort William and I said it would be no problem.

It was the least I could do, having used him as a vehicle to get through my last evening with Angus and Anne.

I made myself some breakfast and then broke camp, loaded all my gear and Carl's into the Capri, said a tense goodbye to Angus and Anne then drove off with Carl to Fort William. I dropped him off on the edge of town, shook his hand and wished him well then drove up to Spean Bridge and took the A86 to Newtonmore and then Kingussie. The weather was once again fine, warm and dry, and I was able to have the sunroof of the Capri open on the drive through. At Kingussie I was bursting for a pee, so I drove round onto the public car park behind the Duke of Gordon Hotel and sought out the toilets there. And what toilets they were, they had an attendant and there was a small charge for using the facility. There was even a shower in there! After I had eased the pressure on my bladder I got talking to the rather pretty attendant. I told her that I was a mole catcher of some note, enquiring if there was a need for the services of such a professional in the area. She said I would have to enquire at the local farms. It was a charming experience and remains the best pee I have ever had.

Afterwards I blasted home, stopping first at Dalwhinnie for petrol and then again at Stirling Services for food and to check my radiator level. I got home around eight p.m. and let Tina out for a run. She was very pleased to see me and I wished I had been able to take her on what had been a good trip, but somewhat traumatic towards the end! I offloaded the Capri, had my supper and went to bed at ten fifteen p.m.

Before I went to sleep, I attempted to analyse my general performance on the trip. Certainly early on my mood had been pretty much as normal, but things had started to get out of shape after the arguments. Physically I had done pretty well. Of course, the medication had restricted me somewhat but it had definitely kept me from going over the edge mentally, when things got difficult in the relationship department. All in all, things had gone well and I went to sleep in a good frame of mind.

The following day I awoke at eight thirty a.m., having enjoyed nine hours of uninterrupted sleep. After breakfast I took Tina for a run out, filled the expenses of my trip into my ledgers and then got a shave and bath. After lunch I drove into Penrith and to a big national cycle retailer to buy a mountain bike. I had been mulling over this purchase for the last few weeks and I finally decided to take the plunge. I was not after an expensive bike and I opted for one in the two hundred pound range, which had full suspension. I also bought a bike pump, some tools, a couple of securing cables and a sturdy padlock. I then loaded the bike and accessories into the Capri and drove home.

During the week that followed, I did some walling with Thomas and a strimming contract for the national park, clearing growth from several footpaths in the Caldbeck area. I also had several opportunities to try out my new bike, riding it up to the top farm of Lobbs and back. However, I soon became disenchanted with my machine. The front suspension was fine but the rear suspension was difficult to come to terms with. The ride quality was shit; it was like being on a rollercoaster. Also, the spare end of one of the brake cables had broken off! I decided to take the bike back and see if I could get my money back.

So on Friday the seventh of July I loaded the bike into the car and headed out, first to Carlisle for nine fifteen a.m., where I had an appointment with the psychologist, Richard, who told me I had handled the stresses of the recent trip very well. Then it was back to Penrith for eleven forty-five a.m., where I had an excellent back massage from a lovely nineteen-year-old girl/woman at the North Lakes Hotel Spa and then it was on to the bike retailer, to do battle with them. I was successful in getting my money back. I gave them the bike back and then it was straight down town to Arragons Cycles, where I should have gone in the first place! This is a very good shop and the staff there were very helpful in guiding me towards the decision of buying a Marin Muirwoods. This bike was a kind of hybrid, which it was explained to me would be good for both on and off road riding. It had a solid frame, chunky tyres, twenty-four gears and only front suspension, but it was also considerably more money than I had paid for the other machine – It would cost four hundred and sixteen pounds! The bike would have to be serviced before I could take possession of it, so I left it with the shop. I then returned home for a lateish lunch before heading out again for my next appointment of the day – a round of golf at the Keswick club, which I had arranged earlier in the week with my pool team member, Steve Butcher. I was due at the club at three p.m. and I set off from the farm at two fifteen p.m. but I didn't get far. I was just opening the gate on the lonnen when I smelled petrol strongly. I looked under the back of the Capri and saw petrol pouring out from the injection pump/tank area. I immediately drove back into the farmyard and parked up. My heart was in my mouth, I could have had a fire and possibly an explosion with the enormous leak being near the hot exhaust!

I left the Capri, as I had no time to deal with it at that moment, and got Dad to give me a lift to the golf club.

Steve was waiting for me as I arrived and we set about preparing ourselves for our round. There were just the two of us for it that day and I knew Steve was very competitive, so I would have to be on good form to beat him. I had not played the Keswick course for some time and I was no longer a member there, so I had to pay the daily green fee along with Steve, which I think was about fifteen pounds in those days. I still had my own clubs and other equipment though, plus I was on the back of my recent day's golf on the Scotland trip, so I was as well prepared to do battle with the crafty Cockney, Steve, as I could be.

It was a fine, dry day and cool, which was ideal for golf. On the first tee, we agreed on a side bet of two pounds to the winner of the round. I can't remember much about the scoring during the round but I do know that I went round in the gross score of ninety-one shots and Steve went round in eighty-seven, so even though Mr Butcher had a lower handicap than me, he still beat me and took the money. There were no hard feelings though and the crack had been brilliant, as it always is with my Cockney friend, who can talk for England! The banter continued on into the clubhouse, where we had a meal, a couple of pints and also a couple of games of pool, in which I was beaten again! Then it was off home to give Tina a walk out before bed.

The following day, Dad and I hatched a rather naughty plan to get my car to Brian Cowperthwaite's garage. I was in the A.A. at the time but I didn't have home start, so Dad got the tractor out and using the heavy tow chain, towed the Capri and me up to the hamlet of Troutbeck where there was a phonebox. Unfortunately, during the journey the heavy tow chain dragged on the tarmac, causing some considerable wear on the chain links, but we got there and I phoned the A.A. to tell them where I had broken down! They came out and the very helpful operative towed me into Penrith, (Dad had of course disappeared by the time the A.A. showed up.)

At Brian's garage the A.A. man dropped my car off and left, then Brian and I discussed the repairs needed on the Capri. A new fuel pump would of course be required and also, Brian knew where to get a new radiator expansion tank to replace the leaky one. So I left the Capri in his capable hands and his dad gave me a lift home.

I spent some of the afternoon watching Venus Williams beating Lindsay Davenport in the Wimbledon final. In the evening, my Mungrisdale friends came for me and we went out in Penrith, exploring the usual haunts, but also the big, new pub called the Warehouse. It has three bars and two dance floors, and it was onto one of these that I was dragged by a bunch of giggling women. I danced with them for a couple of numbers and then, unable to take things to the next level, I returned to my friends! We finished the night off in Toppers Nightclub and then went home. I was full of beer and happy as I went to bed.

Brian Cowperthwaite lent me a courtesy car for the next few days. It was a Vauxhall Cavalier, similar to the one Angus had owned and I used it to get to more strimming jobs for the national park in the Caldbeck area.

On Thursday the thirteenth of July, I was able to get my own car back, fully fixed up and also to pick up and pay for my new bike.

I rode the bike out a few times during the following days, sometimes with Tina running alongside.

Haymaking began on our farm and, this being my favourite job of the year, my mood level was raised correspondingly; in fact I was bouncing! The weather was superb and between mowing the grass and hay baling I worked with Thomas to rebuild the 'bee boles' at Uldale Village. These are two; kind of arched, alcoves built into a dry stone wall that shelter the wicker beehives from the weather. This was yet another national park contract, for which I am eternally grateful to my brother for helping to procure for us!

This particular job was very complex and interesting but it had an added bonus. The hot weather had brought out a lovely young lady in her bikini to sunbathe on the lawn of a nearby house. Phew, I had difficulty concentrating on my work!

We got the bee boles finished and the hay gathered safely in. The hot weather continued and I had another good night out in Penrith, where I had a brief conversation with my favourite gypsy princess; she looked gorgeous in her fine summer dress. I finished the night off with a sweaty extended boogie with a local farmer's daughter in Toppers.

Just after this night out I took the new Marin for its first big ride out, up and over the old coach road to St John's in the Vale and back round home by the A66. The ride took just over two hours and I was pretty tuckered out after it. The bike had performed really well. Afterwards I fitted the Datatag security tracker to the bike by pushing it down inside the frame beneath the seat.

This was a tremendous time for me. I was literally on a high, everything was going right. (Well, except in the department of getting a girlfriend anyway!)

On Friday the twenty-eighth of July, I had another excellent meeting with the psychologist, Richard, in Carlisle, another soothing back massage from the lovely nineteen-year-old in Penrith and the most tremendous round of golf ever on the Keswick course, where I played with Steve Butcher and two of his workmates. I positively burned the course up, scoring a lifetime best round of seventy-nine gross, equivalent to forty-two points Stableford format, which included six pars and a birdie three on the eighteenth. I was literally bouncing. I devastated my fellow players and took quite a few quid in side bets. We finished off the day with a meal and a few pints in the clubhouse.

There was no let-up either, because on the following day I was off to start what could prove to be the biggest hike of my life, excluding those I did when I was manic and ill anyway.

The day started at five thirty a.m. with breakfast and the usual hiking preparations. The plan was that I would rendezvous with Bob Ridehalgh on the A66 at Mungrisdale road ends and then we would take both cars up Borrowdale to the top of Honister pass, leave Bob's car there and then drive on in mine to meet Andrew at Bowness Car Park at the western end of Ennerdale. Then we would attempt to walk the Ennerdale Horseshoe anti-clockwise in a day!

I loaded the Capri with all my gear, which included nearly a gallon (four and a half litres) of water – I had learned from Andrew's and my last attempt on the horseshoe that there were very few places to get water once you were up on the hike. Of course, Tina was going too and she positively leapt into the back of the car, no doubt in anticipation of yet another long overdue adventure.

I met Bob and we drove to Honister, left his car there and then went on in mine to meet Andrew at Bowness carpark at seven forty-five a.m. The weather was perfect for the hike, being dry and fine. Andrew and I donned our heavily laden rucksacks and boots, but Bob seemed only to be burdened with a much lesser pack (I would find out why later).

To get to our starting point, we had to walk around the bottom of Ennerdale Lake, but it was a nice easy warm-up for what was to come. Once we got around the lake, we struck off south east, up onto Crag Fell at five hundred and twenty-three metres (one thousand seven hundred and fifteen feet), then down through some forestry and back up on a gradual rise in a south-easterly direction to Caw Fell at six hundred and eighty metres (two thousand two hundred and thirty-one feet). The weather was still good and a few patches of cooling mist began to envelop us. The going was good, with smooth grassy slopes and Tina gambolled along merrily beside us as we cracked about a variety of different subjects.

From Caw Fell we struck eastwards up onto Haycock at seven hundred and ninety-seven metres (two thousand six hundred and fourteen feet) and then down to a col before climbing out onto Great Scoat Fell at eight hundred and two metres (two thousand six hundred and thirty-one feet). Then, still heading east and all going well, we made the outlying summit of Steeple at eight hundred and nineteen metres (two thousand six hundred and eighty-seven feet) and returned to Little Scoat Fell at a similar height. From here we dropped down to a col and went up north east, on to Pillar, where we had lunch. The mists had cleared again and it was becoming warm. It was at this point that Bob ran out of water and started to use some of my precious supply, which was a bit of a bummer. I had been suspicious from the start that he didn't have enough supplies with him, due to the small size of his pack! Considering that he was an experienced walker, I thought that this was rather an odd state of affairs.

I have of course already detailed the height of Pillar, along with that of most of the summits which follow, during my other account of the horseshoe.

Once we were rested, we descended east, off Pillar to Black Sail Pass and then up the steep scrambly section onto Kirk Fell. By this time, we were all starting to feel the effects of our efforts and my water supply was diminishing. Tina was able to find her own water from the occasional stagnant pool, though.

We came off Kirk Fell to Beck Head and then flogged up onto Great Gable. Then we dropped down north east to the col of Windy Gap, skirted Green Gable and Brandreth to head north west gradually, down to Blackbeck Tarn. During this section, Bob suddenly surprised us by announcing that he was leaving us to walk across below Grey Knotts to his car at Honister, which was only about one and a half miles away at this point. I was flabbergasted, I had thought that he was with us for the long haul, but then it clicked with me as to why he had left his car at Honister; he must have something else planned for that evening. It was now about five p.m. and so without any real explanation as to why he was leaving, Bob departed, wishing us well for the rest of our trip.

Andrew and I were slightly deflated after this, because we had lost one of the main driving forces for our expedition and the going suddenly became even harder as we climbed westwards from Blackbeck Tarn to Haystacks and then down to Scarth Gap. Then we were faced with the steep, daunting ascent of Gamblin End. It was here, on the stone pitched path that we seemed to hit a wall; we were hurting. Andrew was in worse shape than me and began to lag behind. I could hear him mumbling to himself and then suddenly he shouted out, "You're a bloody slave driver, can we not give up? I'm fucked."

I replied, "No, we have to go on. Once we are up this sod of a section, the going will get easier."

He continued to grumble, but kept going and we made it out onto High Crag, then High Stile and stumbled onto Red Pike.

To the west I could see the further summits of Starling Dodd and Great Borne, which I now gather are part of the horseshoe as well (I have climbed them recently as part of doing the Wainwrights). There was no chance of us going on to do those extra two, we were finished and I was close to having a rebellion on my hands from Andrew! Food was getting short too; we were down to my last bag of dried apricots, which I didn't want to open in case we got the shits from them! Our water rations were almost finished as well.

So wearily, from Red Pike we made the long descent southwards into the Ennerdale valley. Evening was coming on as we made the forestry track that runs along the north side of Ennerdale Lake, and although reasonably level this proved to be a real ball breaking section of two and a half miles back to the cars and it nearly finished us!

We got back to our vehicles at Bowness car park at ten fifteen p.m. and it was getting dark. I reckoned we had walked twenty and a half miles (thirty-three kilometres) and it had taken fourteen hours.

I said to Andrew, "The pub in Ennerdale Bridge will still be open. I'm gagging, how about you?" He nodded his head vigorously and I could almost see his tongue hanging out in the gathering gloom. We shook hands heartily, our slight tiff on Gamblin End now largely forgotten, loaded our gear and Tina into our cars and drove to Ennerdale Bridge, where we enjoyed the most gorgeous pint each, before heading to our respective homes; and yes the walk did prove to be the toughest I have ever done, sane, and I will probably never repeat it!

I had a lie-in the following morning and then spent most of the rest of the day sunbathing in the little concrete garden on the south side of the farmhouse. I had done a hell of a lot over the preceding days and although I was high on it, I was forced to admit to myself once again that the medication had kept me from going over the edge!

Shortly after this, I got together with Angus and Anne, whom I had healed relations with, and also Anne's two daughters, my sister Heather and Alex Driver to meet at one of the travel agents in Penrith, where we trawled for several exciting hours through available skiing holiday options for the coming winter. We finally settled on a week in Passo Tonale near the Italian Dolomites, and paid our deposits.

On the evening of Wednesday the second of August, I went on another bike ride on my Marin. I put the bike in the Capri and drove to the Mill Inn at Mungrisdale, where I met Bob, Mac and Ron to resume the camaraderie we had enjoyed on the earlier Scotland trip.

We set off on our bikes at six p.m. along the back road, which skirts Southerfell and brings you out at the White Horse pub at the foot of Blencathra. This road has about five gates on it, which are a bit of a hindrance. We all had small rucksacks with some provisions and also some rudimentary bike lights in case night befell us. The ride to the White Horse was on tarmac and was relatively easy and uneventful. The fun started though when we got onto the path, which skirts the southern foot of Blencathra. As we headed west along this path alongside the fell wall, we encountered our first obstacle; about half a mile from the White Horse we were forced to cross Doddick Ghyll. This is a nasty, rocky cleft, where one of the streams comes down off Blencathra. The weather was cool but with the occasional shower, making the ghyll slippery and treacherous. It was difficult getting across with the bikes and we had to help each other out, but we made it largely unscathed.

We continued on along the fell bottom, managing to ride most of the time, but then the shit hit the fan when Mac got a puncture! I thought we would be held up for ages but Mac is a very experienced cyclist and he soon had the puncture repaired. On we went, crossing three more ghylls, some of them also treacherous and then we made it out to the Blencathra Centre, where the Lake District National Park had its local headquarters.

We then headed north up the valley between Blencathra and Lonscale Fell, on a good track and rode up to Skiddaw House at four hundred and fifteen metres (one thousand three hundred sixty-one feet). Long ago this was a farm, but it is now used as a youth hostel. It is a traditional, stone built structure on the lower eastern slopes of Skiddaw and has only a sparse larch wood to protect it from the storm. It is also miles from anywhere!

We took a rest stop here, taking on food and water, before continuing north east towards the River Caldew. The first stretch was slightly downhill and fast going, but this was where Ron came unstuck; he failed to see a deep drainage channel cut across the track in time, his bike stopped dead and he went clean over the handlebars, landing painfully on his shoulder. Like the trooper he is though, he was soon up and able to continue.

The light began to fail as we rode north east, alongside the Caldew on a good level track, which is part of the Cumbria Way. We made it out to the tarmac road at the head of the Carrock valley and then rode out with our bike lights on, to Mosedale and then back to Mungrisdale, where we had a couple of pints and a few games of pool in the Mill Inn. The crack had been excellent all the way round and we had been equally paced. My bike had performed brilliantly and although tired, I was feeling good. I reckoned up that we had done thirteen point seven miles (twenty-two kilometres). We left the pub, loaded our bikes into our cars and departed for our respective homes to finish a good trip.

Shortly after I had another good night out in Penrith and enjoyed another good boogie in Toppers with the same farmer's daughter. I think she was quite keen on me but I failed to notice, because at the time I couldn't take my eyes off the masseuse from the North Lakes Spa, who was dancing nearby!

The day after was Sunday the sixth of August and I had a lie-in to get over the alcohol excesses of the previous evening. Bob phoned with some intriguing instructions; he said to be at his place at one p.m. and to just dress normally. He was lucky that I didn't have anything else on! So I did as instructed, driving through to Mungrisdale, parking at Bob's house and then we got into his black VW Golf GTI and he drove through to Mosedale. On the way, I asked him where we were going, but he just fobbed me off with a rather vague and devious explanation. We picked our pool team members, Roger Bucknall and Stan Fleming, up at Mosedale and then Bob drove very fast through the back roads to Carlisle and on to the little airport there. Roger, Stan and I were flummoxed as to what was going on but we were soon enlightened by Bob, who told us that his next door neighbour owned a half share in a light plane and this guy had agreed to pilot Roger, Stan and me on a birthday treat flight over our homes. Both Roger and Stan had recently turned fifty and my thirty-ninth birthday had been on the twentieth of July. We were all astonished and were soon on our way out to the plane, which stood waiting on the tarmac. Bob stayed behind in the terminal building, because the plane was only a four-seater. Bob's neighbour, whose name I forget, loaded us into the plane. I sat in the front, next to the pilot and I got my Minolta ready as the pilot started the engine and we taxied out onto the runway (I had brought the camera on anticipation that there might be something unusual afoot). I had of course flown many times but had never before been in a light plane. Roger had flown before but I don't know about Stan.

We took off and headed towards our homes at a fairly low altitude, but as we approached the Skiddaw Range we were forced to turn away, back towards Penrith, because of low cloud. The weather began to improve as we got clear of the fells, with a higher cloud ceiling and some sun. I was in the co-pilot's seat and had headphones on to communicate with the pilot, but for some reason they didn't work and I took them off after a while. It was a lovely feeling, looking down on the green countryside, and then things got even better when the pilot shouted to me above the noise of the engine, "Would you like to take the stick, Steve?"

I nodded and then, smiling like a basket of chips, I took hold of the joystick in front of me and began to actually fly the plane. I didn't try any high jinks or turn, or anything other than just keeping the plane straight and level. After a couple of minutes the pilot took over again and we flew on over Penrith and south to Kirkby Stephen. I took photos out of the window and also of Roger, Stan and the pilot as we went.

We made a long, slow turn at Kirkby Stephen and then we flew all the way back up the Eden Valley to Carlisle, during which I took control of the plane for a second time!

We landed smoothly at Carlisle and Bob came out to greet us on the tarmac. All of us were smiling broadly; it had been a fabulous flight and a very generous treat from Bob and his neighbour. We had all enjoyed it immensely and shook hands with Bob and his pilot neighbour.

Once back in the terminal, we enjoyed a celebratory pint in the bar and then Bob drove us back to Mosedale and Mungrisdale. I had a cup of tea with Bob at his house and he outlined a trip to Northern Ireland he was planning and he asked me if I would like to go. His cousin Walt lived in Newcastle (Northern Ireland) and Bob had not seen him for a while. The Mountains of Mourne are near to Newcastle and Bob said maybe we could get a walk in there. So I jumped at the chance to join his proposed trip, which he said would be around the end of September.

It was shortly after this that my elevated mood took a dive once more. This was largely due to a walling job that Thomas and I had procured whilst working at Caldbeck on other walling projects. This new job was near Uldale, on the northern fringe of the Skiddaw range, and was to repair a wall on a farm intake on the bottom of the fell. We set about the project with our usual gusto, but it quickly became apparent that it was going to be slow work. This was largely due to the walling stones being shaped like dog heads (diamond shaped). The bloody things would not fit, whichever way we put them on the wall, it was the worst stone I had ever worked with and it was awful. Things were not helped by the weather either because it had turned against us, with heavy showers. I quickly became fed up and I moaned constantly, causing Thomas to become sick of me too. Progress was slow – too slow, because the farmer was not happy with what we had got done in the four days we were there and we were thrown off the job. I was devastated, I had never been asked to leave a job before, but also I was kind of relieved – the agony of it was over and we did after all get payment for what we had done.

I went through a low period at this point, though and I was once again blaming my medication for keeping me down, which I know sounds like a direct contradiction from when I considered the medication had kept me from going over the edge while on a high, but that is just the way it was at that time.

Things began to pick up again around the nineteenth of August, when I had another night out in Penrith. I was not driving, but I was a poor drinking fettle and had a couple of Pernods to settle my stomach. I had another good boogie with the farmer's daughter in Toppers, during which I got a date with her for Friday the twenty-fifth of August.

I was out on my bike a lot at this time, often riding the old coach road route, trying to see if I could knock time off the circuit each time I did it.

The day after the night out in Penrith, Heather phoned me just before lunch and asked me if I wanted to go up Blencathra with her and Allan's brother Rob. I jumped at the chance to do a hike and to meet Rob, whom I had heard a lot about. So Allan came up to the farm with Heather and Rob and then he drove us all across to the White Horse and dropped us off to commence our climb on Blencathra.

We walked along the back road from the White Horse towards Mungrisdale, talking as we went. I quickly established a good banter with Rob, who is a nice guy. At Mousethwaite Combe we struck off away north from the road, up the main path to the top of the Combe and then headed northwest to Scales Tarn, where we assessed the prospect of the notorious Sharp Edge. The weather had been okay, but clouds had started to build in the west. Rob was reasonably experienced on the fells but he hadn't done Sharp Edge before. He was keen to give it a try, though and it was still dry, so off we went, north from the tarn and up onto the famed arête. The rock was dry and there was little wind, enabling us to make a reasonably easy passage across the ridge, with only a few hairy moments. Rob managed the traverse well and we were soon heading up the scramble to the side of Foule Crag at the western end of Sharp Edge, out onto the high northern prow of Blencathra. From here we walked south west, passing the large cross on the ground, made from lumps of felspar (I don't know the significance of this cross). We made the summit of Blencathra at eight hundred and sixty-eight metres (two thousand eight hundred and forty-seven feet), and then headed west along the spine of this fine mountain for just over a mile, to the top of Blease Fell. As we did so, the skies darkened and suddenly a mighty hail shower exploded onto us. I was fully equipped and soon had my rain gear on, but Heather and Rob only had light waterproof coats with them and they were wearing shorts. The squall was vicious and it had soon laid the ground white with large hailstones. We descended quickly down towards Blencathra Centre, with Heather and Rob rapidly becoming soaked and chilled! Their boots also filled up with hail and water, squelching as we dropped down to the road into Threlkeld Village. We headed straight to the Horse and Farrier Inn, arriving just as the sun came out once more. We phoned Allan and he came across to join us from his house across at Threlkeld Quarry. Although Heather and Rob were uncomfortable in their wet shorts, they managed a couple of pints with Allan and me before Allan drove us across to his house, where we were able to get dried out and sample some more beer. While we were there I opened up to Rob about my mental health problems and he was very sympathetic. Heather took me home later and I found that it had stayed dry at our place all day. The heavy shower must have been very localized, as our farm is only a couple of miles from Blencathra.

When Steve Butcher and I had last played golf, we had discussed my work on the lime kilns for the national park and Steve was particularly interested in the use of lime mortar on the projects. He asked me if Thomas and I would be able to give him a price to point up the stonework of the western elevation of his house in Mosedale village. So Thomas and I had gone and looked at the job and given Steve a price, which was accepted.

On Wednesday the twenty-third of August, we started the job, taking all the gear we needed to Steve's house in my trailer. Steve's house was a converted byre and it was built out of local Skiddaw slate stone. Over the years the mortar had dropped out of the joints between the stones on the western elevation, causing damp on that side of the house when the prevailing wind blew rain into the stonework during bad weather. We set our cement mixer up in the garden and put one five gallon (twenty-two and a half litre) bucket of lime putty into the mixer, using a trowel to scoop it in, then about a third of a bucket of the same size of sharp sand, followed by a shovel of cement into the mix and started the machine up. Now, lime mortar is queer stuff when you prepare it in a cement mixer. For a while, nothing much happens and then as the mixer turns, the contents start to form sandy balls about two inches across, commonly known as 'donkey shit' in the trade. Then the balls dissolve and the mixture takes on the characteristics of the usual smooth mortar mixes. When the mortar is fully mixed, it displays a fatty type of consistency and is a pleasure to use for both building and pointing work. So consequently over the period of the job at Steve's my mood improved. I was enjoying myself and the crack was good with Thomas as ever, as we worked side by side to point the western elevation of The Byre, as it was called. The weather was largely kind to us too, with several fine, hot days and we only had to put a plastic sheet up over our scaffolding tower on one occasion to protect us from the rain. There was also the added bonus of a can of beer each for Thomas and me, from Steve at the end of each working day, which we glugged down wholeheartedly. I also caught a couple of moles for Steve in his garden while we were on that job.

It was during this period that I forgot to take my medication for two days running and consequently I enjoyed a couple of nights where I dreamed. As I said before, one of the side effects of the drugs I was taking was that all dreaming stopped, so these two occasions of being able to enjoy a normal night's sleep were a real treat!

Friday the twenty-fifth of August came round and I went out on my date with the farmer's daughter. We went to a pub in Penrith for a drink and a crack before going to the local cinema to see *Mission Impossible 2*. We both enjoyed the film and afterwards went to another pub before I took her home and was rewarded with coffee. I didn't feel inclined to take things any further, though and we parted as friends.

On Sunday the twenty-seventh of August, following a night out in Penrith and staying over at Angus and Anne's, I went for a hike with them. It was the first one we'd done together since the difficult Scotland trip. Alex was supposed to go with us but we got our wires crossed and he ended up doing an almost identical hike, but separately.

We parked at Deepdale Bridge, south of Ullswater and then walked south west up onto Hartsop above How Fell and then west, up onto Hart Crag at eight hundred and twenty-two metres (two thousand six hundred and ninety-six feet). After this, we made our way round Dove Crag and visited the feature known as the Priest's Hole. This is a cave in the side of a crag where a local priest reputedly hid out during the religious ructions of the Middle Ages. We had lunch here and then descended back, north east to Hartsop Hall, before walking back down the western side of Brotherswater and back round to the car. It was a good day and the crack had been enjoyable, therefore sweeping away any uncomfortable feelings.

Shortly after this, I had some extra fittings made to my bike at Arragons to prepare for the Northern Ireland trip. I had a new, more comfortable seat fitted, some mudguards and a rear carrying rack. For this last item I bought a couple of good sized pannier bags.

During September, Thomas and I worked on another lime kiln renovation job for the national park. This one was in Mungrisdale village. We were now experienced contractors at this kind of work and the general ins and outs of the job were our usual fare, but things were made slightly difficult by the fact that there were several rare bats roosting in the arched roof of the kiln, meaning we had to be quiet while doing our work to avoid disturbing them. The bat survey people were brought in to study them.

Also during this month, Roger Bucknall hatched a plan to enter an act for the forthcoming Mungrisdale revue show and he asked us as a pool team if we would take part in it. Roger outlined his idea that we would do a piss take of the Gilbert and Sullivan operetta *The Mikado*, and in particular the song *Three Little Maids From School*, except that our version would be *Six Little Maids From Pool*! We were all up for it, apart from Stan, who was embarrassed by the whole idea. This meant that there would only be five of us, but we would still go along with the Three *Little Maids* lyrics. Roger's partner Moira would act as a kind of choreographer for us. We had several rehearsals at Roger's house, usually involving beer drinking and they were hilarious!

Just after the lime kiln job and having attracted the attention of the Mungrisdale Parish Council, Thomas and I were awarded the contract to build a retaining wall in front of the lime kiln, and extending out from the northern end of the village hall. The wall was to be built dry, using local stone and there being none available nearby, it meant that I had to hire out the tractor and trailer from our farm to sort out and transport the stone from a local farm to the job. We also had to hire a digger to excavate the banking in the area the wall was to be built on. It was a very rewarding job, both mentally and financially. The site was duly excavated and the wall built from the hand picked stone and was backfilled with the excavated soil as the wall went up. The weather was unkind to us during the work and we got quite a few wettings.

The village hall has since been completely rebuilt, but our retaining wall still stands!

In the middle of September, I loaded my bike into the Capri and drove across to Bob's, where we took my bike out and fitted Bob's bike rack to the back of the Capri and mounted both our bikes on it. I had never had a rack on the Capri and it was a tricky operation fitting it. From Bob's, I drove us down to Portinscale bridge near Keswick where we parked, offloaded the bikes and then rode them through the back roads to Braithwaite village and then up the B592 to Whinlatter Forest, where we enjoyed a rather tough afternoon exploring the forestry tracks before returning to the car, re-loading the bikes and driving back to Bob's to offload his bike and rack. After putting my bike back into the Capri we went for a couple of pints and some games of pool in the Mill Inn, before I returned home. The crack had been brilliant as always with Bob.

On Friday the twenty-second of September, I had another morning meeting with my psychologist in Carlisle and a back massage in Penrith, before meeting Steve Butcher for a round of golf after lunch on the Penrith course. We played the Stableford points format and he beat me by three points. I have never played well around the Penrith course, which is up on the Beacon Hill and is much drier in nature than the more familiar Keswick course and has the kind of deep rough that wraps itself around your club shaft when you play a shot out of it, and I was in the rough a lot that day!

It was time for the Northern Ireland trip, so I was up at five a.m. on Friday the twenty-ninth of September, got my breakfast and finished packing. I had my big rucksack filled with hiking gear and the two new bike panniers filled with clothes and toiletries. Bob and Ron came at six thirty a.m. in Ron's Nissan Almera, which had Bob's bike rack on the back containing their two bikes. We loaded all the gear and put my bike on the rack. There was barely enough room for it and I was a little concerned with the security of Bob's bungee cords, which held the whole lot to the rack. Bob saw me inspecting the cords and told me to stop worrying, the bikes would be fine!

We set off towards Penrith but we only got halfway there before I, sitting in the back and keeping a nervous eye on the bikes, called a halt to proceedings. My bike was in imminent danger of slipping off the rack, so we pulled into a layby and I got out to tighten the bungee cords significantly. When I was satisfied that my precious bike was not going to fall off and get crushed under a juggernaut, we set off again.

Once in Penrith, we parked up for a bit so that Bob could get a few bits and pieces. We then headed north to Carlisle and then west to reach the port of Stranraer at nine twenty-five a.m. After parking we offloaded all our gear – I had the most stuff, as usual! Then Ron locked his car up to leave it on the park for the duration of our trip. Carrying our rucksacks, we wheeled our bikes, decked out with their panniers, to the Sea Cat ticket office and bought return tickets to Belfast. We joined the stream of traffic and boarded the Sea Cat, which was a hydrofoil. I was intrigued, I had never travelled on one of these beasts before, but had seen them on television and I knew that they were fast. We secured our bikes to a stanchion on the car deck and then made our way up to the passenger lounge. Once there, we settled down as the Sea Cat moved out of the harbour at ten a.m. As we made our way out into open water, the Sea Cat picked up speed and I went outside to the rail to watch as the powerful machine rose up out of the water to glide on its fins. I had been on several ferry rides before and was not troubled by sea-sickness. This journey was even smoother, with the Sea Cat cutting through the waves. It was a great feeling, we were charging across the water! I went back inside and Bob suggested we get a pint at the bar and I, feeling of stout stomach, agreed. We enjoyed the excellent bevvies and then, having approximately one hour to kill, we had lunch in the restaurant. I had fish and chips, which seemed appropriate seeing as we were on the water.

We got into Belfast harbour about eleven forty-five a.m., retrieved our bikes from the car deck and cycled off the Sea Cat into the bustling city. Bob was in the lead and he seemed to have an uncanny sense of direction as we navigated our way through the heavy traffic towards the bus station. It was a hair-raising ride and how we didn't end up under a bus I will never know! Once at the bus station, we had a brew at the café there to kill a bit of time until our bus for Newcastle arrived. When the bus arrived the driver, upon seeing our bikes, kindly opened the boot of the bus and we loaded our bikes in there. We boarded the bus, paid our fare and then settled down in the largely uncrowded vehicle for the hour and a quarter journey to Newcastle. The weather back on the mainland had been a bit drizzly but now, here in the province, it was quite nice, with only the occasional shower about, and so we had a good view of the countryside as we exited the city to head south to our destination.

When we got to Newcastle, we got off the bus, retrieved our bikes from the boot and rode through the town, which is of a similar size to our home town of Penrith, and then Bob led us unerringly to the youth hostel he had booked us into. We offloaded our gear in the comfortable establishment, which would cost us eight-fifty each per night and then I flopped into an armchair in the lounge, but I wasn't there long; there was no let-up. Bob announced that we would go for a bike ride to explore the area. So off we went, with very little gear; I had only my water bottle on the bike frame. We headed northwest, out of town onto quieter roads that led us to Castlewellan and then on into the nearby forest, where there were many good biking trails.

After a good ride around we returned to Newcastle and our hostel for six thirty p.m. Newcastle is a seaside town, so we had a walk on the beach after we had stowed our bikes at the hostel, before getting a shave and shower in our digs. Bob's Cousin Walt had arrived and had also booked into the hostel. We met up and I found him to be a cheery chap, full of good crack!

When we had all had a crack in the lounge, we went out on the town, first to the chippy for some 'good scran' (good eating), and then on to a popular bar, called Diamond Pat's. There was a good band playing country and western type music, which included cover versions of Shania Twain songs, which I was heavily into at that time. We consumed copious quantities of the finest Guinness, a drink that I had never had or have since sampled and it was properly pulled, so I understand, with several half-filled pints standing on the bar settling and then being topped up. Halfway through the evening there was an incident that will live forever in my memory. Bob, who was quite merry by this stage, went to the bar for a round of drinks and upon getting there, spied a handsome looking young woman wearing a cut-off top. She was leaning across the bar, in earnest conversation with one of the bar keeps. Bob sneaked up behind her and kissed her in the small of her bare back. She whirled round and for a moment I thought she was going to give Bob a good clout across the face, but then she laughed and just gave him a playful push. There were several big local guys nearby and they fixed Bob with icy stares; for a moment I thought there was going to be a brawl and things hung in the balance, but then everybody relaxed and things settled down. They were a good natured crowd, fortunately! I had consumed six pints of Guinness and a whisky by the end of the night and I was flying high. We wobbled back to the hostel, had a cup of tea and then went to bed.

Saturday the thirtieth. We were up about eight thirty a.m. and were all feeling a bit muzzy. We managed to cook and eat breakfast from the provisions Bob had bought the night before. Then we got our rucksacks sorted and put on our walking boots, then Walt drove us south around the eastern edge of the Mourne Mountains, which were looking great in the morning sun. We headed on down the coast to the fishing village of Kilkeel, where we walked round the harbour to get rid of the alcoholic haze. Back in Belfast there had been little evidence of 'The Troubles', but here in Kilkeel there were several IRA-related murals painted on the house ends! There were also a few Union Jacks flying.

Once we had got some sea air into our lungs, Walt drove us north and inland to the Silent Valley lower reservoir and dam, nestling in the southern side of the Mourne Mountains. Here he dropped us at the visitor centre with our rucksacks and then he headed back to Newcastle. The plan that we had discussed the night before was that we would walk back to Newcastle from the Silent Valley over the Mournes, bagging as many of the summits as we could on the way. As far as I can remember, we had no map, only compasses and it was a bloody good job it was a fine day or we surely would have got lost before we had walked two miles. As it was, the weather was great and our hangovers diminished as at eleven a.m. we struck off west across the dam, admiring the beautiful vista of the higher summits of the Mournes to the north as we crossed onto heathery/grassy slopes that led us up northwest to our first summit of Slievenaglogh at four hundred and fifty metres (one thousand four hundred and seventy-six feet). Even at this early stage I was struggling with my heavy rucksack, which contained a lot of water. I knew I would need a good supply, especially considering the ravages of the night before, but as it turned out there were several good springs along the way, from which Bob and Ron drank heartily. The views to the north and east were breathtaking, with the Mournes laid out before us in the morning sun. Nearer to us, the two Silent Valley reservoirs nestled serenely beneath the mountains.

We had already passed several dry stone walls, which were the beginnings of the Mourne Wall that keeps livestock out of the catchment area for the reservoirs. These structures were of a simple design, made of large granite stones balanced atop one another in a single skin format, to a height of one and a half metres (four and a half feet), but we would soon come to a more complex and mighty construction. We headed on north, down and then back up again onto the summit of Doan at five hundred and ninety-three metres (one thousand nine hundred and forty-five feet). We continued north towards Slieve Meelbeg, passing little Lough Shannagh as we went.

On reaching the summit of Slieve Meelbeg at seven hundred and eight metres (two thousand three hundred and twenty-two feet), I began to feel a little strange. The effects of my exertions were telling upon me, but also, Bob had begun to talk about kings of Scotland and one of them had apparently been called Stephen. For a few minutes, as we walked, Bob began to call me King Stephen and I started to experience delusions of grandeur, thinking of myself as some kind of long lost descendant of King Stephen! Just at that moment a yellow rescue helicopter of the old Westland Wessex type hove up over the horizon and I thought it had come to take me away to my kingdom. However, it circled us briefly before disappearing again. My euphoric state of mind lasted for only a brief spell and it was maybe only caused by the after effects of the previous night's shenanigans, but it served as a warning to me that maybe I had overdone things on the drinking front, and was maybe now overdoing the physical exertions but I could not do anything about the latter, because we were miles from anywhere and we had to get back to Newcastle before dark, as none of us had a head torch!

As we made our way on north east towards the typical conical peak of Slieve Meelmore, we came up alongside the main Mourne Wall and I steered the conversation away from royalty and people's possible connections to these deities, towards the construction of this extremely robust and finely built wall. I wish I had been able to find out more about the men who built this mighty edifice and about how they had procured the stone for it. (Perhaps this could be done when I finally get on the internet). As a waller myself, I can well appreciate the logistical difficulties of getting the stone to the site and the amount of effort required to build the wall. Also, the workers would no doubt have been out in all weathers and sometimes conditions must have been hellish. These stalwart individuals would likely receive little financial reward for their efforts either! These guys had built the wall out of milled granite blocks to a height of almost eight feet (two and a half metres) and to a width of three feet or almost a metre. It is an awesome example of the drystone walling skill and when we reached Slieve Meelmore at seven hundred and four metres (two thousand three hundred and nine feet) we encountered an even more impressive sight. They had built a watch tower in the wall, not unlike the kind of thing that would no doubt have been present on Hadrian's Wall near the Scottish border, in its time. The Mourne wall is twenty-two miles (thirty-five and a half kilometres) long. It encloses nine thousand acres of land, all of which drains into the Silent Valley and the Ben Crom reservoirs. The wall itself spans over two thousand seven hundred and forty-three metres (nine thousand feet) of ascent, rising and falling over fifteen of the highest peaks in the Mournes. Built over eighteen years between 1904 and 1922, the Mourne Wall is a remarkable structural feat and frames some of the finest mountain views in Ireland.

We ate a late lunch at Slieve Meelmore before heading down south east and back up onto the summit of Slieve Bearnagh at seven hundred and thirty-nine metres (two thousand four hundred and twenty-four feet). Here the topography was somewhat different to the previous peaks, with this summit being kind of crowned with castles of rock. It's a good job I wasn't still dreaming of royalty or I would have regarded this as a propitious place!

From Slieve Bearnagh, we headed down and back up over Slieve Loughshannagh at six hundred and twenty metres (two thousand and thirty-four feet), then down and on up eastwards to Slieve Commedagh at seven hundred and sixty-five metres (two thousand five hundred and nine feet) where there was another watch tower of some ten metres (thirty-three feet) in height. It was exhausting work but the Mourne wall kept us company, seeming to march in step with us as we went.

We dropped down eastwards to a large col, where we contemplated the summit of Slieve Donard at eight hundred and fifty-three metres (two thousand seven hundred and ninety-eight feet) and the flagship peak of the Mournes. It lay to our east and was tantalizingly close, but the day was getting on and we still had a fair stretch to go to get back out of the mountains to Newcastle, so we turned away from this prize rather reluctantly and headed northeast out down the Glen River valley and into Donard Forest. The path was good and it was reasonably dry underfoot, as it had been the whole way.

We battled our way on out to Newcastle, arriving at about eight p.m. It was coming in dark and we were knackered but of good cheer! We had covered some fifteen miles (twenty-four kilometres) in about nine hours and it had been a hell of a good day, with good weather and crack of the highest quality.

Bob, who as ever, seemed to have energy to spare, went out to the supermarket and bought some chicken and some noodles. We cooked this in the hostel kitchen after we had showered and then enjoyed a nice meal. After we had washed up I thought we would just go to bed, but Bob had other plans; we would go out again. So at ten thirty p.m. we hit the town, or rather, just Quinn's bar, where there was live music playing. This band though were not as good as the one in Diamond Pat's had been and after we had drunk three pints of excellent Guinness each, we had had enough and headed back to the hostel to bed. It was one a.m.

Sunday the first of October. We were up at eight fifteen a.m. and were feeling a bit jaded but I had slept well. After cooking and eating breakfast we washed up and then packed up our gear before paying our bills and checking out of the hostel. It really had been a nice stay and the facilities were excellent. I would recommend that hostel if I could remember its name!

After loading the panniers onto the bikes we shouldered our rucksacks and cycled down onto the beach, where I stupidly rode in the surf. (My chain and various nuts consequently rusted!) We rode north and skirted the Royal County Down Golf Course, which I would like to go back and play sometime. Ron had a slow puncture and we had to stop frequently to blow the tyre up. Also Bob had a pedal that came loose – I guess his bikes were prone to that!

We skirted a nature reserve and then rode back into Newcastle, where we met Walt and he guided us to a bike shop, where Ron got his puncture repaired and Bob got a new nut for his pedal. The guy at the shop would not take any money for the repairs and just said to Bob, "I will catch you in the long grass sometime!" This was a rather unusual expression and I have never again heard it used, but I guess the guy meant that someday he would come across us and be in need of a favour himself.

Walt, who lived in the town, (quite why he had spent a night in our hostel eludes me!) invited us to his house for a brew and to meet his family. After we had socialised a bit Walt went with us to the bus station and we said our goodbyes before boarding a bus back to Belfast, our bikes once again went in the boot.

Once back in Belfast, we cycled through the manic traffic and sought out Queen's University, where we had a look around the grounds before getting a meal of chicken and chips at a nearby café, we then made our way in the rain to the ferry terminal. We got out our return tickets and used them to board the Sea Cat when it came in.

The return voyage was somewhat rougher than the outward one but my stomach didn't let me down.

Once back in Stranraer, we loaded up Ron's car and he drove us home. I was dropped off first at the farm and had good, firm handshakes with my friends before I bade them goodbye.

I let Tina out for a run and she was bouncing with enthusiasm at my return. After I had unpacked my gear I had a beer from the small supply that I had started keeping at home and then went to bed around eleven fifteen p.m.

The Northern Ireland trip had left me tired but happy, it really had been a good one! I was however in need of a rest, so I took the following day off.

On Wednesday the fourth of October, I had another of my regular psychiatrist's meetings in Penrith. I went into it with confidence but it did not go well, in fact it went very badly and I nearly ended up in tears. I can't remember why it was so difficult, but I guess I worried my counsellors by continually charging off on trips here, there and everywhere. I suppose most of their other patients were so drugged up that they were unable to carry out such activities, but that wasn't for me. I had to live, for fuck's sake!

This distressing meeting was quickly wiped away though, as I flung myself back into work and then it was time for the Mungrisdale revue. We had continued with our hilarious rehearsals for our act and now our big moment had arrived. In fact, the revue was in the evening following my upsetting psychiatrist's meeting and I gathered with most of the rest of our pool team at Mungrisdale village hall at six forty-five p.m., where we secretly assembled in the kitchen and the womenfolk, including Roger's two daughters, dressed us up in party dresses and used grease paint to decorate our faces in the Japanese style. We had several beers to loosen ourselves up and then when our turn came at eight forty-five p.m. we entered the stage by the little side door, carrying our pool cues. The applause was rapturous as we were introduced to the packed audience by the M.C. There was much giggling and guffawing after the applause and I guess the five of us must have been a very amusing sight. I could see my family and also Stan, sitting in the audience and they were grinning. The piano player struck up and we launched ourselves into song, carrying off our *Six Little Maids from Pool* number with alacrity. We bowed upon completion and Bob lifted up his skirt to flash his bare legs; there was much laughter and applause. We briefly went off stage before being called back on for an encore.

After our performance we got changed and got started on the beer in earnest. There was a buffet laid on too and we got stuck into that. Then we awaited the result of the judges, for the revue had been a competition between about ten acts. The verdict was given. We did not win, much to our disappointment, but were highly placed and just out of the prizes.

It was a great night and remains one of the most memorable and amusing experiences of my life!

In the days following this momentous event, Thomas and I went to work on the Swart Beck retaining wall that we had repaired in 1997. Regular maintenance had to be carried out on the wall and this involved patching up any new holes that had appeared, plus clearing out loose rocks from the channel. Fortunately none of them were of a sufficient size to warrant the use of a winch. I took Tina with us on the job and she enjoyed herself, ratching around the fellside as we worked.

The next job I did was again working with Thomas and it was a walling job at Caldbeck, sub-contracting to Ken Ostle's brother Geoff, who was renovating an old house in the village. We had a twenty-five metre length of dry stone wall to build and then a couple of more complex ornamental sections of wall, built with sand and cement. We also built a flight of stone steps to a height of about two and a half metres. All of this work was in the back garden of the house and the weather was not very favourable towards us!

The winter pool season had started and for home matches I cycled to the Mill Inn. Of course it was dark and I had spent about sixty pounds on a set of lights with a rechargeable battery for the Marin. They were good lights but not good enough to spot that herd of black, semi-wild horses that roamed the area and once again I nearly ended up hitting one of them on the ride home after one match!

I kept up my fitness around this time with regular short bike rides alongside the nocturnal ones to the Mill Inn and back.

I was still on probation and had to attend regular meetings with the probation officer, who was a nice guy and we had a good rapport.

I had several fencing jobs on during October, one of which was up at our top farm, Lobbs, working with Thomas again. They were complex and difficult contracts but Thomas and I were a good team, putting our heads together to solve all the emerging problems.

There were regular nights out in Penrith with the Mungrisdale gang and every time I went, I saw my favourite girl, but she was unattainable and might as well have been on the moon! There was no-one else in my life though and I kept on dreaming.

I paid the balance due, of the forthcoming ski holiday too in October.

In early November, Dad dropped a bombshell on me. He told me he was going to sell everything the following summer and that I had to prepare myself to leave the nest and make my own way from then on! This revelation was not entirely unexpected as he was of retiring age, but it would mean big changes for me.

There was more building work in November with Thomas at Caldbeck. After having made a good job of that one flight of steps we got to build three more flights

On Sunday the third of December, I took Anne's two daughters, Katie and Hannah, down to Kendal dry ski slope, where we hired skis for them (I had my own) and then I gave them lessons for a couple of hours, after we had paid for use of the slope. This would be their first skiing trip and they showed good promise on the gentle bottom section of the plastic slope.

A couple of days after this, Thomas and I did a complex and difficult job for Bob, removing an old fireplace and installing a new wood burning stove. Part of the chimney breast had to be taken down to fit new chimney liners and then it had to be rebuilt, using the Borrowdale slate we had taken out. It was a tough job and took a few days but at least it was indoors. Unfortunately our efforts were not rewarded by an efficient chimney system and the newly installed stove smoked out into the room. A wind operated fan had to be fitted to the chimney pot to help the problem.

I gave Katie and Hannah another ski lesson at Kendal on the seventeenth of December and we spent two and a half hours on the slope. They were quick learners and came on really well, considering the plastic matting is more difficult to ski on than snow.

I got a horrendous income tax bill at this time, which gave me a shock and sent me into a bit of a downer! But my diary for this period is crammed with work information concerning a wide variety of different jobs, so my overall mood must have been pretty good. I even took Anne mole trapping one day, down at Threlkeld village, but the weather conditions were poor. She couldn't keep warm and did not enjoy the experience. I could see that I wasn't going to make a trapper out of her!

On Thursday the twenty-first of December, I went out in the evening on a works Christmas do; it was Ken Ostle's, his brother Geoff and several other workmates of theirs works shindig to celebrate the Caldbeck building contracts completion. Thomas should have been there but wasn't, for some reason. I drove to High Hesket, where Ken now lived with his parents in their new bungalow. I met Ken, Geoff and their other brother Stephen there and also various wives and girlfriends. From here we all got a lift into Carlisle, where we went to the bowling alley. We had a few games of pool there while we waited for the rest of the group to arrive. We had started drinking and continued to do so as the rest of the gang showed up, taking our number to fifteen. We then had three good games of ten-pin bowling, followed by more drink and a good meal at a nearby Indian restaurant. We came out of the restaurant at ten forty-five p.m. and I was feeling decidedly squiffy. Those that were still sober drove us back to High Hesket, where I stayed over, kipping on the living room floor in one of Ken's sleeping bags. It had been a great night and had been my first Indian meal, which was delicious.

Saturday the twenty-third of December. I had a lie-in until nine thirty a.m. and then after breakfast I worked for the rest of the morning to saw up tree trunk sections into logs, using the chainsaw in the wood next to the farm buildings, chop them and then ferry them into the back kitchen, using my quad bike and trailer. While I worked, a sudden impulse to get away came over me. I formulated a plan to go to Scotland that very afternoon and climb one of the mountains; a big Munro called Creag Meagaidh, which lies to the west of the A86, between Spean Bridge and Newtonmore. I planned to take my sleeping bag and kip in the Capri that night, before setting out on the hike at first light the following morning. I felt somewhat naughty because there was no way of informing the probation service of what I intended and I would once again be breaking the law by going up there, but I was further excited by this prospect!

I finished my job, having had Tina out for a run during work, got some lunch and then loaded the car up with all the gear I would need, including my camping stove, which I would use to make myself a hot breakfast the next morning. I knew there was snow in Scotland and therefore I would need good preparation for this hike. I informed my parents of my intentions, hoping that they wouldn't inform on me to the authorities. My dad was particularly non-committal as usual when I was going off on a hike. He hates fell walkers and was then (and still is) of the opinion that if you went arseing about on the fells and hurt yourself, or got lost, it was your own fault!

At four thirty p.m. I set off north and had a trouble free journey up the motorways and then on up the A9, arriving at Kingussie at eight thirty p.m., where I got fish and chips and ate them in the car before driving to Newtonmore and taking the A86 southwest to Aberader farm, which lies just off the main road. There is a good car park here, from which most walkers start the climb on Creag Meagaidh. It was here that I set up camp to spend the night. There was no-one else about but even though it was dark, I could see that there was about three inches of snow lying and it was obviously bitterly cold. I unfolded my sleeping bag and got into it on the passenger seat, with the seat back in the reclined position. I settled down to try to sleep. The car was warm to start with but it soon cooled off and the chill came creeping in from outside. My sleeping bag was not a very good one and I soon began to feel the cold through it. Sleep was impossible and I lay there, looking out at the firmament. Suddenly I saw the most beautiful and bright shooting star I have ever seen and it brightened my grim plight. What was I doing? This was madness and I thought I would be lucky not to freeze to death before the morning came.

As it was, I was up and about at five a.m. I was shivering but set about busying myself with breakfast preparations. It was hard frost but it promised to be quite a fine day on this Christmas Eve. I got the stove going in the back of the Capri and cooked up some spaghetti, plus two mugs of coffee. (I had made a packed lunch before I left home). After tidying away the cooking gear I got my boots on, donned my full winter gear, packed and shouldered my rucksack, then locked the car.

At seven fifteen a.m. I started out on the good path up by Aberader Farm, heading northwest into the long L-shaped valley that takes you up to the Coire Ardair. It was still dark but I was able to pick my way carefully up the valley by the light of the stars. Still shivering, I was aware that I would have to keep moving to generate some body heat. I must have been close to getting hypothermia back in the car!

The going was smooth and only slightly uphill and I had to try and force the pace to get warmed up. The valley I was in is part of the Creag Meagaidh Nature Reserve, so the path is well maintained and any boggy stretches have wooden boardwalks across them, with chicken wire stapled to the planking for grip.

I forced my way up the valley, turning westwards and the dawn began to break, bringing better visibility. The snow lay quite thickly on the ground but it was dry, powdery stuff and was not therefore much of a problem. I had my gaiters on, which prevented snow getting into my boots.

Full daylight came as I approached the head of the valley and the towering Coire Ardair cliffs, with the large Lochan a'Choire nestling at their base. I got my camera out and took a few shots of the great buttresses, with the waters of the lochan in the foreground.

From the lochan I struck out north west up steeper, rockier slopes towards the Window. This is a steep-sided col between the Munros of Stob Poite Coire Ardair and the Creag Meagaidh massif, and is famous for being the col over which Bonnie Prince Charlie escaped from the pursuing English forces.

Large patches of hard frozen old snow began to cover the ground and I thought it a good point in proceedings to dig out my crampons and strap them on. I had not had time to borrow an ice axe off Angus, so I would have to manage without.

When I reached the Window, I started south up the very steep side of the col. Hard frozen snowdrifts covered this slope and the going was treacherous. I became very afraid and was thankful for the grip from my crampons. It was very risky though, especially without an ice axe – if I had tripped I would have slid uncontrollably down onto the rocks below and probably have been seriously injured or even killed, but I did not fall and I made my way out onto the summit plateau safe and sound. I had offered up several silent prayers on the ascent and it seemed my guardian angel was with me. This was borne out as I carefully made my way south west in near whiteout conditions – the mist had come down and a bitter north east wind had got up, blowing the snow around. Suddenly the wind dropped for a moment, the mist lifted and the large summit cairn emerged from the white background about a hundred metres ahead of me. I quickly covered the ground to the cairn and stood on the summit of Creag Meagaidh at one thousand one hundred and thirty metres (three thousand seven hundred and seven feet). Getting my mobile phone out and finding I had a signal, I phoned home and got to speak to Mam. We had a short conversation in which I assured her I was safe and sound, which she was relieved to hear and then after adding I would be home before long, I rang off.

I had brought a map with me and I now had cause to use it for the first time, to figure out how to now get back to the edge of the Coire Ardair cliffs and skirt my way around their eastern end, to be able to descend back to Aberader Farm over a couple of lower summits.

I wasted no time in retracing my steps north eastwards over the flat, snow-covered plateau towards the Coire Ardair drop-off. Visibility again became poor and I became aware that there would likely be great snow cornices on the edge of the cliffs and it would be easy to just step out into thin air and disappear into the void. However, once again my guardian angel must have been with me because the mist cleared for a moment and vicious little snow devils sprang up, forcing me backwards, away from the edge of the cliffs, which yawned very close in front of me! Before the weather closed in again I was able to make my way eastwards, around the cliffs and over the little top of Puist Coire Ardair at one thousand and seventy metres (three thousand five hundred and ten feet) and then north east along a ridge, down to the top of Sron a' Choire at a thousand and one metres (three thousand two hundred and eighty-four feet). Here I ate my lunch in the clearing conditions. Not dallying long though, to keep heat, I was off on down north east, over grass and heather to eventually reach the beck (Allt Coire Ardair), which flows out of the Coire Ardair valley. I found a footbridge to the west of Aberader Farm and crossed this final obstacle to get back to the farm and then the welcoming sight of my car. The hike had taken me six hours, which seemed like a fast time, but I had not hung about, covering the approximately fourteen kilometres (eight point seven miles) at a good pace.

I was pretty tired but felt I had enough reserves of energy to make it back home that day. After all, the next day was Christmas!

I fought my way home through my fatigue, helped by the good driving conditions and after several comfort/fuel stops I made it home for six fifteen p.m. After celebrating my achievement with a few beers I fell into bed at eight thirty p.m. and went out like a light!

I had a very good night's sleep following my trip and was feeling rather good on this Christmas morning. Having been invited to Angus and Anne's for the day, I let Tina out for a run then drove over to Culgaith to share a nice Christmas lunch with the aforementioned and also, Katie and Hannah. In the afternoon, we all played games on the computer and us adults enjoyed some alcohol. I told Angus of my hike the day before and he gave me a bit of a bollocking for going on my own, but also for failing to notify probation.

I stayed over on Christmas night and was up early on Boxing Day, to head home to prepare for an arranged hike up Blencathra with Bob and one of his other friends.

There was snow and ice on the Cumbrian fells by now, too, and this made the hike more difficult, but it was a fine day as we met at the White Horse and set off up Scales Fell, accompanied by Bob's friend's dog. (I didn't take Tina, for some reason.) We walked up to Scales Tarn and then struck up north and onto the notorious Sharp Edge, which I knew was going to be challenging, given the ground conditions. I had put my crampons on early in the walk and was fully prepared as I set off along the arête, but the others had no crampons and struggled to find grip on the 'rimed up' smoother sections of the arête. I sailed across it, followed by the dog and then the others, looking somewhat ashen.

As we made our way out onto the top of the mountain, we were overhauled by another group of walkers, one of whom was recognisable as Sir Chris Bonnington. As he went past us, I heard him describing his crampons, which were apparently made of hard rubber!

There were many people on the summit, which was not surprising, given that the climbing of Blencathra on Boxing Day is a popular endeavour.

We descended from the summit south via Scala Beck Ridge, eating a light lunch at a level spot on the way and made our way back around the foot of the mountain to the cars. Bob invited me to have a brew with him and his friend at Mungrisdale, so we drove round there and had a nice cup of tea, but also a beer, before I returned home.

On Thursday the twenty-eighth of December, Angus, Anne, Katie and Hannah came up to the farm and after they had helped me offload a trailer full of logs into our back kitchen, I took them in the trailer, towed by the quad bike, across the Mosedale beck and we spent the early part of the afternoon sledging on plastic fertilizer bags, down the bank to the bridge over the beck. It was great fun but I hurt my arm on a fallen dead branch. Even though there was about four inches of snow, the sod still managed to get me! Also, Katie was sick due to getting over-excited, but also because she had had no lunch.

Afterwards I tried out the set of new snow chains I had purchased for the Capri. They were a little tricky to fit but gave the car terrific grip, once fitted.

That evening I went down to Heather and Allan's house for drinks, supper and games. Allan's brother Rob was up from Cornwall and was staying with them for a few days. We had good crack and an excellent time all round. I stayed over.

Driving back the following morning, I had cause to use my new snow chains. There had been a good snowfall over night and although the A66 was clear, once I got onto the back roads up to the farm, the going became tricky. I fitted the chains just after I had turned off the A66 and the Capri was kind of transformed, enabling it to fly over the slippery conditions with ease. When I got to the old railway bridge at Highgate Cottages, I found some kind soul had shovelled salt onto the steep switchback, from the council salt heap. I therefore got up it even more easily than expected, but I was reminded of an occurrence a few years earlier, when I had attempted this obstacle in similar conditions when the bridge was unsalted. It was in the Capri but before I had the chains, obviously. The bridge is not normally a problem to front wheel drive cars, but the Capri was rear wheel drive and notoriously nose heavy. There is a straight, uphill approach to the bridge but it is not possible to get a run at the steeper section on the bridge, because the road turns ninety degrees to the left and you have to lose momentum to avoid skidding off at the corner. On that particular occasion, I got around the left hander and with the rear wheels spinning, ground my way up nearly to the level top of the bridge, where there is a right hander. Then all forward motion stopped – I had spun out! I pulled on the handbrake and for a few seconds the car stayed where it was, but then suddenly my much-loved motor began to slide backwards down the bridge. I nearly shit myself, but I was powerless to do anything about it and I sat there in a frozen state as the car slid perfectly back down and around the previous corner, for some thirty metres, to gently come to rest across the driveway into the cottages, only a fraction away from a high kerb, which would have stove in my rear bumper. I breathed an immense sigh of relief. There was no damage, but I had to walk on up to the farm and get Dad to give me a tow up with the tractor.

    Getting back to the twenty-ninth, I got up home, no problem and spent the rest of the day sawing up windblown conifers for fencing materials and firewood. In the evening, I went to a ceilidh at Mungrisdale village hall, which had been organised by Bob. I had been to one of these energetic events before but on this occasion I wasn't feeling up for it. The beer was crap and the heating system in the hall made my fickle nose stream. Consequently I did not stay long and I was home for nine thirty p.m.

Saturday the thirtieth. There was still plenty of snow about and having acquired an appetite for winter walking in the Lakes, I decided to go up Skiddaw this day. I got my gear together and taking Tina, drove to near Millbeck Village, which nestles at the south west foot of Skiddaw. After parking in a little layby on the side of the A591 I got my gear on, put Tina on the chain, left the car and walked up through the village to the fell bottom, just short of Dodd Wood. Once off the road, I strapped my crampons on, let Tina off the lead and she bounded ahead of me as I began the steep climb north east up the flank of Carl Side. I was immediately glad of the grip from my crampons. Although it was only a snow-covered grass slope, it was extremely slippery! I had started from the car at ten thirty a.m. and the weather was fine and clear, with little wind but very cold. I forged ahead up the steep incline with Tina taking the lead and was soon at the summit of Carl Side at seven hundred and forty-six metres (two thousand four hundred and forty-seven feet). From Carl Side I kept on a north east heading, across a level section and then onto a good path known as the Allerdale Ramble, which climbs the western shoulder of Skiddaw itself. An earlier wind had blown snow onto this path and it had been churned to a deep porridge by the feet of the many walkers on the mountain that day. The going became difficult and taxing, with my crampons struggling to find grip in the loose snow. Also I had to keep stopping, to allow people to get past who were coming down from the summit.

After a great deal of toil I made the summit at nine hundred and thirty-one metres (three thousand and fifty-four feet). It had taken just over two hours. Tina had made short work of the porridgy path and was still bouncing with energy, but hungry, so we found a quieter place near the summit cairn and I got out Tina's flaked maize mash that I had brought up for her. She gobbled it down greedily while I ate my sandwiches. We didn't dally long in the freezing conditions and so after taking a few photos of the magnificent views in all directions, we set off south/south east, down to the lower top of Little Man at eight hundred and sixty-five metres (two thousand eight hundred and thirty-eight feet) and then, leaving the path, dropped down steeply in a south westerly direction, straight towards Millbeck Village. The smooth terrain of the higher slopes soon gave way to heather and bracken covered ones, and although there was still snow on the ground I was having trouble with the crampons getting tangled up in the heather/bracken stems, so I took them off. We were soon back down to Millbeck and I put Tina on her chain to walk the last half mile back to the car. I looked at my watch as I was putting the gear and Tina back in the Capri and saw that it was three p.m. We had done the hike in quick time!

I drove to the supermarket at Penrith to buy a pack of Stella Artois beer for the forthcoming New Year's Eve party at Roger Bucknall's house and then drove back to the Mill Inn at Mungrisdale for a couple of swift pints to celebrate my walk. While I drank them I reflected on the day, as there was nobody in the pub that I knew to talk to. There had been quite a strong wind on the summit of Skiddaw and with the low temperatures I judged the wind chill to have been about minus-twenty Celsius, so no wonder we got a move on with lunch. (To this day, I am renowned for being slow at eating my lunch on the fells, but I don't care. I always have plenty to eat, which you should have, but I like to take my time over it. Except of course when it's bitterly cold!)

After the pub I got myself and Tina home, then spent the evening watching T.V. with my folks in their parlour.

Sunday the thirty-first of January. New Year's Eve had arrived. I always got my hopes up for this day, hoping that this year would bring me some nice New Year's kisses (or even more) from some gorgeous available woman!

I was up at nine thirty a.m., got my breakfast and let Tina out before heading out to Hames Hall at Cockermouth to visit my grandma, who was still in that residential establishment. I cracked with her for about half an hour and then drove back to Motherby to fuel the Capri up. I then headed on to Howard Park in Greystoke to visit Thomas and discuss plans for repairing yet more lime kilns for the national park. Afterwards I drove on into Penrith and bought a bottle of good quality red wine at the supermarket, to take to that evening's party, as a present for Roger and Moira. The supermarket was thronged with people buying liquor for the big night and it was a real scrum at the checkout.

Returning home, I had lunch and then Heather came up and we headed off together to the ski shop at Longtown to get Heather's ski boots changed, as the ones she had bought there were too tight. However, we had only got as far as the Sportsman's Inn on the A66 when it came on to snow heavily. We were in Heather's car and she didn't fancy the journey in the rapidly worsening conditions, so we set off home. Just as we were making our way down the back road from Troutbeck to the farm, we came across a couple of large snow dams that some cheeky kids had built across the road. They set off to run away as we got up to these obstacles and I bollocked them from the open car window, shouting, "You stupid little sods, you could have caused an accident!" Heather stopped the car and I got out and got the shovel out of her boot (we always carried one in winter) to clear a passage through the dams, which were constructed of large, wet snowballs.

Once back home, Heather headed back to Threlkeld before she got blocked in by the snow that was still falling, and I took it easy for a few hours before fitting the snow chains to the Capri, getting my supper, bathing, shaving and then getting my glad rags on. I then drove to the Mill Inn in the slippery/snowy conditions. I was glad of the snow chains. Here I met Bob for a couple of pints at seven fifteen p.m. before I drove us up to the party at the Roundhouse. I had with me the wine I had bought and a substantial supply of Stella Artois. Upon being ushered into the Roundhouse cottage I presented Roger and Moira with the wine and then went on in to meet the rest of the pool team, their spouses and one or two other people I had not met before. There was one available woman, and from the outset I set my stall out to try and snare her. The beer flowed and the buffet, which I was not expecting, went down a treat. There was a sing-song, a game of Trivial Pursuit and then dancing. Of course I got the single lady up to dance and was in particularly fine form, especially to T-Rex's *Get It On*, where I moved like a pro. I don't know what it was but I was feeling high as well as quite pissed. Perhaps it was just the strong Stella mixing with my medication. It was a hell of a good night and we all sang *Auld Lang Syne* at midnight. I managed to grab a few New Year's kisses, but no more than that happened with the single lady. Roger and Moira went to bed around two a.m. and consequently everybody else except me went home. I had been allowed to kip over and had brought my sleeping bag to that end. I crept into it in front of the living room fire and went to sleep instantly.

Monday the first of January 2001. It was a new year, but little did I know what the fates had in store for Britain, and for me personally, this year!

I raised myself groggily from my sleeping bag at ten thirty a.m. and for a moment I didn't know where I was, then I remembered and the events of the night before came flooding back, and with them came a terrible hangover. I had never had one quite like it; it was as if a small man was trying to get out of my head with a big sledgehammer! I got up and, realizing there was nobody else up and about, I gathered up my possessions and let myself out of the cottage. It had thawed a bit through the night and I set about taking the snow chains off the Capri. This was made more difficult by my banging head. I managed though and set off home, taking it easy in the still quite slippery conditions.

Once back home, I settled myself in front of the fire I had lit in my living room. Outside, the weather had turned colder again and it was snowing heavily, with large wet flakes.

After lunch Angus, Anne, Katie and Hannah came and they went for a walk in the snow with Tina and me, down the front fields. I was not too communicative due to my hangover, which was still raging.

Once back at the farm, the others went home, leaving me to nurse my woes and spend the rest of the day in front of the telly and the restorative, warming fire.

There is no mention in my diaries for this time about the bullocking on our farm so I surmise that with the reduced number of cattle, my dad must therefore have been doing that work himself.

Leaving the grim New Year's Day behind me, I set about mole trapping for a number of different clients, but this is a bad time of year to trap, as the weather is always against you. It is either freezing the traps solid or blowing a hooley. Consequently I faced some hellish conditions, but got managed somehow.

Heather finally got to Longtown ski warehouse to change her boots and I went with her. Also she and I, accompanied by Katie and Hannah went skiing again on the dry slope at Kendal, where Heather and I gave the two young ones some more instruction.

I ordered my foreign currency (which I think was still Italian Lire back then) at the travel agent for the rapidly approaching holiday and then picked it up a few days later.

I got my skis serviced at Fishers outdoor shop at Keswick, but only just in time for the holiday.

Friday the twelfth of January. In the morning, I finished packing for the imminent ski holiday, gave Tina a final run out, got my lunch and then Allan and Heather came to pick me and my luggage up. We had a bit of a struggle fitting my stuff in amongst all of theirs and getting the three of us into their car as well, but we managed. Then Allan drove us down to Manchester, where we booked into the Cottons Hotel, just outside the city. This was an excellent establishment with a good leisure club, which we took full advantage of.

In the evening, we gathered in the bar for a couple of pints before enjoying a delicious meal in the restaurant and then we turned in around ten fifteen p.m.

Saturday the thirteenth. We were up at four a.m. and I had slept poorly. After a quick coffee in our rooms we packed up our gear, checked out and then boarded the previously ordered taxi, which took us to Manchester airport. We had to endure a queue before checking our luggage in, but we finally managed and then went through customs, where we met Angus, Anne, Katie, Hannah and Alex in the departures lounge.

We boarded the plane (a Boeing 757) at seven a.m. but we waited for an hour on the tarmac before take-off. After finally getting under way we had a good, smooth flight to Bergamo in Italy and landed at ten a.m. (local time). I had taken full advantage of the in-flight meal, being a good flyer and even though I had slept badly back at the Cottons Hotel, I was now on good form and ready to tackle the two and a half hour long coach transfer up to our resort of Passo Tonale.

We cleared customs, retrieved our baggage and then loaded it onto the waiting coach, which was largely and unusually uncrowded. We were all able to therefore sit close to one another and passed the journey up to Passo with good conversation.

The last part of the coach transfer up to Passo Tonale was up a steep switchback out of a narrow valley and it was quite hair-raising.

Once in the resort, we could see that it lay in a high valley at one thousand eight hundred and eighty-three metres (six thousand one hundred and seventy-eight feet) and there was a lot of snow – approximately two metres (six feet six inches). This was the most snow I had yet seen in the village of a ski resort and has yet to be bettered.

The coach dropped us and our luggage off right outside our hotel, the Gardenia, which is situated close to the centre of the village.

Passo Tonale was up until the First World War right on the old Austrian border and there is a monument to mark the old border near the southern edge of the village.

Evening was falling, but we were still able to see that a ragged range of peaks formed up the eastern side of the valley. To the west was a lower range of mountains and this is where I assumed the majority of the ski slopes were. To the north and south, the valley stretched away to open vistas.

After we had got checked into the Gardenia we had enough time to go out to the nearby ski hire shop and acquire the necessary equipment for those of our group that needed it. We got back into the Gardenia just in time to attend the welcome meeting, hosted by our holiday rep. There was a warming glass of the fiery grappa, which is made from distilled grape skins, for each of us during our briefing about the resort. After the meeting we unpacked our equipment into the ski room and our luggage into our rooms.

Dinner was at seven forty p.m. and consisted of five excellent courses, starting with a buffet salad course, where you could load your plate with as much as you wanted. There were also quite a number of bottles of both red and white wine on our table, and although they were only house wines we tucked into them with gusto! We also ordered a few beers each during the meal. This was a bit of an art because the hotel staff did not speak much English.

After my unfortunate experience of the morning after the night before at New Year, I had decided to quit taking my medication for the duration of the holiday. I knew I was taking a risk but how else was I going to be able to let my hair down and enjoy the après ski on this trip to the maximum?

At ten p.m. we retired to bed. The rooming arrangements were that Angus was sharing with Anne, and Heather was sharing with Allan, of course, and in our other two rooms were Katie and Hannah, and then Alex and me.

This was the first time I had been skiing with a large group and certainly the first time I'd shared a room with Alex. I wondered how he would cope with my snoring! I need not have worried though, because we were tuckered out by the long day and went out like lights.

Sunday the fourteenth. We were up at seven thirty a.m. and I had slept well, having knocked myself out with the wine and beer the previous evening. I had a shave and then on exiting the en-suite bathroom, observed a strange sight – it was Alex and he was going through his morning exercise routine, to limber up for the rigours of the coming day. I laughed at first, but then I decided that for him it was probably very sensible. (In those days, I considered myself able to go off skiing at the drop of a hat, without any physical preparation, but alas, nowadays that is no longer the case.)

Breakfast was in the continental style, very similar to that of most European countries, with cereal, bread, meat and cheese, but also, unusually, with large numbers of hard-boiled eggs, which I guzzled, of course!

After our morning meal we got our ski gear and lift passes on (these had been handed out to us on the transfer coach), then headed down into the basement to get our ski boots on and gather up our skis. We stomped out of the ski room and up the steps out to the car park at the front of the hotel.

It was a gorgeous morning and very crisp as we navigated the slippery pavement bordering the main road through the village, to get to the nearest ski-lift.

Heather and I, being the most experienced members of the group, took a shortish drag lift up, next to the nursery slopes to the west of the village, and had a couple of runs to try out the conditions. They proved to be excellent, with only the odd patch of ice in places.

This was Alex's, Katie's and Hannah's first ski holiday, so the whole gang of us spent the morning on the nursery slopes, where Heather and I gave as much instruction as we could to the beginners and they all came on really well.

At lunch time we retired back to the village, where we all had lunch together in the restaurant of the hotel Miramonti, which would come to be a regular lunch stop place for us, as the food and beer were great!

After lunch Alex, Katie and Hannah joined ski school for the afternoon. Heather and I headed out up into the north west part of the ski area, reaching a height of some two thousand five hundred and seventy-seven metres (eight thousand four hundred and fifty-five feet), where we found some great skiing. I was however experiencing some difficulties whenever I encountered a patch of ice; my skis just seemed to skitter off it as though their edges were blunt. This was a disappointment, considering I had just had them serviced!

We returned to the nursery slopes for four thirty p.m. to find that our beginners had done very well in ski school and particularly Katie, who had got into quite a high class! Angus, Anne and Allan had also had a good afternoon finding their feet on the easier, lower slopes.

After returning to the Gardenia to take our gear off, Heather, Allan, Alex and I got our walking boots on and headed up the village, looking for the Ski-Doo meeting place as we had booked ourselves on an evening's Ski-Dooing later in the week, but we couldn't find it, so we retired to the Bar Heaven, which was rumoured to be the best joint in town. (Alex and I would find more seedy but invigorating establishments later in the holiday!) Bar Heaven was right underneath the Miramonti and was accessed only by a long flight of treacherously slippery steps. We had two beers each here and exchanged stories of our day before returning to the Gardenia to do our ablutions before dinner at seven forty-five p.m.

The wine and beer flowed again and they washed the fine food down well. After the meal everybody except Alex and I went to bed. We were eager for action so we headed out into the freezing, starlit night and made our way back to Bar Heaven. Although it was much quieter than earlier, there was a very good looking barmaid on duty. We were both single so we tried our charms on this gorgeous vision, but it was to no avail – she was an old hand and well used to dealing with merry après skiers. We had a couple then returned to the Gardenia bar, where we had a couple more and a good crack. I was enjoying Alex's company again and it would bode well for the coming days. We turned in at eleven forty-five p.m. and it had been a good day.

Monday the fifteenth. We were up and about at seven forty-five a.m. and again I had slept well. After breakfast we all donned our gear in the usual fashion and then Heather and I left the others to do ski school and the like and headed out to the south west section of the ski area to try that out. We reached a height of two thousand four hundred metres (seven thousand eight hundred and seventy-four feet) near the peak of Cima Bleis, where the views were tremendous in the once again perfect conditions. It was bitterly cold though, measuring minus-nine Celsius in the village first thing.

From this lofty viewpoint I eyed up the highest part of the ski area across the valley to the east, the Ghiacciaio Presena, where there was said to be a small glacier. I made up my mind to get up there as soon as possible!

Heather and I were well into our stride by now and skiing well together. Confidence was good between us, which was due to the largely uncrowded slopes. Back home I had bought a fancy ski hat at the ski warehouse and I now exchanged my more dowdy headgear for this flamboyant one. It is bright green and has several long tassels, with fluffy bits on the end. Sometimes the tassels blow into your eyes, but I don't mind as I like looking silly in this hat! I had my small rucksack on my back and in it were the essential water and chocolate.

We returned to the village at one p.m. to meet up for lunch with the rest of the gang at the Miramonti. After another excellent meal Heather joined Angus and Anne, while the beginners went back to their ski school and Allan and I headed for the highest part of the ski area. We took the ski bus to the large car park near the required cable car station. Allan had left his skis back in the village, as the piste down from the top cable car station was a black and beyond his capabilities. Allan walked up to the cable car while I took advantage of the couple of local guys who were offering tows behind their Ski-Doos up the slight incline to the station. I managed to hold onto the tow rope and ski behind the machine without falling over, which would have been a bit embarrassing.

Allan and I rode the cable car up together and took in the view from the windows, back across to the main ski area. On arriving at the top station, I parted company from Allan, as I was going on to take the higher lifts, which required you to have skis on. I left him to potter about round the little hamlet of buildings, including a restaurant and then skied to the chairlift station, took the lift and then went up the final drag lift to the Cima Presena at three thousand and sixty-nine metres (ten thousand and sixty-nine feet). The pistes in this area were nearly all of the more difficult red or black grading, unlike the main area where they were predominately blue and red. The slopes also faced away from the sun for the greater part of the day, and although the snow was crisp, the air was very, very cold. From the top of the drag I went right, onto a snow ledge that took you across the top of a wide red piste. Halfway along this ledge I came across a group of skiers who had taken off their skis and were climbing up a steep snow slope to the left, with the help of a fixed rope. I was intrigued, so I followed their lead and took my skis off to climb the slope. It was a little difficult, wearing ski boots in the soft snow, but after a brief climb I came out onto a ridge and found I was looking down into another valley, which was devoid of habitation. To the east there were spectacular views of the nearby Dolomites range of mountains, which I had longed to visit (I would not do so until 2014).

I took a few photos and then climbed back down to my skis, clipped them on and then tackled the red piste. It was smooth, but of a steepness that would suggest it would turn into a mogul field with heavy use. Although the piste bashing machines had been at work on the slope it was soft, making it a little difficult to make good turns on. It was uncrowded, though and I was able to negotiate it easily. The smooth nature of the slope obviously betrayed the fact that there was a glacier or ice sheet under it. When I got back to the bottom of the drag lift, I went up it again and this time, went left off the top to tackle the other piste, which was a black. This was a trickier proposition and I picked my way down the very steep slope slowly and carefully. Having done that piste, I tried the only other drag in the area, which went up south eastwards and accessed a short blue run, which joined the previous glacier run.

I skied back to the cable car station and looked around for Allan, but could not see him so I set off back for Passo Tonale. Of course, I would ski as far back as I could and this meant tackling the black run under the cableway. It was accessed by a narrow track from the cable car station, which lasted for about two hundred metres before the piste widened out into a series of steep icy pitches. My skis had now bedded in and were working much better as I tackled this difficult run, carving a series of tight turns.

I made it down unscathed, if somewhat breathless, and returned to Passo. I left my skis outside the Miramonti and clomped down the slippery stairs in my ski boots to Bar Heaven, where I found Allan and Heather. We enjoyed a couple of beers together and Allan was keen to learn of my experiences on the higher slopes.

Afterwards we returned to the Gardenia to do our ablutions and prepare for dinner at seven forty-five p.m. Another grand feed was enjoyed by all and then, as per the previous evening, everybody except Alex and I went to bed. We two partook of a couple of beers in the hotel bar and exchanged our stories of the day. Alex asked me if I would take him up to the top of the highest lift in a few days' time when he was further fledged, and I agreed. We turned in at eleven thirty p.m.

Tuesday the sixteenth. We were up at eight a.m., breakfasted and out onto the slopes for nine thirty a.m. For the first time, we all skied together, doing several blue and red runs up to eleven a.m., when our beginners went to their lessons. The rest of us skied together up to lunch time, stopping briefly for a vin brulle (hot spicy red wine) at one of the high mountain restaurants. We had our communal lunch at the Miramonti and then our beginners went back to ski school while the rest of us toured the main ski area. Late in the afternoon, Heather and I broke away from the others and skied a narrow, exciting piste down to an old isolated hotel, where we had a couple of vin brulles and relaxed for a while before making our way back to Passo.

There was the usual evening routine, during which we met our holiday company rep and she told us which evening the Ski-Dooing event would take place.

Later Alex and I went nightclubbing to the bar La Gabbia Erotica, which was justly named! There was a stage with a steel cage on it, in which a gorgeous half naked woman was gyrating to a pulsating disco beat. The bar staff sold raffle tickets and upon the drawing of the raffle, if you won, you got a key, which unlocked the cage and you were able to get in with the sexy girl and dance with her. It was wild, and Alex and I bought several tickets but did not win. For a while I thought it was a fix and a wind up, but then suddenly some guy drew a winning ticket and got into the cage with the girl. She proceeded to undress him slowly, but did not take any more of her own clothes off. The guy was almost naked before she pushed him out of the cage and the show was over. It was very, very sexy and enjoyable for us but it must have been fantastic for the lucky bugger who won the key for the cage!

Alex and I got well tanked up and stayed out till one a.m. before staggering back to the Gardenia, only to find we were locked out. I was fairly sure which was Heather and Allan's room, so I threw snowballs up at their window on the second floor, until Heather staggered blearily out onto her balcony, proving fortunately that I had aimed at the right window. She said, "What are you buggers up to?" and on telling her we were locked out, she came down and let us in at the front door of the hotel with her key. It was a hell of a laugh but we were careful after that to obtain a code from reception, which let us in at the ski room door when punched into the machine there. We went to bed in very good spirits.

Wednesday the seventeenth. On our regular visits to Bar Heaven, we had come across a local guy (who always seemed to be pissed) who had sled dogs and made a living by giving tourists experience of taking out a sled pulled by his dogs. Heather and Hannah were interested in having a go and cut a deal with the guy for one circuit of his track. So after Heather, Allan and I had spent the morning skiing up near the glacier, we had lunch in the usual place and then I skied down out of the southern end of the village with Heather and Hannah, to the place where the sled dogs were housed. The guy who we had met in Bar Heaven came out of his house, looking a bit bleary-eyed, and proceeded to instruct Heather, Hannah and another small group of what turned out to be English people, in the art of sled dogging. I was only there to take photos, being aware that something interesting was about to take place. After the trainees were instructed in the art of helping the dog man to gather up the dog shit (of which there was a copious amount) the real business got under way. Two huskies were attached to each sled and then the trainees were off. My camera clicked as they set off around the track, which was situated on a fairly level field. All went well until the trainees got around to the far side of the track and then all hell broke loose. Hannah's sled collided with one of the others and she lost control. The dogs and sled kept going and Hannah desperately tried to hang on to the back of her contraption but was dragged through the snow for some distance before she gave up and let go. The dog man ran across the field to try to get hold of his dogs before they made for the hills. Hannah walked back slowly to the start/finish line, making it back after all the other sleds had returned unscathed. The poor lass was in tears, she was only a young girl at the time and it was quite a traumatic experience for her. Heather and I comforted her and then we walked back up to the chairlift, which would take us back to the ski slopes to have a few more runs before the lifts closed.

In the evening, after we had wined and dined, some of us (I can't remember exactly who, but Alex was definitely there) went on the Ski-Dooing event. We found the place where the event started and we were separated into pairs, with one pair to each machine. Alex and I joined up and got on our powerful looking steed. A couple of days earlier I had seen a racing Ski-Doo tearing around the cable car station area and it had been very fast. I now wondered what the beast we were mounted on was capable of. We started our engines (there were about ten machines in all) and set off around the lower slopes, just west of the village. Alex was driving, with me sitting right behind him. I think it was his first time on such a machine and buoyed up by alcohol and adrenalin, he set off at a fair lick! We were soon in trouble as he tried to take a corner too fast and threw the machine over, spilling us onto the snow. Luckily the kill cord, which had been attached to Alex, shut the machine down and we were able to haul it back onto its skids and re-mount. I had contributed to our downfall by not leaning into the corner as we came into it. After we had re-started, Alex drove us on without incident, northwards and we got up to quite a speed on the flat because a kind of race had developed between the Ski-Doos.

Eventually we came to the old hotel where Heather and I had previously enjoyed those vin brulles. The place is called Ospizio S. Bartolemeo. Here we dismounted and went into the bar to down a swift grappa before making the return journey to Passo. It was time to change drivers and I mounted, with Alex behind me and we set of with relish. I had first handled one of these beasts during the French holiday in Risoul and I now looked forward to pushing the machine hard on the way back. The race had re-started and before long we were close up behind the organizer of the event and in second place. We were flying, fuck; I was having a good time! We made it back to Passo unscathed and shook hands with the organizer, before going back to the Gardenia and getting our glad rags on to head out on the raz once more. There was just Alex and me up for it, but we were buzzing and ready to paint the town red!

On this evening, we headed to a new haunt that we had heard about. It was a bouncing disco and we were soon fortifying ourselves with pints and chasers. In my case, it was beer followed by shots of Pernod. The music was very good and they played some of the latest numbers, including Black Box's *Right On Time* and the big hit by Anastacia, *I'm Outta Love*. We were soon out dancing to these, and other good disco numbers. The dance floor was a heaving mass of people but it was not easy to get in close with any of the women.

As the night wore on, I began to flag. The pace had caught up with me, but it was at this point that the still-lively Alex (he is twelve years younger than me!) introduced me to the vodka/Red Bull drink. It was very expensive but the caffeine in the Red Bull revived me and I was able to throw myself into the throng on the dance floor once more with renewed vigour.

We partied until three a.m. but returned to the Gardenia without a woman on our arm!

Once more, this day had been better than the last and the weather had again been ideal for skiing, plus the après ski was proving to be the best I had ever known!

Thursday the eighteenth. We were up again at eight a.m. and personally I had slept well but both Alex and I had a hangover, which was really for the first time on that holiday. We managed breakfast though, but Alex had to forgo his morning exercise routine because of his sore head. The other members of our group had learned of our shenanigans but were unsympathetic to the fact that we were suffering a bit.

Alex joined the girls for their ski lessons and I did a few blue runs with Heather and Allan to shake out the cobwebs. Then we returned to the village and went to the ski hire shop, where Heather and I put a plan into place that we had been talking about for a few days. We each hired a pair of snow blades, which are a kind of very short ski (about fifty centimetres), turned up at both ends so that you can kind of go one way and then the other across the slope, and even do tricks. You don't use ski sticks with them.

We headed out onto the slopes with our new gear and the blades took a bit of getting used to. They were particularly difficult on the drag lifts because there was less stability, due to their shortness. However we were soon getting the hang of them and as our confidence increased, then so did our speed.

At some point during the night it had put about eight inches of new snow down and the pistes were positively silky. The morning was cloudy but it got out fine again as we all rendezvoused at a high mountain restaurant for lunch. After we had eaten we all skied together for the whole afternoon, our beginners having finished their ski school. We skied a variety of different runs and I was impressed with how far our beginners had progressed. We did a red piste called the Devil's Run and our beginners tackled it with alacrity. I could see that it was possible that they were ready to tackle the glacier!

When the lifts closed at four thirty p.m., Heather and I took our snow blades back, having enjoyed them immensely.

We all met up for beers in our hotel and enjoyed a good crack, during which I told our beginners that I would take them up on the glacier on the morrow. Then it was time to get showered and changed for dinner.

After yet another good feast it was time to go out on the town yet again. Some of our group stayed in the Gardenia but Heather and Allan, who were feeling adventurous, joined Alex and me for a night on the tiles. We explored a few of the more unfamiliar bars, downing a beer in each and then headed on to the thumping disco/pub. Heather got up for a boogie with Alex and me but Allan declined. The crack didn't seem as good in this place, this night, so at eleven thirty p.m. Alex and I went in search of the other nightclub that we were yet to visit. Heather and Allan were not up for this and went back to the Gardenia.

We found the other club but there were not many women about and we ended up dancing on our own on a sparsely populated dance floor. This, though, had the kind of flashing coloured squares reminiscent of *Saturday Night Fever* and it was great! We stayed out till three a.m. again and had another very good night.

Friday the nineteenth. Up at seven forty-five a.m. Phew, we were really burning the candle at both ends. There were hangovers once more but we were soon out and about. Alex and I took the ski bus to the cable car and I took him up to the top of the glacier. He had a little trouble managing the drag lift up to the top, but didn't fall off. I showed him the climb to the ridge and we did it. He was impressed with the view. Then it was time for him to tackle the red piste. I was a little worried about this because even I had found this to be the most difficult red piste in the resort and there was yet more new snow up here! My fears were somewhat confirmed when Alex failed to make the first turn and fell over on the porridgy slope. He was soon up again though, like a true trooper and started to put a few turns together. It was at this point that I really noticed his headgear; apparently I was not the only one with a silly hat. Alex had on the kind of head garb reminiscent of Deputy Dawg! It was furry with large, loose flaps, stretching down over his ears. These kind of spread out like a pair of wings when he was moving and it was hilarious.

Our hangovers dissipated in the rarefied mountain air as we patiently picked our way down this tricky slope. The piste was again uncrowded though and the weather conditions were wonderful.

We repeated the run and then stuck to the lower chairlift run, which was easier. Towards lunch time I skied down the black under the cableway, while Alex rode down above me in the cable car. I found this piste easier than previously and made short work of it.

We all met at the Miramonti for lunch and then all went up onto the glacier. Katie, Hannah and Anne were somewhat perturbed by Alex's account of his higher piste runs, so they just stuck to the lower chairlift red piste. Angus, though, was having none of it and wanted to do the snow climb at the top and then tackle the porridgy red piste. He would do it alone, though. (He probably didn't want any witnesses if he came a cropper!) So off he went and the rest of us skied the lower run to give him a bit of space. He appeared again a little later and seemed unscathed!

Later in the afternoon, Heather and I skied the black down under the cableway and then her and I took Alex up the big chairlift in the main ski area and skied that piste with him a couple of times, right up to the last lift, as it was our last day. Alex had made amazing progress, considering he had not even had a pair of skis on prior to that holiday!

Back at the Gardenia, we had a beer and then all went up to the Bar Heaven for the ski school presentation, where our beginners picked up their awards. After this and a few beers we returned to the Gardenia to get cleaned up and dine. After the excellent meal, it was time to pay the bar bill, which was quite large as we had supped considerable amounts of the house wine with our evening meals. Then it was time for getting on the raz once more and this last time was phenomenal! There was only Alex and me, but we supped the rest of the group's share as well. We frequented the usual haunts and then ended up in the Antares Nightclub, staying in there until four a.m. and enjoying the most tremendous boogie ever! Then it was back to the Gardenia in an inebriated condition to get only one hour's sleep (from which we nearly didn't awaken in time to leave the resort).

Saturday the twentieth of January (nine years to the day since I gave up smoking!). There was frantic activity at five fifteen a.m. in our room to get packed, because we were leaving for home in an hour! We literally crammed our stuff into our suitcases, but we must have left some items behind, because I can't find them to this day! We had been in bed such a short time that our hangovers had not yet kicked in. Scrambling down to reception with our luggage, we only just had enough time to grab our packed breakfast before it was time to board the coach. As we were about to do so, I suddenly remembered my skis and raced back to the ski room to get them. Fortunately I had packed them away in their bag the night before. I dragged them out to the coach and then joined the rest of our gang on board. There were disapproving looks from Angus and Anne, but also complaints from some of the rest of our group, about the strong smell of alcohol emanating from us!

Once we were under way, Alex and I slept most of the way to the airport. When we woke, though, our hangovers were raging and we became a bit grumpy, naturally.

We got checked in okay but after clearing customs we had to wait an hour and a half before we could board the plane. During this time I got a lecture from my brother in which he told me my behaviour of the last few evenings could have, or even might still, lead to another episode!

He said, "Another few days of carrying on like that and you would have been off on one!"

I just shrugged and said nothing. Hell's teeth, we had had a good time and I felt fine, except for my hangover, that is!

We flew out of Bergamo and once under way, I enjoyed the in-flight meal, having picked at my packed breakfast at the end of the coach transfer. Sitting all fairly close together on the plane (again a Boeing 757) we were able to have a good crack. Alex told me he would like to do this again sometime, as it had been a blast.

Having landed after a good flight, we quickly cleared customs, retrieved our luggage and then myself, Heather and Allan parted company from the others, hailed a taxi and were taken back to the Cottons Hotel, where we loaded up Heather's car and set off back north. There was a brief stop at Charnock Richard Services and then we went on, straight back up home. The weather back in England was grim, as it usually is when you get back from a skiing holiday, and this had been the best ever, but I was never again able to push the boat out like we did on the après ski. Christ, I was getting too old for such shenanigans!

I was not long for my bed that evening and left the unpacking until the next day.

The first few days after the holiday were quiet as everything was frozen up and I couldn't trap or really get anything else done workwise. I was able to give Tina several good walks and take some films into town to be developed.

On the evening of Tuesday the twenty-third of January, we had a pool match against the Sportsman's Inn team and things got a bit rowdy. There were several contentious fouls committed by the opposing team and there was bad blood between us. Nick from our team got himself particularly upset (nowadays we have referees, which cuts down disputes but does not entirely eradicate them). We won the match, though, eight-four and we were through to the final of the consolation plate, which was one of the lesser cup matches. We did not go on to win the plate though!

The following day, Thomas and I started work on what would prove to be our last lime kiln repair job. It was at High Ireby, which was a bit of a drive for both of us and would prove to be our most notorious job together! We used my trailer and took turns at ferrying materials to the site using both our cars. The kiln was just off a little back road between High Ireby and Ireby itself. There was limited parking on the roadside and also, we had to cut a good stock fence to get our tools and materials to the kiln face. This fence had to be temporarily re-erected each evening to prevent the sheep from getting out of the field and onto the road.

There was the usual clearing of small trees, the rebuilding of the arched 'eyes' of the kiln with the help of wooden formers and the repair of the kiln face, using the 'donkey shit' lime mortar mixes. One day while we were working, a white pickup truck pulled up on the road, which was only about twenty metres from the kiln, and the occupants regarded us with interest. I thought nothing more of it at the time, being of the opinion that it had just been a couple of farmers on their rounds. The work continued and things went well for a while.

I had an excellent meeting with Richard, my psychologist, on the twenty-sixth of January, in which I described to the full extent the details of my recent holiday. We had a good laugh about it but he said I should be careful when pushing the boat out. Afterwards I had another great massage back at Penrith, from my favourite masseuse and we enjoyed a good crack.

That afternoon, I took a break from the lime kiln work and did some trapping at a farm just across the valley from our place. I had been trying to find time to do this job for a while and I now took advantage of some open weather to do it. I caught most of the moles for the farmer but there was one crafty bugger that outwitted me – I tried everything but I couldn't catch the sod!

Sunday the twenty-eighth of January. Andrew and I had arranged another hike and on this day he came through from Workington and met me at the road end below the old railway. There was a good covering of snow on the high fells, so I had with me my full winter gear and Tina. We took both our cars to Patterdale and then left mine just off the road, in a field up the Grisedale valley. The field belonged to a farmer whom I trapped for, and I left a note inside the front window to tell him what I was up to if he saw my car. (Parking in this valley is very hard to come by!) Leaving my motor, we went on in Andrew's car, south up to the top of Kirkstone Pass, where we parked, got our gear on and got Tina on her chain. From the car park we struck off north west, in good spirits, up Red Screes. It was steep going but the ground conditions were quite good, with not much snow and there was a good, if faint, path. Things became more difficult though, by the time we got out onto the southern end of Middle Dodd at six hundred and fifty metres (two thousand one hundred and thirty-two feet) where we found more snow and where it had thawed slightly, it had then re-frozen into verglass. This frozen slush is very slippery and I called a halt to put my crampons on. Unfortunately Andrew still didn't have any and proceeded on, sliding about all over the place. However, it was now fairly level going as we headed north west to the crossroads of paths at Scandale Pass.

Tina, who had been let off the chain after we got away from the road, was now enjoying herself but also sliding around quite a bit. The weather was fine, with little wind, but very cold. We continued north west, past Little Hart Crag at six hundred and thirty-seven metres (two thousand and eighty-nine feet), then on past Black Brow, Dove Crag at seven hundred and ninety-two metres (two thousand five hundred and ninety-eight feet), up to Hart Crag at eight hundred and twenty-two metres (two thousand six hundred and ninety-six feet) and then westwards up onto Fairfield at eight hundred and seventy-three metres (two thousand eight hundred and sixty-four feet), our highest summit of the walk. There were quite a few other walkers out and about, some with crampons and some without. It was the finest Sunday for a while and it had brought people out like flies. The wind had scoured the snow off the gravelly, round-topped summit of Fairfield and it was once more getting up again, making us glad we had stopped for lunch a while back in the shelter of some rocks. We only stopped briefly before descending westwards down a good, if loose, path to Grisedale Tarn. From the tarn we turned north east and walked right back out down the Grisedale valley to my car, which appeared untouched. I reckoned we had walked about twenty point nine kilometres (thirteen miles), which was pretty good going. I have no record of how long it took us but it must have been dusk by the time we got back to my car.

I drove us back to Kirkstone and we had a pint of Stella (a poor one) in the Kirkstone Pass Inn before taking both our cars back north, to the Brotherswater Inn for another, much better, pint.

We returned to our farm, where I lent Andrew my Tomb Raider 2 computer game along with the memory card for it, which contained all levels in the game. I hadn't used my Playstation to play the games for a while and Andrew was interested in trying them out. He then went home to Tracy. We had venison for supper that evening at the farm; Allan had shot a fallow deer as part of a cull, with a friend and we had been given some of the meat.

It was back to the lime kiln job, me having finished the trapping for the time being. I had had to leave that crafty mole, which I nicknamed 'The Stinker' and I never did catch it.

Work on the kiln went well up until Tuesday the thirtieth of January, when we arrived on site to get a shock – some bastard had stolen our precious, beautifully maintained cement mixer. It had been some days since we had been at the job and we had left the mixer chained and padlocked to various other pieces of equipment in the kiln. We had ummed and ahhed about leaving it and had finally decided to do so, thinking it would be safe, but we were wrong. The bastards had cut through the chain, hauled it over the fence and gone with it, probably in that bloody white pickup we had seen. I was boiling mad; of all the tools we had, that mixer had been our favourite. The situation looked hopeless but I was not about to let things stand at that. Being as there was no mobile phone signal at the kiln I drove to a nearby farm and asked to use the landline phone to contact the police. The farmer was only too glad to help and I asked him if he had seen anything suspicious going on at the kiln, but he hadn't. The police were very interested and sent a scenes of crime officer out to have a look. When the officer came, he told Thomas and me that there had been a lot of that sort of theft going on in the area. There was not much he could do in the way of fingerprints but he did take a plaster cast of a boot print left in the mud by one of the perpetrators. We never heard any more about it though, or saw our cement mixer again and had to finish the job with a beat up old mixer borrowed from the national park depot.

That job was the last one I did with Thomas Arkle for some years and it was a very poignant one. Now, as I write this in early 2015, I have just received the distressing news that Thomas has died very suddenly! His son Paul telephoned to tell me the sad news and how much his dad had enjoyed working with me on the national park contracts and all the other jobs we did together. His death has affected me deeply and it is all the more difficult to bear because he was a clean living man who was very fit and had never been in hospital in his life! I will always cherish the memory of our time together and regard the world as having lost a true gentleman. Here's to you, Thomas Arkle.

Shortly after that last lime kiln job I had a prang in the Capri. I was driving down the back road from Troutbeck, in the snow, when I came to the hairpin left-hander on the Gills Bridge over the old railway. I was probably going too fast, but anyway I failed to make the turn and the car went straight on and I hit the fence. The front wheels dropped over the edge of the road and the car bellied out, rendering me stuck and partially blocking the road. I was unhurt though and apart from pulling the plastic corner off the front bumper, there didn't seem to be any other damage. I phoned home on my mobile and Dad came out with the tractor and chain. Another farmer stopped to help as well and together we pulled the Capri out backwards, by attaching the tow chain to the ball hitch, disentangling it from the wire fence. I was able to reattach the piece of bumper and drive the car home.

Sunday the eleventh of February. I had spent the night at Allan and Heather's after an evening's telly watching and drinking. I drove home and got my hiking gear and Tina, then drove down to the Coledale Inn at Braithwaite, where I met Andrew, having previously organised our plan to do the Coledale Horseshoe together. We left one car at the inn and then, having loaded our gear and Tina into the other, we drove up Newlands to the foot of Rowling End Fell, where we parked on the roadside, donned our gear, let Tina out and set off up the steep eastern prow of Rowling End.

We left the car at ten thirty a.m. in dull, cold and generally rather grim conditions. There was a stiff west wind blowing, but the cloud base was above the highest summits, making for quite good visibility.

Tina raced in front of us as we toiled up the steep path through heather, out to the top of Rowling End at four hundred and thirty-three metres (one thousand four hundred and twenty feet). Heading westwards, the going then levelled out for half a mile before we began to climb the steep east end of Causey Pike. The odd sleety shower came blowing in around this stage and we had to don our wet weather gear. We made the summit of Causey – six hundred and twenty metres (two thousand and eighty-nine feet) and found it to be typical of most of the tops of those fells formed from Skiddaw slate, therein stony but fairly round topped. From Causey, we dropped down to the crossroads of paths, where we two and Tracy had had lunch on that previous epic, where Tracy had hurt her pelvis. We decided that this was a poignant place to eat again on this day. Lunch was taken quickly though due to the conditions. Because it was a big walk I had brought a tin of Whiskas especially for Tina and she gobbled it down greedily.

From the lunch stop we climbed steeply up to the summit of Sail at seven hundred and seventy-three metres (two thousand five hundred and thirty-six feet). The path to here was about three metres wide and must have been visible from outer space. Heading on up westwards, we reached the summit of Crag Hill at eight hundred and thirty-nine metres (two thousand seven hundred and fifty-two feet) and then dropped down into a shallow valley, where our route took us west on a good, wide path. This was one point in the walk where we were able to hold a conversation quite easily, due to the less strenuous going, and the crack flowed. Subjects ranged from women and sex, through food to the state of my mental health, which was quite good at that time.

We got through the valley and walked on to our highest summit of the trip; Grassmoor at eight hundred and fifty-two metres (two thousand seven hundred and ninety-five feet). This great bulk of a mountain offers views out to the west over Buttermere and Crummock Water towards Melbreak and the Haystacks/Red Pike range of fells. However on this day the view was less inspiring.

We turned back and headed across the broad summit in a north westerly direction, to then drop off down grassy slopes to the major path crossroads at Coledale Hause. Then it was up again to the north west, to the summit of Grisedale Pike at seven hundred and ninety-one metres (two thousand five hundred and ninety-five feet). Here we came across more people than we had seen all day, proving it was a very popular peak. It has a conical profile. Amongst the folks we saw was Heather Larcombe (a news presenter off Border TV). We didn't dally long before dropping all the way east down, Sleet How and on back to the Coledale Inn. It was four thirty p.m., meaning we had done the hike in six hours, which seemed like a fast time. The total distance covered was about fourteen and a half kilometres (nine miles). We loaded our gear and Tina into the car and drove up Newlands to retrieve the other car, before returning to the Coledale Inn for a couple of well-earned pints. One of my old golfing buddies was in the pub and he tried to take the piss out of our hiking activities, but I shut him up by saying, "We didn't see you up there, did we?" We set off home after a good crack in the pub and being pretty knackered, I was in bed by ten fifteen.

The next few weeks were filled with trapping work mainly, the weather being quite open. There was another hike on Sunday the eighteenth of February, when a group of us climbed Skiddaw, through the forestry from the car park near Mirehouse on the A591. A severe problem developed early on in the walk though, when Tracy had to turn back, due to the re-emergence of her hip/pelvis problem. She got Andrew's keys and spent several uncomfortable hours in the car, waiting for us to return. When we did, she was not amused and the atmosphere between her and Andrew in the pub after was distinctly frosty!

Little did I know it, but this would be the last organised hike I would go on for some considerable time!

Five days later, all hell broke loose and I use 'hell' in the most meaningful terms. On Friday the twenty-third of February, reports began to come in on the news about foot and mouth disease breaking out at a number of locations around the country. I was once more feeling a bit down and this grim news only served to consolidate my mood. My dad had lived through the last major foot and mouth outbreak, in the 1960s and he told me what it would mean if the outbreak was not controlled quickly. He said that people's movements on and around farms would be severely restricted and that because of the modern pace of life in general, the disease was likely to be widespread. He was not wrong!

The weather turned bitterly cold and everything froze up, meaning I could not trap anyway. What with the weather and the foot and mouth, I worried about my contracting work, especially as I was coming into my busiest time of the year!

On the twenty-sixth of February, the first cases of foot and mouth were confirmed in Cumbria. One case was just to the south of Penrith. Hundreds of animals were slaughtered and burned in a big pyre on the farm. I was having dental treatment done in Penrith at the time and as I drove in by Stainton on the A66, I could see the massive pall of smoke drifting across the fields towards the town. It was like a scene from a war and sure enough, when I got out of my car in town to walk to the dentist's I could smell the smoke from the pyre. It was a mixture of burning flesh, straw and the creosote from the burning railway sleepers. It was terrible and is a smell I will never forget. The people who lived near the Nazi death camps must have smelled something similar!

I got Brian Cowperthwaite to carry out work on the Capri before everything ground to a halt around our farm. My motor had to have new bearings put in the rear differential, the prop shaft and one of the back wheels and it was quite a costly job.

I busied myself with work around the farm, as the government were advising people on farms to travel as little as possible. All farms by now had straw in the farm entrances, which was disinfected and all vehicles going in or out had their wheels sprayed with disinfectant. This was all very well but what about the wildlife moving around? Badgers, for instance, they ranged over wide areas. There were no more hikes as all the footpaths were closed, causing an outcry from the people who served the tourist industry; surely the local economies would collapse!

I was getting more depressed and decided that my medication was making me worse, so I stopped taking it!

Heather still came up to the farm to try and cheer us all up. She even brought a few cans of Stella for me to drink each week. She also purchased tickets for herself and me to go and see the Eagles live in concert on the twenty-second of July at Hampden Park, as my fortieth birthday treat, and I tried to raise my spirits by looking forward to that. It was difficult to get any good feelings going, though, as the foot and mouth crisis deepened. The travelling shop still came each Saturday and Philip Brown left his van out at the farm gate and carried the groceries into our big cattle shed, where we picked them up and paid him out at the shed. He brought us horrific tales of what was going on in the Eden Valley. It was rumoured that apparently some farmers had been deliberately trying to get the disease so that they could cash in on the government compensation. Aligned to this was the rumour that severed, diseased cow tails from slaughtered beasts were being thrown into the fields of unaffected farms. I thought at the time that any bastard found to be doing this should at the very least be horse whipped!

Vast sums were purported to be being made out of the transportation of slaughtered animals and the disinfecting of culled out farms by other contractors. There was an outcry about the number of pyres and the air pollution coming from them. So it was decided that a massive burial site for the culled stock would be constructed at Great Orton near Carlisle, into which truckloads of dead animals would be transported.

There were heart-rending stories on the news about people with pet lambs and other cloven footed pets, having their animals carted off and killed!

All our pool matches were cancelled and we put ourselves under lockdown on our farm. Up until then the disease had been quite far off, but it was getting closer and then suddenly, on the third of March, the frightening news came to us that one of my customer's farms only two miles away had contracted the disease, but that proved to be untrue. The crisis deepened even further and the reports of farms not far away started to come in; there was a farm at Berrier infected and culled. A pyre was built and we could clearly see the smoke from it from our place, then the disease caught hold around to the north of the Skiddaw range and a pyre was constructed and lit there, somewhere around Uldale. The weather was still bitterly cold and the wind had swung into the north, therefore blowing the smoke from this pyre in our direction. One evening in particular, we could clearly see the smoke drifting over the top of Blencathra towards us and then we caught its unmistakable stench – Christ, it was like World War Three!

We had few cattle left on our farm and these were all in the sheds, but we did have two hundred and twenty sheep. These consisted of a hundred and twenty yearlings (hoggs), and they were in the large rough grazing area above our Lobbs farm. Then there were a hundred lambing ewes and we decided to bring these as close to the farmstead as we could, to thereby create a kind of firebreak of empty fields on our boundaries. This wasn't difficult because we had three hundred and fifty acres to play with.

There was an outbreak of moles in the bottom field below the old railway and I dealt with this as and when the frost allowed. There was one crafty bugger that I couldn't catch though and I became paranoid that somebody had caught it in their garden, in a live catch trap and set it free on our land. Thinking back, this would be a sign that my mental health was deteriorating once more. Somehow I contracted a strange kind of 'flu, which made my hands go numb slightly. Perhaps it was just a reaction to stopping my medication though.

On the nineteenth of March, foot and mouth was announced to be out of control in Cumbria! A cull of uninfected sheep within three kilometres of infected farms was announced by the government and this caused outrage amongst farmers who were unaffected, leading to rumours of militant action and violence! Shortly before this, the first lambs were born on our farm.

The Prime Minister, Tony Blair, paid a visit to Carlisle to try to press a few palms and soothe the situation, but he got a nasty reception!

On the second of April, Bob rang me to tell me the awful news that one of the farmers in our pool team, Nick, had got foot and mouth at his farm and been 'taken out.' Bob got me out to the Mill Inn for a few pints. (I had to break our lock-down to go, which was risky, but my folks thought it would be good for me to get out.) Some of the other pool team members were present at the pub, but neither of the farmers were there. I got quite a few pints down me but the atmosphere was decidedly subdued and I returned home in a miserable mood.

Lambing began in earnest and there was a good crop of lambs, but it kind of felt empty. What was the point if they were all going to be culled anyway? The Sword Of Damocles was literally hanging over us!

I did quite a bit of walling in amongst the lambing work and while doing so, sighted the first swallows of the year on Saturday the twenty-first of April. This was usually an uplifting event on the farm, but this year the sight of these brave birds failed to lift the gloom.

I had been in the middle of my dental treatment all this time and a crown was due to be fitted, so the dentist came out to the farm and I met him at the lonnen gate with a chair. The kind chap fitted me with the crown as I sat on the chair. It was somewhat bizarre, but that was just one example of the lengths we were prepared to go to try and prevent the disease from getting onto the farm!

By the end of April, the progress of the foot and mouth had started to slow and there was an outcry by the tourist industry to get the footpaths on low ground opened again, to get people visiting the county again. The clamour, supported by a famous mountain climber, soon extended to the high fells. The government took notice and restrictions eventually began to be eased, but Cumbria was the last to feel the benefit of this.

Up until this point we had had it relatively easy, compared to a lot of other places anyway. There had been reports of suicides amongst the farming community around the country.

And then, just when we thought we were going to get away with it, the shit hit the fan. A nearby farm contracted the disease and they had sheep grazing on the fell adjacent to where our hoggs were being kept. These fell sheep, it was rumoured, included some fat lambs that had been bought at the infected auction mart at Longtown and had been turned out to the fell, thereby supposedly infecting the other sheep out there! Disaster was doubled for us when our close neighbour went to the fell to help the other farmer gather in these so-called infected sheep, and after he did so the authorities were said to have followed him home and then classed his farm as infected too. A cull was ordered on both farms and when it took place, we could clearly hear the sound of the humane killing bolt guns from our farm. It was most distressing!

The government vets phoned us and came to see us, as we were regarded as a dangerous contact. Dad would not let them onto the farm until our own vet came. A 'D Notice' was served on us, which I am not sure of the meaning of, but I guess it meant that unless we allowed our stock to be inspected, we would be culled out! We were terrified; we knew that baby lambs had been slaughtered all over the place and we had hundreds, never mind the adult sheep!

On Saturday the nineteenth of May, our vet came and we had to gather all the lambing ewes and their offspring into the sheep folds, where they were thoroughly checked over for signs of foot and mouth. Then the cattle were checked and afterwards, to our enormous relief, we were given a clean bill of health! It had helped that we had kept the fields clear of stock next to our boundaries, but also, the killing out of farms within three kilometres had had to be stopped because there had been a public outcry about the staggering number of uninfected stock being killed.

We were not out of the woods yet by a bit, though; there was the matter of the hundred and twenty hoggs. They were judged to be close enough to the infected area of fell to be likely to have caught the disease. The one hopefully saving grace was that apart from a narrow strip of land, the Mosedale Beck separated our land from the fell and very few sheep crossed this obstacle.

I had wrenched my shoulder badly at this point and even though I was in pain, I managed to help with the stock handling, because it was so important to me. Obviously I couldn't get to town for treatment, so Mam gave me what massage she could manage.

One of my farmer friends from near Hesket New Market phoned me and told me that they had not yet been 'taken out' and I told him we were the same. It was good to be able to talk to somebody outside the family who was in the same predicament.

On Sunday the twenty-seventh of May, the authorities came to inspect our hoggs. Our vet was present, but there were also vets from Canada and America on hand. (There were vets from all around the world working on the foot and mouth crisis!) We gathered the hoggs down into the old byre at the Lobbs farm, where they were thoroughly inspected. We had to hold the animals so that the vets could check for the tell-tale lesions between the cleats of their feet and in their mouths. One of the foreign vets, who was a bit trigger happy, thought she had found a lesion, but it turned out to be nothing. (She was probably overworked.) It was a heart-stopping moment though! Blood samples were also taken from the hoggs and then from the lambing ewes back down at the main farm. It was a nerve-wracking experience and we were worn out at the end of the day. Initial examinations did not reveal any real signs of the disease, but there was another inspection to come!

I phoned another of my Mungrisdale friends, who was also a farmer and he told me that although his farm in the village was clear of foot and mouth, he had lost six hundred sheep to the disease that were being away-wintered out near Carlisle. Also, they had been unable to let their holiday cottage, so there was no income from that. It was all very distressing news.

On Monday the fourth of June, we had our third inspection of the stock, this time by our own vet only and again we were given a clean sheet. Our vet was brilliant all through the crisis!

Strangely, the Ministry of Agriculture, Fisheries and Food (or DEFRA as it is now known) would not give us the results of the blood tests carried out on our animals unless we wrote to them. It was all very weird and smacked of a conspiracy. There were other rumours flying also; one of these was that the Lake District National Park had helped orchestrate and worsen the outbreak of the disease to get stock numbers cut on the fells. Whatever the authenticity of this, there have still never been as many sheep back on the fells, in Cumbria anyway!

Because no vehicles had been in through our farm gate, we had not yet had cause to disinfect the wheels of our, or anyone else's, vehicles, but now our agricultural supplier brought us a specialist sprayer to disinfect when we decided to venture out once more

In mid June, Dad and I started a fencing project between the two farms. Logistics were complicated by the fact that we could not use the connecting road between the two farms to ferry tools and materials to the site, because it meant going out of our farm gate into the non-disinfected area. So we had to use my quad bike and trailer to take the stuff two thirds of the way to the site via the fields, but it was not possible to get all the way because there was an unbroken stone wall and a deep ditch, blocking further vehicular progress. Consequently we had to carry everything up the last four hundred metres to the site. It was exhausting work and as the weather grew hot, the bastard horseflies (cleggs, as we call them) came out and took their share of blood out of me, in particular. The swine literally drove me mad!!

Word came in that Andrew and Tracy had split, but thankfully it was only temporary. Also, Alex had a new woman in his life! Anne's son Kevin and his wife were expecting a baby. Life was moving forward apace

On Wednesday the twenty-seventh of June, I ventured out for the first time in what seemed like ages. In the evening, I loaded my golfing gear into the Capri, disinfected the wheels and then drove out to Brayton Park near Blennerhasset, where I met Andrew and some of his other friends for fourteen holes of golf. I played particularly well, taking a few quid in side bets. Afterwards we had a couple of pints in the bar and I was feeling quite high! I talked a load of geese shite (rubbish) and was aware that Andrew was scrutinizing me quite closely! I guess this was because when I had arrived at the golf course I had been in a pretty low mood, and now suddenly I was transformed. This phenomenon, I have now learned, is known as 'rapid cycling' in the understanding of the bipolar condition.

It was great to be feeling 'up' again, though, after all the horror we had endured. After the golfing experience my mood stayed fairly high and a few days later, Bob phoned and asked me to a meeting with him, Mac and Ron at the Sportsman's Inn on the evening of the twenty-ninth of June to discuss a biking trip to Scotland. The meeting went well and we decided on the idea that we would stay at a youth hostel at Pitlochry for the first night, then take the train with our bikes up to Kingussie and cycle through the Cairngorms to Braemar, stay in a youth hostel there for a night and then cycle back out, down Glen Tilt to Pitlochry once more. Friday the sixth of July was the date set for the trip and at that point I was looking forward to it.

On the evening of Saturday the thirtieth of June, I went on a night out with Alex and Lee – a friend of his and an old golfing associate of mine – and also Angus and Anne. We had supper at the Stoneybeck Inn and then hit the drink, big style. Considering I had had little alcohol for several months, suddenly drinking a large amount was not wise, but I was feeling reckless and was undergoing an experience, post foot and mouth, which must be somewhat similar to being let out of prison! We had a few drinks with the meal and then moved into Penrith, where we trawled the pubs and then ended up in Toppers. Lee could fairly put the drink away and I tried to keep up with him, getting very drunk indeed. I was so pissed I couldn't even manage a boogie, which was unusual for me. I can also remember talking a load of geese shite to Anne towards the end of the night out.

I stayed over at my brother's after and it was nearly four a.m. when we got in.

I had a tremendous hangover next morning, on a par with the one I had at New Year!

Back on our farm once more, the cattle were still inside due to the continuing nervousness about the foot and mouth and they had to be seen to. The fencing job continued and along with it the constant battle against the cleggs. Also, although it seemed strange with the cows still in the sheds, we started haymaking.

I didn't seem to notice at the time but looking back, I can appreciate that my psychologist's analogy of the glass that was being filled with the various ingredients that would lead to a breakdown was at work. There was the recent intense stress of the foot and mouth, poor sleep and sudden excess of alcohol, just to start with, and then I was about to embark on what would be likely to be a very physically taxing bike trip to Scotland!

In short, my mood was in a raised condition!

Friday the sixth of July arrived; a red letter day! In the morning, I did some last minute routine farm work and gave Tina a run out. After lunch I loaded the Capri with my walking/cycling gear and my bike, which was newly serviced and thoroughly disinfected. At three p.m. I disinfected my car wheels at the farm gate and then drove into Penrith, where I visited my new dentist to book an appointment to have a loose filling replaced. At four p.m. I set off for Pitlochry and drove fast up the M74, M80 and A9. On the way, I decided that after the traumatic experience in the Loch Ossian youth hostel of recent times, I would steer clear of the Pitlochry hostel and get a B&B for the night. I was scheduled to meet the other members of our gang at the hostel. They would be going up under their own steam as I had no room in my car for anyone, or anything else.

Once up at Pitlochry, which is just off the A9, I cruised around looking for a B&B. I eventually found a nice place up the hill on the edge of town and it was relatively cheap at twenty-five pounds for the night. There was a nice garden at the back and the proprietors told me that if I was lucky, I would see the red squirrels that regularly visited their garden.

When I had got my stuff sorted, I went out in the car again to find a chippy. On locating one I got some nice fish and chips, ate them in the car and then found the supermarket, where I bought some supplies. These included four five hundred millilitre bottles of the fine real ale, Old Speckled Hen!

After I had stocked up and asked the checkout lady where I could find the youth hostel, I followed her instructions and drove up the hill to find the hostel, which was just a few streets away from my B&B. I parked up and went inside to find that Bob, Mac and Ron had arrived and were busying themselves with the preparation of their evening meal. When I told Bob I was staying in a B&B, he immediately went into a strange mood. He told me that the hostel was very busy and therefore he had had difficulty in getting the four of us in there. Now I was telling him I had bailed out, and he was not best pleased! I told the gang I had eaten, but that I would spend a few hours with them after their meal to iron out some of the fine details of the expedition on the morrow.

Following their meal, the discussion began and we agreed that we would not be breaking the law by cycling anywhere that was still under the foot and mouth restrictions. (Bob had made enquiries as to this.) Things had eased first in Scotland, concerning access to the mountain and moorland areas. All went well until we started discussing unrelated topics, one of which was Bob asking me what I thought about secret societies. I would not be drawn on the subject and began to feel decidedly uncomfortable. Bob was needling me and I didn't like it; in fact, it was freaking me out! I got up suddenly and said, "I'll see you at the train station at eight thirty-five a.m.," and with that I left them to it. The events of the evening had left me feeling paranoid (IT WAS BEGINNING ONCE MORE!) and I drove back to my B&B in a grim mood. From that point on, I christened the other members of our group the 'Three Wise Monkeys' (3.W.M.).

Back at the B&B in my room, I cracked open two of the bottles of Old Speckled Hen and glugged them down, before retiring at eleven p.m.

Saturday the seventh of July. I was up at six a.m. after a disturbed sleep and I went for a walk in the garden, where I did indeed see the squirrels. I had a nice Scottish breakfast, packed my gear, paid the bill and then drove to the railway station. The 3.W.M.s were there already, having cycled to the station from the hostel. I told them I would drive to Kingussie and join them there. I was still feeling paranoid and had begun to distrust the others; it was as if a barrier had gone up between us! Without any more ado, I rushed off to my car. The train was in the station and I knew I would have to get my foot down if I wanted to arrive in Kingussie at the same time as the others. I had approximately a hundred and six kilometres (sixty-six miles) to cover and the driving conditions weren't ideal; there were intermittent light showers!

I set off from the railway car park and quickly got out of Pitlochry. Once out on the A9 and heading north I put my foot down. The showers kept slicking up the windscreen, but there was not much traffic and I pushed the big Capri hard, sometimes at speeds approaching a hundred miles per hour. The railway ran alongside the road and at intervals I glanced across to the left to catch sight of the train, which must have been doing sixty to seventy m.p.h. I got held up a couple of times by traffic on the two-way stretches of the road, but forged ahead on the dual carriageway sections. Christ, it was exciting!

I arrived in Kingussie, just ahead of the train and parked next to the toilet block in the big car park behind the Duke of Gordon Hotel. I was able to get my bike, complete with its panniers plus my medium sized rucksack out of the car, lock up and cycle down to the train station before the others came looking for me. I found them just getting their gear together near the platform.

As I approached, Mac in particular gave me a piercing look and then he said, "Bloody hell, how did you get here before us? Do you know how difficult it is to race a train to a given point, in a car?"

I replied, "Yes, it's difficult, but I have just done it, haven't I?"

"Yes," he snapped, "but you must have been exceeding the speed limit!"

I just grinned and left it at that. (Mac was of course still a speed cop, but he had no jurisdiction up here). There would be no more grinning from that point on!

After this little exchange I received grim looks off Bob and Ron, too.

Then it was time to set off into the mountains. It was nine forty-five a.m. as we departed eastwards across the railway tracks on the road to Feshiebridge. We were all pretty much laden down with gear; even Bob had a couple of panniers, him not normally being known to carry much stuff!

The showers had cleared up for the time being and it had got out into quite a pleasant day as we passed the old Ruthven Barracks. We rode on for several miles on the level, heading for the northern end of Glen Feshie. I just followed where the others led, though I had a map myself. Presently Bob called a halt and got his map out to take a look, to see if we could take a short cut across a low, forested fell and access the glen quicker. It was plain that this plan could work and we set off once more, again eastwards, leaving the road at a place where there was a break in the trees. We all had off-road bikes, but the going soon became tortuous, with soft ground and old tree branches underfoot. We fought on uphill for what seemed like miles, before we got to the top of the low fell and started to drop down the other side into Glen Feshie. I was feeling the pace and was glad of the downhill going. We got down onto the floor of the valley and hit the road coming from Feshiebridge. Riding south along it, we passed several fairly new properties and then we crossed the River Feshie, thereby exchanging the tarmac road for a gravel track, which took us on south on fairly level going.

Time seemed to slow for me. I was tired and hungry and as the miles passed I became more and more disenchanted with the whole idea of this trip. The track deteriorated into a rough path and we began to climb from the quite bonny glen, with its scattered Caledonian Pines, out onto high moorland. The weather closed in, bringing mist and rain. The crack was already subdued, but now it became non-existent as we forged on across peaty ground. Just as the way turned east again we came across an old shack, where we stopped for something to eat. Little was said and I kept myself to myself. I was starting to feel decidedly weird, alongside my paranoia. I looked at my map and saw that we had reached a height of approximately five hundred and forty metres (one thousand seven hundred and seventy-one feet). Visibility was poor and although I was trying to distance myself from the others, I was glad in a way that they were there. I would have had difficulty navigating this terrain alone!

We set off again and the land levelled out. The ground became boggier, forcing us to wheel our bikes over the worst areas. Eventually we encountered the Geldie Burn and I'm sure that by this point, we were all thoroughly soaked to the skin with perspiration and by the nagging, driving rain. If we had not kept moving, we surely would have quickly become chilled!

We had passed the watershed and the Geldie Burn flowed down towards Whitebridge and into the River Dee. We followed this water course and soon struck a well-surfaced gravel track, taking us on east. Another old shack appeared out of the gloom and the others stopped here to do something with one of their bikes. I rode on and encountering a very straight, slightly downhill stretch of track, a sudden desire to make a break for freedom came over me. I accelerated and shifted the bike up into top gear. Finding energy I didn't know I had, I flew down the track and kept going until I was 'blowing out of my arse!'

I heard a noise behind me and looked round to see Bob, hard on my back wheel. His grinning face unnerved me and he said, "Where the hell do you think you're going? We have to stick together, you know!" My sudden exhilaration evaporated, leaving me deflated. I stopped, got off my bike and sat down on the side of the track, with my head in my hands. Bob got off his bike and sat next to me, but said nothing more.

Presently Mac and Ron rode up and Mac said, "Is everything okay?"

I issued the outburst, "Yes everything is fucking brilliant, thank you!" But of course, it was far from it. Feeling angry suddenly, I snatched up my bike, mounted and with the words, "Let's get this fucking show on the road again, shall we?" I rode off towards the Linn of Dee. Riding at a much more sensible pace, I was well aware that the others were right behind me as we continued on to Whitebridge and joined the River Dee, where it flowed down out from the high pass to the north, known as the Lairig Ghru. Another six point four kilometres (four miles) saw us reach the Linn of Dee and there we found tarmac again. It was eleven point two kilometres (seven miles) of hard up and down riding in the constant rain before we reached Braemar.

I was now beyond caring and almost exhausted. We had ridden some fifty kilometres (thirty miles) over some very difficult terrain and I was cleaned out!

We cycled through Braemar Village and found the youth hostel on the southern outskirts. It was a big rambling place with quite a large garden. I had little option but to follow Bob inside. He was rushing around organising us, not unlike a strutting rooster shepherding his flock of hens! We checked in, and even in my numb/paranoid condition I was able to produce my Scottish Youth Hostels loyalty card.

Strange forces were at work within me; the rational, reliable and honest side of me was warring with the uncontrolled and angry side. In short, I was in turmoil!

Bob led the way to our dormitory after we had checked in. It was quite large, sleeping about ten people, and it was nearly full. I felt claustrophobic and wasted no time in getting my gear sorted. There was a good shower/toilet room in the dormitory and I took a quick shower while it was relatively empty. After this I put some fresh clothes on, from the two panniers I had brought in. The contents of these had remained dry due to the good quality rain covers I had put over them. However, I only had one set of footwear -- the heavy-duty trainers, and these were soaked. There seemed little point in putting a dry pair of socks on in them, so I went without.

Bob was trying his best to coax me out of my shell and he asked me if I would give him a hand to make supper. I however was in no mood for 'niggle naggle' and said sharply, "I'm going out!" So I grabbed my coat and went out into the evening air. It was drying up again and looked promising for the morrow, but I daren't think about what the coming day had in store for me. The urge to get out and away from the others was stalking me! I walked into the large village and found a nice chippy, where I waited patiently for my ordered fish and chips. I was on my own again and started to relax a bit.

I ate my nice meal at the single table available and then continued on down the street. I was searching for a good pub and found a popular public bar at one of the larger hotels.

A thirst was upon me and I got stuck into a good quality ale, drinking four pints in rapid succession. There was a tipsy, obviously single, older woman at the bar and she sidled over to me. She started chatting me up and she was not unattractive. On another day, I might have gone for it, but I was in a fragile condition, so on downing my fourth pint, I made my excuses and slipped away back to the hostel at eleven p.m.

On entering the building, I found the others (I will stop calling them the three wise monkeys now because it really is unkind) sitting drinking Stella Artois in the lounge. They were engaged in animated conversation and didn't seem to notice me standing in the room, so I slipped away to bed.

Sunday the eighth of July. I was up at six thirty a.m. and felt I had slept well in the crowded dormitory. It must have been the alcohol that had knocked me out and I was grateful for it. I packed up all my gear and noticed that the others were up and about too, but there was little interplay between us.

Breakfast was made in the spacious kitchen, but the bacon and eggs tasted strange. (Bob had bought some groceries at a nearby shop the previous evening.) This should have been a severe warning to me that one of the other symptoms of my condition was emerging; I was going off my food!

Again conversation was stilted, but we managed to get ourselves ready for the ride back to Pitlochry. Mac had been missing for a time, just before breakfast and in my continuing paranoid state, I thought he had been off liaising with the local police. To what end? I don't know.

We loaded up our bikes in the dry/fine conditions and rode away from the hostel at nine fifteen a.m., heading westward, retracing our route of the previous evening. I was feeling tremendously energised and from the rear, I slowly began to overtake the others. I found myself in the lead and gradually I began to stretch it out, until the point where I looked back to find there was nobody behind me. Suddenly the urge to make a clean break for it came over me and I pedalled even faster. The River Dee flowed not two hundred metres on my right and finding a large stand of pine trees coming up on that side I turned off the road and plunged into the trees. I rode through the relatively open woodland for a hundred metres or so and then hopped off my bike and dived behind the trunk of a large Caledonian pine tree, which gave me cover from the nearby road. I peeped around the tree trunk and shortly I saw the others riding on past. When I was sure they had gone on by, I picked up my bike and wheeled it on through the trees, towards the river. A great sense of relief flowed through me; I had got away from the others. Now all I had to do was make good my escape!

I came to the river bank and contemplated the swirling, brown water. The Dee at this point was more than fifty metres wide and there was no bridge. (I had not yet reached the bridge at the Linn of Dee.) However, the water didn't look very deep and the river bed looked gravelly, so bravely I wheeled my trusty bike down the bank and entered the flow. I was soon up over my knees and the swift current tugged at me. The bike gave me stability as I wheeled it alongside and I slowly picked my way across. I made it to the opposite bank and climbed it, at the same time breathing a sigh of relief!

I got my map out and located my approximate position. Then I plotted a route through to join the valley, which led to the Lairig Ghru pass. I had no intention of heading back for Glen Feshie and I worked out that the Lairig Ghru would take me through to Loch Morlich and then on to the A9 and back to my car at Kingussie. It was obviously a very long way, but I tried not to think about that, at that point.

Once I had forded the river I found a good, fairly level track that took me through Glen Lui in a north-westerly direction to Derry Lodge, where there was presumably a hunting lodge of some description. I was able to ride the track and make good time. My mood began to become more rational again and I started to enjoy myself.

I passed Derry Lodge, which was partially obscured by trees and then the track petered out into a rough path. The gradient began to increase as I swung more westwards and I was forced to dismount and wheel the bike. I stopped and got out my brick of a mobile phone, with the idea I would call home and let my folks know I was okay. When I switched it on, though, it displayed the message, 'not allowed', which I thought was strange and I got it into my head that it meant that you were not allowed to use mobile phones here because of the proximity of Balmoral Castle. Looking back now, the message would simply mean there was no signal!

As I climbed, the country opened out and I was soon entering the 'U' shaped valley than ran south to north towards the Lairig Ghru. I descended into this valley and turned north to once more join the River Dee. The path here was well worn and some sections were rideable. I made good progress with the river to my left. Also on that side, across the river was the impressive, towering peak of the Devil's Point at a thousand and four metres (three thousand two hundred and ninety-four feet). This is a Munro and one which I have not yet climbed.

I entered the Lairig Ghru and forged on north, climbing gradually. I had seen few other people up to that point, but now I spied a lone figure coming towards me down the path. We met at a place where I had stopped to examine an area where the rocks seemed to have been thrown around and smashed. Two Tornado jets had recently crashed near Ben Macdui, which was just east of where I stood, and I wondered if the disturbed ground had something to do with that.

The figure revealed itself to be a woman about forty years old and she was quite attractive. Naturally we stopped for a crack, as lone travellers are apt to do in the Highlands. She was fully decked out in good quality hiking gear and as we talked, she told me that her husband had dropped her near Loch Morlich in the north and she was walking through to the Linn of Dee, where her husband would pick her up again, having driven around via Braemar. She had obviously come over the Lairig Ghru and I asked her what it was like up there, telling her I was heading over it to join the A9. Her eyes widened as she heard my plan outlined.

She said, "You are a brave man, taking a bike up there. It's very rough going and you will certainly have to wheel it, and maybe even carry it some of the way!"

She eyed my panniers and rucksack, rolling her eyes. She must have thought; this daft bugger is mad. Little did she know; I was mad!

We wished each other well and went our separate ways. As I flogged on up the pass, I felt the presence of the mighty Ben Macdui at one thousand three hundred and nine metres (four thousand two hundred and ninety-four feet) above me to the right. I ate little; in fact, I can't remember having much in the way of supplies with me anyway, which was not normal. I gave the occasional thought towards the others, who must by now have realized that I had taken off. But I wasn't bothered really, things had become impossible with them and it was better for both parties that I was out on my own.

As I approached the top of the pass, the 'U' shaped valley tightened in even further and the mountains pressed in from either side. The source of the River Dee was up here and I soon came to the Pools of Dee, which are three small lochains, one after the other. In one of the pools, I could clearly see what appeared to be a piece of a wrecked aircraft. As I skirted these crystal clear pools, the going became very difficult indeed. I had entered a boulder field and as the lady had told me, I had to pick the bike up, complete with panniers, and carry it on my shoulder over this daunting obstacle. It was hair-raising stuff as I stepped from one boulder to the next and I was extremely glad of the fine, dry, benign conditions. Each of the gaps between the boulders could easily have broken my leg if I had fallen, but I did not and once more I could almost feel the presence of my Guardian Angel as I tip-toed through the boulders like a mountain goat.

I got through this nightmare area and reached the summit of the Lairig Ghru, the height of which I am not sure of, but it must be around eight hundred and thirty-five metres (two thousand seven hundred and thirty-nine feet). From here I could see out towards Loch Morlich and it seemed a long way off, but undaunted, I set off towards it down the well-used path. It was some time and distance before I came to a stretch of path that was safe enough to ride my bike again. I was tired but in good spirits and felt able to pass the time of day with the occasional group of walkers I encountered.

Eventually I got down out of the mountains, into the flat forest area around Loch Morlich, which is known as being an area that the Commandos trained in during WW2. There were good, well-surfaced tracks here and I made my way swiftly out onto the road between Aviemore and the Cairngorm Ski Centre.

Once out onto the tarmac, I was soon at the roundabout at the southern end of Aviemore and here I found a pub. It was busy but I was able to get a pint of Carlsberg lager and find a seat. I had a hell of a thirst on and the first pint hardly touched the sides. It was swiftly followed by two more and then it was time to get moving as it was getting late. I would have to be quick getting down the last stretch to Kingussie, if I wanted to get a bed for the night. I set off south, initially on the A9, but there was a lot of traffic and I soon abandoned it for the B9152, which ran alongside the A9 but was much quieter. Buoyed up by the alcohol, I pushed myself and the bike hard to cover the nineteen point three kilometres (twelve miles) between Aviemore and Kingussie. Halfway there I ran out of steam and ate some chocolate I had bought at the pub. This sustained me for the last leg and I arrived in Kingussie at about nine p.m.; thus it had taken me about twelve hours to travel from Braemar, an approximate distance of fifty-six point three kilometres (thirty-five miles). I parked my bike outside the Duke of Gordon Hotel and enquired within to check availability of accommodation, but the hotel was full. The receptionist told me to try over the road at the Osprey guest house, so over I went and luckily there was a room available. There was car parking at the back so I left my bike and gear at the back door of the Osprey and walked round to the big car park behind the Duke to bring my car to the Osprey. Once I had got myself sorted, I used the en-suite facilities to get a shave and a bath. When I had got cleaned up, I cracked open the last two bottles of my stash of Old Speckled Hen and wrote up my diary. Remarkably, I managed to keep doing this to catalogue events!

There was a funny smell in my room, but otherwise it was good accommodation. I got into bed and before I nodded off, I thought through the events of the day. I was glad I had got away from the others and then kind of proud that I had come through the Lairig Ghru unscathed. Christ, it was higher than the nearest mountain to our farm, Clough Head. The feeling that somebody was watching over me had been strong. Perhaps that was because the previous evening, I had found a church on the way back from that bar to the hostel and as the door had been open, I had gone in and said my prayers!

I had, however, not eaten anything substantial all day. I was running on raw nervous energy and adrenalin, plus the alcohol I had consumed near the end of the day. It was a recipe for disaster!!

I tried to sleep but it was a hell of a struggle and I awoke on Monday the ninth of July having probably only had a couple of hours of sleep. I packed up my gear and went down to join the other guests at breakfast. A nice looking Scottish breakfast was put before me but I had little appetite and only picked at the food; in fact I was suspicious of it. Perhaps there was something in it that would harm me. This was of course ridiculous, but the paranoia was in me again. I left the meal virtually untouched and left the table. The staff were busy making breakfasts and were a little disgruntled when I asked to pay the bill and check out. I loaded my gear into the Capri and drove off south to Newtonmore and then took the A86 to Spean Bridge. I drove steadily and sensibly, almost mechanically, but inside I was again in turmoil. Strange, ridiculous thoughts and emotions raced through my head. As had happened in the other episodes, it was me against the world and I felt hunted!

I drove on through Fort William and down to the Ballachulish Bridge, crossed it and took the A828 coast road south towards Oban. Before I got to Oban, though, I was passing through a village when I experienced a terrible hallucination. Any people I saw had pigs' faces, with vicious-looking tusks. It scared me to death!

I was shaken by this, obviously, and instead of going on into Oban I turned east onto the A85 and then something else happened to scare me even more. The car bonnet catch sprang and the bonnet popped up slightly. Fortunately the second catch caught it, or it would have blown back over the windscreen. I nearly had a bloody heart attack and quickly pulled over to get out and re-catch the bonnet. In my paranoid state, I thought somebody back at Kingussie had fiddled with it, to deliberately cause an accident.

Things settled down a bit after that and most of the rest of the journey back home was uneventful. I took the usual route back past Stirling, but I didn't stop at the services for something to eat; my appetite had gone completely. I drove on down the M80, M73 and M74, but as I was approaching Carlisle I turned off to drive through Longtown, which had reputedly been one of the sources of the foot and mouth outbreak. Part of me was still operating normally and I was curious to see what things were like in the worst affected areas.

Driving through the little town, things appeared to be normal, but as I left Longtown and headed south I drove through a landscape devoid of livestock!

I headed on through Carlisle and took the A595 towards west Cumbria. I passed Wigton and took one of the minor roads to Caldbeck and here the fields were again empty.

When I got home, I learned that Dad was out hay baling, so rather mechanically I offloaded my gear, got changed and went to help. Angus, Anne and Heather arrived soon after and I immediately came under scrutiny. Together we stacked the hay bales in the front fields and questions were fired at me, to find out what had happened in Scotland and how I was feeling. This was obviously because Bob would have got back and told my family that I had taken off. In my paranoid state, though, I was reluctant to tell the tale of what had happened and later, when I was attaching the bale carrier to the tractor, my sister came to me and pleaded with me to go to the hospital. There were tears in her eyes, but I remained unaffected and did not heed her advice!

We led (brought in) and stacked the bales on one of the lofts until about ten thirty p.m., during which time I was unapproachable and then angry when anyone tried. I went to bed and tried to sleep, but I was up again about three a.m.

Tuesday the tenth of July. Up in the early hours, I packed my rucksack, put on my hiking boots and without eating anything I set off, south from the farm. I had given Tina little thought, as well as everyone else since I got back and fortunately, I didn't take her with me on this particular jaunt. Even though my stomach was empty I seemed to have plenty of energy, so was obviously in a very manic state.

I headed due south, up out of our land and onto Matterdale Common. Then without any real idea of direction I headed on south, up Great Dodd, over the other Dodds, then Raise and then over Helvellyn, Nethermost Pike and Dollywagon. By this point, the weather had closed in and it was a foul morning. There was a stiff south west wind blowing, the mist was down and it was raining! I was soon thoroughly soaked and had to keep going to stay warm.

I headed down to Grisedale Tarn and then west out to the A591 at Dunmail Raise. It was warmer down here, thank God, but it was still raining and I sought shelter in the little A.A. emergency phone box by the side of the road. The idea came to me that I would head for my grandpa's place down in Kent, so before I got into the A.A. box I checked the bus timetable on the board nearby, to see when I could get a bus to Lancaster, from where I could get a train on south. The buses ran every hour, so I waited patiently in my dripping clothes, which wet the floor of the box. I kept the box door ajar so that I could watch for a bus coming over the raise from the north.

Eventually a double decker appeared and I went out to flag it down. I boarded, bought a ticket for Lancaster and then took a seat on the lower deck. The water from my soaking clothes puddled at my feet and then ran down the aisle. The other passengers eyed me with suspicion, but I tried to ignore them. Even though I was wet, the bus was warm and I began to thaw out, even managing to doze a bit as the bus headed south to Kendal and then Lancaster.

Once in Lancaster, I sought out the railway station and bought a ticket for London. I can't remember exactly how much it cost, but it would have been in excess of fifty pounds! I waited patiently for a train, but then when one came I failed to board it and just went out of the station and made my way up to the castle, where I sat on the castle lawns amongst dozens of other people. The rain had cleared now I'd got out of the Lake District and it was sunny and hot. I spread my rain gear out on the grass to dry, and my other clothes dried on me. After dozing for a bit and getting my clothes dry I headed down into the city and drifted into an antique shop, where I kind of browsed around like any other potential customer.

It was like there were two different beings inside me. On the one hand, there was the paranoid, terrified person and on the other was the rational, calm person, just going about his everyday business.

I had caught the eye of the shop owner and, worried that I might damage something by knocking it over with the rucksack on my back, she asked me to leave. So I did as I was asked and started to head back north again, having by now abandoned all plans to go to Kent!

I walked out of Lancaster and crossed a bridge over the River Lune. Turning right I headed north east and followed the river until I came to what I thought was Kirkby Lonsdale (looking at the map of the area now, I must have been mistaken). It was here that I hid myself away for several hours, in a large culvert under a road. I had my diary with me and I must have kept it in a plastic bag to keep it dry at the time, because I am reading from it as I write this, and it is undamaged. This is some of what I wrote in it that day: 'This is a hell of a time; I'm writing this tucked up in a nettle bed, next to a bridge in Kirkby Lonsdale. There is evil all around and I only just got out of Lancaster. I think it's Tuesday, but I'm that tired I hardly know, I've been on the run so long. I'll wait until dusk to make my next move and hope meantime that I remain undiscovered. Weather is fine with normal spells for a bit and then there is very heavy weird showers, it's warmish.'

The reader will be able, I hope, to appreciate the level of instability in my mind at the time, from the kind of things I have just detailed.

I didn't stay put in that culvert until dusk though, rather I got up and continued back north, sometimes on the roadside and sometimes across country, until I came to Carnforth, where I found a kind of Travelodge in the middle of the town. I took a room here and tried to tidy myself up by getting a shave (a wet one) from the razor I had bought at a nearby chemist's, and a bath, but it took enormous effort. In a sense, I was trying to fight what was happening to me.

There was a restaurant attached to the establishment and after I had got cleaned up, I ordered a meal there and tried to eat it, but was only able to get half of it down. I had paid for the accommodation up front by debit card; this I had also used to buy the train ticket in Lancaster, so as well as everything else, I was spending money indiscriminately! After my attempted meal I went to bed and tried to sleep again, but was only partially successful.

Wednesday the eleventh of July. Once again, I was up in the very early hours and after packing up my rucksack I left the Travelodge by a back door and set off up the A6.

It was still dark when I came across an articulated lorry parked in a layby. My feet were hurting and I guess I was looking for transport, so I climbed onto the footrest below the passenger side door and looked in. I assumed the driver was asleep inside and fearing his wrath if awoken, I got back down and trudged on.

I arrived in Milnthorpe (home of the Milnthorpe Bachelors' Society, which was fitting for me) and this is where events took a very serious turn. On exiting the village, I came across a little, isolated cottage and outside it, a little red VW Polo was parked. It must have been around five a.m. because it was certainly daylight, but the occupants of the house were not yet astir. Something made me stop at the car; maybe it was sheer exhaustion, I don't know. But I found myself checking to see if the little car was locked; it wasn't. I opened the driver's door and checked the ignition for keys, but there were none there. There was, however, what looked like a house key in the little alcove behind the gear lever. I picked it up and walked to the front door of the cottage and tried the key in the lock; it fitted. I unlocked the door, opened it and walked into the living room. There was nobody about, but lying on the coffee table were the car keys. I took them, went back out, re-locking the front door as I went and put my rucksack in the back of the car. I got in the driver's seat, put the keys in the ignition and started the car. It fired up eagerly and I wasted no time in driving off before I was discovered. There were shades of some of the things I had done in Switzerland in 1994 developing!

I quickly got the hang of the gearbox in the little car and drove east towards the M6, with the plan in mind to drive home. I got to the motorway, but I took the southbound carriageway by mistake and I had driven some miles before I realized I had gone wrong. Luckily there was a service area not far ahead and I then pulled in there. Up until then I hadn't noticed the fuel gauge level, but now I saw that the needle was in the red, so I pulled up at the petrol pumps. Now I was faced with a quandary; was the car a diesel or a petrol? And if it was a petrol, did it use leaded or unleaded fuel? My own car used leaded fuel but it was older than this one. I got out and walked round the back to see if anything was written there to solve my problem, but there was nothing there, other than the make and model plates. I made an educated guess and plumped for unleaded fuel. I put ten pounds' worth of fuel in from the pump with the green hose and went to pay – again by debit card.

I was somewhere near Garstang, so I had a bit to go to get back home and I hoped that I had put enough fuel in to get me there. The weather was cloudy, but dry and quiet as I pulled out of the service area and located the northbound carriageway. I drove steadily, keeping to the speed limit. The law would be after me soon enough, but perhaps I could just get home and then take it from there.

I got home, unmolested by the police, at nine a.m. and parked the little Polo on the grass verge just below the farm gate. I got my gear out, locked the car and walked up to the farm. I even remembered to dunk my boots in the disinfectant bath at the farm gate as I went in. Once in the house, I went straight upstairs and ran myself a bath. After I had bathed I went to bed and I must have slept to some extent. Five hours later I got up, got dressed and went down to the kitchen, where I managed to eat a light lunch. Mam and Dad were there and asked me many questions. They were obviously worried, bless them, but I was off in another world and avoided their enquiries. After I had eaten I put my rucksack together again, this time with my electric shaver in it, got my own car keys, having left the Polo keys in the back kitchen, and went out to load the Capri up with the rucksack, my bike and this time, Tina, who was bright eyed, bushy tailed and pleased to see me.

The recent sleep had refreshed me somewhat and I was feeling sociable, so after driving out to the farm gate and disinfecting my car I drove across to Mungrisdale to visit one of my farmer friends. My reception was somewhat strange, as you might expect; the foot and mouth was still at large and I was probably being perceived as behaving strangely by others, and correctly so. After a rather stilted conversation, I left their farm and drove to Motherby. During the short journey I thought about the visit to my farmer friend and realized it had not gone well, concluding that it was he who was behaving strangely!

At Motherby I got the Capri filled up with fuel at my regular petrol station and I had a crack with the owners, to whom I am related. Again it was a strange conversation and I remember thinking that the foot and mouth had driven everybody mad. This was probably true in a lot of cases!

I drove off and headed into Penrith and then out towards Carlisle on the A6, but when I was approaching the roundabout over the M6 I saw a sign, which I probably mistakenly read as 'motorway closed', so I turned around and went back south for a mile or so and then turned east towards Cotehill. I headed through the back roads and turned north towards the A69. I was driving through the area that had been most heavily devastated by the foot and mouth. On a whim, I pulled over on the roadside and got out of the car. There were fields and woods all around but they were empty of all life. I switched the car engine off and listened. There was total silence, not a single bird was singing. It was as if the countryside had been wiped out, and it had been, to all intents and purposes! It was eerie and scary, and I wasted no time in getting back in the car and driving on.

I found my way out to the A69 and drove east to Haltwhistle. Here I took a road out of town northwards, but my progress was halted by the level crossing on the railway being closed. My paranoia was suddenly back and I thought the authorities were trying to stop me getting out of Cumbria. I turned around and drove back to the A69, turned east again, drove for a few miles and then turned off northwards again. This time I crossed the railway by a bridge and drove on for some time. Presently I found myself at the Kielder Reservoir and I pulled onto one of the car parks, where I let Tina out for a run. She rushed around, shaking her back end and then she did a shit, which I kicked into the long grass. Tina always seemed to sense when I was in distress and did her best to try and cheer me up, thus I valued her company immensely.

From Kielder, I drove on north (funny how this was the direction I mainly seemed to be heading in when unwell) through southern Scotland, eventually arriving in Edinburgh, where I found the traffic light system and road signs difficult to master, so I got the hell out of there and headed on north over the Forth Road Bridge. On I went up through Dundee and onto the A90 to Aberdeen. Time seemed to blur and from here on (at least for a while anyway) I lost track of the days, but my diary is still full of information, which complements my memory.

In Aberdeen, I drove round the hospital and found a freshly run over, relatively undamaged rabbit, which I got into the car and kept to feed Tina with later. Her trust in me with the car had been reinstated after that incident racing down the A6 towards Kendal in late 1997 and now, as I drove sensibly, she remained unperturbed in the back of the car.

I left Aberdeen and continued on north to Frazerburgh, where I got out and walked around the harbour, with Tina on her chain. There were many redundant fishing boats there and it was a rather depressing sight. When I got back to the car, I gave Tina the dead rabbit and she crunched it down herself.

From this point I couldn't go north or I would have ended up in the Moray Firth, so I turned west to Inverness and then, exhaustingly, on north west, all the way out nearly to the fishing port of Kinlochbervie on the north west coast of Scotland. I turned around and went back all the way to Edinburgh, where I tried to get accommodation, but was unsuccessful, so I headed back north west to Kincardine, where I found a Travelodge that accepted pets and had a room. It cost forty-nine pounds and I again paid by debit card up front. The room was pretty ordinary, but it was somewhere to crash for a bit. Again I tried to sort myself out by getting a shave, a bath and a bit of kip, but I was really beyond reason and was literally like a metronome; I kept going and going!

I left the Travelodge in the early hours and headed north to Braemar, where I arrived at the same hotel that I had enjoyed a few pleasant drinks in previously. I parked up and went into the dining room, where I politely enquired about buying some breakfast. A nice waiter told me it was a little unusual but he would see what he could do. After a short wait, the waiter came back and sat me at one of the tables, where I was served with a nice

Scottish breakfast. I had by now attracted the attention of the other guests and they were giving me quizzical looks. I became nervous and after I had only eaten half the breakfast I signalled the waiter. He came over and I asked to pay by card, at the same time apologising for not finishing my meal. I was able to pay by debit card again and then I hightailed it out of there, got in my car and drove out of the village, heading east on the A93 towards Balloch.

I had not gone far; however, when looking in the rear view mirror, I saw a small black car come tearing up behind me. I could clearly see the driver and his face was a mask of concentration. He pushed his car right up behind me and I became annoyed and touched the brakes. My red brake lights suddenly coming on must have given him a shock because he backed off for a bit. He was soon back on my tail though, and then we came to a straight section of road and he pulled out to overtake, without signalling. I was having none of this, so when he got alongside I accelerated. The powerful Capri leapt forward and we went down the straight side by side. His car was obviously quite powerful as well and he kept pace. There was a sharp right hand corner coming up though and seeing he was not going to get past in time, the young buck backed off and pulled back in behind me. I slowed down, took the corner and ahead I saw a layby on the left. I braked hard and shot into it. The young buck nearly ran into the back of me, but then went on down the road, flicking two fingers up at me as he went. I did a U-turn in the road and drove back to Braemar, feeling annoyed and het up, along with everything else.

I drove on through Braemar and headed south on down towards the Glen Shee Ski Centre. Again, I had not gone far when I came upon a car travelling quite slowly in the same direction as me. I signalled to overtake on a straight and pulled into the right hand lane to do so. Suddenly the car moved into the middle of the road and blocked my manoeuvre. I followed for a bit and the other car stayed in the middle of the road. Obviously there was nothing coming the other way at this point. I again indicated and pulled across to the right but this had no effect. I sounded my horn but again there was no response, so I carefully drove right up behind the car and purposely nudged it with my front bumper. The driver responded immediately and pulled over to the left. I went past slowly and stared across at the driver, who was a woman; her face was as white as a sheet, she must have nearly wet herself when I nudged her car!

I drove on thinking that Braemar was not as nice a place as I thought – there were obviously some idiots living there! Then I very nearly became an idiot myself. I was heading down a straight, just before the ascent to the ski centre and coming down the road towards me was a large truck. As we drew closer, I took my hands off the steering wheel for a second to fiddle with something in the car, thereby taking my eye off the road. When I looked up, I had drifted across the centre line, the truck driver was frantically flashing his headlights at me and preparing to take evasive action. I grabbed the wheel and regained control just as the truck flashed past! This incident panicked me and after driving over the pass, past the ski centre, I resolved to get the hell off this road before I killed myself.

Then after a couple more miles and unable to find somewhere to pull off, I met another vehicle, this time a pickup and something strange happened. The driver was frantically pointing to my side of the road! I took this to mean he wanted me to turn off to my side as soon as possible; perhaps the police were coming! Anyway, I found a little lane going off to the left shortly after and I turned into it. It led up to a croft and nearby was an open fronted, modern barn. There was an empty bay in the barn and I drove the Capri into it, parking it next to some large fertilizer bags. I quickly got my hiking gear on, letting Tina out, who rushed about ecstatically, but I left the bike in the car. Then I locked the car and left it to the supposed care of the farmer. It was no more use to me at that moment; if I had kept driving I surely would have died, or worse still, killed somebody else!

From the barn I climbed over a wall and fled up onto the hillside; the hunted feeling was upon me again and I feared the law would descend on me at any moment!

I walked for hours, up hill and down dale in a roughly northerly direction, with Tina gambolling along happily beside me. I began to approach the Glen Shee ski area and climbed the steep southern flank of a mountain to the east of the ski centre. It must have been Glas Maol, which is a Munro and stands at a thousand and sixty-eight metres (three thousand five hundred and four feet) high. There were definitely the pylons of a ski tow on its northern side, so it must have been Glas Maol that I was on, and remains the most unorthodox Munro that I have climbed. It was here that I saw the most amazing thing, and to this day I don't know if it was real or another hallucination. I was just approaching the summit when I caught sight of a mountain hare and as I walked on there was another and another, until I was surrounded by hares. There must have been around fifty and they were all in their brown summer coats (they turn white in winter). They seemed to pay Tina and me little heed; perhaps they were used to being around the many skiers up here in the winter. I think Tina fancied her chances at getting a quick meal and tried to snatch one of the wily creatures, but they were way too quick for her!

It was an extraordinary experience. I felt privileged to have witnessed the sight of so many hares together in one place; you are lucky if you catch sight of more than one hare at a time in the Scottish mountains! I was lifted by it and for a little while things seemed almost normal, and then the despair descended on me again, accompanied by the paranoia. I was descending north from 'Hare Mountain,' as I nicknamed it, when I spied a white helicopter coming south above the nearby A93. Thinking it was a police helicopter, looking for me, I dived for cover behind a rock. The machine went on past to the west of me without altering its course though, and I got up and continued on down the grassy slope, which then became heather-covered.

It was at that point that I hit a wall, physically and mentally, that is. I had literally run out of gas! I stumbled and fell in the tangling heather and I couldn't get up again. I lay there exhausted and Tina came over and licked my face, perhaps trying to comfort me. The weather was dry and relatively warm and I dropped off to sleep.

I awoke some hours later, feeling stiff and abused. It was getting late in the day and I realized that I would be out here all night unless I got going. My survival instincts were the only thing that kept me going. I nibbled on a bit of emergency chocolate and pushed myself wearily to my feet. Off I went unsteadily and Tina fell in step beside me, she must have taken the opportunity to get a rest as well. As I went on down into a valley that ran out towards the north west, some measure of energy began to flow back into me and I strode forth with more purpose.

I made my way out of the valley and came to the A93 once more. I was fading in and out of psychosis, sometimes suspicious and paranoid and sometimes quite rational. I was in the rational state when, as I was walking north beside the road towards Braemar again, a green Land Rover pulled up and a kind farmer gave me and Tina a lift to the village. I told him I was going to the youth hostel, so he dropped me outside it.

I went in cautiously and asked if I could stay. The woman on reception said, "Yes, there is a bed for you, but you will have to leave your dog tied up outside!"

This was not a very satisfactory state of affairs and later I did something about it. I got a shave and shower and then feeling more normal I went out to the same bar I had visited previously and had a pint. This was not a good idea!

It must have been around eleven p.m. when I got back to the hostel and there being nobody still up, I moved Tina from her chained up position next to the front door and put her in the enclosed porch. She was used to her little hull (small stone built shed) on the farm, so this porch would suffice; at least she would be inside if it came on wet.

Tina was probably the only thing, or being, that was keeping me from complete insanity and I knew I had to look after her!

I went to bed in the little dormitory that I was sharing with two other guys. There had been little conversation earlier and they were asleep when I got in.

I must have slept a bit, but I was up long before dawn and I packed my gear, went and got Tina and made my way out through the back garden of the hostel. The paranoid, hunted feeling was with me again, probably fuelled by the alcohol I had consumed the previous evening. I'd not had much of that, but it had been on an empty stomach. Anyway, I was anxious not to be discovered as I left the hostel. As I neared the back fence of the garden, a squeaking sound came to my ears. There was a little ambient light and I was able to make out something moving by the fence. I approached it and found it to be a half grown duckling that had got its leg stuck in the wire. I freed it and it limped off into the wood at the end of the garden. I got over the fence, went through the wood, with Tina beside me, and climbed over another fence into a large field.

I was heading north again across this field when I disturbed a pair of roosting oystercatchers and they took off, setting up a tremendous clamour with their cries. Their distinctive call has annoyed me ever since. The racket they were making spooked me and I ran off across the field eastwards, got myself and Tina over the boundary wall and ran into some more forestry. This was a dense stand of trees and it was almost pitch black as I forced my way through the claw-like lower branches.

Presently I came to a break in the trees. There was more light here and I was able to make out a faint path. I followed it and came to a sign and although I used the light from my digital watch, I couldn't see what was written on it.

I went on up the path and Tina kept running ahead and then coming back to make sure I was following. A strange delusion came over me. I was on a quest to find Balmoral Castle and when I found it, the Queen would receive me! I went on uphill, and looking at the map now as I write, it must have been the hill called Creag Choinnich, to the east of Braemar Village. The trees thinned out as I climbed this hill and the light began to strengthen as the dawn approached. I turned south around the shoulder of the hill and found a good path leading away ahead of me. I became animated; I was nearly at the castle and about to meet the Queen. Then, as suddenly as the delusion had started, it was shattered. Ahead of me I could see in the growing light that the land fell away towards the A93 at the southern side of Braemar. Thus in fact I had walked round in a circle and I was nowhere near Balmoral Castle!

Dejectedly I walked down to the road and returned to the hostel. It was dry so I chained Tina up outside again, as people would be up soon and I would get into trouble if they found her in the porch. I went in and returned to my bed. The other two guys were up soon after that though and I didn't sleep.

Things kept rolling forward and I got up and went down to the kitchen, where I searched the leftover food compartment and found some useable items, from which I made a mish-mash of a meal. This I actually managed to eat! Then I was off again with my rucksack and Tina. I paid for my accommodation by debit card on the way out and the receptionist gave me a funny look, as though she knew what I'd been up to in the night!

I headed through the village, found the shop and bought some supplies for myself and Tina; these included some tins of Whiskas and four tins of Caffrey's ale. Obviously this haul added considerably to my rucksack weight, but I was feeling energised by my hodge podge of a breakfast and I thought I could cope with the extra load.

I headed out to the western outskirts of the village and came across a large double garage next to the lane I was walking along. On an impulse, I tried the door; it was unlocked. I opened the up-and-over door and went inside, taking Tina with me. I closed the door again behind me. There was a Renault saloon in the garage and this too was unlocked, but there were no keys. I had no idea of how to hot-wire a car, so I searched it for any items that might be of use to me.

I hope that the reader will understand that in my right mind I would never do any of these kinds of things, but I was in an altered state and like in the earlier episodes, the world had gone to hell in a hand cart! Therefore I was in full survival mode.

Suddenly the garage door began to open and my heart skipped a beat. I shot out of the car, grabbed my rucksack and, as an old lady entered the garage I shot past her, shouting to Tina as I went to, "Come out of there."

The astonished woman shouted after me as I ran off down the lane, in a broad Scottish voice saying, "I'll get the police on you, you thieving young bugger!"

I didn't look back but turned up a track towards the nearby hillside. Tina ran with me and we didn't stop until I was clear away. I was out of breath and my heart was pounding. I threw myself down in the cover of a hazel bush and feeling in need of sustenance; I pulled off my rucksack and got out the tins of Caffrey's. I opened one and took a long slurp from it. This proved to be an unfortunate move because the ale came straight back up and I was violently sick.

After I had purged myself I got my stuff together again, left the tins of Caffrey's in a tree fork and began to walk south across the partially wooded hillside.

I forgot to state that ever since leaving the Capri, I had been wearing my Wellingtons and as you can imagine, by this point my feet were starting to get into a bad state. (Let alone what they must have smelled like, but such things were of little concern to me at that point!)

I made my way down to the river that flows out of Glen Clunie in the south – the Clunie Water. It was on the western bank of this river that I procured a useful tool. There was a good stand of hazel here and like I had done in Canada, I made myself a stout staff from it. This time however I had my Swiss Army knife and I used the saw blade on it for the first time to cut the staff out of the hazel bush. When I had trimmed up my staff, I used it as a third leg to help me cross the river. This was not as wide or as deep as the Dee had been, but the river bed was rougher and I had to watch my footing. I made it across and found myself on Braemar Golf Course. There were a few groups out playing, but none were close, so, anxious not to come into contact with any of them, I scuttled across the course, heading east towards the A93 once more. Tina had crossed the river easily and now stuck to me like glue. As we approached the road, I spotted a difficult obstacle. Between us and the road was a high deer fence, presumably erected to keep the deer off the course. I went up to it and looked for a place where Tina and I could possibly squeeze under the wire. I found a place, but there was only enough of a gap to admit Tina's small body. Suddenly it was as if I was back in Canada again and facing that deer fence by the side of the Trans-Canada Highway. So what, I had got over that one, hadn't I? This would be a piece of piss! I said to myself. So with my rucksack on my back I started to climb the wire netting, next to one of the posts. Up and over the top of the eight foot high fence I went, but then, halfway down the other side I lost my footing and fell heavily, almost twisting my ankle! I was quickly up again though and encouraging Tina through the gap under the fence. Once she was through we tackled the road. There was quite a bit of traffic, but we waited for a gap and then crossed safely. Then we climbed east up onto the Queen's Drive, which was an old road, heading towards the Creag Choinnich Hill we had been on during the night. This road isn't marked on the map as the Queen's Drive, so there must have been a sign by the side of it, describing it as such.

We followed this road north east around Creag Choinnich Hill and dropped down past a little crag called the Lion's Face. Suddenly we were back down at the A93 again, where it had turned east from Braemar. I was faced with a quandary now. Did we go on east towards Balmoral Castle or did we go back to Braemar again? I chose the latter option. It meant we were going around in circles, but I was very weary once more and was looking for a place to crash out.

There was a path heading back towards Braemar, so off we went along it. On entering the eastern side of the village, I did a bit of exploring and found a caravan on the roadside, which looked as though it hadn't moved for some time. The door was unlocked so I went inside and found that there was a mattress on the little bed. I got Tina to come inside the caravan, shut the door and crashed out on the bed. Tina climbed up beside me, curled up and went to sleep.

Again I felt my guardian angel was looking after me (and I guess Tina as well) and had led me to this place to hole up.

I went to sleep immediately, being careless of the fact that we may be discovered! When I awoke, it was pitch black in the caravan; darkness had fallen! It took me a few moments to work out where I was. Perhaps I thought I would awaken in my own bed and what had gone before was just a nightmare. But no, this was real enough and it was time to get going again. I was strangely angry as I gathered my rucksack up and felt my way to the door. Why the fuck was life doing this to me?

I exited the caravan and Tina followed, she was rejuvenated by her sleep. Working by starlight I opened a tin of Whiskas for her, shook it out on the ground and she cheerfully wolfed it down. Thankfully the weather was fine and settled or we would otherwise have been in a hell of a pickle; perhaps the gods were smiling down on us, but they were certainly testing us too!

We headed east out of the village along the A93 and we came to the northern side of that big field where I had disturbed the oystercatchers. There were sheep in it now and it was then that I did something completely irrational and stupid, for which I should have been horse whipped! My anger drove me to open the gate into the field, which I was able to locate by the light of the last street light on the village edge. I then proceeded to issue my command to send Tina out to round up the sheep. She shot off with gusto and gathered the sheep to me (she was the best working dog I have ever owned and this manoeuvre was meat and drink to her). I held the gate open and Tina drove them out onto the main road. I closed the gate and then proceeded to drive the flock of sheep back into the village. I left them to spread out amongst the houses and lanes and then walked back out eastwards again. God knows I am sorry I did this incredibly stupid prank and I apologise most profusely to the farmer, who would have to gather up his flock again. I just hope and pray that my actions didn't result in an accident!

I got Tina on her chain and walked down the roadside. There was not much of a grass verge and the occasional car passing made our situation very dangerous. The moon had risen and by the light of it I was able to see we were coming to a kind of council depot by the side of the road. Needing to get off the highway, we entered the apparently deserted depot and spotting a line of parked machinery, I decided on another rash course of action. There was a tractor of a similar make and size of our own tractors back home, parked amongst the other assorted machines. The cab door was unlocked so I climbed up into the cab and looked for an ignition key in the gloomy interior. Sure enough, I found one above the windscreen wiper console (just where we would have kept it back home). I found the ignition slot, inserted the key and turned it. The engine didn't fire but the revolving beacon light on the top of the cab roof sprang into action, flooding the depot with flashing yellow light. This proved to be unfortunate, because I didn't know how to stop the beacon and start the engine. I ended up smashing the beacon with a wrench I found, before it alerted anybody to my position, but it was too late. I saw the lights of an approaching vehicle and it turned into the depot. I quickly got down from the cab and shouted Tina to me; she was busy, off exploring and looking for smells as dogs are apt to do! The approaching vehicle was almost on me before I succeeded in getting Tina to me and we just managed to escape in time, into the woods at the eastern end of the depot. It was a close shave and I wondered if the vehicle had been a police car. Perhaps the balloon had already gone up with the sheep incident; it was not too far away.

We went through the trees and back to the A93. I had Tina back on the chain again and we continued east, crossing a bridge over the River Dee, which was by now a very large waterway. To the north I could see the twinkling lights of a house and finding a side road turning off towards it, we took it. There was a gate off the road into what looked like a large flat field on the left and I took Tina off her chain and we went through the gate into the field. I closed the gate behind me and set off in the direction of the house, which although was a couple of hundred metres away appeared to be, by the light of the moon, a large country house. Now, looking on the extreme right hand edge of the only map of the area I have, I can see that it must have been Invercauld House.

Tina, rather annoyingly, was off exploring. I hoped she wasn't going to become a liability! I shouted to her in as quiet a voice as I could to, "Come in." She immediately appeared beside me and sensing something else exciting was about to happen, she stayed with me as we approached the house. As we got up to it, I could see that an outside light was burning, but all else seemed quiet. I found the field gate and we went through it out onto the drive. There was a little open fronted shed just ahead and closing the gate behind us, I went to the shed. In it were a number of bicycles and they weren't chained up. I selected one with well-inflated tyres and procured it. Once I had got it out of the shed, I could see that it was a woman's bike of a sort of crossover mountain/road bike design. It was a little small for me but I thought it would do, so I mounted up and off I went back down the drive, with Tina trotting alongside.

Dawn was breaking as we headed out onto the A93 once more and headed on east. There was no traffic but I kept Tina on her chain and rode slowly, so that I didn't exhaust her. I could not have gone much faster anyway, because I was having difficulty mastering the bike's gear system!

The light strengthened and the occasional vehicle began to appear on the road. This was going to make things dangerous for us on this major highway, so I kept my eye out for an alternative. Presently we came to a little side road on the right and I turned the bike into it. I still had my staff with me and had it kind of fixed to my rucksack like an ice axe. We went a little way along this slightly overgrown side road and then found ourselves at a stone bridge, which obviously crossed the River Dee. There was a plaque at the entrance to the bridge and I read it. I learned from the plaque that this was the Old Bridge of Dee and I was obviously on the old road. We crossed the bridge, with its several impressive arches, and continued on along the old road on the south side of the Dee.

My earlier anger had given way to a kind of peaceful acceptance and I drifted along on my bike, pedalling slowly on the level surface, heading east with Tina trotting happily along beside me, now off her chain. She must have been thinking that this was a tremendously exciting adventure!

I decided it was time for a rest so I pulled over on the roadside and got off my steed to take the weight off my feet. I sat down rather heavily after taking my rucksack off. We were in partly wooded country with a lot of deep heather under the trees, which appeared to be Caledonian pines. I took my Wellingtons off and inspected my feet. They were red and getting sore, and blisters were starting to form! I wasn't too bothered though, the day was fine and warm and I was relaxed for the first time in what seemed like ages. I lay down in the deep heather and went to sleep.

I was awoken some time later by a sound. It was a woman's voice and she was asking me if I was okay. I sat up and observed a rather attractive lady of about the same age as myself, standing on the road nearby.

"Yes, I'm fine, thanks," I said in reply to her question.

"Do you know you are on the Balmoral Estate?" she asked.

"No, I didn't know I was. Is that a problem?" was my enquiring reply.

The lady went on to tell me that people didn't normally walk or cycle on the Queen's estate, but she didn't go on to say it was illegal. I wondered what she was doing, walking out here and then came to the conclusion that she may be one of the staff from Balmoral Castle. Our conversation continued for a little while, but I became guarded when I was asked where I was from. I told quite a few porkies (lies) and generally made up a cock and bull story about where I was heading and what I was doing. I thought this was okay, because after all, I didn't really know what I was doing or where I was going anyway!

The woman said, "Oh, well, I'd better be going, but make sure you keep your dog under close control when you get near the castle!"

She was fondly stroking Tina's head. Tina had returned from obviously fussing around in the undergrowth nearby and was pleased to greet this new person.

I said, "Yes I'll be careful with my dog, she's very well trained." And with that we parted company.

I gathered up my belongings, put my wellies back on, mounted the bike and continued down the road. Shortly, I came to a little turnoff to the right and being curious, I took it. The little track took me to a finely built wooden chalet in a clearing. I approached it rather warily and got off my bike. I went up onto the porch and tried the front door, but it was locked.

My meeting with the woman had told me one important thing. I was obviously on the Queen's estate and I would have to behave myself, therefore there would be no breaking into houses or cars here!

I sat down on the veranda and whittled at my staff for a bit with my knife, trying to decide what to do next. After a while I got up, mounted my bike and rejoined the old road to head on east. I began to experience the uneasy feeling that I was being watched and it stayed with me as the miles passed. I passed over several wooden bridges spanning small becks or burns and at one of these I got off the bike to look at the bridge construction. It was very solidly built, of wooden sleepers on massive steel girders and I concluded that it was strong enough to carry the weight of a battle tank!

I continued east, with Tina in close company and finally the scattered woodland gave way to good farmland. Balmoral Castle came into view on my left. There was no Royal Standard flying, so I guess none of the Royal Family were in residence. However, I became conscious of the fact that I had the stout staff on my back, which might have been perceived as a weapon, so I left it behind a wall on the roadside.

The road I was on now gave way from gravel to tarmac and it dropped down to join the main drive up to the castle. I still had the feeling I was being watched, but continued on unchallenged. The grounds of the castle were obviously extensive and to the east of it was a golf course. I assumed this was a course for the exclusive use of the Royal Family and their guests! I wandered across the course, finding it deserted and presently I came to the clubhouse, which was a small wooden construction. It must have been somewhere about eight a.m. when I walked up to the main door and tried the handle. To my surprise the door opened easily and I went inside. There I found a comfortably furnished lounge, a bar and a little kitchen. I explored cautiously and finding nobody at home, I set about making myself a cup of coffee and I raided the biscuit tin. I had left Tina outside while I investigated the building and I was worried she would attract attention, so after spending a short while enjoying my beverage and biscuits I signed the visitor's book, adding the comment 'Thank you for your hospitality,' and then I went out and continued on eastwards through the course. As I walked along the green fairways, wheeling my 'borrowed' bike into the early morning sun, I reflected on the last few hours. They had seemed quite normal: I had held a reasonable conversation with that woman back on the estate; I had seen Balmoral Castle, but my delusion/fantasy of meeting the Queen had not come to pass; and I had enjoyed a brief break in the Balmoral Golf Club facilities without damaging anything.

I do apologise to the Royal Family, though, for helping myself to their coffee and biscuits in the clubhouse!

I liked the look of the golf course I was walking through and maybe, just maybe I will get to play it one day. I availed myself of a scorecard while in the clubhouse and I still have it now. I can see that there are no par five holes on the course.

I made my way out from the golf course and passed through what I assumed to be the main gates of Balmoral Castle. There was a small tourist information building just outside the gates and also nearby was a phone box. My mobile was still not registering a signal, so I rustled up a few coins and phoned home. I can't remember exactly what I told my mother during that brief call, but I expect that because I was feeling a little better I therefore told her that I was okay and that there was no need to worry! This was all a delusion, though and as I rode away from the phone box things began to darken in on me once more. I was tired and although I had eaten a little, I was literally running on fresh air. I rode in a generally south easterly direction down a quiet road, with Tina trotting alongside. My feet were sore and deep inside myself I must have been crying out for somebody to help me. The survival instinct in me was strong though, as it had indeed been throughout all of my episodes, and it now forced me into a chain of drastic acts.

The first of these acts was played out shortly after leaving Balmoral. I came to a village, and around the back of one of the houses I found a little red van with the keys in the ignition! I quickly put the bike and Tina in the back of the vehicle, got into the driver's seat, started it up and drove off. Nobody tried to stop me and I drove north for some distance, before abandoning the van in a long distance haulier's yard. Weirdly, I even took the keys out of the ignition and put them up on top of the sunshade. I got the bike and Tina out of the van and made to exit the yard, but just then my curiosity was drawn to an HGV trailer that was parked nearby. I approached it and on an impulse, used my knife to cut a small opening in the curtain side of the trailer. I exposed part of a crate of bottled water, which was incredibly fortunate because I was thirsty. I guess my guardian angel was still with me. I took one of the bottles of water and drank from it, before putting it in my rucksack.

The brief drive in the van had given my feet a rest, but as I cycled out of the yard they soon began to bother me again and I was soon on the lookout for another means of transport.

The land I was passing through was now largely good farmland and there was a green combine harvester parked just inside a field gate near the little back road I was on. I got off my bike and investigated the large agricultural machine. I climbed up the steel ladder into the open cab area and found the keys in the ignition. I turned the key, but there was nothing; there was no electrics working on the machine and I assumed perhaps that there was no battery on it. It was a very old machine and had obviously not moved for some time. I took the key out though and kept it; perhaps it would come in useful for something, further on.

I abandoned the combine harvester and returned to my bike. I rode on towards a distant farm. There was still nobody about and I had seen few people yet that day; that was because it was now Sunday the fifteenth of July (looking now at my diary, in which I had now caught up with the correct date).

I turned off down the farm lonning, with Tina in close attendance, and part of the way down this lonning I came to an open fronted barn. I stopped and eyed up a massive 4WD Ford tractor, parked just inside the barn. I approached the machine, which must have been over a hundred horsepower, because it had a forage harvester on the back and it takes a lot of power to drive one of those. The tractor was blue and the harvester was red; my favourite colours. I was like a little kid in a sweet shop. What if I could start this machine and borrow it? One way or another, I couldn't go any further on the bike, that was impossible. So I tried the tractor cab door. It was open, and lo and behold, the keys were in the ignition. I sat on the seat and inspected the controls. It was an old tractor with a simple high/low gearbox, like I was most familiar with. Just like I would have done at home with our own tractors, I made sure the gear levers were in neutral, depressed the clutch pedal and turned the key. The engine turned over a couple of times and then roared into life! I got off the machine again and used some handily placed baler twine to tie my bike to the front of the forage harvester. Then I caught hold of Tina and lifted her into the back of the tractor cab, next to my rucksack, closed the cab door, put the tractor in gear, released the handbrake and drove the outfit out of the barn, and away from the farmstead.

Once out on the tarmac road I moved up through the gears and headed east and then north. I soon came to a two-lane highway and I stopped at the junction to remove my wellies, because my feet were burning up, and kind of itching at the same time. This meant I was operating the metal pedals virtually barefoot and I would soon come to regret this!

I got my wellies stowed, waited for a gap in the traffic and then turned right and east. I was quickly up into top gear but the tractor seemed strangely underpowered on the hills. I soon had a queue of traffic behind me and I kept politely pulling off into laybys to allow the logjams to get by.

I entered a small town, and that is when the shit hit the fan. I had been trying for some time to get the revolving spout of the forage harvester turned in line with my outfit. Because it was pointing over to the left, it was catching the hedges at the side of the road. I couldn't master the electric servo controls for it though and now, as I entered this town, the spout began to strike the lamp posts. There was a loud clang every time I hit one and I was forced to drive further out to the right to avoid hitting them. Then, of course, I caused on-coming traffic to take evasive action. This was getting dangerous and somewhat ridiculous, so after clearing the small town, and noticing I was getting low on fuel, I turned up a farm lonning. As I approached the farm buildings, I passed over a disinfected straw area (foot and mouth precautions) and this kind of brought me back towards reality.

I pulled up in the farmyard and a baffled-looking farmer came out of the farmhouse. I thought, *fuck, what am I going to do now?* I got down from the tractor and launched into a cock and bull story about me being an agricultural contractor from Cumbria, who had come north looking for work, but I was low on fuel, could I please borrow some? The farmer's bafflement quickly turned to anger and he raged at me. "What the hell do you think you're doing? You could have brought foot and mouth onto my farm! Get the hell out of here." I rather ashamedly got back on the tractor and drove out of the farmyard, but I didn't go all the way back to the main road, I pulled off onto the verge, stopped the engine and put on the handbrake. I got Tina and my rucksack, put my wellies back on, untied my bike from the forage harvester and saddled up once more. The farmer I had enraged was not going to leave it at that, though and he came down the lonning in his Land Rover, shouting, "You can't leave that bloody thing here, where the hell are you going now?" I ignored him and rode across the main road onto a footpath, which headed up between two fields. It became too narrow for the farmer to follow in his vehicle, so he stopped and shouted after me, "I'm getting the police!" This statement chilled me to the bone; the game was up, now I was really in the shit!

I rode as fast as I could and followed the footpath across country for a few miles, but it eventually brought me back to the road. Tina had stuck close to me and had obviously been scared by the tirade from the farmer, and now as we came back to the road I put her on her chain again, so that I could keep her close.

I rode north on the two-lane road and I felt hopelessness envelop me. I heard the sound of police sirens and when I looked round I saw no fewer than four police cars rapidly approaching. I pulled into a gateway and the police cars screeched to a halt beside me. Officers piled out of the cars and I panicked. I threw the bike and my rucksack down, released Tina to whatever fate may await her, jumped over the field gate and started to run across the field of ripening wheat. I looked back briefly as I fled and saw an officer in hot pursuit. I was no match for him in my weakened state and he soon caught me. He rugby-tackled me and I went down like a bag of shit. The officer then rolled me onto my back and started to punch me in the face, shouting, "I'll teach you to run from the law."

I tried to grab his flailing fists, responding with, "There's no need to punch my lights out, you bastard, I'll come quietly now!"

The copper got me to my feet after ceasing his onslaught on me and clapped me in irons. He walked me slowly back across the field to the waiting police vehicles, at the same time reading me my rights. I was put into the back of a police car and I saw Tina being put into a police van nearby. I wondered if I would ever see her again!

I was very grateful to be off my feet, they were burning up from my flight across the field and also sore from the abrasive effect of working the tractor pedals in my stockinged feet.

I was driven to the police station in Banchory and put into a cell, where I remained for a number of hours, during which I was searched and questioned and then a kind officer brought me a cup of tea.

Eventually I was taken from the cell and put into the back of a cage van. I was then transported to Aberdeen. During the journey I was quite passive, unlike that other time when I had been in the cage van in Carlisle. I even managed to hold a conversation with the two officers in the cab, through the connecting grill. I asked them what would become of Tina and they said they weren't sure at that time.

Evening had fallen by this time and as we approached the glow from the lights of Aberdeen City, I experienced another delusion/fantasy. We were some of only a few people left on earth and we were heading towards a spaceship that would take us to another planet! This state of mind persisted as I was taken to a brightly lit building, which I thought was some kind of departure lounge, when it was really the psychiatric wing of the Royal Cornhill Hospital!

I was put in an interview room and released from the custody of the police into the care of the hospital. I was then interviewed by a psychiatrist, to no doubt ascertain the extent of my madness!

It is at this point that I would like to thank the Aberdeenshire Constabulary for their generally kind and sympathetic treatment of me. I would also like to express my sincerest apologies to all those people whose vehicles I 'borrowed'. Christ, I must have made them a lot of work. Apologies also go to anyone else who was affected by my actions during this crisis.

From the interview room, I was moved to a locked ward, similar to the Rowanwood Unit, at the Carleton Clinic in Carlisle. I was put into a single room and made to undress and get into bed. As I lay there, I came back to reality, realising that I was of course in a mental hospital and I began to cry. The room door was open and a nurse sat on guard in the doorway as I bawled my eyes out. Eventually I cried myself to sleep.

Monday the sixteenth of July. I awoke about six thirty a.m. and when I lifted my head I saw that the nurse was still in the doorway. She must have been there all night. I got up and the nurse encouraged me to go to the bathroom to get cleaned up; I must have been stinking. The nurse supervised me as I ran a shallow bath and she kept a close eye on me as I attempted to cleanse myself.

Afterwards I dressed myself and went through to the dining room, where I managed to eat a little breakfast.

Part of me still thought I was on a spaceship and I regarded the staff with a little mistrust, especially in regard to my sore feet, which I saw fit to treat with Vaseline and they tried to encourage me to use E45 cream. I eventually agreed to this. I wore some disposable slippers on my sore feet and towards lunch time I was allowed to meet the other patients, who were of both sexes and of varying degrees of states of mental illness. I was allowed out in the yard, which was again similar to the one at Rowanwood, with sloping window ledges and high walls to prevent escape. I tried sunbathing on the grass, but I couldn't bear the hot sun on my feet, it burned me even through my socks!

I had several lie downs in the afternoon and around four p.m. the medications were dispensed. I was encouraged to go back onto the Risperidone and then in the evening I was given Sodium Valproate as well, but right from the word go, I had little intention of continuing on this medication and reiterated to the staff that these drugs did not agree with me. In fact, during the days that followed I tried to pursue a ruse by which I would put the pills under my tongue, leave the medication room, go to the toilet and flush them down the loo. The staff were wise to these tricks though and they soon put me on an injection, which was an old drug (but new to me) called Depixol and was administered through a long needle jabbed into my arse.

I went to bed early and was soon asleep; I had a lot of sleep to catch up on!

Tuesday the seventeenth of July. I was up around seven thirty a.m., having been observed only at intervals through the window in my bedroom door during the night, which was a step in the right direction from being under close guard the previous night.

I ate a reasonable quantity at breakfast and there were loads of scrambled eggs available, which suited me down to the ground. Unfortunately, the loose filling in my mouth finally dropped out and I experienced excruciating pain as the hot food came into contact with the nerve of the damaged tooth. From then on, I had to be careful when eating, but even so, every now and then I made a mistake while chewing and food got into the hole in the tooth; the pain nearly lifted the top of my head off! (I was either unwilling or unable to get the tooth filled while I was in that hospital.)

The common room of the unit had a huge television set with digital channels and I soon found my way to the music channel, to watch music videos and listen to such hits as Robbie Williams's *Eternity* and Travis's *Sing*.

There was also a reasonable selection of books and board games, and from breakfast to lunch on this particular day I played Scrabble with one of the nurses. It was no ordinary game of Scrabble though, because it was an amalgamation of three different sets and you could make some very large words indeed. Words just kept appearing on my rack and at the end of one game I scored a massive two hundred and sixty points!

The strange, pervading feeling that I was on a spaceship was still with me.

Lunch was at eleven forty-five a.m. and I began to eat heartily again. In the afternoon, I started to get to know some of the other patients a bit better. I did a bit of sunbathing out on the lawn and I began to notice a pair of herring gulls that had a nest up on the roof at the far end of the yard. You could see that these cheeky birds had a couple of young ones in the nest and I made it my mission to make sure the family didn't go hungry; I smuggled bread out of the dining room when I could and fed the adult birds on the lawn.

I was moved to a room down at the end of the main corridor, where it was a bit quieter and there was a bathroom right next door. The view from my window was out onto a road around the back of the unit. There were houses, too and I watched people going about their daily business and was envious of their freedom.

I had been placed on Scotland's equivalent of England's Section 3 and was being detained for at least four weeks. This made me worry even more about the fate of Tina and also, my car!

In the evening, I found that the staff had confiscated my passport. I asked to see it and on being allowed, I found that the two tickets for the Eagles concert at Hampden Park were in it. The concert was on the twenty-second of July and I asked if there was any chance that I could be allowed to go and see it, supervised of course, but the staff said there was no chance. I was willing to give the tickets to anyone who would go, and the staff said they would ask around.

I watched the very good and patriotic film towards Scotland, *Braveheart*, before I went to bed.

Wednesday the eighteenth of July. I was up around seven thirty a.m., breakfasted and then used the laundry room to wash and dry some of my stinkier clothes. The rest of the day was spent playing Scrabble and sunbathing out in the yard. This was less painful on my feet now, as they were healing quickly. I found a quiet place away from the others at the end of the yard, where I could stretch out in peace.

In the evening, a new member of staff came on duty and he took a special interest in me. His name was Bob and he bore an uncanny resemblance to the Bob I knew. For many days after I thought this was Bob Ridehalgh in disguise, so I guess my paranoia was still in evidence, to some extent anyway.

The medications were administered and I was on two milligrams of Risperidone and two hundred milligrams of Sodium Valproate per day, some of which I swallowed and the rest I flushed down the toilet!

Thursday the nineteenth of July. Again I was up around seven thirty a.m. It was the start of the Open Golf Tournament and I watched it on the big telly, on and off all day, when the other patients would allow me. I had begun to feel an overpowering urge to write and I got a notepad off the staff to enable me to write the story that was racing through my head. It was about a farm lad who went to Switzerland to work and climb. He had many adventures, some of them sexual, and he fell in love with a beautiful Swiss miss.

I have not yet typed out this story but intend to do so in the future. It is largely autobiographical!

Most of the nurses in the ward were very nice and helpful, but there was one that I would soon come to dislike!

In the late afternoon, I had a bath and this time I was allowed to take it privately. I sang in that bath (probably an Eagles number) and I suspected that there was a nurse listening at the door. Anyway, my spirits must have been lifting.

Friday 20th July. My birthday, and a special one, my fortieth! Obviously, I would have liked to have gone out on the piss to celebrate but there was no chance of that, given my circumstances.

I spent the first part of the day writing my story and watching the second round of the Open Golf. Then in mid-afternoon I got a nice surprise; I was presented with a large birthday cake, it was about a foot square and four inches thick. It was iced and written on the top in blue icing were the words, 'Happy birthday, Steve'. When I cut into it, I found it was a Battenburg. All the staff and patients shared it with me; there was a lot to go around.

The next few days passed in a largely uneventful way, apart from the fact that the Eagles concert came and went without any takers for the tickets. Also I phoned home and I was told that rescue missions were being mounted to come up and get Tina home before the police put her down, plus Brian Cowperthwaite was going to bring a trailer up and get my car home!

During this time I also wrote many letters to my friends and customers, some of which were probably a bit weird, especially the one to Bob Ridehalgh, which was positively defamatory as I blamed him partly for my predicament at the time. I apologise for this!

David Duvall won the Open Golf on ten under par.

On Monday the twenty-third of July, the staff told me that the Eagles concert had been a sell-out, with forty-five thousand people there (there was one that wasn't) and the performance had rave reviews!

I had learned from home and the staff where I was that no further action was going to be taken by the police. I had been lucky and was greatly relieved.

There were two male patients that I did not like or trust and they were liable to turn nasty at any time. I had a drawer in my room where I kept my most private possessions and I kept it locked.

Tuesday the twenty-fourth of July. It was five twenty-five a.m. and I had been awoken by a wracking cough coming from one of the adjacent rooms, I thought it was one of those guys I didn't like. However as I sat on my bed I looked out of the window onto a scene of such peace. There were three wild rabbits grazing on the lawns and a herring gull picking about, with more in the air.

Of course I couldn't get back to sleep and got up to continue writing my story. In the coming days, I would write so prolifically that I would exhaust the unit's supply of notepads and they would have to get more in.

My feet were recovering very well and the blisters had now turned to callouses and were itching.

I had an interview with a social worker to get me fixed up with incapacity benefit. During this time one of the other patients kicked off and had to be tranquillized!

The herring gulls in the yard provided much entertainment with their antics in trying to catch the two mice that had been attracted by the bread I put out.

Another of the patients kicked off and he was a big guy, meaning it took six staff to hold him down to administer the tranquillizer.

At one point during the following days I got a phone call and thinking it was just my folks calling, I picked up the receiver in a relaxed manner, only to get a shock. It was Bob Ridehalgh calling and he seemed casual in his regard for me; too casual! I was cold towards him, and I can't remember what was said but I do know that the call upset me greatly and I burst into tears afterwards. One of the nurses comforted me and says she would make sure I didn't speak to him again.

I saw one of the psychiatrists and she told me I would lose my driving licence because she was duty bound to tell the DVLA about the driving antics I had admitted to. Also, she told me I was going to start on the new injection, Depixol, and it would start on the twenty-seventh of July. This was when I started to develop the dislike for the nurse who administered the injection into my arse through the inch-long needle that he waved in front of me like a sword. He took a sadistic delight in banging the needle in with little warning and then waggling it about in my arse. The pain was excruciating, but worse was to follow. The drug was slow release and the nurse seems to be amused by the side effects that begin to manifest themselves. My sex drive went completely and I lost control of my lower jaw and lips, causing me to drool. There is a drug called Orphenadrine that you can take to control these side effects but it was some days before I was given it, during which time the nurse gloated over my discomfort (I will not forget you, pal!). My writing suffered when under the early effects of the Depixol and I could see it now as I looked at my spidery handwriting in my diary.

I was delighted to receive a large package at this time though, from my sister's partner, Allan. When I opened it, I found a Discman and several of my own favourite C.Ds. I put the machine on to play immediately and listen to the strains of Abba and the Eagles through the headphones. Good old Allan!

There was a third kick-off amongst the other patients when a young guy who was in for drug use and subsequent mental illness wrecked the smoking room, and he too had to be sedated. It was all happening!

I received several packages and get well cards from my grandpa in Kent.

My routine continued on through Friday the third of August, when I received my first large weekly dose (forty milligrams) of Depixol from my 'trusted friend', the nurse. The drug knocked me down even more and I tried drinking a lot of tea and coffee to get a fix of caffeine, but this did little to liven me up. Perhaps it was de-caff I was drinking!

My sleep was uneven and full of strange dreams. Well, I suppose I was at least dreaming, unlike when I was on the Risperidone!

I got the chance to attend a sheriff's meeting to ascertain if I was fit to be moved onto a Section 18, which would have meant I was moved to a less secure ward, but I was persuaded out of this course of action by one of the psychiatrists.

One morning I was told that some of my family were coming to see me, while they were up rescuing Tina. I waited with anticipation, but when they came I felt able only to deal with my dad. Angus and Anne were the other members who had come up, but I couldn't face them. Dad and I had a good crack though and he told me Tina was safe and that Brian Cowperthwaite had recovered my car, if at great expense! I was much relieved by this news. The family left and I was once more alone, a long way from home.

I was considered to be too high a risk to be allowed outside the confines of the unit for a walk, unaccompanied, like I had been at Rowanwood, but one day I was able to visit one of the less secure wards with a couple of nurses in tow. I found a pool table and had a few games on that. One of the nurses who was supervising me was the sod that was injecting me and I beat him several times at pool, which gave me intense satisfaction.

On Thursday the ninth of August, I was told that I was to be moved back to England in a week's time, but then only to Rowanwood. This was, however, a step in the right direction and it lifted my flagging spirits.

I spent what would be my last week in the Royal Cornhill Hospital making a thousand-piece jigsaw of two Scottish pipers and when I finished it, I tried to get the staff to give me a sheet of hardboard so that I could glue the jigsaw to it and make it into a picture, with a view to taking it home, but they wouldn't agree to it. I didn't think I was asking too much, was I?

My ears blocked up with wax during this last week and I had to have drops put in them and then get them syringed. Perhaps I had been playing the Discman too loud through the earphones!

On Wednesday the fifteenth of August, I was allowed to pack my gear into my rucksack, taking my stuff that had been locked away in a side room. However, I couldn't find my good pair of Karrimor gaiters or my waterproof trousers and they never did show up. Some bastard probably nicked them!

Thursday the sixteenth of August. I was up at seven a.m., shaved, washed and breakfasted. Then two nurses came for me (one was my favourite injection nurse), and I got my rucksack together. Then they escorted me through the hospital. On the way, I was allowed to visit the bank and draw out thirty pounds, which had to be given to the nurses with my other personal effects, to be looked after for me during the journey south. Just before we exited the hospital to the waiting taxi, my injection nurse, Paddy as I called him, because he was an Irishman, showed me the syringe of 'Cosh' (a heavy duty tranquilizer) that he would jab me with if I tried to make a run for it!

The three of us got in the taxi and it took us to Aberdeen airport, where we boarded a small, twin-engined turbo prop plane, along with a number of other, ordinary passengers.

We took off and had a good, if short, flight down to Newcastle, where there was another taxi waiting to take us through to Carlisle.

Once back in Carlisle and at Rowanwood, my two nurses did the paperwork to transfer me over from the Scottish system and then supposedly handed over my personal effects to the Rowanwood staff in the office next to the airlock entrance way. It felt strange to be going in through this again. However, when later I asked the Rowanwood staff if I could have my thirty pounds they said, "We weren't given any money of yours by the Scottish nurses!" It had disappeared, the bastards had stolen it! I bet it was that fucking Paddy, trying to get the last laugh on me. I was very annoyed, as you can imagine and this final nail in the coffin severely reduced any respect I had held for the Royal Cornhill Hospital!

I got a nice room in Rowanwood, looking out towards the M6 and dossed around until evening, when I was examined by a doctor and given a clean bill of health. I had supper with the other patients, who were a mixed bunch, but there were one or two really dangerous-looking characters. My key worker gave me an Orphenadrine pill for the side effects of my Depixol and then I went to bed.

Friday the seventeenth of August. I was up at six forty-five a.m., wrote up my diary and had breakfast at eight a.m. I spent the rest of the morning getting my dirty laundry into the washer. I had lunch, then dossed around until three thirty-five p.m., when I had a meeting with the same psychiatrist I had had back in 1998. It went well but I was told I would be in there for a week for accurate assessment, before possibly being transferred down to Penrith and the Beacon Unit. I was a bit deflated by this but I was getting there slowly.

In the evening, I was given another depo injection by a much gentler nurse. This time it was the slightly reduced dose of thirty milligrams. I went to bed and slept reasonably well.

Saturday the eighteenth of August. The little birds woke me with their cheerful chirping in the trees outside my bedroom window at seven ten a.m. I got ready for the day in the normal fashion and then after breakfast, my key worker told me that she would take me for a walk down to the old Garlands hospital, providing I behaved myself. I positively jumped at this plan, it was a huge step in the right direction and they obviously thought I was doing well.

I enjoyed the walk but it was kind of sad in a way, because the old Garlands buildings were being knocked down to make way for a new housing estate.

I was still having trouble with my bad tooth and it continued to make mealtimes a trial!

In the afternoon of this day, I was taken out into the central yard by the ward manager, who was a real hard nut, but kind of nice at the same time. He told me I was 'too well' to be in this unit and that if I wasn't moved to Penrith soon, there would be a danger of the other patients causing me to become unwell again. This was again another encouraging sign for me, and I really was feeling better again. The feeling that I was going up on a spaceship had faded by now. The Orphenedrine was working nicely against the side effects of the Depixol and I felt ready to face the world again.

I was in bed early that evening, because I was trying to keep out of the way of some of the other patients. Rowanwood did not seem as safe a place this time round!

Sunday the nineteenth of August. I was up by seven ten a.m. and quickly did my personal jobs, breakfasted and then my key worker came to see me to ask if I wanted to go for another walk, but because it was raining I declined. Instead we had a long talk, she was keen to hear of my experiences in Scotland, especially those in the Royal Cornhill Hospital; she was interested in the different systems between the two countries.

Lunch was at twelve noon. And after, I went for a kip. I was woken a little later by one of the staff, who told me I had visitors. I went through to the main concourse and found Mam, Dad, Angus and Anne waiting there. An emotional reunion followed and Mam especially gave me a big hug. We got the vacant meeting room, went in and had a good crack. I was keen to learn how Tina was and I was told she was fine, but pining for me.

My visitors went at four p.m. and I spent the rest of the day relaxing and talking to one of the nurses, who was administering the Orphenedrine.

The following few days were pretty much routine, apart from a big meeting with various psychiatrists, doctors and other counsellors present. This went fairly well, but they had learned that I had run up a bit of a debt while I was on my 'wild ride'. I was asked what I intended to do about the situation and I told those present that the only way I could clear my debts was by being allowed to get out and go back to work. I was told that that would not be possible for a little while yet!

The pool table was still in Rowanwood and I passed some of the time on that, thrashing those other patients who were adept at the game. I read a Patrick O'Brian seafaring book that had been brought by my visitors from Allan. I did a bit of pottery work in the O.T. department and made the figurine of a cat, which I painted grey and white, like our much loved Tiny. I don't know what happened to the clay cat but I haven't got it now. I was allowed out unescorted around the grounds, but only for five minutes at a time at first. A local farmer was combining one of the fields next to the Carleton Clinic and I took an interest in that. The length of time I was allowed out was increased when the staff saw that I was not going to run off and I was able to relax around the grounds in the late summer sunshine.

I picked up a nasty athlete's foot infection that had to be treated with special cream.

Heather came to see me on the twenty-fifth of August and we enjoyed a good crack. John, the social worker, also visited and he told me he was sad that I'd had another breakdown, but that there had been much mental illness and obvious distress in Cumbria, due to the foot and mouth crisis, especially amongst the farming community.

One of the Rowanwood staff helped me with the mountain of paperwork associated with claiming incapacity benefit.

During the following week a bed became available in the Beacon Unit at Penrith and on Thursday the thirtieth of August, I was taken down to Penrith in a taxi by one of the nurses. It felt a bit strange in the Beacon Unit at first, with it being the scene of my attack on the nurse, but nobody seemed to bear me any ill will and I soon relaxed into a similar routine to that of Rowanwood. The Beacon Unit differed, however, in atmosphere from both Rowanwood and the Royal Cornhill by being much more relaxed. I liked my room and most of the other patients. There was also a pool table but decent opposition was in short supply.

On Saturday the first of September, England beat Germany five-one, which was a great result. I watched the match in the T.V. room. I am not a great football fan but I like to watch England play.

I was allowed out almost immediately for walks around the grounds. Then on the third of September I was allowed to go into town unescorted for three to four hours and spent the time doing bank work and picking up my books from my accountants. Also, on the way back I visited one of my old customers, who had sold his farm and moved into town. He was pleased to see me and made me tea before driving me back to the Beacon Unit.

Thursday the sixth of September. I was up a good time, breakfasted and then went for a long walk up around the castle. I returned for lunch and was told there was going to be a big meeting with various counsellors and my family, to discuss my illness and whether I was well enough to be allowed home for a few days. I of course attended this meeting that afternoon and the upshot of it was that I would indeed be allowed home leave there and then. I gleefully packed up enough gear for a few days at home and then returned to the farm with my family.

The first thing I did when I got out of the car was let Tina out. She positively pronked about around me, she was so pleased to see me again and I was very pleased to see her. I owed her a lot, possibly even my life!

I spent the next few days trying to sort out my paperwork for my business. This was a tricky job and I had to use my memory and my diary to get my affairs in order. After this was done, I generally relaxed and took Tina for long walks.

On Sunday the ninth of September, Angus, Anne and Hannah came and took me to see Grandma at the old folks' home at Cockermouth. She was pleased to see me but did not really understand what had been going on with me.

Dad had been haymaking during my incarceration in the various mental hospitals and it was good to see that at least some of life had been progressing normally.

That evening Angus took me back to the Beacon Unit and I was in bed by eight thirty p.m. It was surprising how tired the last few days had made me.

The following day I had another big meeting with the various counsellors and it was agreed that I would be allowed out for home leave again on the evening of the next day (Tuesday the eleventh of September). Most of the rest of the day was routine but what was to come would turn the world upside down!

Tuesday the eleventh of September. I was up at seven fifteen a.m., abluted and breakfasted. I then went down town to attend the appointment with my new dentist at nine ten a.m. I had a check-up and some X-rays and was given another appointment for two weeks' time. I was wishing I had got some treatment there and then on my bad tooth but it wasn't to be; the agony would be prolonged for a little while yet! While I was in town I went to the D.S.S. to get some benefits details sorted out. I returned to the Beacon Unit for lunch and then dossed around for the early part of the afternoon.

It must have been around three p.m. when one of the other patients came to get me from my room. She was very excited, blurting out, "Quick, come and look at the television, something terrible is happening!" I rushed into the T.V. room to witness one of the most stunning pieces of broadcasting I have ever seen; one of the World Trade Center buildings in New York was in flames. Reporters were saying that it had been hit by an airliner! And as I stood in the room, crowded with patients and staff alike,

I saw another airliner plunge into the other World Trade Center building. For a second, as the impact ripped through the building I thought it had been cut in half, but no, it still stood! We were all transfixed with horror at what was happening; there was footage of people jumping from the burning buildings. Then after much debate amongst us and the reporters at the scene about whether the buildings would stand up to their devastating damage, we witnessed the fall of both buildings and the massive blast of dust and debris that followed. As we continued to watch, we learned that another airliner had crashed into the Pentagon and yet another had crashed in open countryside. It transpired that the airliners had been hijacked by terrorists and deliberately aimed at their targets like giant missiles. It was the most incredible thing I have ever witnessed, but I suppose ever since, most people will remember where they were when the twin towers went down.

I send a quiet prayer up now in remembrance of all those who died in the tragedy as I sit writing this!

Later that day Heather came to take me home, and this time I hoped it would be for good.

During the days that followed what became known as 9/11, I busied myself doing small jobs round the farm, trying to slowly acclimatize myself back into work. Tina accompanied me during my various tasks and in between jobs we played her favourite game of me running, with her jumping up to grab my forearm in a light bite. It was great fun.

The television news was filled with the aftermath of the terrorist attacks in America and there was much harrowing footage of the tragedy.

I was sleeping pretty well and also, the new medication allowed me to dream again; consequently I was even gladder to be rid of the other bloody stuff!

I have the Scottish system to thank for this change in medication. I think that if I had been looked after in England during the entire recent crisis I would have still been suffering on the same drugs.

All through this period, Brian Cowperthwaite had been looking after my beloved Capri, which he had recovered from Scotland, and he now phoned me up to ask if we could remove it from his yard as it was getting in the way of business, so Dad took Heather to Brian's garage and she brought the Capri home for me. I put it away in the back of the silage clamp with a sheet over it, just like I had done when I was banned from driving in 1993. I had no idea when the authorities would deem me fit to drive again and of course, this raised the problem of how I was to be able to continue my contracting work. Dad told me that for the time being, I would be able to get some work on the farm, which would bolster up my income from the incapacity benefit I was now receiving, by way of the 'permitted work' initiative.

Heather surprised me with a late fortieth birthday present of a Timex Expedition watch, which had a built in compass to help me on my fell walking escapades.

My expected permanent return home was interrupted by one more day and night back in the Beacon Unit on the seventeenth of September. On this day, I was assessed by a team of various health professionals and deemed fit to be allowed home on long leave.

On Saturday the twenty-second of September, I went out for an evening meal with the Mungrisdale gang. Angus and Anne were there too and we ate a fine Italian meal at Gianni's in Penrith. It was a kind of dual celebration really; firstly to mark my return to health and then secondly to give Ken Ostle a good send-off. He was making the quantum leap from farming to joining the Metropolitan Police down in London!

It was the first opportunity I had had for quite some time to have an alcoholic drink, but I indulged carefully and sparingly. I had been advised to take it easy on the alcohol after the recent breakdown, but not cut it out entirely as I had following the other hospitalised episode.

It was a good night out and I had a nice lie-in the following morning. Later in the day, Heather arrived at the farm with some forms to re-apply for my driving licence, which I had previously surrendered. The forms required four photographs so we went into Penrith to get them from a photo booth. Heather was keen to get me back on the road so I could get out earning a proper living again and stop 'Living the life of Riley', as she put it. I have always ever since considered this comment as hurtful!

A few days later my social worker (who was still John) came to see me at the farm. He told me for a second time how disappointed he was that I had relapsed again following his involvement with me in the 1998 episode, but at the same time pleased to be visiting the farm once more. I guess he kind of saw his visits to me as a sort of mini-break!

After John and I had enjoyed a walk down the front fields with Tina, John took me, along with my driving licence forms, to see the psychiatrist in Penrith, where I was given even more forms, which had to be countersigned by various health professionals (including my own doctor) and then posted with my passport to the D.V.L.A.

All through this period following my hospitalisation, I had been aware of Bob Ridehalgh's concern for me. He had phoned the farm several times but I had been loath to speak to him. However, now, with my mental health obviously on the mend I felt obliged to make bygones be bygones. After all, he had not really done anything wrong, had he? I phoned him up and arranged to meet him at the Mill Inn. The meeting was awkward to start with but we soon both thawed out and enjoyed a few pints and games of pool together, while indulging in the crack. I had gone to the pub on my bike and Bob was pleased to see I was still using it. He was also impressed with my story of carrying the Marin, complete with panniers, over the Lairig Ghru. By the end of the evening, things were just like old times between us.

I now had a community psychiatric nurse (C.P.N.) coming out to visit me at the farm once a fortnight, with a forty milligram injection of Depixol for my backside. I shall call him Jim, although I'm sure he wouldn't have minded me using his real name as he is such a nice bloke. He always stayed for at least half an hour following the administering of the jab, to determine whether my improvement was continuing. He was brilliant crack and gave me regular updates about his gigs with the rock band that he was the bass player in.

I finally got my bad tooth sorted at the new dentist but it was so badly damaged that it had to be extracted, which proved to be a bit of a mauling.

A terrorist group called the Taliban had claimed responsibility for the 9/11 attacks and a guy called Osama bin Laden was said to be in charge of them. The Americans had reacted like a disturbed hornets' nest to the attacks (quite understandably so) and now set about bombing the shit out of targets in Afghanistan, where the Taliban were said to be based. The R.A.F. joined in the bombing and once more Britain was involved in another foreign conflict!

It was now October and I continued with my farm jobs, which included a lot of walling and quite a bit of routine stockwork.

Jim arrived every two weeks to administer my injection and counsel me. I couldn't help noticing that in spite of working fairly hard, I was starting to put on weight. Also, the tremendous drive that I had always counted on to keep me going was starting to be eroded. I mentioned these concerns to Jim and he didn't think the medication would be to blame for my troubles.

This attitude towards the side effects of the medication by the health professionals I have always found typical and is opposed to my own feelings!

In the middle of October, Dad took me to the Carleton Clinic for my first appointment with a psychotherapist, this being a course of treatment recommended by my other counsellors. The meeting seemed to go okay but I was slightly unnerved by the practitioner's approach to regressing me into my childhood, with a view to searching out some early life trauma, which might explain my more recent mental health condition.

I came away from the meeting slightly befuddled and actually I only attended two more of these meetings before I knocked them on the head. I had become more and more uncomfortable and actually began to feel it was having a negative effect on my wellbeing!

Towards the end of October I received some forms from the D.V.L.A. to fill out, in regard to my alcohol consumption. I duly completed the forms, with the information that I was drinking very little alcohol at that time, which was true, and then posted them back to the D.V.L.A.

Despite my lowering energy levels, I must have had some left over because on Sunday the twenty-eighth of October I cycled down to my sister's house at Threlkeld and then, after loading my and her bikes (Heather had recently bought a Marin similar to mine) into her car, we travelled to Whinlatter Forest and spent most of the day exploring the tracks there.

This escapade had an impact upon me the following morning however, because I had a hell of a job getting out of bed. I felt that my injections were really starting to impact upon my physical performance and set about trying to encourage Jim to reduce the dosage, but I had little initial success.

It was round about this time that Dad was approached by a neighbouring farmer, Mr W Wilson of Gillhead Farm, who wished to buy what remained of our breeding ewes and tup them with his Blue Faced Leicester tups. Dad agreed to sell the ewes and look after the flock and four tups on our land for the duration of the mating period. We know the Wilson family very well, they are very nice people. Indeed I have done a lot of mole trapping for them and it was actually while working for them that I caught the first of my white moles!

I bought a good set of lights with a rechargeable battery for my Marin and began cycling to the home pool matches at the Mill Inn, where I had a few pints and then came home by the excellent beam from my new lights. I still had to watch out for the semi-wild fell ponies on the Mungrisdale road though.

My persistence with Jim paid off and although he injected me with the same dose of Depixol, the interval between jabs was extended to a month.

Consequently my energy levels picked up again to some extent and on Sunday the eighteenth of November Andrew picked me up and drove us to Patterdale from where we climbed Place Fell at six hundred and fifty-seven metres (two thousand one hundred and fifty-five feet) via Boredale Hause, just east of the head of Ullswater. We were up and down it in not much over three and a half hours but I struggled a bit on the steeper sections. Afterwards we enjoyed a couple of pints in the White Lion and caught up with the crack. I hadn't seen much of Andrew since before my breakdown. Tina didn't go with us on this occasion.

Foot and mouth, although now over, was not forgotten and one of the after effects was that all the remaining sheep on our land had to be blood tested as a further precaution. One of the bonuses of this for me was that one of the lady vets who came to do the testing was very good looking, so I tried my chat up lines on her, but to little effect!

At the end of November, word arrived from the D.V.L.A. that I would be given a licence to drive for the probationary period of six months. This was good news; I was on my way back towards normality.

Alongside Jim's regular visits, I also had to continue getting visits from John and although I liked him, he was not the most reliable of people. Sometimes I waited round for him for half a day and he never showed up! I suppose he was a very busy person.

On the evening of Saturday the first of December, I went out on the town with my Mungrisdale mates and saw my favourite girl for the first time in many months. I was captivated; the flame had burned low but had not gone out entirely.

The following morning I was up at eight a.m. having got in at one a.m. I quickly got myself breakfasted and packed my rucksack for an arranged hike with Andrew and one of his other friends from West Cumbria. I carried my gear down to the road-end below the old railway and waited for the others. It was a fine, cold morning but quite windy from the south west. The others arrived and we drove to Patterdale and then some way up the Grisedale valley road, where we went through a gate into the field of a farmer I had worked for and parked next to a rough track. Then, as I had done on that previous occasion, I left a message on the dashboard to say who we were, in case the farmer came by. Then we donned our gear and struck off south westwards up a good path, ascending the prow of the fell known as Birks. It was very steep going and exhausting, especially for me. Also, as we climbed higher the wind got even stronger.

We topped out on Birks at six hundred and twenty-two metres (two thousand and forty feet) and then continued westwards and up onto St

Sunday Crag at eight hundred and forty-one metres (two thousand seven hundred and fifty-nine feet). It was frighteningly windy here and we almost had to crawl into the teeth of the gale. We forged on though and dropped down to Deepdale Hause, where we ate a hasty lunch.

It would have been nice to have had Tina with us but I didn't like imposing her on somebody else's car and she would probably have been blown off the mountain!

After the brief lunch stop we flogged on westwards up the steep rocky ridge known as Cofa Pike and out onto the windswept summit of Fairfield at eight hundred and seventy-three metres (two thousand eight hundred and sixty-four feet). There was a light dusting of fresh snow up here and it was bitterly cold, so we didn't dally long before dropping off the west side of the mountain towards Grisedale Tarn.

We skirted round the southern shore of the tarn, which was complete with white-tipped waves and then walked right back out down the Grisedale valley to the car. I felt exhausted as we put our gear away and I suggested we retire to the nearest hostelry for a much needed pint. Before we did so, though, we sat in the car and ate the rest of our food supplies, at the same time comparing views of how scared each of us had been on the exposed summit of St Sunday Crag.

We drove down to the White Lion and had a couple of refreshing pints there before heading for home. It had been a good day but I was running low on energy.

In the days that followed, I took up my usual farm tasks, including shepherding the Wilson's purchased flock of sheep. The four tups were also being fed concentrates (cake); also the coloured ochre raddle was applied to the tup's chests, so that when each ewe was tupped the colour would be transferred to the back end of the ewe to show it had been mated. The colours were changed after a period of time so that when lambing time, came you could sort the ewes into their respective colours so that the ones that were due to lamb earliest could be given priority.

On Sunday the ninth of December, Andrew and I were out hiking again. This time we parked at Glenridding and did Striding Edge up onto Helvellyn and down Swirral Edge onto Catstye Cam at eight hundred and ninety metres (two thousand nine hundred and twenty feet). From here we dropped down northwest off-piste, so to speak, and down to the old Keppel Cove Dam, with its large hole in the bottom of the western end.

Returning down the Greenside Valley, we had a couple of pints at the Traveller's Rest before heading home. It had been another great day and the weather had been superb, with a strange temperature inversion i.e. it had been frosty in the valleys but mild high up. The views had been stunning. I was not yet driving again so Tina was left at home.

The regular walking trips were starting to build up my fitness. As for the state of my mental health, well, I guess you could say that it was fine.

A few days later I caught the bus to Penrith to go and meet my new accountant, Chris Dent of Graham and Dent partnership. Chris was a couple of years older than me but I had known him from school. He is a very nice man and he immediately made me comfortable about taking on my accounting affairs (his firm had been recommended by my workmate, Thomas).

Christmas was a bit low key for me because I went down with a very bad cold and therefore had no nights out on the town. However, I did go to Carlisle on the twenty-seventh of December to see the new *Lord of the Rings* film, *The Fellowship of the Ring* and it was very good. I saw it at the big new cinema in Botchergate with Heather, Allan and his brother Rob. Allan got the hip flask out mid-film, which spiced up the evening somewhat.

THIS IS THE END OF THE FIRST PART OF MY STORY. READ MORE IN 'THE WHITE MOLE – RELOADED'.

Author's Note

I don't really believe I suffer from bipolar disorder. Rather, I think this diagnosis is a smokescreen for the fact that my mental health has been severely damaged by over exposure to organophosphorous sheep dips and cattle wormers in the 1980s and 1990s. These chemicals contain nerve agents and have been linked to Gulf War Syndrome. Back in the days when I did a lot of sheep dipping, the task always took place on fine days and it was impossible to wear all the protective clothing that was advised because dipping is very hot and strenuous work. What with the splashes from the dipping tub and breathing in the noxious vapours, I positively bathed in the stuff! As for the police and the trading standards officers who oversaw the compulsory dipping, well, I think they were there just to see who was wearing protective clothing in the light of any future claims for side-effects emerging. As for the cattle wormers, which were used to kill warble fly larvae, roundworms and tapeworms etc, these chemicals made the air in the cattle sheds thick with their oily, sickly stench once you had poured them along the backs of the animals, and obviously you were breathing this in while you worked with the beasts.

Compulsory worming of cattle and compulsory dipping of sheep all took place over the period when I was most ill!